The Meaning of Marxism

The Meaning of Marxism

Paul D'Amato

Chicago, IL
Haymarket Books

First published in 2006 by Haymarket Books.
This revised and updated edition published in 2014 by
Haymarket Books
PO Box 180165
Chicago, IL 60618
773-583-7884
info@haymarketbooks.org
www.haymarketbooks.org

ISBN: 978-1-60846-250-6

Trade distribution:
In the US, Consortium Book Sales and Distribution, www.cbsd.com
In the UK, Turnaround Publisher Services, www.turnaround-uk.com
In Australia, Palgrave Macmillan, www.palgravemacmillan.com.au
All other countries, Publishers Group Worldwide, www.pgw.com

Special discounts are available for bulk purchases by organizations and
institutions. Please contact Haymarket Books for more information at
773-583-7884 or info@haymarketbooks.org.

This book was published with the generous support of Lannan Foundation
and the Wallace Action Fund.

Cover design by Samantha Farbman.

Printed in Canada by union labor.

Library of Congress CIP data is available.

10 9 8 7 6 5 4 3 2 1

Contents

Introduction to the 2014 Edition

The Return of Marx

Modern bourgeois society, with its relations of production, of exchange and of property, a society that has conjured up such gigantic means of production and of exchange, is like the sorcerer who is no longer able to control the powers of the nether world whom he has called up by his spells. For many a decade past the history of industry and commerce is but the history of the revolt of modern productive forces against modern conditions of production, against the property relations that are the conditions for the existence of the bourgeois and of its rule. It is enough to mention the commercial crises that by their periodical return put the existence of the entire bourgeois society on its trial, each time more threateningly. In these crises, a great part not only of the existing products, but also of the previously created productive forces, are periodically destroyed. In these crises, there breaks out an epidemic that, in all earlier epochs, would have seemed an absurdity—the epidemic of overproduction. Society suddenly finds itself put back into a state of momentary barbarism; it appears as if a famine, a universal war of devastation, had cut off the supply of every means of subsistence; industry and commerce seem to be destroyed; and why? Because there is too much civilization, too much means of subsistence, too much industry, too much commerce. . . . The conditions of bourgeois society are too narrow to comprise the wealth created by them. And how does the bourgeoisie get over these crises? On the one hand, by enforced destruction of a mass of productive forces; on the other, by the conquest of new markets, and by the more thorough exploitation of the old ones. That is to say, by paving the way for more extensive and more destructive crises, and by diminishing the means whereby crises are prevented.
    —Karl Marx and Frederick Engels, *The Communist Manifesto*

A year or so after this book was first published in 2006, the world was hit by the worst economic crisis since the 1930s, from whose effects millions are still reeling. Modern readers cannot help reading these words above, from a little 1848 pamphlet by Karl Marx and Frederick Engels called *The Communist Manifesto*, and not have them jump off the page. The crisis reinforces the value of Marxism both as a way of understanding the world we live in and in sensing the urgency of changing it.

When the crisis came, the "neoliberal" ideology that told us that markets solved everything, crises were avoidable, and governments should keep their hands off business was itself thrown into crisis. Suddenly, capitalists and their mainstream press mouthpieces were extolling the virtues of government intervention—to save capitalism. Once the banks were bailed out, however, the talk faded. Once the banksters had fed at the state trough, it was back to business as usual. No bankers went to jail. Very few new economic regulations to prevent the emergence of new crises were put into place. Deregulation, rampant spoliation of the environment, privatization of everything that moves, drastic cuts in wages, pensions, government services, and "entitlements" (which, apparently, we're not really entitled to anymore)—all these processes continued apace. It is apparently the "medicine" we are meant to take after our tax dollars were appropriated to pay to restore the banking system.

What's different is that neoliberalism has lost its luster. Nobody believes anymore that a rising tide of corporate profits lifts all boats. More and more people are acutely aware of the fact that the wealth at the top comes at the expense of the labor and health of the vast majority. In spite of decades of media pundits and politicians telling us that we are to blame for our poverty, low wages, and lack of social opportunities, more and more people understand that the system is set up deliberately to benefit a tiny minority.

The signs of dissatisfaction are growing—best exemplified by the fact that the framing introduced by the Occupy Wall Street movement that spread across the country in 2011—the 1 percent versus the 99 percent—is now everywhere. The crisis has produced questioning, disillusionment, and also resistance. A study by the Initiative for Policy Dialogue finds a world wracked by significantly higher levels of protest starting in 2006.[1] A 2011 Pew poll found that almost half of young Americans ages eighteen to twenty-nine had a favorable view of socialism, and 47 percent a negative view of capitalism.[2] While the majority of Americans may not have a clear idea of what socialism is, and despite the history of phobia around the word *socialism*, it is significant in this country that so many young people are not happy with the way wealth is distributed upward. As author Naomi Klein notes, "The fact that the business-as-usual pursuit of profits and growth is destabilizing life on earth" is prompting some climate scientists to draw anticapitalist conclusions, and is fueling a growing ecological activism across the planet.[3]

Not even the mainstream press can ignore these developments. In March 2013, *TIME* ran a story called "Marx's Revenge: How Class Struggle Is Shaping the World," which commented, "With the global economy in a protracted crisis, and workers around the world burdened by joblessness, debt and stagnant incomes, Marx's biting critique of capitalism—that the system is inherently unjust and self-destructive—cannot be so easily dismissed."[4] The article continues:

> Marx theorized that the capitalist system would inevitably impoverish the masses as the world's wealth became concentrated in the hands of a greedy few, causing economic crises and heightened conflict between the rich and working classes. "Accumulation of wealth at one pole is at the same time accumulation of misery, agony of toil, slavery, ignorance, brutality, mental degradation, at the opposite pole," Marx wrote.
>
> A growing dossier of evidence suggests that he may have been right. It is sadly all too easy to find statistics that show the rich are getting richer while the middle class and poor are not. A September study from the Economic Policy Institute (EPI) in Washington noted that the median annual earnings of a full-time, male worker in the U.S. in 2011, at $48,202, were smaller than in 1973. Between 1983 and 2010, 74% of the gains in wealth in the U.S. went to the richest 5%, while the bottom 60% suffered a decline, the EPI calculated. No wonder some have given the 19th century German philosopher a second look.

Hopefully, this book will help people who want to take a second—or first—look at Marx. I've not changed everything. Some if it remains as it was in the first edition. But I have tried throughout, in using modern illustrations to highlight the applicability of Marx, Engels, and other Marxists' ideas to the present, to update my examples to take into account the changes that have occurred over the past several years. There are some chapters I've substantially revised, like the one on Marx's economics and the chapter on Marxism and oppression, and some I've added bits to. There are also chapters I've almost completely rewritten, like the chapter on the Marxist views of organization and the one on capitalism and ecology. It makes for a somewhat longer but, I hope, better book.

As someone new to writing a book, I didn't have any acknowledgements in the first edition. So I figured I'd better include them here. I'd like to thank Anthony Arnove, who gave me helpful guidance and comments on the first edition; Tithi Bhattacharya and Chris Williams, who helped me with parts of the second version; and Phil Gasper, who helped me with both versions. I'd also like to thank the good folks at Haymarket Books, Julie Fain, Anthony Arnove, and Ahmed Shawki in particular, who pushed me to get this second edition done. (Whether it was because I was expanding my mind or just procrastinating I'm not sure, but I constantly felt the urge to read one more book.) I'd also like to thank my wife Bridget Broderick for her insight, friendship, love, and encouragement. Finally, I'd like to thank my cats, Leon, Lupe, and Felix, meow more than ever. It goes without saying that I didn't create any of the main ideas in this book myself. Marx and a bunch of other great Marxists did.

Introduction

Every so often—usually after a period of economic instability and crisis that has given way to stabilization and growth—some talking head comes along and declares that Marxism is dead and capitalism is the final form of human fulfillment. As the late socialist author Daniel Singer aptly put it, "The purpose of our pundits and preachers is to doom as impossible a radical, fundamental transformation of existing society."[1]

The most common theme is that socialism has failed to make inroads, especially in the United States, due to the prosperity and social mobility that even the lowliest members of society can experience. "On the reefs of roast beef and apple pie," wrote the German writer Werner Sombart in his famous 1906 book *Why Is There No Socialism in the United States?,* "socialistic Utopias of every sort are sent to their doom."[2] The Depression years of the 1930s made these pro-capitalist ideas harder to swallow, but variations on the argument were dusted off and refurbished during the economic boom after the Second World War. Daniel Bell's *The End of Ideology* told us that postwar Western prosperity and the rise of Stalinism signaled "the exhaustion of the nineteenth century ideologies, particularly Marxism, as intellectual systems that could claim *truth* for their views of the world."[3]

Writers on the left, too, like German radical philosopher Herbert Marcuse, could write, "Independence of thought, autonomy, and the right to political opposition are being deprived of their basic critical function in a society which seems increasingly capable of satisfying the needs of the Individuals through the way in which it is organized. . . . Under the conditions of a rising standard of living, non-conformity with the system itself appears to be socially useless, and the more so when it entails tangible economic and political disadvantages and threatens the smooth operation of the whole."[4] For Marcuse, whose ideas were typical of a whole generation of post–Second World War left-wing thinkers, working-class struggle was no longer the connecting link between our society and a future socialist society. Workers were either bought off or simply so enmeshed in capitalism, and unable to see beyond it, that they were now part of the problem rather than the solution.[5]

The mass general strike of ten million French workers in May 1968 offered strong evidence to the contrary, as did a whole period of working-class and student rebellion that spanned the globe in the late 1960s and early 1970s (Poland's Solidarność in 1980 and the major role played by Black workers in the downfall of apartheid South Africa are two other examples). But those movements receded and capitalism found its footing again, utilizing a period of economic crisis to begin an assault on working-class living standards that has continued unrelentingly to this day. Ideologists once again sprang forward to justify capitalism in its most naked, brutal, "free market" form.

Then came the collapse of the bureaucratic regimes in Russia and Eastern Europe in 1989–1993. We were told then that the "free market" and liberal democracy had triumphed over "totalitarian" systems like fascism and communism. Historian Francis Fukuyama came forward and argued that society had indeed evolved, as Marx argued, from lower to higher forms of human social organization. However, instead of that evolutionary process leading to socialism, Fukuyama argued, liberal free-market capitalism constituted the "end point of mankind's ideological evolution," and the "final form of human government"; as such, it constituted the "end of history."[6]

In a flush of exuberance, Western pundits waxed lyrically about a new era of endless peace and prosperity. But if this was the end of history, it didn't seem things were ending all that well. Instead, we entered a world of incessant war, where the United States, as the world's sole superpower, felt free to throw its military weight around, and did; a world of growing disparities between rich and poor (even in the midst of the economic growth of the 1990s); and a world—as we moved into the twenty-first century—of economic and social instability. It was a world in which the much-touted benefits of free trade and "globalization" dramatically enriched a very few but left tens of millions in ever-worsening conditions. In short, it seemed like we had returned to the days of the robber barons and sweated labor of the late nineteenth century, only on a more colossally destructive, global scale.

The obscenity of capitalism today is expressed in a few simple facts:

- The combined wealth of the world's 1,210 billionaires in 2010 (410 of whom were in the United States) was more than half of the total wealth of the 3.1 billion people with a net worth of less than $10,000.[7] Between 1982 and 2011, the Forbes 400—the magazine's list of the world's richest individuals—increased its combined wealth by a factor of fifteen.[8]
- More than a third of the world's people—2.6 billion—live on less than two dollars a day, and 1.44 billion people live on less than one dollar a day.[9]

The statistics for the United States reveal a society that is certainly rich—but only for a minority:

- The average compensation in 2011 for the CEOs of US companies in the S&P 500 index was $12.94 million. On average, CEOs in that year made 380 times what a production worker made, up from a 107:1 ratio in 1990 and a 42:1 ratio in 1982.[10] The compensation package for Walmart CEO Lee Scott Jr. in 2007 was $29.7 million—1,314 times that of the average full-time Walmart employee.[11] Two-thirds of US companies paid no income tax between 1998 and 2005.[12]
- CEO pay increased by 300 percent between 1989 and 2004, whereas wages increased in the same period by only 5 percent (and minimum-wage workers have seen their pay fall 6 percent). If wages had kept up with the percentage increase in CEO pay, in 2004 the average pay for production workers would have been $110,136, instead of $27,460.[13]
- The top 1 percent of the US households controls 34.5 percent of the nation's wealth, and the top 10 percent controls two-thirds, whereas the bottom 90 percent controls 26.9 percent. The average income of the top 0.1 percent of the households is $23.8 million; for the bottom 90 percent it is $29,800.[14]
- 46.2 million people, or 15 percent, live below the poverty line—an increase from 11.3 percent in 2000.[15] Twenty-six percent of Blacks live below the poverty line, and 40.9 percent of all households headed by a single mother live below the poverty line.[16] The poverty level is set at $21,000 for a four-person household—an absurdly low figure. In truth, millions more live in poverty in the United States than these official numbers indicate.

Poverty is always horrible. It only becomes an obscenity when the material means exist to eliminate it, yet it persists. But the priorities of world capitalism are such that the two things—unimaginable wealth and great misery—exist side by side, the one dependent on the persistence of the other. The priorities of capitalism are starkly revealed by the fact that the per capita income in sub-Saharan Africa is $490, whereas the per capita subsidy for European cows is $913.[17] These massive disparities of wealth, moreover, are buttressed by various forms of oppression—national, racial, and sexual—designed to reinforce inequality and maintain the dominance of the many by the few.

These obscenities make the case, if not for Marx and Marxism, then at the very least for some project to change the world. That is why, try as the pundits may to bury him—Marx keeps resurfacing. His ideas are alive because his indictment of capitalism—though first penned in the 1840s—is still confirmed on a daily basis. As the misery worsens, the glaring class divisions give rise to what Marx argued was the motor of historical change—the class struggle. Everywhere around the world, the working class (called the "proletariat" in Marx's day)—those whose labor produces society's abundant wealth in exchange for a pittance—continues to organize, demonstrate, strike, and resist in various ways.

Marx not only exposed the ills of society—many had done so before him—but he revealed how capitalism developed, how it went into crisis, and how it would meet its end. At Marx's gravesite in 1883, Marx's friend and lifelong collaborator Frederick Engels said that Marx "discovered the special law of motion governing the present-day capitalist mode of production." Even Marx's critics sometimes acknowledge that he had brilliant insights into the nature of capitalism. But, Engels continued, "Marx was before all else a revolutionist. His real mission in life was to contribute, in one way or another, to the overthrow of capitalist society and of the state institutions which it had brought into being, to contribute to the liberation of the modern proletariat, which he was the first to make conscious of its own position and its needs, conscious of the conditions of its emancipation."[18]

Of course, much has changed since Marx's day. But the essence of capitalism—the exploitation of the many by the few for profit—remains, and wreaks its damage on an ever-expanding scale. The insane anarchy of a world market that can produce enough food to feed everyone but fails to feed the six million children who die every year from malnutrition remains with us.[19] The unplanned character of capitalist production, with its incessant drive for profit, has created an environmental crisis that threatens the earth's inhabitants like a runaway train threatens its passengers. Indeed, many of the trends described by Marx and Engels—the creation of an increasingly interdependent world market; the system's tendency toward periodic economic crises; increasing productivity and wealth on one side and poverty on the other; the concentration and centralization of capital and the growth of monopolies—give their writings an almost prophetic air.

The task today, set out so long ago by Marx and Engels, also remains the same—to replace competition with association, to build a society in which all wealth is produced and held by its producers in common, and distributed according to human need rather than profit. "In place of the old bourgeois society, with its classes and class antagonisms," wrote Marx and Engels in *The Communist Manifesto*, "we shall have an association in which the free development of each is the condition for the free development of all."[20] Only in such a society can humankind develop its full creative capacities, using our scientific knowledge to enhance lives rather than destroy them.

Moreover, those who loudly applauded the fall of Stalinism left out one important factor: The death of what passed for communism in the East—but what was in reality bureaucratic, state capitalism—paved the way for people to rediscover the real Marxist tradition hidden behind years of distortion in both the East and the West during the Cold War era—that is the tradition of working-class self-emancipation. Far from being dead, therefore, Marxism is experiencing a rebirth.

This book began as a series of articles written for a biweekly column in *Socialist Worker* newspaper called "The Meaning of Marxism." It aims to provide a basic introduction to Marxist ideas, and to show how these ideas remain crucial to our understanding of the world today and the task of changing it.

There is, of course, no substitute for reading Marx and Engels, or the great revolutionary socialists who followed them, such as Rosa Luxemburg, Vladimir Lenin, and Leon Trotsky. I've read and reread works such as Marx's *Civil War in France*, Engels's *Socialism: Utopian and Scientific*, Rosa Luxemburg's *Reform or Revolution*, Trotsky's *Lessons of October*, and Lenin's *State and Revolution*, among many others, and each time I reread them I learn something new in light of fresh experiences.[21] But, as Lenin said in a postscript to *State and Revolution*, "It is more pleasant and useful to go through the 'experience of revolution' than to write about it."[22] Marx and Engels, like Lenin, were not armchair thinkers. First and foremost, they were revolutionaries who fought for a world free of oppression and exploitation. They understood that to change the world, it is necessary to understand how that world works, and to learn from past struggles to distinguish the effective levers for its transformation.

Chapter One

From Millenarianism to Marx

The Dream of a New Society

The idea of socialism is as old as class society itself. So long as there were high priests, kings, lords, nobles, emperors, magistrates, and generals, there were also people who envisioned, and sometimes fought for, a world in which the minority who enriched themselves at the expense of the majority would fall, and the world's wealth would be held in common and shared by all.

Often, radical ideas were couched in religious form, but their content was nonetheless unmistakable. "Grace was among them, because none suffered lack. . . . For they did not give one part and retain another part for themselves. . . . They abolished inequality and lived in great abundance," wrote the patriarch of Constantinople, St. John Chrysostom, in the late fourth century of Christ's apostles.[1]

The fourteenth-century English radical preacher John Ball, a leader in the great agrarian rebellion of 1381, sermonized:

> If we are all descended from one father and one mother, Adam and Eve, how can the lords say or prove that they are more lords than we are—save they make us dig and till the ground so that they can squander what we produce?
>
> They are clad in velvet and satin, set off with squirrel fur, while we are dressed in poor cloth. . . . They have beautiful residences and manors, while we have the trouble and the work, always in the fields under rain and snow. But it is from us and our labor that everything comes and with which they maintain their pomp.

He concluded that "things cannot go well in England nor ever shall until all things are in common and there is neither villein [serf] nor noble, but all of us are of one condition."[2]

Seeing that the French Revolution of 1789 ended feudal tyranny but not economic inequality between rich and poor, nor the rule of the wealthy, Gracchus Babeuf organized a "conspiracy of equals" and called for a new revolution to establish a society in which all goods would be held in common storehouses and distributed according to need. "Everything will be blended together," he wrote, "and on the footing of a perfect equality."[3]

The United States had its share of early radical movements, thinkers, utopians, and socialists. The American Revolution engendered a radical democratic, pro-labor, and antislavery tradition. For example, Thomas Skidmore, author of *The Rights of Man to Property!*, wrote in the 1820s, "Inasmuch as great wealth is an instrument which is uniformly used to extort from others their property, it ought to be taken away from its possessors on the same principle that a sword or pistol may be wrested from a robber." Skidmore believed that new inventions like the steam engine, though "likely to greatly impoverish or destroy the poor," could be beneficial to them on the condition that they "lay hold of it and make it their own."[4]

Emerging industrial capitalism had its insightful critics before Marx. The Swiss economist Jean Charles Léonard Simonde de Sismondi wrote in the 1830s: "Exertion today is separated from its recompense; it is not the same man that first works, and then reposes; but it is because the one works that the other rests."[5] Sismondi grasped the essence of all class societies. It is not simply that some are wealthy and others are not. It is the labor of the many that accounts for the wealth of the few.

In the years following the great French Revolution, a group of socialists emerged who came to be known as utopians. The utopian socialists concocted plans and schemes for a rationally organized society. They were brilliant critics of the iniquities of industrial capitalism, which they argued worked against the better part of human nature. The French utopian Charles Fourier, for example, wrote, "Social progress and historic changes occur by virtue of the progress of women toward liberty, and decadence of the social order occurs as the result of a decrease in the liberty of women."[6]

The utopians sought to create islands of social or communal living that would set an example for the rest of the world to follow. Their aim was to convince everyone—including the wealthy—of the superiority of their system. Human reason—the sheer logic of their position—would convince the well born in society to adopt their plans. Indeed, Fourier was actually opposed to revolutionary change from below. For the utopians, the working class was only a "suffering class," not a class capable of transforming society by its own actions. Engels put it this way:

> The solution of the social problems, which as yet lay hidden in undeveloped economic conditions, the Utopians attempted to evolve out of the human brain. Society presented nothing but wrongs; to remove these was the task of reason. It was necessary, then, to discover a new and more perfect system of social order and to impose this upon society from without by propaganda, and, wherever it was possible, by the example of model experiments. These new social systems were foredoomed as Utopian; the more completely they were worked out in detail, the more they could not avoid drifting off into pure fantasies.[7]

Virtually all of these utopian experiments—many of which were established in the United States in the 1800s—failed. Rather than changing the wider world, the social and economic priorities of the capitalist world changed them. These experiments, though they sometimes offered a glimpse of alternative ways of organizing society, succumbed to the surrounding hostile capitalist environment. Worker-owned cooperatives, by the way, have also faced the same problem as utopian colonies, and for the same reason: you can't build little islands of socialism in a sea of market capitalism.

Various strands of utopianism remain influential today, often justified on the grounds that such experiments "prefigure" a better world. The idea that you can create autonomous islands of liberation fails on two counts—first, because the "real" world finds a way to impinge on, and therefore undermine, the relations that the autonomists try to establish; and second, because they pose no challenge to the capitalist system as a whole by their existence.

He Was a Young Hegelian

Marx and Engels did not start their political lives as socialists. As young, well-to-do German university students, they were drawn to the philosophical youth movement called the Young Hegelians in the late 1830s. Hegel was a highly venerated German philosopher who argued that the course of human history proceeded "dialectically," that is, through constant change based on the clash of contradictory ideas, toward the "absolute idea." Conservative Hegelians considered the highly repressive and bureaucratic Prussian state to be the embodiment of this "absolute idea."

The left Hegelians to which Marx and Engels were attracted, interpreted Hegel's dialectic as a clash of ideas leading to human freedom. Some of the Young Hegelians spent a great deal of time splitting metaphysical hairs, while others looked to constitutional and democratic reforms. After Prussia's new king legally barred the Young Hegelians from taking university posts, a job to which Marx had aspired, he became an editor of an important liberal paper, the Cologne *Rheinische Zeitung*, in 1841, and for the first time moved from the abstract realm of philosophy into the realm of, in his words, "material interests" and "economic questions," such as the theft of wood, free trade, and the conditions of the peasantry.[8]

In this period he could be described as an extreme democrat. He wrote, for example, that "every form of freedom conditions the other," such that if one freedom is taken away, then freedom in general "is deprived of any semblance of life."[9] As editor, Marx saw how laws, for example those against wood theft, were used against the poor on behalf of wealthy forest owners, and that the state did not stand above class interests. He also saw how liberals were the first to desert the struggle and find compromises with the status quo. The liberal backers of the newspaper failed to defend press freedom when the state banned the *Rheinische Zeitung* in 1843. Marx saw this as an example of "the natural impotence of half-hearted liberalism," which fears anything that might threaten its petty interests.[10] But he also criticized himself, vowing never to place himself again in a position as he did as an editor, where he would have to engage in "bowing and scraping, dodging, and hairsplitting over words," which, he felt, led to self-corruption.[11]

Marx stood for the fullest democracy, and denounced those who argued that the masses were too "immature" for it and needed to be kept in swaddling clothes. "If we all lie in a cradle," he asked, "who is to cradle us? If we are all in jail, who is to be the jail warden?"[12]

For a time, however, he continued to see workers and peasants merely as suffering beings rather than the shapers of their own destiny—for he still saw "spirit," or philosophy, as the prime mover of change. He held on to the Hegelian idea that the state could be "perfected" to represent the whole of society rather than just narrow, bourgeois interests, and that the clash of theories was more important than the "crude" material struggle.

The cowardly timidity of the German liberals had convinced Marx that the bourgeoisie in Germany was incapable of leading a process of social and political transformation as he believed the bourgeoisie had done in the French Revolution of 1789. So after being fired from the paper and moving to Paris in 1843, he was informed by two inclinations—to see practical struggle, rather than ivory-tower disputes, as the key to social change, and to look for a new class, or social force, that could play the key role in transforming society.

When he first became aware of the socialist and communist ideas that were developing in France, Marx first did not embrace them. He felt that he would first need to delve into and study them carefully before he decided what he thought. They were, he surmised, ideal constructions that bore no relationship to existing conditions and possibilities when what was needed was a way to combine a theoretical understanding of the world with practical participation in struggle:

> Nothing prevents us from making criticism of politics, participation in politics, and therefore *real* struggles, the starting point of our criticism, and from identifying our criticism with them. In that case we do not confront the world in a doctrinaire way with a new principle: Here is the truth, kneel down before it! We develop new principles for the world out of the world's own principles. We do not say to the world: Cease your struggles, they are foolish; we will give you the true slogan of struggle. We merely show the world what it is really fighting for, and consciousness is something that it *has* to acquire, even if it does not want to.[13]

While in Paris Marx for the first time made contact with the workers' movement, and was impressed by the French workmen's nobility of spirit and commitment to the struggle. "You would have to attend one of the meetings of the French workers," he wrote to Ludwig Feuerbach in 1844, "to appreciate the pure freshness, the nobility which bursts forth from these toil-worn men. . . . It is among these 'barbarians' of our civilized society that history is preparing the practical element for the emancipation of mankind."[14] He was also influenced by his new friend Engels, who in Britain was witness to the struggles of the country's rising industrial working class, and before Marx's own awakening had begun to draw conclusions about the role of workers achieving socialism through their own struggles.

At the end of December, he expressed his new views—that the path to a new society in Germany lay in revolutionary struggle, and that the class capable of carrying it out would be the newly forming working class, the class "with radical chains" that cannot acheive it own liberation "without emancipating itself from all other spheres of society and thereby emancipating all other spheres of society."[15]

Then, in 1844, he witnessed the first stirrings of mass workers' protest in Germany, the Silesian weaver's revolt—a two-day battle between weavers and state militia—which confirmed his views. In a debate with another Hegelian, Arnold Ruge, who criticized the revolt from the sidelines, Marx declared that rather than be a "schoolmaster," one must not only study the struggle but also sympathize with it.

A New Kind of Socialism

What made Marx and Engels's socialism, when they decided to embrace it, different from the utopians was that their socialism (actually, they chose to call themselves communists because communism was associated more closely with the workers' movement, whereas socialism was more associated with the utopians who stood apart from workers' struggles) was rooted in real, rather than ideal, conditions. Marx and Engels showed that the desire for and vision of another world wasn't enough. The utopians, in criticizing existing social relations and proposing elaborate social plans for a better society, simply counterposed what is with what *ought to be*. But there had to be something that connected the future with the present. The seeds of a future society had to already exist in the soil of the present for it to spring forth. The material conditions and social actors had to exist to make that change both possible and necessary for society to move forward.

"Communism is for us," wrote Marx and Engels, "not . . . an *ideal* to which reality [will] have to adjust itself." It is "the *real* movement which abolishes the present state of things."[16] The starting point for Marx and Engels, therefore, was not "what men say, imagined, conceived, in order to arrive at men in the flesh." Instead, they wrote, "We set out from real, active men, and on the basis of their real-life process we demonstrate the development of the ideological reflexes and echoes of this life-process."[17]

The point was not that it was impossible to have ideas about freedom before the conditions for their realization existed, or that there was a mechanical one-to-one relationship between people's ideas and their material conditions of life. However, "one cannot be liberated," if one is "unable to obtain food and drink, housing and clothing in adequate quality and quantity." "Liberation," Marx and Engels argued, "is a historical and not a mental act."[18]

Socialism, in short, must be more than a good idea. There must be material and social forces created within the framework of capitalism that have the potential to make it a reality. Put crudely, if there isn't enough food to go around, equality simply means a slow death for everyone—an equality of suffering. Sharing on a sustained basis implies that food is plentiful. Revolutionary change, moreover, comes not from the actions of a few social engineers remolding society but through the actions of masses of people.

Marx and Engels were able to move beyond the utopians for a number of connected reasons. Like other socialists, Marx and Engels saw the tremendous increase in wealth that sprouted up during the rise of industrial capitalism that promised, but did not deliver, a world free of want. But they also witnessed something else: workers' strikes and demonstrations in Germany, Britain, and France. The working class ceased for them to be only a "suffering class" and became before their eyes the active agent of its own liberation—the class whose own emancipation could act as the basis for the liberation of all.

This is the central component of Marxism, so we'll come back to this. But for now a couple of points need to be highlighted. The "discovery" of the working class was an important breakthrough, because it identified a social force capable, through its own actions, of transforming society. Before this point, there had been, roughly speaking, two views about radical social change, and both saw in the mass of the exploited, at best, a passive element that might aid more enlightened minorities to transform society.[19] Marx and Engels had originally held these views, but they broke with them—based on their own observations and experiences of the class struggle itself.

The radical French eighteenth-century materialists, like the utopians, argued that the mass of the people, as products of their social and material conditions, were incapable of getting beyond it. For how can someone molded by his or her environment step outside that environment to change it? What was required, therefore, was an exceptional man, or a group of enlightened *men*, standing above or outside society—that these philosophers thought enlightened men would change the world was, ironically, proof that they, too, were products of the prevailing circumstances—or even an enlightened despot, who would make change from above. Even radicals such as the French revolutionary Auguste Blanqui saw workers as part of a more or less unconscious mass that could provide muscle, but not leadership, to the revolution, which would be made by a group of conscious conspirators.

Idealist thinkers, who believed that great ideas shaped the material world, held equally elitist theories that relegated the masses to either no role whatsoever in historical change, or to a completely passive role. For the left Hegelians in Germany, for example, of which Marx and Engels were members in the early 1840s, spirit (or ideas or philosophy) was the active element, whereas the material, the "mass," was the passive element in social change, if it played any role at all. The point is that most radicals adhered to the "great man" theory of history—every great event in history was brought about by the great ideas and great actions of great men. French radical nineteenth-century historian Augustin Thierry ridiculed this approach:

> It is highly singular that the historians stubbornly refused to attribute any spontaneity or creativity to the masses of people. If an entire people migrates and makes itself a new home, that means, our annalists and poets assert, that some hero has taken it into his head to found a new empire to add luster to his name; if a city is established, it is some prince that has given it life. The people, the citizens, are always material for the thinking of a single individual. Do you really wish to learn who founded an institution and who conceived a social enterprise? Search among those who really needed it; it was to them that the first idea of it, the wish to act, and a considerable part of the execution belonged.[20]

Historians and poets may write history, but it is great masses of people in motion—in particular, social classes—that make history. Marx came to this conclusion in a series of notes, or "theses," he jotted down in 1845. First, he argued that the mechanical, or one-sided, materialists who said that people were products of their circumstances, and that to change people you only had to change their circumstances, inevitably divided society into two parts: the passive majority (who were victims of their circumstances and therefore trapped within them) and a thinking elite that could somehow stand outside society and act on it. Like the famous behavioral scientist B. F. Skinner, who set up various experiments to elicit certain predictable responses from his subjects, this minority would mold the passive majority by changing its circumstances.

The problem with this view is that the special minority who are meant to change things are themselves products of their material environment, so there is no logical reason why they also should not be subject to the same circumstances that constrain everyone else's behavior—in which case change would be impossible. As Marx put it, "The materialist doctrine concerning the changing of circumstances and upbringing forgets that circumstances are changed by men and that it is essential to educate the educator himself. This doctrine must, therefore, divide society into two parts, one of which is superior to society."[21]

In criticizing Hegel's idealism, therefore, Marx did not fall back on the old mechanical, one-sided materialism that presented human history as something that just "happens" behind the backs of human beings. Rather, as we shall see later in more detail, he presented history as something that is made by people themselves, and, at the same time that historical possibilities are *constrained* materially in such a way that human will and historical outcome do not coincide.

"The chief defect of all hitherto existing materialism," argued Marx, "is that the thing, reality, sensuousness, is conceived only in the form of the *object or of contemplation*, but not as *sensuous human activity, practice*."[22]

To the idealists who argued that conditions didn't matter, and that only ideas were important, Marx argued that ideas without any connection to the real world were immaterial, and therefore incapable of changing social conditions. The validity of any idea about society could only be tested in practice—the practice of masses of people attempting to change society. The way Marx got around this dilemma was to say that historical change could only be conceived as the self-conscious activity of masses of people; that the oppressed changed their ideas, and their own conditions, by acting on the world to transform it. "The coincidence of the changing of circumstances and of human activity or self-changing can be conceived and rationally understood only as *revolutionary practice*."[23]

Chapter Two

Marx's Materialist Method

Why Theory Matters

The last "thesis" that Marx jotted down in 1845 was this: "The philosophers have merely interpreted the world; the point, however, is to change it."[1] One way to interpret this statement is as an argument against theory. We don't need theory—that's for professors and intellectuals who like to debate to no particular end—we just need to fight for what we know is right. "You don't need a weatherman," goes the 1960s Bob Dylan song, "to know which way the wind blows."[2]

While people might declare that ideas about society are a waste of time, they wouldn't say the same thing about what we call the hard sciences. No one would ever say: Who needs physics? (Except maybe bored high school students.) All of our modern technology—from electricity to airplane engines and computers—was developed on the basis of science.

Scientific theory helps us get beneath the surface appearance of things to understand the underlying laws that govern their behavior. "All science would be superfluous," wrote Marx, "if the outward appearance and the essence of things directly coincided."[3] Scientific theories are explanations about why and how things happen that are not apparent through immediate observation. We can't, for example, know what processes are at work that make water boil simply by observing water boiling.

"If we lived on a planet where nothing ever changed, there would be little to do," wrote science writer Carl Sagan. "There would be nothing to figure out. There would be no impetus for science. And if we lived in an unpredictable world, where things changed in random or complex ways, we would not be able to figure things out. Again, there would be no such thing as science. But we live in an in-between universe, where things change, but according to patterns, rules, or, as we call them, laws of nature."[4]

How do we know whether or not a theory is right or wrong? It has to be tested in practice. A scientific theory can be invalidated if examples or results are found that the theory cannot explain. Wrong theories produce bad, if not useless, practical results; or they cannot explain every case they are meant to explain. Indeed, the proof of a scientific theory's soundness lies, with some exceptions, in its ability to predict behavior, whether practical experiments can reproduce what it predicts will happen, or whether the practical applications developed out of the theory actually work.

That isn't to say that the application of science is completely neutral. Obviously, the fact that governments and businesses spend more time and money on things like nuclear weaponry and designer drugs than on curing deadly diseases tells us something about the way capitalism shapes scientific inquiry today. Scientific practice is not an objective pursuit that takes place outside of society; it is largely harnessed to the interests of profit-making and military competition between states. "Modern science is big business," writes David B. Resnick. "Like any other business, science is influenced by economic forces and financial interests."[5] Nevertheless, the whole purpose of science, for good or ill, is to assist in changing reality. Scientists, in other words, must be able to "interpret the world" in order to "change it." This holds true, perversely, also with the atomic bomb, if we were to replace "change" with "destroy."

Can there be, however, any talk of "science" in regard to understanding, or changing, society? Marx's little quip quoted above about philosophers only "interpreting the world" when the point is to "change it" was written as an attack on armchair thinkers, people who talked but did nothing. He didn't really think that there was no point interpreting the world—rather, he thought that there was no point interpreting the world *unless* you were trying to change it. Ideas divorced from practice are free to float in the stratosphere, where one is as good as the next—or as useless, as anyone who has been to a graduate-student wine-and-cheese party can attest.

Science can be harnessed to suit the needs of corporations attempting to improve production techniques and outsell their competitors. But we live in a society that is divided into a small minority of very wealthy exploiters and a majority of people who work or starve. All societies that are divided into a minority class of exploiters and a majority class of exploited require for their functioning a set of ideas that reinforce class domination. "The ideas of the ruling class are in every epoch the ruling ideas, i.e., the class which is the ruling material force of society, is at the same time its ruling intellectual force,"[6] Marx and Engels wrote in 1845. "The class which has the means of material production at its disposal, has control at the same time over the means of mental production, so that thereby, generally speaking, the ideas of those who lack the means of mental production are subject to it. The ruling ideas are nothing more than the ideal expression of the dominant material relationships."[6]

Consequently, the closer we get to lines of inquiry that involve human society, the less scientific, and the more apologetic, the inquiry becomes. The ruling, capitalist class (whom Marx and Engels referred to as the "bourgeoisie") certainly harnesses social ideas to its needs. But it does so for the purpose of justifying its rule—not changing the unequal relations between rich and poor in society, but keeping them the way they are. The fact that the United States was founded on conquest (of Indians and Mexicans) and enslavement (of Africans), or that the legal system favors the rich over the poor and the white over the Black, or that workers here had to go on strike to get an eight-hour day, is not going to be prominent in most high school textbooks. History reflects the "ruling ideology."

The "ruling ideas" are ideas meant to bolster the status quo, not explain or challenge it. An example of this would be the idea that "outside agitators" cause strikes and social movements, a common refrain among employers and their political hirelings throughout the history of the US labor movement. The argument conveys the idea that ordinary people are too happy with their lot to want to fight against their own oppression, but are gullible and therefore easily duped by "Machiavellian" leftists. The assumption is also "that the victims of injustice lack the wit or the will to challenge their superiors, that they are incapable of acting on their own grievances and rationally choosing their allies," writes radical British author Mike Marqusee.[7]

Historians and sociologists usually make more sophisticated arguments than this, but their sophistication does not necessarily indicate greater insight. Indeed, often less crude, more superficially impressive arguments are more useful in bolstering the status quo. Marx challenged the bourgeois economists of his time, saying that for them, it wasn't a question of whether "this theorem or that was true, but whether it was useful to capital or harmful, expedient or inexpedient, politically dangerous or not."[8] More than that, the social science practitioners and theorists routinely set out to discredit anyone who puts forth the idea that class and class struggle are central to history. Lenin put it this way:

> Throughout the civilized world the teachings of Marx evoke the utmost hostility and hatred of all bourgeois science (both official and liberal), which regards Marxism as a kind of "pernicious sect." And no other attitude is to be expected, for there can be no "impartial" social science in a society based on class struggle. In one way or another, *all* official and liberal science *defends* wage slavery, where Marxism has declared relentless war on wage slavery. To expect science to be impartial in a wage-slave society is as silly and naive as to expect impartiality from manufacturers on the question of whether workers' wages should be increased by decreasing the profits of capital.[9]

Those most committed to fundamentally transforming capitalism are in the best position to understand it. It is no accident, therefore, that the academics and researchers whose writings contain the most useful insights and revelations about history and society are those who have, at least in some point in their lives, been directly involved in, or at least closely connected with, radical and revolutionary attempts to change society.

Marx argued that insofar as a real critical understanding of society represents a class, "it can only represent the class whose vocation in history is the overthrow of

the capitalist mode of production and the final abolition of all classes—the proletariat."[10] By this Marx did not mean that you just walk up and ask a UPS worker to
get an accurate answer to various social questions. He meant that only movements
of workers in struggle, seeking ways to challenge the world, require as a condition of
success a real picture of the dynamics of society. Only among the working class and
the oppressed, and all those who stand with them in struggle—where there is "no
concern for careers, for profit-making, or for gracious patronage from above"—can
we find the potential to understand the real life-processes of capitalism.[11]

Common sense tells us that truth is about impartiality, finding the golden mean
between different positions. The irony is that it is only by taking sides in a fight to
change the world—on the side of the oppressed and exploited—will you have both
the *need* and the *capacity* to understand how things work. For example, if as a worker
I believe that bosses are reasonable people who are looking for ways to improve my
wages, I will act accordingly: I'll go and ask politely at the manager's door for a raise.
But I will quickly learn that my "theory" about the bosses won't get me very far. Employers raise wages in response to labor shortages or to labor struggles, but—all other
things being equal—they aren't interested in cutting into their own profits by increasing the wages of their workers.

Unfortunately, when looking at society, it is often accepted that one "theory" is
as good as another. Imagine if physics or astronomy were approached this way. You
say the earth revolves around the sun, I say the sun revolves around the earth—who's
to say what's correct? But if we are to intervene in society practically, and actually
change it, "flat-earth" sociology won't do. We'll need to go beyond "commonsense"
ideas that help bolster the status quo—like "people are poor because there isn't enough
to go around," "immigrants steal our jobs," "poor people are poor because they are
lazy," or "our government invades other countries to liberate people."

What is there to recommend one view of society over any other view? For Marx
and Engels, the question of whether this or that view of the world is correct was
something that had to be tested against experience. "The question whether objective
truth can be attributed to human thinking," Marx wrote, "is not a question of theory
but is a practical question. . . . Man must prove the truth, i.e., the reality and power,
the this-worldliness of his thinking *in practice*." Debating the truth or non-truth of
any idea without reference to the real world was "purely a scholastic question."[12] Society isn't a laboratory or a test tube where controlled experiments can take place to
test our theories. Life itself is the experiment.

Working-class people are not blank slates, but carry with them a variety of different, often contradictory ideas, some of which reflect the ruling ideas, and some which
challenge them. For example, the same person who supports unions as a way to better
conditions on the job may also hold racist ideas. Another may oppose racism, but
accept sexist ideas about women. They may not be conscious that these ideas—some

reinforcing solidarity and liberation, others reinforcing division and oppression—are contradictory. The importance of clear ideas becomes more obvious in the course of mass action, when there are all kinds of debates about which way forward. The founder of Russian Marxism, Georgi Plekhanov, wrote, "Without revolutionary theory there can be no revolutionary movement."[13]

By this he did not mean that we have to have all of our ideas sorted out before we can fight for a better world. You can't sort your ideas out about the world without engaging in struggle. What he did mean is that if our side—the side of the downtrodden, the mistreated, the exploited—is eventually to triumph and build a new society, it must have its own set of coherent ideas, its own worldview that counters that of the ruling class. A coherent worldview is shaped in part over the course of challenging capitalism, but it is also shaped by coming to grips with the historical experience of past struggles and by scientifically investigating the way our society works. "In the eyes of a philistine, a revolutionary point of view is virtually equivalent to an absence of scientific objectivity," observed Russian revolutionary Leon Trotsky.

> We think just the opposite: only a revolutionist—provided, of course, that he is equipped with the scientific method—is capable of laying bare the objective dynamics of the revolution. Apprehending thought is in general not contemplative, but active. The element of will is indispensable for penetrating the secrets of nature and society. Just as a surgeon, on whose scalpel a human life depends, distinguishes with extreme care the various tissues of an organism, so a revolutionist, if he has a serious attitude toward his task, is obliged with strict conscientiousness to analyze the structure of society, its functions and reflexes.[14]

Materialism and Idealism

In the history of philosophy, idealism and materialism have very different meanings from their popular usage—where idealism means having unrealistic ideas (or unrealizable goals), and materialism refers to a desire to possess property and wealth. By that definition, Marx was an idealist and Bill Gates is a materialist. According to their traditional usage in philosophical writing, however, idealism and materialism represent the two main divergent ways of looking at the world we live in. For the idealist, the mind—or the spirit, sometimes God—is the origin of all material things. The ancient Greek idealist philosopher Plato, for example, argued that the world and the things in it were determined by universal, ideal categories. Therefore, every real tree was a copy derived from the universal, ideal "tree." In fact, according to Plato, the universal ideal was "real," whereas the material manifestation was merely a shadow, or weak copy, of the universal. Plato separated the mind from matter, and argued the former ruled over the latter.

Idealism permeates much popular thought. For example, the idea that historical change comes about because great men (women don't usually get any credit) come along with great ideas is widely accepted. But this doesn't explain why it is that anyone bothered to follow these leaders or where the great ideas of these "great men" came from.

For the materialist, all of reality is based on matter, including mental activity, which is itself a result of the organization of matter in a particular way. Whereas the idealist places the mind above and outside of nature, the materialist argues that the mind itself is a product of natural developments. Minds cannot exist apart from the material world, and the material world existed long before any human mind was able to contemplate it. In this view, the abstract "tree" derives from our experience of actual trees. Universal categories are just generalizations that human beings made out of their experience of the real world. "It is not consciousness that determines life," wrote Marx, putting it another way, "but life that determines consciousness."[15]

One of the most common forms of idealism is the view that humans have unrestricted "free will"—the idea that individuals can do anything they set their minds to regardless of economic, social, and cultural obstacles placed in front of them. The view that "you can beat poverty if you really try hard" implicitly accepts free will. Poverty, in this view, is not a social phenomenon caused by, for example, a factory closing or a chronic illness in the family (itself perhaps caused by a pollutant spewed into the air by some corporation). Rather, poverty is a personal failing.

The most famous example of this kind of thinking came from former US president Ronald Reagan, who once argued that the "people who are sleeping on the grates . . . the homeless . . . are homeless, you might say, by choice." The dramatic rise in homelessness in the 1980s naturally had nothing to do with the fact that Reagan halved the public-housing budget and reduced federal spending to local governments.[16] The flip side of this argument is that businessmen and wealthy professionals derive their social status from their brilliant personal qualities, not because of the silver spoons stuck into their mouths at birth.

No one has ever argued that companies go bankrupt by choice. Yet every year, in spite of the intentions of individual businesspeople, thousands of companies do go bankrupt. The same applies to unemployment. Unemployment goes through cyclical rises and declines. There was a massive spike in unemployment after the 2007–8 financial crisis, and it remained high for several years following. It stretches logic to argue that it was caused by a sudden outbreak of mass laziness. The truth, as we shall show later, is that unemployment has economic causes that are beyond the control of individual workers or capitalists.

Marx and Engels ridiculed the view that ideas determine reality. "Once upon a time, a valiant fellow had the idea that men were drowned in water only because they were possessed with the idea of gravity," they wrote. "If they were to get this notion out of their heads," they could avoid drowning.[17] Behind the humor lay an important point: Thought that bears no relationship to reality is impotent thought. The will to action is important, but if that will does not correspond to material possibilities, it doesn't count for anything. This can apply in obvious ways—willpower cannot overcome a shortage of food on a deserted island. Or it can apply in more subtle ways. Willpower alone cannot convince everyone at my workplace to walk out with me on strike—other conditions are required.

What people say and think about themselves and the world must not be taken on its own merit but must be judged in light of the underlying social and economic relations that govern their behavior. We must go beneath the surface of what often appear to be religious disputes, for example, to see that these conflicts express deeper class conflicts. "A distinction must be made," wrote Marx, "between the material transformation of the economic conditions of production . . . and the legal, political, religious, aesthetic or philosophic—in short, ideological forms in which men become conscious of this conflict and fight it out."[18]

Another popular idealist premise is that human behavior is shaped by universal morals. Ideas of right and wrong, which exist above society and above time, govern human behavior. This fails to address the fact that different societies have very different moral standards. A more current form of idealism is the idea that the international relations between states are not governed by military and economic competition but by universal norms of human behavior: rules of trade, rules of war, and so on. All the glaring deviations in reality from these universal norms merely reflect that the real world is an imperfect copy of the ideal world from which it derives.

The abstract morality of good versus evil is used by opposing classes, and by opposing nations in wartime, to justify their own actions and condemn those of their opponents. The truth is, as Engels argued, people "consciously or unconsciously, derive their ethical ideas in the last resort from the practical relations on which their class position is based—from the economic relations in which they carry on production and exchange." Morality, in the final instance, either justifies the domination of the ruling classes, or represents the oppressed classes' "indignation against this domination and the future interests of the oppressed."[19]

Sometimes the indignation manifests itself as a belief that the world should live up to the abstract moral ideas that various world leaders prattle on about. Sometimes it finds expression in the idea that we as individuals should live by a certain moral code. Many young people who are horrified by the inequalities of capitalism are motivated by a belief that one can change the world by changing one's own moral outlook and behavior. One need only reject greed and selfishness, refuse to eat and buy certain products, and then impart this outlook to others. But this approach, though it might help its practitioner feel better about himself/herself, doesn't change anything. Greed and selfishness are not the result of bad individual choices, but are engendered by the competitive and profit-driven nature of capitalism. A capitalist who is not greedy for profit is a capitalist who will lose out to his more greedy competitors.

The problem with the notion that it is only necessary to change people's ideas in order to change society is that this leaves the social structure intact. "This demand to change consciousness amounts to a demand to interpret the existing world in a different way, i.e., to recognize it by means of a different interpretation," Marx wrote of some German idealists of his day. In doing this "they are in no way combating the real existing world," but are "combating solely the phrases of this world."[20] The materialist view is exactly the opposite. Morals are derived from particular forms of human social organization. Capitalism breeds greed, not vice versa. In societies that foraged for food and shared it as a collective, greed was frowned upon because it disrupted the functioning of the group.

Marx and Engels subjected idealism itself to a materialist analysis, showing that it had historical roots in the separation of material and mental labor that came with the overall division of society into classes—those who engage in back-breaking work, and those who are free to engage in mental pursuits (priests, for example, in the earliest class societies). It was no accident that Plato developed his idealism in a slave society, where physical labor was denigrated. "From this moment onwards consciousness can really flatter itself that it is something other than consciousness of existing practice," wrote Marx and Engels, "that it *really* represents something without representing something real; from now on consciousness is in a position to emancipate itself from the world and to proceed to the formation of 'pure' theory, theology, philosophy, ethics, etc."[21]

But ideas are not suspended in air—they have real material roots. To understand why people think and behave the way they do, you must understand the way in which they work together to procure their means of existence. On this basis arises a superstructure of ideas and concepts that people form in their everyday intercourse to explain and influence the world around them.

"You Can't Change Human Nature"

There is another kind of materialism that Marxism rejects outright, and that is the biological or genetic materialism that presents human behavior as determined either solely or primarily by our genetic inheritance. This line of reasoning, which goes back to such social Darwinists of the late nineteenth century as Sir Francis Galton and Herbert Spencer, presents us with the argument that human nature is the fixed and unchanging result of our biological makeup. Why do people behave the way they do? It's part of our genetic coding. Greed, selfishness, xenophobia, racism, male domination, violence, and war are all attributed to something innate to all of us. Needless to say, this is a very convenient argument for someone who is trying to uphold the status quo, for it places the blame for all sorts of nasty behavior on human traits that are beyond anyone's power to change.

The early advocates of social Darwinism, which can be summarized as a theory advancing "survival of the whitest and the richest," were blatant in their racism and disdain for the poor. In addition to arguing that white Anglo-Saxons were superior to the dark-skinned people of the world, Spencer also opposed universal education, free lunches for the indigent, and any laws regulating wages or working conditions.[22] A popular idea among historians in the United States and Britain in the late nineteenth century was that the allegedly superior form of government existing in Britain and the United States resulted from the biological characteristics of the Anglo-Saxon and Teutonic people from which they descended. During a lecture tour of the United States in 1881, Oxford professor Edward A. Freeman, a proponent of the "Teutonic" school, remarked, "The best remedy for whatever is amiss in America would be if every Irishman should kill a Negro and be hanged for it."[23] Anglo-Saxon racial superiority was one of the key justifications used by religious leaders, statesmen, newspaper editors, and professors for the God-given right of the United States, indeed, its responsibility, to expand its empire overseas. "Fitness [for self-government]," declared Theodore Roosevelt, "comes . . . only to those races which possess an immense reserve fund of strength, common sense, and morality."[24]

Racial theories fell into disrepute after the rise of Nazism and the Holocaust, but began to revive in various forms starting in the 1960s and culminated in the publication of *The Bell Curve* in 1994. In addition to arguing that people rise to the top of the society because they are intelligent, an attribute that they said was primarily based on genetic inheritance, the authors unabashedly argued that Blacks were inherently less intelligent than whites.[25]

The late Stephen Jay Gould rightly noted that these purportedly scientific ideas are ideology, not science, providing the justification for various right-wing policy initiatives that attack the poor and the oppressed. "Why struggle and spend to raise the unboostable IQ of races or social classes at the bottom of the economic ladder?" he asked. "Better simply to accept nature's unfortunate dictates and save a passel of federal funds (we can then more easily sustain tax breaks for the wealthy!). Why bother yourself about under-representation of disadvantaged groups in your honored and remunerative bailiwick if such absence records the diminished ability or general immorality, biologically imposed, of most members in the rejected group, and not the legacy or current reality of social prejudice?"[26]

The argument that our behavior is based on evolved genetic traits was presented most systematically by sociobiologist E. O. Wilson in the 1970s, and has since become widely accepted. "The most distinctive human qualities have emerged during the phase of social evolution that occurred through intertribal warfare and through genocide,"

Wilson asserted. "Among general social traits in human beings are aggressive dominance systems with males dominant over females."[27] Richard Lewontin, another Harvard geneticist, calls sociobiology "the latest and most mystified attempt to convince people that human life is pretty much what it has to be and perhaps even ought to be."[28] The method of sociobiology is to look at the world as it is—our capitalist world—and from that distill a set of fundamental human traits that it claims apply to all human beings throughout history. These claimed universal traits, according to sociobiology—male dominance, hatred of strangers, systems of domination, competition for resources, even a hankering for religion—have their origin in our genes.

The modern incarnation of sociobiology, evolutionary psychology, claims that human beings possess genetically programmed behavior that developed over a long period of time in the Paleolithic era. Psychologist Cordelia Fine, a critic of this ideology, argues that evolutionary psychologists promote the idea that "we are the luckless owners of seriously outdated neural circuitry that has been shaped by natural selection to match the environment of our hunter-gatherer ancestors."[29] But as biologist Steven Rose points out, in an argument that also applies to Wilson, "The descriptions that evolutionary psychology offers of what human hunter-gatherer societies were like read little better than 'Just So' accounts, rather like those museum—and cartoon—montages of hunter-dad bringing home the meat while gatherer-mom tends the fireplace and kids. . . . There is a circularity about reading this version of the present into the past, and then claiming that this imagined past explains the present."[30]

These fashionable ideas, though continually offered as fact, have no scientific foundation. Search as they may, biologists will never find a war gene—because war isn't innate to humans any more than is nonviolence. It's not that there is no biological basis for our behavior. But for every example of aggression in human behavior, we can also find examples of peaceful cooperation and sharing. Moreover, how these things are even defined depends on the historical and cultural setting. Neither violence nor sharing is genetically programmed—they are socially shaped and conditioned. As the evolutionary biologist Theodosius Dobzhansky noted, "Heredity does determine that a person can learn to speak a language or languages, but it does not determine which language he will learn or what he will say."[31]

If there is a fixed human nature, then how can it be that human societies have differed so much between different regions and historical times? How is it that some societies were egalitarian, sharing societies, while others were competitive and class divided? How is it that some were warlike and violent, while others were relatively peaceful? How is it that some accorded women a high position, and others a subordinate one? How is it that some societies proscribed same-sex intimacy, while others embraced it?

The French Jesuit missionary Le Jeune lived among the Montagnais-Naskapi Indians on the Labrador coast of Canada in the early 1630s. "Alas!," he lamented, "if someone could stop the wanderings of the Savages, and give authority to one of them to rule the others, we would see them converted and civilized in a short time."

"They have neither political organization, nor offices, nor dignities, nor any authority," he observed of the Indians, "for they only obey their chief through the goodwill toward him, therefore they never kill each other to acquire these honors. Also, as they are contented with a mere living, not one of them gives himself to the Devil to acquire wealth."[32]

The Jesuits who proselytized among this society considered it healthy to beat children into submission, while the Indians considered the practice barbaric. Consider an incident described by LeJeune cited in Eleanor Burke Leacock's book *Myths of Male Dominance*: A French boy struck and injured a Montagnais boy. Alarmed, the Indians demanded gifts. But the French missionaries instead prepared to punish the French child by whipping him in front of the Indians. According to the report of a Jesuit, "One of the savages stripped himself entirely, threw his blanket over the child and cried to him that was going to do the whipping: 'Strike me if thou wilt, but thou shalt not strike him.' And thus the little one escaped."[33] In another telling incident, when the missionary tried to tell a Montagnais-Naskapi man that women should love only their husbands so that men could be sure of who their children were, he responded: "Thou hast no sense. You French people love only your own children; but we all love all the children of our tribe."[34]

The "human nature" view of the world assumes that humans have a built-in nature—shaped genetically by their physical attributes—in the same way that other animals have a nature that determines their behavior. The wolf has sharp teeth to tear raw meat, and the bear has fur to keep warm, and fish have gills to breathe under water and special muscles adapted for swimming. But we humans have none of these special adaptations. The reality is that our brains are not "hard-wired" for certain behaviors and not others; we possess a great deal of neuroplasticity. Human beings shape their environment, and the environment shapes our brains. It is this that explains our infinite adaptability. As Fine notes,

> Our brains . . . are changed by our behavior, our thinking, our social world. The new neuroconstructivist perspective of brain development emphasizes the sheer exhilarating tangle of a continuous interaction among genes, brain, and environment. Yes, gene expression gives rise to neural structures, and genetic material is itself impervious to outside influence. When it comes to genes, you get what you get. But gene activity is another story: genes switch on and off depending on what else is going on. Our environment, our behavior, even our thinking, can all change what genes are *expressed*. And thinking, learning, sensing can all change neural structure directly.[35]

Our peculiar genetic inheritance that make us all human—in particular, our upright gait, larger brain size, opposable thumbs, and the capacity for language—gave us the ability to make tools to manipulate our environment cooperatively and to pass those skills on to our offspring. Humans can make fur coats, build shelter, and catch, grow, and cook food; that is, we can create the things nature did not physically endow us with, things that allow us to exploit virtually every environment on the planet.

There is a human nature—we are naturally cooperative, naturally social creatures. But what makes us human—language, cooperative labor, and tool-making— are precisely the things that make human social relations, and therefore our modes of behavior, so malleable. The point is, what makes humans distinct from other animals—though we are still animals—is that we are social creatures who possess an ability to artificially reproduce our means of existence, a fact that creates a plasticity of behavior that other animals do not possess. In short, we adapt culturally.

Human beings have changed relatively little genetically or biologically over the last forty thousand years. Yet our social forms of organization—the way that we organize ourselves to procure food, shelter, clothing, and other necessities—have changed tremendously, and in recent centuries, at an accelerating rate. It is this that accounts for the changing "nature" of humans—our morals, our ideas about the world and about ourselves—from one society to the next.

The Russian Marxist Georgi Plekhanov noted, "Human nature can no longer be regarded at present as the ultimate and most general cause of historical development; if constant, it cannot explain the extremely changeable course of history; if changeable, its changes are obviously themselves determined by the historical development."[36]

In attempting to attribute extremely variable human behavior throughout history to a relatively fixed constant—a genetically determined human nature—the biological materialists fall into the same trap as the idealists who believe that society is governed by universal ideals or norms. They are both incapable of explaining historical change and evolution.

Marx and Engels rejected both idealism and the old, static, deterministic materialism. If you recall, Marx criticized the French materialists' view that human beings were a product of their circumstances because it was one-sided and left no room for human beings to shape their own history. These materialists always let idealism in the back door, in the form of a liberator standing somehow outside society. Marx and Engels's materialism was historical and, consequently, *dialectical*.

Dialectics: It's Not a New Religion

A lot of confusing ink has been spilled about this strange word, *dialectics*. People may have only a vague idea, if any, of what it is (something to do with an old German philosopher named Hegel, something to do with contradictions), but the question is of considerable importance. For the question of dialectics is about method—about how we go about looking at the world, how it works, and how it changes—and ultimately, how we can consciously transform it. To put it most plainly, wrote Engels, dialectics is "nothing more than the science of the general laws of motion and development of nature, human society, and thought."[37] That is, it is the form of thinking about the world that best corresponds to the way in which the processes of natural and social evolution work.

The ancient Greek philosopher Heraclitus is the first recorded thinker who stressed a dialectical view of the world. For Heraclitus, nothing was fixed, fast, or frozen. "Everything flows," he wrote. "Strife is the father of all things. . . . The fairest harmony is born of things different, and discord is what produces all things."[38] These are key concepts of the dialectic: Constant change and movement is the natural order of things, and change comes about through the conflict of contradictory forces ("strife"). Everything is in a state of either coming into being or passing away.

The Marxist dialectic developed by way of a German philosopher by the name of Georg Friedrich Hegel, who wrote his greatest works in the early part of the 1800s. His philosophy is extremely difficult to read, and though the young Marx, in a letter to his father in 1837, called Hegel's philosophy a "grotesque craggy melody,"[39] he was won over (as was Engels) and became a disciple for several years.

Hegel's ideas were a major breakthrough in philosophical thought. He developed his philosophy in the shadow of the French Revolution, and in many ways his philosophy is an ideal expression of the spirit of that age—a period of almost unceasing conflict and change, of the death of old feudal relations and the birth of the new. At the heart of Hegel's dialectic was the idea that history is a process of the unfolding of the "absolute idea." Ideas and concepts are not static things, Hegel argued, but move through contradiction in a continual process of development. Hegel counterposed his dialectical approach to what he called the "metaphysical" approach, which holds that things are to be viewed as separate, static, and without any contradiction. A is always A, B is always B, and A can never become B. This method had a value, within limits, but it stopped working as an approach once you started to analyze things in their movement and transformation. This is how Engels summarized the difference between the two approaches:

> To the metaphysician, things and their mental reflexes, ideas, are isolated, are to be considered one after the other and part from each other, are objects of investigation fixed, rigid, given once and for all. . . .
>
> [T]he metaphysical mode of thought, justifiable and necessary as it is in a number of domains whose extent varies according to the nature of the particular object of investigation, sooner or later reaches a limit, beyond which it becomes one-sided, restricted, abstract, lost in insoluble contradictions. In the contemplation of individual things, it forgets the connection between them; in the contemplation of their existence, it forgets the beginning and end of that existence; of their repose, it forgets their motion.[40]

Engels noted that the great merit of Hegel's philosophical system was that in it, "the whole world, natural, historical, intellectual, is represented as a process—i.e., as in constant motion, change, transformation, development; and the attempt is made to trace out the internal connection that makes a continuous whole of all this movement and development."[41] The quote below will give you an idea of Hegel's approach. Here he's talking about the unfolding of philosophical ideas, but he uses an analogy from nature to make his point:

> The bud disappears in the bursting-forth of the blossom, and one might say that the former is refuted by the latter; similarly, when the fruit appears, the blossom is shown up in its turn as a false manifestation of the plant, and the fruit now emerges as the truth of it instead. These forms are not just distinguished from one another, they also supplant one another as mutually incompatible. Yet at the same time their fluid nature makes them moments of an organic unity in which they not only do not conflict, but in which each is as necessary as the other; and this mutual necessity alone constitutes the life of the whole.[42]

Each form is "negated," in Hegel's terminology, only to give rise to something that is qualitatively different from what it emerged from. You could take the analogy even further back and say that the seed and the plant it becomes seem to bear no resemblance. The seed goes through a series of stages of growth in which its old form is destroyed and a new form takes its place, yet through all its forms, it is still the same plant. Things can only be fully grasped not as separate, static entities, but as conflicting or contradictory elements of a unity or whole, a process involving birth, life, decay, and death. The contradictory elements combine in an appearance of fixity or stability, but those very same conflicting elements produce movement or development. In the process of this development, new forms burst forth and negate or supersede previous forms, yet are clearly also dependent for their development on those previous forms. That is the main idea of dialectics that Marx took from Hegel.

"It is said," Hegel writes in his work *Science of Logic*, "*natura non facit saltum* [there are no leaps in nature]; and ordinary thinking when it has to grasp a coming-to-be or a ceasing-to-be, fancies it has done so by representing it as a gradual emergence or disappearance. But we have seen that the alterations of being in general are not only the transition of one magnitude into another, but a transition from quality into quantity and *vice versa*, a becoming-other which is an interruption of gradualness and the production of something qualitatively different from the reality which preceded it."[43]

Hegel himself acknowledged that his view that quantitative changes could, at a certain point, give way to qualitative leaps was an idea influenced by the revolutionary age in which he lived. In his 1807 book, *Phenomenology of Spirit*, he writes:

> It is not difficult to see that ours is a birth-time and a period of transition to a new era. . . . Just as the first breath drawn by a child after its long, quiet nourishment breaks the gradualness of merely quantitative growth—there is a qualitative leap,

and the child is born—so likewise the Spirit in its formation matures slowly and quietly into its new shape, dissolving bit by bit the structure of the previous world, whose tottering state is only hinted at by isolated symptoms. . . . The gradual crumbling that left unaltered the face of the whole is cut short by a sunburst which, in one flash, illuminates the features of the new world.[44]

A dialectical approach sees change not simply as a series of quantitative changes that leaves the thing intact, but argues that quantitative changes can give way to, as Hegel describes, qualitative leaps. The acorn transforms itself into an oak. A fertilized egg becomes a full-grown dog—the egg was not a little tiny microscopic dog that grew slowly to a big dog. An element, water for example, at different temperature points turns from a solid to a liquid, and from a liquid into a gas, and so on. These changes do not happen gradually, but almost instantaneously once a certain temperature is reached—and yet through all the different transformations, the substance continues to be H_2O.

Dialectics views fundamental motion and change emerging from contradictory forces acting against each other, creating an unstable unity. Dialectics therefore allows for temporary states of stability or equilibrium, but also for qualitative leaps or breaks in which the equilibrium breaks down and gives way to something new.

In criticizing the metaphysical view, dialectical logic does not claim that there are no "things" because all is fluid motion, and therefore not definable. Darwin's eminently dialectical theory of evolution did not overthrow the system of classifying animals, for example. It merely showed that these classifications do not describe species that are fixed and separated through all time, but species that die out or change and become something else. Evolution is the continual formation and transformation of species through history. Nevertheless, species are a category that corresponds to a real phenomenon: groups of populations with similar biological characteristics that are able to mate with each other and not with other population groups. Yet it is also true that species are not fixed, but rather evolve—each new form negating the old— through the process of natural selection of random mutations.

It's easy to see how Hegel's ideas influenced Marx. But Marx transformed the dialectical method and applied it in a consistently materialist way to human history. For Marx, the dialectic was not a system delineating the unfolding of the history of thought toward the absolute idea, but a method to be used that best corresponded to the workings of the material world. Human history, he argued, was dialectical, in that it was fluid, rather than static, with one form of human social organization giving way to another, the transformation being effected based upon the contradictory forces at play in each phase of development. In one of the prefaces he wrote to *Capital*, his most famous work, he makes clear his debt to Hegel:

> The mystification which the dialectic suffers in Hegel's hands by no means prevents him from being the first to present its general forms of motion in a comprehensive

and conscious manner. With him it is standing on its head. It must be inverted, in order to discover the rational kernel within the mystical shell. . . .

In its rational form [the dialectic] is a scandal and an abomination to the bourgeoisie and its doctrinaire spokesmen, because it includes in its positive understanding of what exists a simultaneous recognition of its negation, its inevitable destruction; because it regards every historically developed form as being in a fluid state, in motion, and therefore grasps its transient aspects as well; and because it does not let itself be impressed by anything, being in its very essence critical and revolutionary.[45]

Hegel himself ended up as a defender of the conservative Prussian state, but at the heart of his philosophy nevertheless was a radical concept: as Engels noted, the idea that "all that exists deserves to perish."[46]

So, the dialectic involves change, movement. But it isn't simply the gradual change, like erosion of a riverbank over millions of years—sometimes a catastrophic flood can do what slow erosion took eons to accomplish. The dialectical model says that things can be in temporary equilibrium, but they are never static and unchanging. Indeed, the equilibrium is always formed by the interaction of conflicting, or contradictory elements, which break apart at a certain threshold.

Marxism applies the dialectical method to understanding historical change, to understand that it is not just a gradual process. Our schoolbooks would like us to believe that social change must always be gradual and peaceful. Sudden, abrupt changes are seen as disruptions of a "normal" functioning society. "Respectable" society looks upon mass protest, civil disobedience, strikes, disruption, and revolution with horror. But fundamental social change rarely comes gradually. Industrial unions didn't come to this country by the gradual addition, year after year, of a few new unions. On the contrary, mass industrial unionism came in an explosion of organizing and mass strikes over a period of about five years, from 1934 to 1938. The gains of the civil rights movement were achieved through heroic civil disobedience and mass protest in the face of systematic racist terror.

While governments caution the governed to act peacefully and refrain from drastic action, they themselves reserve the right to use overwhelming force. There was nothing gradual about the invasion of Iraq or the coordinated suppression of the Occupy movement in the United States. Moreover, the modern capitalist class in many countries rose to power on the basis of revolutionary violence—the heirs of 1776 are no exception. Gradualness and big leaps are complementary and contradictory aspects of history, one preparing the conditions for the other. As Trotsky wrote, "For us it is enough to know that gradualness in various spheres of life go hand in hand with catastrophes, breaks and upward and downward leaps. The long process of competition between two states gradually prepares for war, the discontent of exploited workers gradually prepares a strike, the bad management of a bank gradually prepares a bankruptcy."[47] We could add, the quantitative increase in the earth's surface temperature gradually leads to a leap toward ecological catastrophe. In short, without understanding dialectics, it is difficult to make sense not only of natural processes but of history. This is how Trotsky summed up the dialectic:

> Hegel's logic is the logic of evolution. Only one must not forget that the concept of "evolution" itself has been completely corrupted and emasculated by university professors and liberal writers to mean peaceful "progress." Whoever has come to understand that evolution proceeds through the struggle of antagonistic forces; that a slow accumulation of changes at a certain moment explodes the old shell and brings about a catastrophe, revolution; whoever has learned finally to apply the general laws of evolution to thinking itself, he is a dialectician, as distinguished from vulgar evolutionists. Dialectic training of the mind, as necessary to a revolutionary fighter as finger exercises to a pianist, demands approaching all problems as *processes* and not as motionless categories. Whereas vulgar evolutionists, who limit themselves generally to recognizing evolution in only certain spheres, content themselves in all other questions with the banalities of "common sense."[48]

Chapter Three

The Marxist View of History

The Materialist Conception of History

We have established that Marxism does not view history as something that is governed either by eternal ideas or by some biologically fixed conception of human nature. Just as life has evolved, so has human history, since evolution is really just change through time. But what governs that change?

"The writers of history," wrote Marx, "have so far paid very little attention to the development of material production, which is the basis of all social life, and therefore of real history."[1] What was important for Marx was not "what is made but how, and by what instruments of labor, that distinguishes different economic epochs."[2] It is through labor, Marx wrote in *Capital*, that man appropriates and reshapes the products of nature in accordance with his own needs and wants. "By thus acting on the external world and changing it, he at the same time changes his own nature."[3]

Marx called this view of human history "the materialist conception of history." It began with the idea that social change and social progress are determined, first and foremost, by the ways in which human beings come together to produce their means of survival. "Men can be distinguished from animals by consciousness, by religion or anything else you like," wrote Marx and Engels. "They themselves begin to distinguish themselves from animals as soon as they begin to produce their means of subsistence."[4]

In an English preface to one of his most important works, *Socialism: Utopian and Scientific*, Engels summed up succinctly what he and Marx meant by "historical materialism": "I use . . . the term 'historical materialism' . . . to designate that view of the course of history which seeks the ultimate cause and the great moving power of all important historic events in the economic development of society, in the changes in the modes of production and exchange, in the consequent division of society into distinct classes, and in the struggles of these classes against one another."[5]

Marx's basic premise was that the way people organize with each other to produce their subsistence, the technologies they use and corresponding forms of labor, determine the kind of social organization they have: "In the social production of their existence," Marx wrote, "men inevitably enter into definite relations, which are independent of their will, namely relations of production appropriate to a given stage in the development of their material forces of production. The totality of these relations of production constitutes the economic structure of society, the real foundation, on which arises a legal and political superstructure and to which correspond definite forms of social consciousness."[6]

Each stage of human development in history has had its own corresponding "mode of production," its own distinct economic laws of motion, which are independent of the wills of those caught up in it. Each mode of production—slavery, tributary, feudalism, capitalism—has had its own set of social relations, that is, the social arrangements by which people interacted in production and reproduction of their lives. Each has had its dominant, exploiting class and its oppressed, exploited class. (The exception is in foraging societies that relied on gathering and hunting sources of food provided by nature without human labor, where there were not class divisions, as we shall see.) Each mode of production has been defined by the specific form in which the laboring class produces a surplus for the dominant class—that is, the extra wealth produced by the laboring class over and above its own subsistence needs, and to each system of class relations there has arisen the entire social and political structure. Or, as Marx put it:

> The specific economic form in which unpaid surplus labor is pumped out of the direct producers determines the relationship of domination and servitude, as this grows directly out of production itself and reacts back on it in turn as a determinant. On this is based the entire configuration of the economic community arising from the actual relations of production, and hence also its specific political form. It is in each case the direct relationship of the owners of the conditions of production to the immediate producers—a relationship whose particular form naturally corresponds always to a certain level of development of the type and manner of labor, and hence to its social productive power—in which we find the innermost secret, the hidden basis of the entire social edifice.[7]

The transformation from one mode of production to another was not smooth or automatic, primarily because different modes of production were not walled off from each other, but interpenetrated each other, so that the elements of some could exist, in different forms, side by side with others. Moreover, simply changing technology did not automatically produce changes in the relations of production. Each new mode of production first acted as a spur on the development of society's productive forces. But gradual changes in the development of society's productive powers over time came into conflict with the existing social relations. Social relations established at each stage of development blocked the development of new relations, restricting the further advancement of society. Each ruling class at first acted to lead society forward, then, as their rule progressed, acted to prevent any changes to the system from which they benefited. They shifted from being a class that was historically progressive into a class that was historically regressive. (By "progressive" or "regressive" Marx simply meant whether a particular mode of production advanced or retarded the development of society's productive forces, and therefore humanity's control over its destiny.)

In each phase of human history, this contradiction between what Marx called the "forces of production" (the productive power of society, including labor itself) and the "relations of production" (the form of social organization under which production took place) grew to a point at which the tensions within society became unbearable, and there would begin a period in which these contradictions, manifested in an antagonism between contending classes, would burst forth. Then the clash of ideas, organizations, and classes would determine whether society moved forward or backward.

"At a certain stage of their development," Marx continued, "the material productive forces of society come in conflict with the existing relations of production, or—this merely expresses the same thing in legal terms—with the property relations within the framework of which they have operated hitherto. From forms of development of the productive forces these relations turn into their fetters. Then begins an era of social revolution. The changes in the economic foundation lead sooner or later to the transformation of the whole immense superstructure."[8] In short, molecular economic changes produced economic contradictions, which in turn produced social and political conflicts—class struggle—in which the old relations were overthrown and replaced by new ones. The most poetic and succinct description of this process is found in the first section of *The Communist Manifesto*: "The history of all hitherto existing society is the history of class struggles. Freeman and slave, patrician and plebian, lord and serf, guild-master and journeyman, in a word, oppressor and oppressed, stood in constant opposition to one another, carried on an uninterrupted, now hidden, now open fight, a fight that each time ended, either in a revolutionary reconstitution of society at large, or in the common ruin of the contending classes."[9]

By rejecting the idealist notion that people can achieve whatever they "will," however, Marx didn't embrace "economic determinism"—the idea that human beings are slaves to the blind forces of history—or that the revolutionary transformation of society is as inevitable as the sun rising every morning. As Marx noted, the "legal and political superstructure . . . to which correspond definite forms of social consciousness" arises, or is based upon, basic economic structure of society—a structure that is organized around the relations of exploitation between dominant and subordinate classes. However, it is at the level of this superstructure that people "become conscious of this conflict and fight it out."[10] Hence Marx's emphasis on the role of the struggle between contending classes in the transition from one mode of production to the next.

For Marx, history consisted, therefore, of the changes brought about by human beings in the process of producing their existence. In a now famous passage, Marx summarized his views that people "make their own history." "But," he added, "they do not make it just as they please; they do not make it under circumstances chosen by themselves, but under circumstances directly encountered, given and transmitted from the past."[11] That sums up Marx's materialism in a nutshell.

The limits of human activity are always circumscribed by the material constraint placed on them by the way in which they are compelled to obtain their existence at a given level of production. This dictates a certain social division of labor and ways in which people relate to each other. The weight of the old customs and ideas corresponding to that level of development also press on those attempting to challenge the old. So long as humankind does not have complete conscious mastery over production, full freedom is impossible.

Humans act with purpose, with will, but their individual intentions interact in such a way as to produce outcomes that are not consciously willed. This contradiction becomes most pronounced in capitalist society, in which individual wills appear powerless over the blind workings of the market. But once humanity has created a means of production that can provide for the needs of humanity, the necessity of a division of society into classes is abolished, and the foundation of a society based upon the conscious mastery of production and distribution becomes possible for the first time. A society democratically and consciously planned by the associated producers, on the basis of the application of the most sophisticated scientific knowledge, has long been within our grasp.

The socialists who followed Marx and Engels tended to read into Marx and Engels's historical materialism a kind of schematic list of stages that every society must pass through according to its level of economic development. Stalinism took this to the height of absurdity and turned Marxism into its opposite. Instead of being a guide for workers to achieve liberation, it became, in Stalin's hands, an ideological screen that justified his dictatorship over the proletariat. Marx castigated those who caricatured his argument, seeking to "metamorphose my historical sketch of the genesis of capitalism in Western Europe into a historico-philosophical theory of general development, imposed by fate on all peoples, whatever the historical circumstances in which they are placed."[12]

Engels felt compelled on more than one occasion to clarify to both critics and supporters that his and Marx's materialism was not mechanical or one sided:

> According to the materialist conception of history, the ultimately determining element in history is the production and reproduction of real life. Other than this neither Marx nor I have ever asserted. Hence if somebody twists this into saying that the economic element is the only determining one, he transforms that proposition into a meaningless, abstract, senseless phrase. The economic situation is the basis,

but the various elements of the superstructure—political forms of the class struggle and its results, to wit: constitutions established by the victorious class after a successful battle, etc., juridical forms, and even the reflexes of all these actual struggles in the brains of the participants, political, juristic, philosophical theories, religious views and their further development into systems of dogmas—also exercise their influence upon the course of the historical struggles and in many cases preponderate in determining their form. There is an interaction of all these elements in which, amid all the endless host of accidents (that is, of things and events whose inner interconnection is so remote or so impossible of proof that we can regard it as non-existent, as negligible), the economic movement finally asserts itself as necessary.[13]

Material conditions inherited from the past do not predetermine what will happen in history; they merely indicate the constraints on what is possible at any given moment. A certain set of social arrangements gives rise to a corresponding set of ideas. But that does not mean that ideas are merely a passive reflection of material relations. Ideas can act back on those relations to change them—provided they are ideas that correspond to what is materially possible at that moment, and that those ideas embrace a sufficient number of people to effect a social change. As Marx and Engels noted, "*Ideas* can never lead beyond an old world order but only beyond the ideas of that old world order. Ideas *cannot carry out anything at all*. In order to carry ideas men are needed who can exert a practical force."[14]

That Marxism is the furthest from mechanical materialism is most clearly demonstrated by its understanding that revolutions are the midwife of history. For what are revolutions but the more or less conscious political movement that, having achieved political power, proceeds to transform social relations? As the Russian Marxist Georgi Plekhanov, fending off critics of Marxism who claimed that it was a mechanical doctrine that left no room for human agency, wrote:

> Had Marx and Engels, from the very start of their political careers, not attached importance to the political and the "intellectual" factors and precluded their impact on the economic development of society, their practical program would have been quite different: they would not have said that the working class cannot cast off the economic yoke of the bourgeoisie without taking over the political power. In exactly the same way, they would not have spoken of the need to foster class consciousness in workers: why should that consciousness be developed if it plays no part in the social movement and if everything takes place in history irrespective of the consciousness, and exclusively through the force of economic necessity? And who does not know that the development of the workers' class consciousness was the immediate practical task of Marx and Engels from the very outset of their social activities?[15]

Capitalist development has made a society of cooperation and democratic planning possible but not inevitable. One form of society does not emerge from the other like a snake sloughs off its old skin. It is class and political struggle, the clash of social forces, that determines whether and to what extent social change happens. The more or less conscious and willful activity of social actors must burst the shell of the old society for a successful revolution in social relations to take place. Nevertheless, however much human beings may will something, it cannot happen unless the material conditions exist for its emergence. "New superior relations of production never replace older ones before the material conditions for their existence have matured within the framework of the old society," writes Marx.[16] Yet the ripeness of those conditions does not automatically guarantee that a new society will be born. For that, there must exist social forces "conscious, organized, and powerful" enough—to quote Trotsky—to carry through the social transformation.

Trotsky summarized this argument in a 1921 speech to a gathering of the Communist International:

> The proposition that conditions . . . for a social revolution which replaces one economic system by another are created only when the old social order no longer leaves room for the development of productive forces—this proposition does not at all mean that the old social order unfailingly collapses as soon as it becomes reactionary in the economic sense, that is, as soon as it begins to retard the development of the technological power of man. Not at all. For while the productive forces constitute the basic driving force of historical development, the latter nevertheless occurs not separate and apart from human beings, but through them. The productive forces—the means whereby social man dominates nature—take shape, it is true, independently of the will of any single individual and are only slightly dependent upon the common will of human beings alive today, because technology represents the accumulated capital inherited by us from the past, which impels us forward, and which under certain conditions also holds us back. But when the productive forces, when technology become too restricted within an old framework, say that of slavery, or feudal or bourgeois society, and when a change of social forms become necessary for the further growth of mankind's power, then this is not accomplished automatically, like the sun rises and sets, but must be accomplished through human beings, through the struggle of human beings welded into classes. To replace a social class, governing an old society that has turned reactionary, must come a new social class which possesses the program for a new social order meeting the needs for the development of productive forces, and which is prepared to realize this program in life. But it by no means always happens when a given social system has outlived itself, i.e., has turned reactionary, that a new class appears, conscious enough, organized enough, and powerful enough to cast down life's old masters and pave the way for new social relations. . . .
>
> It has more than once happened in history that a given society, a given nation, or people, or a tribe, or several tribes and nations, living under similar historical conditions, have run up against the impossibility of developing any further on a given economic foundation—slavery or feudalism—but inasmuch as no new class existed among them capable of leading them out to the main highway, they simply fell apart. The given civilization, the given state, the given society disintegrated. Mankind has

thus not always moved upwards from below in a steady, rising curve. No, there have been prolonged periods of stagnation and there have been regressions into barbarism.[17]

The materialist understanding of history is not like the law of gravity. We know that anything we drop in a vacuum, where there is no friction or wind resistance, falls at the same rate. Human history's welter of variables cannot be isolated in that way, but can only be observed in their messy totality. Natural events are blind, that is, they involve no intervention by any conscious will. Human history, on the other hand, involves people, or groups of people, acting together or in conflict to achieve definite, more or less conscious goals.[18] Yet in spite of—or perhaps because of—those competing wills, history produces results neither intended nor foreseen by its participants. There are, in other words, driving material forces beneath the surface that shape the consciousness of historical actors and also shape and limit the scope and character of their actions. But it is also the case that capitalism creates the potential for a society in which human activity can be consciously planned and directed. Even in the most modern human societies there remains a big gap between conscious aims and practical results. Writes Engels,

> This cannot be otherwise as long as the most essential historical activity of men, the one which has raised them from bestiality to humanity and which forms the material foundation of all their other activities, namely the production of their requirements of life, that is today social production, is above all subject to the interplay of unintended effects from uncontrolled forces and achieves its desired end only by way of exception and, much more frequently, the exact opposite. In the most advanced industrial countries we have subdued the forces of nature and pressed them into the service of mankind; we have thereby infinitely multiplied production, so that a child now produces more than a hundred adults previously did. And what is the result? Increasing overwork and increasing misery of the masses, and every ten years a great collapse. . . . Only conscious organization of social production, in which production and distribution are carried on in a planned way, can lift mankind above the rest of the animal world as regards the social aspect, in the same way that production in general has done this for men in their aspect as species. Historical evolution makes such an organization daily more indispensable, but also with every day more possible. From it will date a new epoch of history, in which mankind itself, and with mankind all branches of its activity, and especially natural science, will experience an advance that will put everything preceding it in the deepest shade.[19]

The Rise of Class Inequality and the State

Marx and Engels's materialist account of historical change placed class division and class struggle at its heart. But Engels added an important addendum to the famous phrase in *The Communist Manifesto* that "the history of all hitherto existing society is the history of class struggles."[20] He noted that this was true only for written history. For most of our existence as a species, humans lived as the Montagnais-Naskapi did—without any class divisions, without armies, courts, or bureaucracies. For tens of thousands of years, humans lived in societies "without soldiers, gendarmes or police; without nobles, kings, governors, prefects, or judges; without prisons; without trials."[21] All things beyond personal possessions were communally owned and shared in what some have called "primitive communism." In these egalitarian societies, people foraged for food in small bands, moving wherever food was most plentiful. These societies necessarily emphasized reciprocity and sharing, and knew no formal or permanent hierarchies.

The Jesuit historian Pierre Charlevoix, who lived among Indians in French Canada in the early 1700s, wrote in his *History of New France*: "The fraternal disposition of the Redskins doubtless comes in part from the fact that mine and thine, those icy words, as St. John Chrysostom calls them, are as yet unknown to the savages. The care that they take of orphans, widows, and the infirm, the hospitality they practice in so admirable a manner, are but a consequence of their view that everything ought to be common for all men."[22]

The Iroquois Indians, who engaged in a simple form of agriculture and hunting, were also far more egalitarian than our present-day society. "All quarrels and disputes are settled by the whole body of those concerned," Engels wrote of the Iroquois. "There can be no poor or needy—the communistic household and gens [clan or group of families] know their obligation toward the aged, the sick, and those disabled in war. All are free and equal—including the women. There is as of yet no room for slaves, nor, as a rule, for the subjugation of alien tribes."[23]

The status of women in communal societies was far higher than in class societies that followed. Among the Iroquois, a woman could dissolve her marriage simply by placing her husband's belongings outside the household door—a practice that was common in many pre-class, pre-state societies. "No matter how many children, or whatever goods [the husband] might have in the house, he might at any time be ordered to pick up his blanket and budge; and after such orders it would not be healthful for him to attempt to disobey," wrote the anthropologist Louis Henry Morgan, who studied the Iroquois in the 1870s. Women also had the power to remove chiefs they did not like.[24] This was due in part to the fact that women in Iroquois society did most of the labor in the fields (having previously been the gatherers, and therefore knowing the most about edible plants), which accounted for more of the group's food than did hunting.

Subsequent anthropological research has reinforced Morgan's and Engels's view that most societies that foraged for food—as well as many societies that engaged in simple agriculture (sometimes called "horticulture")—were free of class division and of women's inequality. Such societies had no need for a group of people who were elevated above society and ruling over it. It is common still to describe pre-agricultural societies as constantly living on the edge of scarcity and starvation, always in desperate search of food—kind of an ancient equivalent of living paycheck to paycheck. Yet far from engaging in a brutish, relentless struggle for existence, people in foraging societies probably only spent on average something like two to four hours a day procuring an adequate subsistence.[25] A 1960s study calculated that the !Kung Bushmen of Dobe, one of the handful of surviving foraging societies in the modern world, "despite their harsh environment, devote from twelve to nineteen hours a week to getting food."[26] And the !Kung had been pushed to more marginal lands from the regions more abundant in food where their ancestors had thrived.[27] Moreover, peoples in ancient pre-agricultural societies, archeological studies show, were significantly healthier and taller, and lived longer than the agricultural peoples who came after them, because they lived in less crowded conditions and had a more plentiful and varied, lower-starch diet.[28] "Hunter-gatherers," writes Jared Diamond, "practiced the most successful and longest-lasting lifestyle in human history."[29] Why, then, if people lived for so long without bosses or cops, in relative ease and health, in a society based on cooperation and sharing, did class divisions and the state ever emerge at all?

Starting about ten thousand years ago, some societies, as a result of the depletion of their food sources, moved to domesticating plants and animals instead of foraging for plants and animals. This is commonly known as the Neolithic revolution. Foraging people had already accumulated an enormous amount of knowledge about the plants they gathered, and in some places, about certain species of animals they hunted. In foraging societies, the small bands necessarily produced only for immediate needs, with little thought of creating a surplus very much above what was necessary from day to day. When food became scarce in one area, they simply picked up and moved elsewhere.

Some societies turned to food domestication, perhaps prompted by climate change or the depletion of plants and game due to over-harvesting resulting from population growth. Once people began to produce their food rather than just forage for it, they could sustain bigger populations that could stay in one place. In turn, this new, growing, more sedentary population had need of a surplus store of food as a hedge against disasters. (There were also cases in which the food supply in an area was so abundant—fish, for example—that it allowed for the development of larger, sedentary populations without the invention of agriculture.)

Early agricultural societies therefore tended to reward those who worked the hardest to increase food production. The prestige of these "redistributor" chiefs—called in some cultures "big men"—rested on their ability to produce, and exhort their followers to produce and give away more than anyone else. Still, their status as providers placed them in control of society's surplus. As the surplus grew, such chiefs could take some of the extra surplus and use it to pay for specialists—craftsmen, priests, servants, and warriors.[30]

"Under certain circumstances," writes anthropologist Marvin Harris, "the exercise of power by the redistributor and his closest followers on the one side, and by the ordinary food producers on the other, became so unbalanced that, for all intents and purposes, the redistributor chiefs constituted the principal coercive force in social life. When this happened, contributions to the central store ceased to be voluntary contributions. They became taxes. Farmlands and natural resources ceased to be elements of rightful access. They became dispensations. And redistributors ceased to be chiefs. They became kings."[31] In other words, a figure who begins as a giver turned into its opposite, a taker—that is, an exploiter.

This was one possible path toward the emergence of classes. Classes arose in different ways, but always for the same underlying reason. In ancient India, for example, the first state evolved from those individuals "responsible for the collective maintenance of irrigation throughout the river valleys."[32] Elsewhere, the first class division was between masters and slaves—the expansion of the old family structure to include war captives who could produce extra wealth. In any case, classes emerged on the basis that "production had developed so far that the labor-power of a man could now produce more than was necessary for its mere maintenance."[33]

Once agriculture was established, society began to produce a surplus over and above what was needed for subsistence, as well as the technical means of storing and maintaining such a surplus. Indeed, once society became more sedentary, and hence, subject to potential crop failures, such a surplus became a necessity. But that surplus was only possible on the basis of the hard toil of the majority, and could only sustain a small minority who were freed from that labor. As Jared Diamond notes, though "farming could support many more people than hunting," it did so "with a poorer quality of life."

> Besides malnutrition, starvation, and epidemic diseases, farming helped bring another curse upon humanity: deep class divisions. Hunter-gatherers have little or no stored food, and no concentrated food sources, like an orchard or a herd of cows: they live off the wild plants and animals they obtain each day. Therefore, there can be no kings, no class of social parasites who grow fat on food seized from others. Only in a farming population could a healthy, non-producing elite set itself above the disease-ridden masses.[34]

Once a society moved from foraging to horticulture to sedentary agriculture, class division was a necessary result of society's low level of productivity. As Engels put it, "So long as the total social labor only yields a produce which but slightly exceeds that barely necessary for the existence of all; so long, therefore, as labor engages all or almost all the time of the great majority of the members of society—so long, of necessity, this society is divided into classes. Side by side with the great majority . . . arises a class freed from directly productive labor, which looks after the general affairs of society."[35]

Classes are therefore defined by their relationship to the production and control of society's wealth, and in particular, the surplus product. Each ruling class used its position of control over the surplus to increase its own wealth and power over those it exploited—that is, to maximize the appropriation of surplus wealth. In any society, discover who appropriates and controls the surplus wealth produced in society and you have discovered the ruling class of that society. Find the class that produces the surplus wealth for the ruling class, and you have found the exploited class.

Along with class differences arose gender inequality. The relatively high status of women in foraging societies, closely connected to their key role as food gatherers, was overturned, the sexual division of labor now assigning to men the key productive roles in agriculture and domestication. In the transition from communal to private property, men became the owners of property, and women became a subordinate part of the household. "The first class antithesis which appears in history coincides," wrote Engels, "with the development of the antagonism between man and woman in monogamian marriage, and the first class oppression with that of the female sex by the male."[36]

Human progress—the advance of our ability to produce an expanding surplus over and above our basic needs—was impossible without the rise of class society. But the rise of class society has meant that every advance in human productive power has been made at the expense of the majority of humanity. "The power of these naturally evolved communities had to be broken," Engels wrote of pre-class societies,

> and it was broken. But it was broken by influences which from the outset appear to us as a degradation, a fall from the simple moral grandeur of the old [pre-class] society. The lowest interests—base greed, brutal sensuality, sordid avarice, selfish plunder of common possessions—usher in the new, civilized society, class society; the most outrageous means—theft, rape, deceit and treachery—undermine and topple the old, classless gentile society. And the new society, during all the 2,500 years of its existence, has never been anything but the development of the small minority at the expense of the exploited and oppressed great majority.[37]

The rise of class society also necessitated the development of an institution which is often portrayed as something eternal and "natural" to all human societies: the state, "a public power distinct from the mass of the people," wrote Engels.[38] A special coercive power wasn't necessary for classless society, in which everyone shared common interests. In classless foraging societies, where food was shared, no separate body arose out of society, standing over it, which maintained, by coercion if necessary, rules of social conduct that protected the wealth of the minority. Engels noted that in ancient Greece out of kinship-based, relatively egalitarian and democratic societies, there began to arise differences in household wealth, accentuated by slavery and plunder. And as elected forms of chiefdom gave way to hereditary succession,

> Only one thing was wanting: an institution which not only secured the newly ac-quired riches of individuals against the communistic traditions of the gentile order, which not only sanctified the private property formerly so little valued, and declared this sanctification to be the highest purpose of all human society; but an institution which set the seal of general social recognition on each new method of acquiring property and thus amassing wealth at continually increasing speed; an institution which perpetuated, not only this growing cleavage of society into classes, but also the right of the possessing class to exploit the non-possessing, and the rule of the former over the latter.
>
> And this institution came. The state was invented.[39]

Once society is divided into classes, there needs to be a body that can moderate class conflict and keep it from threatening the economic interests of the dominant class. Wrote Engels, "This power, arisen out of society, but placing itself above it and increasingly alienating itself from it, is the state."[40] The state, in other words, is at its core a political institution that concentrates in its hands the coercive power of society and removes as much as possible the means of coercion from the majority, exploited class.

The most popular rationale for the existence of this "public power" is that without it human nature is such that everyone would be at each other's throats. "During the time men live without a common power to keep them all in awe," wrote the seventeenth-century philosopher Thomas Hobbes, a great supporter of monarchy, "they are in that condition which is called war; and such a war as is of every man against every man."[41] In short, the state is a referee in a social brawl. But once we acknowledge that a coercive state apparatus did not emerge until very late in human history, then this view can be seen for what it really is—more of a justification for state power than a real explanation of it.

Hobbes merely observed superficially that the state regulates conflict. The truth is that it arises to regulate a certain kind of conflict—class conflict, itself a historical product. But that doesn't mean that the state is an impartial referee. It always rigs the game in favor of the wealthy classes in such a way that it always wins. As Engels put it:

> Because the state arose from the need to keep class antagonisms in check, but be-cause it arose, at the same time, in the midst of the conflict of these classes, it is, as a rule, the state of the most powerful, economically dominant class, which, through the medium of the state, becomes also the politically dominant class, and thus ac-quires new means of keeping down and exploiting the oppressed class. Thus, the state of antiquity was above all the state of the slave owners for keeping down the slaves, as the feudal state was the organ of the nobility for keeping down the peasant serfs and villeins, and the modern representative state is an instrument for the exploitation of wage labor by capital.[42]

The essence of state power is its coercive power. But no class system can survive by naked force alone. By definition, a class society involves the exploitation of the many by the few. What is to stop the many from seizing back the wealth they have produced? Unless there are to be endless rounds of conflict, class rule must at least to some degree rest on the consent of the exploited. And for that to happen, historically, elaborate ideologies have been promulgated—not only by state actors, but by other non-state institutions and "intellectuals"—to convince people that the world they live in is in some way necessary and unavoidable. As we shall see later, this complicates the issue of how revolutionary change can come about, but it does not render it impossible, as the history of mass revolts and social revolutions over the past centuries shows us.

The Rise of Capitalism: Greed Unbounded

"Long, long ago there were two sorts of people; one, the diligent, intelligent and above all frugal elite; the other, lazy rascals, spending their substance, and more, in riotous living." This "insipid childishness" of this historical fairy tale, wrote Marx, is what usually lies behind explanations of why capitalist society is divided between the very rich and the rest of us. The true explanation is far less flattering to the so-called elite. "It is a notorious fact that conquest, enslavement, robbery, murder, in short, force, play the greatest part" in the rise of capitalism.[43]

All class societies are defined by the fact that there is a majority that works to keep a minority in idleness—a majority that slogs away and a minority that skims all the extra wealth over and above the subsistence needs of the majority. As Marx wrote, "Wherever a part of society possesses the monopoly of the means of production, the worker, free or unfree, must add to the labor-time necessary for his own maintenance an extra quantity of labor-time in order to produce the means of subsistence for the owner of the means of production, whether this proprietor be an . . . Etruscan theocrat, a civis romanus, a Norman baron, an American slave-owner, a Wallachian boyar, a modern landlord or capitalist."[44] Each class society has its own character, defined by the form that the exploitation takes, "the form in which . . . surplus labor is in each case extorted from the immediate producer, the worker."[45]

Under slavery and feudalism, the way in which a surplus was extracted was completely transparent. Anything produced over and above the costs of purchasing the slave and maintaining him or her (which varied depending on whether the owner profited more from working the slave to death or stretching his service out longer) was taken by the slave owner as surplus product. The feudal peasant or serf was required either to hand over a portion of his crop to the lord and/or the state in rent, tithes, or taxes, or to perform unpaid labor for the lord. The vast majority of the population produced what they needed to live on rather than buying it from others.

Whereas serf and slave labor was to varying degrees forced or bonded labor, modern capitalism is dependent on "free labor." This sweet-sounding term, however, disguises a bitter truth. The "free" does not only refer to the fact that the wageworker is no longer owned body and soul like a slave, or tied to the same land like a serf. Marx noted that "free" also means the worker is free of any possession of land or tools or any guaranteed means of livelihood, and therefore compelled on pain of destitution to hire himself or herself out piecemeal, "unencumbered," as Marx facetiously wrote, "by any means of production of their own."[46]

Whereas in previous societies trade was secondary, if not marginal, capitalism is the first system of production in which all economic intercourse involves the buying and selling of commodities and in which other economic activities are marginal. But capitalism is also more than that. It is a system where *labor itself—or a person's capacity to work—becomes a commodity that can be bought and sold on the market.* Under feudalism, people were tied to the land or owned their own tools and workshops. A condition for capitalism to develop fully, then, was the separation—by force, fraud, and legal sanction—of the direct producers from land and tools on one side, and the concentration of all the land and instruments of production in the hands of a few rich capitalists on the other. Both processes—the development of an extensive world mar ket *and* the dispossession of the laboring classes—were necessary for modern capitalism to emerge.[47]

There were several social groups from which the capitalist class emerged: merchants, who amassed great wealth from the trade in commodities, including spices, cloth, and slaves; lords or rich peasants, who were able to buy land and become capitalist farmers by producing and selling crops on the market; and master craftsmen in the towns, who "transformed themselves into small capitalists, and, by gradually extending their exploitation of wage-labor and the corresponding accumulation, into 'capitalists.'"[48] Far more important in the development of the bourgeoisie (or capitalist class), though, were the merchants, who moved beyond pure buying and selling to become full-fledged capitalists, that is, exploiters of labor as well as sellers of commodities. First, they "put out" material to artisans and laborers to be worked up, initially in the home or in small, scattered workshops, where the material would be made into finished commodities and sold for a profit. Later, these merchants would bring the laborers under one roof to work—the precursor of the modern factory.

This process was dependent upon two developments—the capacity of merchants and investors to amass fortunes in order to build larger capitalistic enterprises, and the availability of a labor force for these new enterprises. The key development to keep uppermost in mind was the separation of the workers, whether they were peasants working the land or craftsmen making various wares, from their land and their instruments of production. A period of "primitive accumulation" (or "original expropriation," as Marx also called it) was necessary, involving "the expropriation of the agricultural producer, of the peasant, from the soil" (as well as the destruction of the old skilled handicrafts of the towns, villages, and farms).[49] The merchants were also able to build up their immense fortunes through conquest and forced labor in the colonies, with considerable aid from the state.

The new class of wageworkers was created by forcible theft of the common lands that the peasants had depended on for their livelihood. English landed gentry and big farmers, for example, taking advantage of the high price of wool, simply "enclosed" common lands, claiming them for their own, and turned them into sheep pastures. Soldiers were sent to drive tenants and small landholders by force from land they had tilled for centuries. Laws were then enacted in the fifteenth and sixteenth centuries that punished unlicensed begging and vagrancy with whipping, imprisonment, and, for a third offense, death.[50] "Thus were agricultural folk forcibly expropriated from the soil," wrote Marx, "driven from their homes, turned into vagabonds, and then whipped, branded and tortured by grotesquely terroristic laws into accepting the necessary discipline for the system of wage labor."[51]

In the history of capitalism, this process has never been repeated in exactly the same way. In colonial America, for example, the issue was not how to "free up" peasants to be workers, because there weren't any peasants to be had. Moreover, free immigrants tended to seek land rather than work in the towns and cities. Any employer who wanted to get around paying the relatively high wages that such a tight labor market allowed looked in two directions, both involving forced labor. Initially, the colonies imported indentured servants from Europe—people who signed a contract compelling them to work for several years for a master in exchange for passage. Sometimes American Indians were enslaved and forced to work, but they often escaped, and European diseases thinned their population, making them an unreliable supply of labor.

In the South (and in the Caribbean), a system of plantation exploitation based on the use of slaves from Africa became the preferred method for securing a cheap and plentiful supply of labor. Alongside the creation of this new class of "free" laborers in Europe came the development of unfree labor in the New World. "In fact," noted Marx, "the veiled slavery of the wage-workers in Europe needed, for its pedestal, slavery pure and simple in the new world."[52]

Marx and Engels's condensed description of the rise of the bourgeoisie and of a world market in *The Communist Manifesto* emphasizes capitalism's dynamism, explaining how exploration, the discovery of the New World, and the spread of colonies gave a tremendous boost to commerce and industry.[53] But these proceedings, wrote Marx in *Capital*, were in truth "written in the annals of mankind in letters of blood and fire."[54] "The discovery of gold and silver in America," wrote Marx, "the extirpation, enslavement and entombment in mines of the indigenous population, the beginnings of the conquest and plunder of the East Indies, the turning of Africa into a warren for the commercial hunting of black-skins, are all things which characterized the dawn of the era of capitalist production. These idyllic proceedings are the chief moments of primitive accumulation."[55]

These methods of primitive accumulation did not end with the abolition of slavery, but continued with the emergence of modern imperialism in the late nineteenth century. The European powers, in their carve-up of Africa in the late nineteenth century, were not only interested in robbing Africa of its raw materials but also in creating a cheap and plentiful labor supply in Africa. For example, the Dutch and the British invaders, after militarily defeating various African kingdoms and peoples in South Africa, dispossessed Africans of 87 percent of their lands, squeezed them onto unproductive "reserves," and used pass laws, hut and poll taxes, and other coercive means to compel Blacks to work as cheap migrant laborers in white-owned gold and diamond mines, farms, and other concerns.[56] In these instances, Black workers were neither slaves nor completely "free" wageworkers, but something in between.

The development of capitalism spurred the growth of mass industry and an integrated world market. Through sheer economic weight, and also by outright force, capitalism compelled the world to follow in its own image. "In one word, for exploitation, veiled by religious and political illusions," Marx and Engels wrote in the *Manifesto*, "it has substituted naked, shameless, direct, brutal exploitation."[57] Profit at any cost became the all-consuming, driving force of all economic activity. In *Capital*, Marx cites a trade unionist's chilling observation made in 1860: "With adequate profit, capital is very bold. A certain 10 per cent will ensure its employment anywhere; 20 per cent certain will produce eagerness; 50 per cent positive audacity; 100 per cent will make it ready to trample on all human laws; 300 per cent, and there is not a crime at which it will scruple, nor a risk it will not run, even to the chance of its owner being hanged. If turbulence and strife will bring a profit, it will freely encourage both. Smuggling and the slave trade have amply proved all that is here stated."[58]

Abundance and the End of Inequality

Notwithstanding the "sordid avarice" and "selfish plunder" of class society, human productivity has advanced. As Marx and Engels so brilliantly summarized in the *Manifesto*, the rise of capitalism has created a world market, where each part of the world is dependent on the other; it has concentrated populations in large cities, subordinating the country to the town; and it has, by the development of centralized and expanded, machine-based mass production, created productive forces that far surpass all previous societies. The bourgeoisie "cannot exist without constantly revolutionizing the instruments of production, and thereby the relations of production, and with them the whole relations of society."[59]

Abundance is the first material premise that makes socialism more than just a utopian dream and makes its achievement really possible. As Engels explained:

> It is precisely this industrial revolution which has raised the productive power of human labor to such a high level that—for the first time in the history of humanity—the possibility exists, given a rational division of labor among all, to produce not only enough for the plentiful consumption of all members of society and for an abundant reserve fund, but also to leave each individual sufficient leisure so that what is really worth preserving in historically inherited culture—science, art, human relations—is not only preserved, but converted from a monopoly of the ruling class into the common property of the whole of society, and further developed.[60]

The decisive point for Engels is that this abundance has removed every excuse for the existence of a handful of exploiters, or for any kind of privation. Indeed, the existence of a ruling class has now long been a positive hindrance on human development.

Organized rationally, modern technology would lessen the burden of toil and free up the majority to participate fully in the running of society, by limiting "the labor-time of each individual member to such an extent that all have enough free time left to take part in the general—both theoretical and practical—affairs of society."[61]

Chapter Four

Marxist Economics: How Capitalism Works

N ot long after the first edition of this book appeared in print, the worst economic crisis in decades hit the United States and the world. "By every significant measure," writes Canadian Marxist David McNally,

> the Great Recession was the deepest and longest decline experienced by global capitalism since the catastrophic collapse of 1929–33. The 30 large economies of the Organization for Economic Cooperation and Development (OECD) underwent a 6 per cent contraction in Gross Domestic Product (GDP) with jobless rates jumping two-thirds higher on average. World industrial output fell 13 per cent; international trade dropped by 20 per cent; global stock markets plunged 50 per cent. A wave of bank collapses swept the United States and Europe, generating a financial panic unlike anything witnessed since the 1930s, and inducing an intense intellectual crisis in ruling-class circles, as confidence in free market nostrums staggered. Not only was the contraction of 2008-9 deeper than any since the 1930s, it also lasted nearly twice as long as the average recessions of the last 80 years.[1]

The question, therefore, of what causes crises, is a crucial one. Yet for most people, economics is a mystery better left unsolved. Economists are viewed alternatively as impenetrable geniuses or snake oil salesmen. Either way, economics is dismal, boring, hard to understand, and ultimately a waste of time.

These suspicions are not unfounded. The majority of mainstream economists, on the whole, seem incapable of explaining economic trends, or extrapolating what might happen in the future. The reason is not hard to discover. It is not possible for bourgeois economists, first of all, to engage in an impartial inquiry into the inner workings of capitalism, because "all treatises on political economy take *private property* for granted"—that is, they assume that capitalism is the best and only form of society whose fundamentals have existed since the beginning of humankind.[2]

In the early phases of capitalism's development, when it was emerging in conflict with feudalism, political economy had some important scientific insights into the workings of capitalism. However, the emergence of more threatening and organized forms of class struggle between workers and capitalists, in Marx's words, "sounded the death-knell of scientific bourgeois economy." From here on, economics became transformed into what Marx called "vulgar economics"—shallow justifications for the system as it is. "In place of disinterested inquirers, there were hired prize fighters; in place of genuine scientific research, the bad conscience and the evil intent of apologetics."[3]

Economics for the past thirty years, for example, was dominated by theories that denied the possibility of economic crisis and insisted that the "the unrestrained pursuit of self-interest leads to the optimum allocation of resources."[4] According to the popular Efficient Market Hypothesis (EMH), competition between "profit-maximizers," each with good current information about the market, "should cause the actual price of a security to wander randomly about its intrinsic value."[5] Markets are, in this scenario, "self-correcting" and tend toward equilibrium. The model cannot account for, and in fact positively excludes, the possibility of either a "bubble"—an extended period of the inflation of the price of assets—or a collapse in their value.

Not even the 1998 collapse of Long-Term Capital Management, at the time the largest hedge fund in the world, operated by two men who won the Nobel Prize for devising economic models based on EMH, convinced economists to alter their basic approach. "In the summer of 2007," writes McNally, "such models utterly discounted the possibility that house prices might stop rising steadily, never mind decline."[6] And yet not only did housing prices decline—the decline triggered a world economic crisis. It would be like examining a working car and predicting that, based on a week of test drives, it will never break down. The prediction will be right—the car will go on working for quite some time, possibly even several years—until it is wrong, and the car breaks down.

Most economists typically proclaim the end of crisis when times are good, and explain away the crisis when it comes as a disturbance in an otherwise well-balanced system. In flush times, bourgeois economists offer upbeat forecasts of endless prosperity ahead. "American industry and business have reached that status of well-being," wrote one economist not long before the Wall Street crash in 1929, "where it no longer has to fear a recurrence of the radical spreads from prosperity to depression that formerly afflicted business and industry."[7] Similarly effervescent claims were made during the Clinton boom of the 1990s: "The big, bad business cycle has been tamed," proclaimed the *Wall Street Journal* in 1996.[8] This was a few years before the outbreak of the Asian crisis, which caused a wave of worldwide bankruptcies.

When mainstream economists are finally forced to recognize the obvious, that capitalism periodically lapses into crisis, they explain it not as an inherent feature of capitalism but as "an exceptional deviation from the norm," brought about by some external factor not intrinsic to the market.[9] Economists Olivier Coibion and Yuriy Gorodnichenko, in a January 2010 blog post, for example, called the 2007 financial crisis "a violent storm in otherwise temperate times."[10]

In a speech he made after the outbreak of the Great Recession, after admitting that "almost universally, economists failed to predict the nature, timing, or severity of the crisis," chairman of the US Federal Reserve Ben Bernanke argued that the standard economic models based on the idea that markets are efficient and "self-regulating" should not be abandoned. "Economic models are useful only in the context for which they are designed," he explains. "Most of the time, including during recessions, serious financial instability is not an issue. The standard models were designed for these non-crisis periods, and they have proven quite useful in that context."[11] It is as if Bernanke thought there are two entirely separate economies—one that works, which we have models for; and one that doesn't, which we don't have models for! Economists, then, must be like meteorologists: they can loosely predict economic trends for today and possibly a couple of days in advance, but they get less and less reliable the further away you get from today. Clearly, an economic "science" that fails to predict crisis—indeed, whose theoretical models either preclude the possibility of crisis or claim to not cover that aspect of economic reality—isn't really much of a science.

This wishing away or externalizing of crises goes back to the eighteenth- and early-nineteenth-century economists like J. B. Say and James Mill, who said that supply creates its own demand. There can be no "superfluity of commodities," argued Mill, because everything that is produced will find a buyer.[12] Marx was scornful of this idea. "Nothing can be more childish," wrote Karl Marx in *Capital*, "than the dogma that, because every sale is a purchase and every purchase a sale, therefore the circulation of commodities necessarily implies an equilibrium of sale and purchase."[13] It may be a comforting idea, but it hardly accords with reality, where economic crisis, at its core, consists precisely in the rupture between purchase and sale.

Marx rescued economics from these economists and turned it into a tool for explaining inequality, exploitation, and crisis—as well as a way to end all three. He was able to do this because he viewed capitalism from a historical standpoint as a system that came into being and would, like all previous modes of production, pass away. At the heart of Marx's understanding of the economics of capitalism is the "labor theory of value." This concept is the foundation for the whole edifice of his theory of capitalism.

The Labor Theory of Value

At the beginning of his most important work, *Capital*, Marx described capitalist wealth as an "immense accumulation of commodities."[14] In order to get a handle on how capitalism worked, Marx began with this basic cell of the capitalist organism—

the commodity—and worked from there, adding more features to present a systematic picture of the whole. It is similar to the method used by scientists, who, if they want to figure out a problem, devise an experiment that eliminates as many variable factors as possible to isolate the phenomenon they want to investigate. In one respect, Marx started this way because he wanted to isolate key factors of the system and then put them back together to show how they worked in their interaction and movement. Another reason, however, was that he wanted to show how the appearance of "equal exchange" of commodities in the market camouflaged inequality and exploitation. At its most superficial level, capitalism can be described as a system in which production of commodities for the market becomes the dominant form. The problem with most economic analyses is that they don't get beyond this level.

Commodities, Marx argued, have a dual character, having both "use value" and "exchange value." Like all products of human labor, they have use value, that is, they possess some useful quality for the individual buyer or a given society. The commodity could be something that could be directly consumed, like food; it could be a tool, like a saw, a hammer, or a lathe, that could be used to make other useful things; or it could be a material worked on by tools, like wood or thread, that form the raw material for making another commodity. A commodity doesn't have to be a material thing—it can also be a service sold on the market, like health care, cleaning, playing an instrument, or hairstyling. A commodity must be useful to some potential buyer—it must have use value—or it cannot be sold. Yet it also has an exchange value, that is, it can exchange for other commodities in particular proportions. Commodities, however, are clearly not exchanged according to their degree of usefulness. On a scale of survival, food is more important than cars, but that's not how their relative prices are set. Nor is weight a measure. I can't exchange a pound of wheat for a pound of silver. Yet there must be some quantitative relation that all commodities have. "Despite their motley appearance," Marx noted, commodities "have a common denominator."[15]

That common denominator is human labor. Not particular types of labor, but labor in the abstract. All commodities are products of labor. What makes them exchangeable in certain proportions is not the type of product they are, which differentiates them according to their qualities, but what they all have in common—that they are all products of labor. Marx argued that the action of buying and selling mass quantities of commodities in the market reduces them, behind the backs of the producers, to quantities of abstract labor-time. The value of a commodity, that is, how much of it can be exchanged for another commodity, is determined by the amount of labor-time necessary to produce it. "Necessary labor-time" simply means the amount of time something should take to make, more or less, using prevailing techniques of production. If, for example, I build a kitchen cabinet with my hands in a day, when a cabinet of the same quality can be built in a factory in an hour, I can't sell mine for twenty-four times the price of the factory-made cabinet. A great portion of the time it took me to build the cabinet is therefore not "socially necessary" labor; it is, as far as the market is concerned, wasted labor.

The labor theory of value explains why, for example, a car is more valuable than a radio, or a computer is more expensive than a pencil. If you add up all the labor-time it took to make all the elements that enter into the process of production as well as the time to assemble each into the final product, then it is clear that one took more labor-time to make, under prevailing conditions of production, than the other, and that this, logically, is what determines their different exchange values.

Marx was influenced by the new economic analyses of the world presented by political economists like Adam Smith and David Ricardo. Writing in a period before the political triumph of the bourgeoisie, these economists wrote with a scientific rigor and honesty that later economists did not possess. "The value of a commodity," wrote Ricardo, "depends on the relative quantity of labor which is necessary for its production."[16]

This "labor theory of value" was dropped by later economists and replaced with the idea that value is equal to price, and price is determined by a commodity's relative scarcity or abundance. The idea that labor is the measure of value was too dangerous because it acknowledged that labor is the source of a capitalist's profit. But as Marx pointed out, supply and demand "regulate nothing but the temporary *fluctuations* of market prices. They will explain to you why the market price of a commodity rises above or sinks below its *value*, but they can never account for the *value* itself."[17] The price of a shoe and the price of one of its components, like the leather sole, might fluctuate, but the entire shoe will always cost more than sole because the shoe embodies more labor-time than its sole.

Economists of his day tried to discredit Marx by pointing out the divergence between prices and values. But prices and values cannot coincide because production is unplanned. The point is to determine the underlying laws that govern the production and exchange of commodities under capitalism. "The vulgar economist," writes Marx,

> has not the slightest idea that the actual, everyday exchange relations and the value magnitudes *cannot be directly identical.* The point of bourgeois society is precisely that, *a priori*, no conscious social regulation of production takes place. What is reasonable and necessary by nature asserts itself only as a blindly operating average. The vulgar economist thinks he has made a great discovery when, faced with the disclosure of the intrinsic interconnection, he insists that things look different in appearance. In fact, he prides himself in his clinging to appearances and believing them to be the ultimate. Why then have science at all?[18]

Of course, you can't look at a commodity—a car or a book or a shoe—and find any exchange value in it. All you'll see is that it is a useful object fashioned by human hands. That's because value isn't really a quality that any object intrinsically possesses, like color, shape, or taste. Value is not really a thing, but a historically evolved relation between human beings that takes "the fantastic form of a relation between things."[19]

Marx called the way in which capitalist society appears to imbue objects with characteristics they do not materially possess "the fetishism of commodities."[20] Value is a meaningless category outside of market relations, that is, outside a society in which independent, separate producers of commodities meet each other in the marketplace. All human societies produce useful things, but not all societies throughout history have produced them for exchange, that is, as items to be bought and sold. As Marx notes, "articles of utility become commodities, only because they are products of the labor of private individuals or groups of individuals who carry on their work independently of each other."[21]

It should be noted, however, that for Marx, labor was not the only source of use value—that is, of material wealth. "*Nature*, Marx wrote, "is just as much the source of use values (and it is surely of such that material wealth consists!) as labor, which itself is only the manifestation of a force of nature, human labor power."[22] This point will become more important in the chapter on the impact of capitalism on the environment later in this book.

There Is Nothing Quite as Wonderful as Money

"Yellow, glittering, precious gold," says Timon in Shakespeare's *Timon of Athens*, has the power to "make black white" and "foul fair," "wrong right, base noble, old young," and even make the "coward valiant."[23]

Money seems to possess mystical powers—pieces of paper or of metal that confer on their bearer the power to convert them into real objects of need or want. It has become a kind of fetish or idol that we bow down to. We are so accustomed to money's role in society that it appears to be the natural state of human society. But there's nothing magical about money. Indeed, while the Spanish conquistadors killed for gold because it was the quintessential form of money, in Inca society the metal, though highly valued, was not used as currency, as Inca society did not use any currency for the purposes of exchange.

"All the illusions of the monetary system," wrote Marx, "arise from the failure to perceive that money, though a physical object with distinct properties, represents a social relation of production."[24] What does that mean? Money arises first as a means of exchanging commodities between independent producers. In a community where all goods are produced and shared in common, everyone contributes their work as they can, and everyone takes out what they need from the common storehouses. Such a society does not need money, because there is no exchange of commodities taking place.

The earliest exchange took the form of barter. Different communities would occasionally come together and exchange surplus products they did not need or want for goods produced somewhere else that they needed or wanted but could not produce themselves. One community would take some surplus salt and trade it to a community that needed it, in exchange for that other community's surplus obsidian or fur pelts, for example. The barter would be roughly based on the amount of labor it took for each community to produce its particular product. This kind of barter existed probably even in the earliest hunter-gatherer societies. But it was incidental trade, not essential to a group's survival. To put it another way, most of the use values a society produced never became commodities, but were directly consumed without being exchanged. As Marx wrote in *Capital*, a "relationship of reciprocal isolation," that is, a society of independent producers "does not exist for the members of a primitive community of natural origin, whether it takes the form of a patriarchal family, an ancient Indian commune or an Inca State. The exchange of commodities begins where communities have their boundaries, at their points of contact with other communities."[25]

At first trade was incidental and haphazard, but then became regular and habitual, and on that basis communities could calculate roughly how much one sort of thing would exchange for another. Further economic development that came with the accumulation of an agricultural surplus led to a greater division of labor between agriculture and the manufacture of weapons, tools, and luxuries, for example. This in turn gave rise to more commodity exchange, not just between communities, but also within them—to the rise of a market for various goods, in other words. As trade became more regular, some kind of medium became necessary to facilitate exchange—a commodity that could be used to buy all other commodities, agreed upon by all. At first it was usually whatever moveable commodity was most coveted and in abundance: cattle, horses, shell beads, and later, with the development of metal work, precious metals like silver and gold. It should be kept in mind, however, that only with the rise of capitalism did commodity production—production for the market—become the dominant form of production. In ancient Rome, for example, where the landowning class accumulated enormous estates that exploited great slave gangs, trade accounted for a small fraction of overall revenue.

Because of their malleable character, gold and, to a lesser degree, silver became the preeminent money commodities. States began producing silver or gold coins in various weights, stamped with the face of a particular ruler. There is nothing magical about gold. It is a commodity like all others, whose value is measured by how much labor-time is necessary to produce it. By convention, it became what Marx called the "universal equivalent"—the commodity against which all other commodities express their value.[26] It is, in other words, not merely a medium of exchange, but also a measure of value. We could, by agreement, make shoestrings money, and then all prices would be quoted in shoestrings. The problem is that it would take too many shoestrings to buy something valuable, and so it's not a practical commodity to use as money. For related reasons, lead never became money. Lead money would require that we throw away our wallets for wheelbarrows.

The mystery of money is compounded by the fact that, as capitalism developed, money as a means of circulation and exchange was replaced by paper symbols of money, and coins debased with cheaper metals. But these coins and paper symbols were originally named after the gold or silver weights they were supposed to be symbols for (a pound note, for example, originally represented one pound of sterling silver). Until the early 1970s, the value of a paper dollar was pegged to gold—one dollar was worth a thirty-fifth of an ounce of gold. Since then, paper money is not directly convertible (at a legally defined rate) into gold or silver—a fact that distances money even further from its origins from the world of commodities and makes it appear to be an even more mysterious thing. That paper notes are ultimately, however, symbols of real value is demonstrated clearly by the fact that if a government prints money at will—that is, if more money is pushed into circulation, and the supply of money increases faster than the supply of goods and services—its value depreciates and prices go up.

In modern capitalist society, where everything can be bought and sold, money's historical origins are completely invisible, and it appears to possess a power independent of human will. "Men are henceforth related to each other in their social process of production in a purely atomistic way," wrote Marx of capitalism. "Their own relations of production therefore assume a material shape which is independent of their control and their conscious individual action. This situation is manifested first by the fact that the products of men's labor universally take on the form of commodities. The riddle of the money fetish is therefore the riddle of the commodity fetish, now become visible and dazzling to our eyes."[27]

Capitalism's Driving Motive

Today, scarcely a few hundred years after the rise of industrial capitalism, the complete dominance of the market has become such a normal feature of economic life that it is hard to conceive of any other economic mode of existence. Yet on the scale of human history it is a recent phenomenon. That has never stopped economists, however, from projecting capitalist relations of production into the distant past. The noted eighteenth-century economist Adam Smith put it most famously when he wrote of the "propensity in human nature" to "truck, barter and exchange."[28] Marx ridiculed one economist who discovered the "origin of capital" in the "first stone which the savage flings at the wild animal he pursues."[29]

Marx criticized the bourgeois economists who tried to ascertain modern economic laws from "the individual isolated hunter and fisherman" stranded on a deserted island—an "unimaginative conceit" he called constructing "Robinsonades."[30] According to the nineteenth-century French economist Bastiat, for example, the same economic laws apply equally to a "totality of lonely persons" or an isolated individual.[31] Human beings are, however, social creatures, not hermits. "Production by an isolated individual outside society—a rare exception which may well occur when a civilized person in whom the social forces are already dynamically present is cast by accident into the wilderness—is as much of an absurdity as is the development of language without individuals living *together* and talking to each other."[32]

Ironically, Marx observed, "the epoch [capitalism] which produces this standpoint, that of the isolated individual, is also precisely that of the hitherto most developed social . . . relations." The whole concept of human beings as individuals rather than as part of a social group derives from "a society of free competition" where "the individual appears detached from the natural bonds . . . which in earlier historical periods make him the accessory of a definite and limited human conglomerate."[33]

Such views serve to make it appear as though capitalism and the market were eternal features of human society, intrinsic to our very nature.

In addition to seeing trade as eternal, bourgeois economists also try to argue that the purpose of the capitalist market is simply to facilitate the distribution of products where they are needed. The famous US economist Paul Samuelson described economics as "the study of how men [sic] and society end up choosing . . . to employ scarce resources . . . to produce various commodities and distribute them for consumption."[34]

The main things to note here are that, one, Samuelson equates economics with commodity production, and two, he sees the capitalist market as simply a distribution mechanism—a means to get goods to consumers. The early economists, like Adam Smith and David Ricardo, were far more honest in their appraisal of the capitalist system that was growing up around them than were its later apologists like Samuelson. "It may very justly be said," Adam Smith explained in one of his lectures, "that the people who clothe the whole world are in rags themselves"—an observation that could be made today as much as in the eighteenth century.[35] Samuelson failed to define the most important thing that distinguishes capitalism from all previous forms of production—that it is a system whose main purpose is profit making. "Use-value," that is, the production and distribution of useful things, wrote Marx, "must therefore never be treated as the immediate aim of the capitalist."[36]

All societies, in order to survive, must produce and distribute necessities. The question is, what is the specific form in which this happens and how does it change? In a letter to a friend, Ludwig Kugelman, Marx quipped:

> Every child knows that any nation that stopped working, not for a year, but let us say, just for a few weeks, would perish. And every child knows, too, that the amounts of products corresponding to the differing amounts of needs demand differing and quantitatively determined amounts of society's aggregate labor. It is self-evident that this *necessity* of the *distribution* of social labor in specific proportions is certainly not abolished by the *specific form* of social production; it can only change its form of manifestation. Natural laws cannot be abolished at all. The only thing

that can change, under historically differing conditions, is the *form* in which those laws assert themselves. And the form in which this proportional distribution of labor asserts itself in a state of society in which the interconnection of social labor expresses itself as the *private exchange* of the individual products of labor, is precisely the *exchange value* of these products.[37]

Samuelson would only be right if capitalism were a system of independent producers whose sole purpose for bringing their wares to market was to get other things (of equal value) they needed but did not produce. I make a pair of shoes, sell them for money, and use the money to buy some carrots you produced in your garden. Marx simplified this economic circuit with the formula C-M-C (commodity-money-commodity, the conversion of one commodity into money, and the conversion of that money into another commodity), or selling in order to buy. It is true that this describes in a way what *most* of us, who are not capitalists, do—we sell (our labor) in order to buy (our necessities).

But for capitalists the purpose of selling is not to end up with other things of equal value. That would be a waste of time. What would be the point of selling x number of widgets in order to buy y amount of hammers? I didn't produce the widgets to personally consume them, and I can't personally consume a large number of hammers. My aim as a capitalist is to end up with more money than I started with. The process of buying and selling commodities is merely a means to achieve this end. Capital, after all, is, in Marx's aphorism, "self-expanding value."[38] Though capitalists must produce something useful to someone in order to find a market for it, they are selling it merely for its value, that is, for the profit it can bring them. Capitalists buy in order to sell. Marx described the basic circuit of capital M-C-M′ (money-commodity-money, investing money to produce a commodity and then selling the commodity for an amount that exceeds my original investment), the M′ representing the original investment plus the extra value realized after sale, or "surplus value."

To his contemporaries, who argued along the same lines as Samuelson would many years later, Marx admonished: "It must never be forgotten, that in capitalist production what matters is not the immediate use-value but the exchange value and, in particular, the expansion of surplus value. This is the driving motive of capitalist production, and it is a pretty conception that—in order to reason away the contradictions of capitalist production—abstracts from its very basis and depicts it as a production aiming at the direct satisfaction of the consumption of the producers."[39]

"Nothing Will Come of Nothing"[40]

We have already shown how in a market economy commodities are exchanged as equivalents, that is, according to how much labor-time they contain. Yet, if equal values exchange on the market, according to the amount of labor-time they embody, where does profit come from? How is it that something can be sold for more than it was purchased for?

Perhaps that's all profit is—setting a price above cost. But if everyone selling commodities simply marked up the cost of their products, they would have to pay the inflated prices of other sellers who were doing the same thing. The nominal price of everything might go up, but the relative value of each thing wouldn't change, and no one would gain. In other words, the markups would cancel each other out, and still there would be no extra value. To use Marx's terms, no "surplus value" is added to commodities during the process of circulation. Surplus value has to come from somewhere else—in the process of production.

As already discussed, the evolution of capitalism not only involves a division of labor in which isolated individuals produce for the market, but also the separation of the means of production—the tools, machinery, materials, and physical plant necessary for production—from the mass of workers. Once this separation takes place, the majority, the working class, are forced to sell their labor power to the minority, the capitalist class that has concentrated land and means of production into its hands. And the owners of these means of production also, therefore, own the products of labor and the proceeds from their sale.

As Marx jokingly related, the marketplace where goods are exchanged is seen as "a very Eden of the innate rights of man" where "alone rule Freedom, Equality, [and] Property," because each "exchange equivalent for equivalent."[41] The exchange between labor and capital, where workers are forced by their very survival needs to seek employment, is portrayed as a fair exchange between two equal partners.

But if the value of a commodity is determined by the amount of necessary labor-time embodied in it, then what is the value of labor? Here we have to make a distinction between the value of labor expended (that is, as it is contained in an amount of work or product), and the value of someone's capacity to labor. Marx argued that the value of this particular commodity, labor power, is equal not to what a worker can produce, but to the labor-time necessary to make up what it costs to keep a worker and a worker's family alive and functioning—the cost of producing, and reproducing, labor power. Marx put it this way:

> The value of labor-power is determined, as in the case of every other commodity, by the labor-time necessary for the production, and consequently also the reproduction, of this special article. In so far as it has value, it represents no more than a definite quantity of the average labor of society objectified in it. Labor-power exists only as a capacity, or power of the living individual. Its production consequently presupposes his existence. Given the individual, the production of labor-power consists in his reproduction of himself or his maintenance. For his maintenance he requires a given quantity of the means of subsistence. Therefore the labor-time necessary for the production of labor power reduces itself to that necessary for the

production of those means of subsistence; in other words, the value of labor-power is the value of the means of subsistence necessary for the maintenance of its owner.[42]

Marx added that the value of labor power not only includes the costs of the training and subsistence of the laborer, but also of the workers' replacements; that is, his children, "in order that this race of peculiar commodity-owners may perpetuate its presence on the market."[43]

In order to set the production process into motion, capitalists must bring together means of production (machinery and raw materials) and labor power, by purchasing them on the market. The workers, using the machinery, then work up the raw materials into a finished product to be sold. The value of the used-up raw materials together with the amount of incremental wear and tear on machinery is only part of the final value of the product. These things are products of past labor, and as they are used up they pass their value onto the new product.

But new labor-time is needed to work up the final product by current, living labor, and this also goes into the final value of the product. In other words, the value of a commodity is made up two parts—dead, or accumulated labor, which is wholly or incrementally passed on to the finished commodity, and living labor (the labor-time added by the worker using the "dead" labor embodied in machinery and materials). Marx calls machinery and materials "constant capital" because in its use it merely transfers existing, but adds no additional, value to the final product. He calls the value of labor power, or wages, "variable capital." Why variable? Because labor power, when set in motion, can add new value to the product over and above its own cost. The capitalist pays for all the value added by accumulated, or "dead," labor—but only part of the value added by living labor. If a capitalist sold a product by the cost of wages plus materials and machinery wear and tear, there would of course be no profit—the capitalist would merely get back what he or she paid out.

It is, Marx noted, a "piece of good luck" that labor's use is greater than "what the capitalist pays for that use."[44] The value of labor power—that is, wages—is less than the value of output that this labor can produce. Put another way, workers produce enough value to cover the cost of their wages (variable capital) in just a part of the working day. The labor performed for the rest of the working day does not have to be paid for—it is "surplus labor," which produces "surplus value," and therefore when the product is sold, this unpaid portion goes into the pocket of the capitalists. Here is how Marx puts it in *Capital*:

> The capitalist pays the value of the labor-power (or, if the price diverges from this, he pays the price) and receives in exchange the right to dispose of the living labor-power itself. The length of time during which he utilizes the labor-power is divided into two separate periods. During one period, the worker produces a value that only equals the value of his labor-power, i.e. he produces its equivalent. Thus the capitalist receives, in return for advancing the price of the labor-power, a product

of the same price. It is the same as if he had bought the product ready-made in the market. During the other period, the period of surplus labor, the utilization of the labor-power creates a value for the capitalist without costing him any value in return. He is thus able to set labor-power in motion without paying for it. It is in this sense that surplus labor can be called unpaid labor.[45]

So the source of surplus value—and thus profits—is *unpaid labor*. The appearance of equality in the market, whereby a capitalist buys labor at a "fair price," as we now see, hides good, old-fashioned exploitation. Capitalists don't really care whether they're producing steel girders or computers, green beans or golf balls—as long as they end up with more money than when they started. And they can't do that without exploitation—drawing from labor power more than its cost of maintenance and production. Such exploitation was transparent in previous societies. It would be difficult to deny that feudal lords and slave masters' wealth did not come from the surplus that they appropriated from the labor of their serfs or slaves. The capitalist class, likewise, appropriates the surplus wealth of society produced by the working class. The mediation of this process through money and market exchange disguises this fact, but the process is nevertheless in its essence identical.

Bourgeois economists squirm around this fact. They have long tried to portray profit as the capitalist's "reward" for being a capitalist, for being so kind as to employ people who otherwise would starve, and for "risk-taking." Profit, according to the nineteenth-century economist John Stuart Mill, writing in 1848, represents a "recompense" for the capitalist's "forbearing to consume his capital for his own uses"— his "remuneration for abstinence."[46] According to this logic, if the capitalist is going to be so altruistic as to skimp on his own needs in order to invest his hard-earned capital, he should get a little back in return. Yet Mill is forced to admit that the surplus that accrues to capitalists must come from somewhere. "The cause of profit," he acknowledges, "is that labor produces more than is required for its support."[47] When put this plainly, the logic is hard to argue with.

The capitalist's "reward," in fact, results from workers' "forbearing to consume" the fruits of their own labor. Whether capitalists reinvest the surplus to expand production, or whether they spend it on their own personal luxury—and they do both in extravagant proportions—they are making use of wealth they did not produce. It is not abstinence on the part of the bosses but on the part of the workers that explains profit.

Competition: The Big Fish Eat the Small Fish

"The bourgeoisie," wrote Marx, "cannot exist without constantly revolutionizing the instruments of production, and thereby the relations of production, and with them the whole relations of society."[48] Capitalists invest money to make more money, to make a profit. Their aim is "the unceasing movement of profit-making," as Marx put it.[49]

To make money, capitalists must sell their products on the market. There must be a demand for them. Yet individual capitalists don't control the market; rather, the market controls them. There is no central control, no planning in the economy as a whole—only the anarchy of the market, where individual producers are forced to compete with one another for market share, and they will only know once they've brought their products to market whether they will sell or not. This competition is what drives capitalists to continually revolutionize the means of production—to reduce production costs in order to cheapen their product and outsell their competitors. On pain of being driven into extinction by their competitors, capitalists must be able not only to sell most of what they produce they must be able to sell it at a profit. In turn, they must be able to reinvest a part of this profit to expand production and beat out their competitors. As Marx wrote, "Accumulate, accumulate! That is Moses and the prophets! . . . Therefore, save, save, *i.e.*, reconvert the greatest possible portion of surplus-value, or surplus-product into capital! Accumulation for accumulation's sake, production for production's sake: by this formula classical economy expressed the historical mission of the bourgeoisie."[50]

Capitalists do this in two ways. First, they fight to lower wages and reduce benefits as much as possible, to the barest minimum if they can get away with it. The smaller the portion of investment that goes to labor costs, the bigger the portion of a day's labor that goes unpaid and therefore counts as surplus value. Another way to do this is to make workers work longer hours for the same pay.

In the early days of capitalism, low wages and impossibly long hours (not to mention child labor) were the norm. But as capitalism developed, workers began organizing for and winning a shorter working day, and many capitalists came to realize that if workers were going to successfully reproduce and raise the next generation of workers and minimally educate them to take on their role as future workers, they couldn't be worked to death through twelve-, fourteen-, or sixteen-hour workdays.

Capitalists increasingly turned to finding ways to increase productivity—the output per worker per hour. They did this first by making workers work harder to produce more in less time. "Taylorism," or the misnamed "scientific management"—named after Frederick Winslow Taylor, an early-twentieth-century engineer devoted to improving industrial efficiency—was all about managers observing workers and timing their movements in order to eliminate all "dead time" and "superfluous motion." The aim was to turn the worker into a streamlined automaton.[51] Capitalists think that by paying wages they earn the right not only to set a worker to work but to determine the way in which the work is performed. A worker's own ingenuity in finding the most efficient way to perform a task, which he or she naturally uses to lighten the burden of labor, is taken by capitalist managers and used to squeeze out every last drop of work. One author describes the militarized methods of "scientific management" used on workers at United Parcel Service: "As every UPS employee works, every motion, every step, every turn has been studied, measured and timed. Drivers must work exactly according to UPS methods: enter the truck with the right foot, not the left; carry the package with the left arm, not the right; carry the truck keys on the little finger of the right hand, and on no other finger." One worker tells of how his wife calls him a "UPS robot."[52]

Amazon employs similarly inhuman techniques to squeeze every last drop of work from their employees, as author Simon Head explains:

> Amazon's system of employee monitoring . . . combines state-of-the-art surveillance technology with the system of "functional foreman," introduced by Taylor in the workshops of the Pennsylvania machine-tool industry in the 1890s. . . . [A]t Amazon's center at Rugeley, England, Amazon tags its employees with personal satnav (satellite navigation) computers that tell them the route they must travel to shelve consignments of goods, but also set target times for their warehouse journeys and then measure whether targets are met.
>
> All this information is available to management in real time, and if an employee is behind schedule, she will receive a text message pointing this out and telling her to reach her targets or suffer the consequences. At Amazon's depot in Allentown, Pennsylvania . . . , Kate Salasky worked shifts of up to eleven hours a day, mostly spent walking the length and breadth of the warehouse. In March 2011 she received a warning message from her manager, saying that she had been found unproductive during several *minutes* of her shift, and she was eventually fired. This employee tagging is now in operation at Amazon centers worldwide.[53]

Bosses also squeeze out more work by investing in more and more productive machinery, thereby cutting down the cost per unit of production and undercutting the competition by underselling it. Going back to the labor theory of value, if machinery cuts down the time it takes to produce something, the product's value will go down. It is this that permits the capitalist to sell at or below the value of the competition. With each new invention, some capitalists will go bankrupt and others will adopt the new technology, wiping out the advantage of the capitalist who introduced it first. Then the whole process starts again.

Over the history of capitalism, productivity has soared astronomically compared to the sluggish pace of technological change in previous societies. "From the beginning of the nineteenth century to the end of the twentieth," writes economic historian Michel Beaud, "worldwide per capita production was multiplied by a factor of six; since world population during this time span rose from one billion to six billion, we may estimate that total world production was multiplied by a factor of thirty-six."[54]

To give some examples, between 1973 and 1990, according to one study, world machine productivity increased by more than 50 percent.[55] Over the past three decades, changes in steel production methods have reduced by as much as 90 percent the time it takes to produce a ton of steel.[56] The ratio between the least productive manual agriculture and the most productive mechanized agriculture has increased "from 1 to 10 at the beginning of the twentieth century to 1 to more than 100 today."[57]

Another result of capitalist competition is that individual capitals get bigger and bigger, not only by growing in size as profits are reinvested in bigger and more productive operations but also because the big fish swallow the little fish. This happens when bigger firms buy out smaller ones, and when profitable enterprises buy out and scoop up ones that have failed. "One capitalist always kills many," as Marx wrote in *Capital*, calling this process the concentration (bigger units) and centralization (fewer units) of capital.[58] This process doesn't mean that small businesses disappear as a phenomenon (although small business fail at an alarming rate), but it does mean that they become less and less economically significant. As a result, a relatively small number of large companies in the United States account for a highly disproportionate share of economic activity. The top ten corporations in the United States, for example, with a total of about 3.6 million employees, had a combined 2012 revenue of more than $2 trillion—the equivalent of the total GDP of California.[59]

What therefore began as more or less "free" competition (although, as we shown, there have never been markets that have not been manipulated by state policy and violence) over time has led toward the growth of trusts, cartels, and monopolies, where a small number of huge corporations control an entire market.[60] This process took off dramatically among the leading capitalist nations—the United States, Britain, Germany, France, and Japan—in the late 1800s. For example, a wave of mass mergers during "the 1890s produced significant industrial concentration. For the US economy as a whole there were more than three thousand mergers during 1898–1902. In 1901, US Steel Corporation was formed through a series of mergers involving about 165 separate companies. It became the world's first billion-dollar company and controlled over 60 percent of the US steel market."[61]

As these capitalist concerns grew, they became so large that they were driven beyond national boundaries, more and more into the creation of an integrated world market where investment, production, and commodities cross borders as a matter of routine. Capitalism is the first economic system that is truly a world system that draws all corners of the planet into its "cash nexus."[62] Today, giant multinational corporations have production and distribution networks that span the globe, employing hundreds of thousands of people and with net worths that rival the total GNPs of entire countries. The materials, parts, and labor that go into many manufactured products involve sometimes dozens of countries. As David McNally explains, "The production of a personal computer . . . involves more than 1,000 discrete acts of labor, typically conducted in ten to twenty countries."[63] An electric toothbrush made by Philips involves assembling thirty-eight components produced in twelve countries across five time zones.[64]

Capitalism creates tremendous wealth unheard of in previous times, but it does so in such a way as to deny the wealth it creates to the majority it exploits. In theory, the growth of machine-based manufacturing should be a means to lessen the burden of work, shorten the workday, and provide everyone with jobs. Instead, "Machinery in itself shortens the hours of labor, but when employed by capital it lengthens them; . . . in itself it lightens labor, but when employed by capital it heightens its intensity; . . . in itself is a victory of man over the forces of nature but in the hands of capital it makes man the slave of those forces; . . . in itself it increases the wealth of the producers, but in the hands of capital it makes them into paupers."[65]

In spite of the astronomical growth in labor productivity, our hours of work never seem to hover far below, and often are higher than, the eight-hour day, forty-hour week. Using Bureau of Labor Statistics data, the late biophysicist and ecologist Erik Rauch calculated in 2000 that "an average worker needs to work a mere 11 hours per week to produce as much as one working 40 hours per week in 1950."[66] Yet no worker today works anything close to a 2.2-hour workday! What happens instead is that, since the rate of wages doesn't keep up with increases in productivity, the rate at which capitalists exploit workers—the ratio of paid to unpaid labor, continues to rise.

Urban planner and historian Lewis Mumford, though no Marxist, could see how the vast gulf between the promise of technological progress and its capitalist application was a glaring contradiction at the heart of the system: "Those machines whose output was so great that all men might be clothed; those new methods of agriculture and new agricultural implements which promised crops so big that all men might be fed—the very instruments that were to give the whole community the basis of a good life, turned out, for the vast majority of people who possessed neither capital nor land, to be nothing short of instruments of torture."[67]

From its inception, capitalism has depended on there being a pool of unemployed and semi-unemployed workers that could be drawn on when growth is on the upswing and tossed into the streets when growth slows down. This unemployed "reserve army" varies from country to country, but nowhere is it below 6 or 7 percent of the population, and in most places it is far larger. The onset of crisis in 2007 initiated a period of high unemployment that has barely abated even after five years, hovering in the United States in 2012 above 8 percent and in Europe above 11 percent—these figures increase dramatically for young people and if "discouraged" workers are included.

The growth of capitalism creates jobs—a fact frequently touted by presidents and pundits. However, over the long haul, capitalism is also a job-killer, as a result of the shrinking of the role of labor in the production process. Unemployment is an inbuilt feature of capitalism, one which capitalists depend on to discipline workers who have jobs. Instead of lowering everyone's hours and providing jobs for all, capitalism maximizes the hours and intensity of work, using the threat of unemployment, or the threat that other workers can always be hired for less, as a means for keeping the working class in check, cheapening labor costs, and thereby boosting profits. In other words, the very process that improves productivity, and therefore the potential for a greater standard of living and less work for all, becomes under capitalism a means to increase exploitation at the worker's expense and to leave millions without a means of any livelihood.

The fanatical intent of the capitalist to accumulate in order to accumulate more, which is imposed on him as an external necessity, acts as a spur to the growth of society's productive forces, even as it denies the benefits of this development to the vast majority whom it exploits and casts aside. This system is only justified to a point in that it creates the material conditions of production, "which alone can form the real basis of a higher form of society, a society in which the full and free development of every individual forms the ruling principle."[68]

Chapter Five

Marxist Economics: How Capitalism Fails

The Crisis of Overproduction

The unplanned, explosive growth that takes place under capitalism does not happen smoothly, but runs in cycles of boom and slump. Each phase of capitalist expansion is accompanied by a crisis that leads to a disruption in production and distribution, a collapse of prices and lending, mass bankruptcies, and unemployment. From Marx's day to the present, the system has been prone to periods in which growth suddenly gives way to stagnation and even decline, economic crises that "put the existence of the entire bourgeois society on trial, each time more threateningly."[1] These crises, absurdly, are not the result of shortages, like a crop failure or some other disaster, as was the case in previous societies. They are crises of *overproduction* or *overaccumulation*. "Society suddenly finds itself put back into a state of momentary barbarism," wrote Marx and Engels in the *Manifesto*. "And why? Because there is too much civilization, too much means of subsistence, too much industry, too much commerce."[2]

Capitalism, Engels wrote in 1877, is "thrown out of joint every ten years or so":

> Commerce is at a stand-still, the markets are glutted, products accumulate, as multitudinous as they are unsaleable, hard cash disappears, credit vanishes, factories are closed, the mass of the workers are in want of the means of subsistence, because they have produced too much of the means of subsistence; bankruptcy follows upon bankruptcy. . . . The stagnation lasts for years; productive forces and products are wasted and destroyed wholesale, until the accumulated mass of commodities finally filter off, more or less depreciated in value, until production and exchange gradually begin to move again. Little by little, the pace quickens. It becomes a trot. The industrial trot breaks into a canter, the canter in turn grows into the headlong gallop of a perfect steeplechase of industry, commercial credit, and speculation,

which finally, after breakneck leaps, ends where it began—in the ditch of a crisis. And so over and over again.[3]

This was written in 1877, when the world was in the midst of what until the 1930s was called the "Great Depression," which began in 1873 and lasted, with ups and downs, until 1896. At that time, the capitalist world had already experienced six major recessions in the nineteenth century; it experienced another in 1907, 1921, and then the other Great Depression, beginning in 1929, which only ended during World War II. After the long postwar boom, crisis struck again in the mid-1970s, early 1980s, 1991, 1997–2001, and, of course, the most recent period of crisis, which began in 2007, and from which there has been weak, jobless recovery. Another recession looms as I revise this book for a new edition.[4]

Economic crises underline the fact that in our society production is not for human need but for profit. Crises happen because capitalists can't sell their goods profitably, not because there aren't millions who could use the "overproduced" goods. Eight hundred million people go hungry every year. Yet economists can speak of a "grain glut" or a "pork glut." Steel is used to make so many essential products that literally hundreds of millions of people desperately need, yet the financial press can talk of a "steel glut." Millions can be homeless, yet there can be talk of a "real-estate glut."

Supply and demand under capitalism have nothing to do with human need. In India, for example, 200 million people are malnourished. Yet in 1995, India exported $625 million worth of wheat and $1.3 billion worth of rice (a total of 5,000,000 metric tons).[5] Profit alone "determines the expansion or contraction of production, instead of the proportion between production and social needs, the needs of socially developed human beings. . . . Production comes to a standstill not at the point where needs are satisfied, but rather where the production and realization of profit impose this."[6]

Overproduction refers solely to production exceeding what can be sold profitably on the market, not that there is an overabundance of goods compared to human need. As Marx put it:

> So long as the most urgent needs of a large part of society are not satisfied . . . there can of course be absolutely no talk of an *overproduction of products*—in the sense that the amount of products is excessive in relation to the need for them. On the contrary, it must be said that on the basis of capitalist production, there is constant *under-production* in this sense. The limits to production are set by the profit of the capitalist and in no way by the needs of the producers. But overproduction of products and overproduction of commodities are two entirely different things.[7]

Capitalist crises arise first of all from the unplanned competitive drive toward accumulation. Overproduction of commodities is a regular feature of a system in which production and distribution are regulated not by a plan but blindly through the market, where each capitalist concern is driven by competition to outpace its competitors. Because individual capitalists or corporations produce without knowing in advance what they can sell, and moreover, because they strive to expand production and capture more market share, and thereby, more profit, there is a built-in tendency for capitalists "to produce without regard to the limits of the market."[8] There is a constant tension, writes Marx, "between the restricted dimensions of consumption on the capitalist basis, and a production that is constantly striving to overcome these immanent barriers."[9]

Capitalists invest in the necessary conditions for mass production with the expectation that the entire product, or most of it, will be sold, and at a price that will guarantee a sufficient rate of profit. But if these conditions aren't met—if only part of the products sell, or if they sell at a price lower than the costs of production, then profits will not be realized, and crisis will ensue. Crisis—that is, a disruption in the process of production and circulation—takes place in the same way that trains become held up, one behind the other, if too many are launched on the same line. In fact, it is only through crisis, ultimately, that the system is able to restore a temporary balance in the economy—a balance that is continually being disrupted and then reestablished.

The cycle of boom and bust begins with an upswing or boom—a period of unrestrained growth in which capital investments in new technology and labor spur growth, more and more workers are hired, more and more goods are sold, and more and more profits are raked in. As capitalism reaches the height of its boom phase, prices and wages start to go up in response to the increasing demand for labor and goods. Hungry for profits, capitalists borrow huge sums of money from banks and other lenders in order to get in on the profit bonanza, thereby taking on huge debts that they expect to pay off from windfall profits. With the boom comes speculation—making short-term profit on changes in the prices of commodities and securities. The frenzy for money reaches spectacular heights, as corporate stocks and other financial instruments are traded at increasingly astronomical values that bear no relationship to their actual value. As long as the prices of stocks and other securities go up—and in this manic betting phase everyone becomes intoxicated by the idea of ever-expanding prices, and therefore profits. An orgy of gambling and speculation, feeding a cycle of increasing stock prices, accelerates just at the point when the boom is reaching its apex, profits are being squeezed, and investment is slowing down. Indeed, as capitalists find fewer profitable outlets for investments, they shift more and more "idle" funds into speculative stock, currency, and debt trades. "Business is always thoroughly sound, and the campaign in fullest swing, until the sudden intervention of the collapse," wrote Marx.[10]

As capitalists begin to worry about their profit rates—as the overaccumulation of capital leads to an expansion of capacity beyond the ability of the market to absorb it—they begin to cut back on investments, producing first a crisis in what Marx called "department one," the department that makes the means of production (producer goods). Workers are then laid off in this sector, which restricts consumption and begins to produce a slump in sales in department two, the production of means of consumption (consumer goods).[11] Banks and other lenders begin calling in loans and refusing to grant new loans, which leads to bankruptcies, more layoffs, more slumps in sales, and so on in a vicious downward spiral. "The chain of payment obligations at specific dates," writes Marx, "is broken in a hundred places, and this is still further intensified by an accompanying breakdown of the credit system, which had developed alongside capital. All this therefore leads to violent and acute crises, sudden forcible devaluations, an actual stagnation and disruption in their production process, and hence to an actual decline in production."[12]

Crises can be mild or harsh, producing either stagnation or a decline in production (negative growth) for a shorter or longer period. But they always lead to mass layoffs, wage cuts, and social spending cuts, and therefore increased misery, for the working class and the poor.

But capitalism never permanently stagnates. "How are the relations corresponding to a 'healthy' movement of capitalist production to be restored?"[13] Marx asks. Growth can only be restored after a certain amount of capital is destroyed or drastically devalued and profit rates return to a point where capitalists are willing to invest again. This happens in a number of ways. First, unemployment brought on by the crisis allows the employers to drastically lower wages and benefits without fear of retaliation. Second, the machinery and physical plant of bankrupt businesses is destroyed and/or devalued. Some of the oldest, least productive plant and equipment are simply tossed on the scrap heap or are left idle. The rest can still be operated, but not profitably by their owners, whose investments can't be recouped because prices are too low. The capitalists that have survived the crisis best now swoop in and buy up on the cheap the unprofitable or bankrupt businesses. The now cheaper capital inputs and wage costs mean that the remaining capitalists—larger, leaner, and meaner—can once again begin to operate profitably. Then the whole cycle begins again, only now with fewer, even bigger, more centralized and more concentrated firms dominating the market.

This process operates internationally, involving constant changes and restructuring of networks of production and distribution. The onset of crisis in 1973 after the long postwar boom, for example, triggered a massive restructuring of industrial production worldwide, buttressed by an assault on trade unions and working-class living standards. The restructuring involved "major downsizing, scrapping of old plants and equipment, and dramatic reorganizations of the work processes and technology."[14] Take steel for example. The number of steel workers in the United States declined by 350,000 throughout the 1980s, as the center of world steel production began to shift from the United States, Europe and Japan to newly industrializing countries like Brazil, South Korea, Mexico, and later, China, which is today the world's largest steel producer.

"Across the globe," writes McNally, "geographic relocation, wage cutting, downsizing, and new technologies contributed to a halving of the cost of making flat-rolled steel."[15] The result of this kind of restructuring, which affected all industries, is that in the United States the rate of profit doubled between 1982 and 1997.[16] This massive restructuring "produced a new wave of capitalist expansion (centered on East Asia) that began to exhaust itself in the late 1990s."[17]

A much deeper economic depression was only averted in the last crisis (2007–08) through massive intervention by states and central banks to shore up the collapsing financial sector. This in turn led to massive state indebtedness and what became known as a "sovereign debt crisis." The cost of the crisis was diverted to the states. After big business clamored for, and received, enormous cash infusions courtesy of the taxpayer, capital then turned around and demanded austerity—severe cuts in public jobs, public pensions, wages, and social services in order to restore "fiscal responsibility." While financial firms began to restore their profitability as a result of practically free money (for example, in the United States banks could borrow from the government for next to nothing and then loan it back to the government at a higher interest rate) and to again dish out unimaginable bonuses to their CEOs and traders, workers in the public and private sector were being asked to absorb the costs. The new debt crisis, which has hit Greece, Spain, Italy, Ireland, and other European states particularly hard—and the harsh austerity being imposed in those countries in order to placate investors—threatens to bring the world economy back into recession. The bailouts—which amounted to considerably more than $21 trillion worldwide—did not solve the underlying problem of overaccumulation in the world system, but rather shifted the way in which the crisis expresses itself.[18]

State intervention, then, can alter the character or the impact of the boom-bust cycle. States can manipulate the supply of money or try to influence interest rates in order to make it easier or harder for capitalists to get loans. Because these manipulations attack the symptoms rather than the causes, they cannot eliminate crises but can only change their form.

Buy Now, Pay Later

Credit plays an important role in the development of capitalism. Historically, it has allowed for large concentrations of otherwise idle funds that could be used to make large investments that no single capitalist could make on their own. Credit accelerates the concentration and centralization of capital, and therefore the growth of monopolies—huge corporations dominating entire industries. Government debt (bonds)—which is really just placing a portion of tax money into the hands of the capitalists—has also been a key to funding the development of transportation, energy, and other infrastructures necessary for the functioning of the system.

Credit also transforms many capitalists into mere "money capitalists"—that is, investors seeking profit without any relationship to the production process. To quote Marx, credit "reproduces a new financial aristocracy, a new kind of parasite in the guise of company promoters, speculators and merely nominal directors; an entire system of swindling and cheating with respect to the promotion of companies, issue of shares and share dealing. It is private production unchecked by private ownership."[19] In other words, credit allows for a great deal of financial gambling that appears to have no relationship to the "real" economy—that is, the production and distribution of goods and services—but seems to live and breathe in its own realm.

In a chapter in *Capital*, volume 3, Marx talks about the mysterious quality of financial capital, or what he calls "interest-bearing capital"—money that makes more money—as the capital relationship "in its most superficial and fetishized form."[20] With interest we enter a realm in which, seemingly, money can generate more money from itself, without any intervening factors (for example, the actual production of goods). Somehow, an investor can throw money into a fund, and draw out of that fund more money (M′) than he or she put in. So long as this keeps happening, the investor is happy to believe that money does indeed come from money. Indeed, for capitalists, such an opaque understanding coincides perfectly with their self-interest in denying the role labor plays in generating surplus value. "Capital appears as a mysterious and self-creating source of interest, of its own increase," continues Marx. "The thing (money, commodity, value) is now capital even as a mere thing, and capital appears as a property inherent in the thing itself. . . . Thus it becomes as completely the property of money to create value, to yield interest, as it the property of a pear-tree to bear pears."[21]

Interest, however, is not the magical increase of a sum of money into more money, but a claim to a portion of the total surplus value produced in the economy. Marx explains it "is nothing but a particular name, or special title, for a part of the profit which the actually functioning capitalist has to pay to the capital's proprietor, instead of pocketing it himself."[22] Interest is a claim on profit, which is, in turn, the product of unpaid labor. As Marx writes, though "interest is only a portion of the profit, i.e., of the surplus-value, which the functioning capitalist squeezes out of the laborer, it appears now, on the contrary, as though interest were the typical product of capital, the primary matter, and profit, in the shape of profit of enterprise, were a mere accessory and by-product of the process of reproduction." This apparent "capacity of money, or of a commodity, to expand its own value independently of reproduction," Marx concluded, "is a mystification of capital in its most flagrant form."[23]

This mystification reaches its apex at the height of a period of business expansion, when hothouse price inflation encourages capitalists to engage in wild speculative adventures, which are really nothing but pyramid schemes based on gambling and swindling. At this point, the amount of wealth sloshing around appears to be almost limitless, and yet there are limits. The limits to the amount of real wealth capitalists can obtain is based on the amount of surplus they can extort from the working class. "The identity of surplus-value and surplus-labor," Marx continues, "imposes a qualitative limit upon the accumulation of capital. This consists of the total working-day, and the prevailing development of the productive forces and of the population, which limits the number of simultaneously exploitable working-days. But if one conceives of surplus-value in the meaningless form of interest, the limit is merely quantitative and defies all fantasy."[24]

It is only when the crash comes that everyone realizes that many of these values were "fictitious," that is, had no real value. In the 2008 financial meltdown, for example, world stock markets contracted by 50 percent, wiping out $35 trillion in financial assets.[25] This does not mean that more than half the world's GDP was wiped out. In a boom, stocks, bonds, and other financial instruments trade at prices that are far above the value of the assets underlying them. The crisis forcibly asserts the reality that paper wealth must ultimately bear a real relationship to the wealth actually produced.

Credit both encourages and accelerates the boom; and, at a certain point, can both trigger and make the crises worse. As the Polish-born Marxist Rosa Luxemburg wrote, "When the inner tendency of capitalist production to extend boundlessly strikes against the restricted dimensions of private property, credit appears as a means of surmounting these limits in a particular capitalist manner."[26] Yet credit does so by allowing production to extend beyond the limits of the market, that is, beyond the point at which goods can be sold profitably. In addition, credit allows for more extensive market speculation—buying and selling based on price fluctuations. Credit ties capitalist investors together in a web of relations, so that when some capitalists go bankrupt, it threatens the health of the whole system. "Credit," concludes Luxemburg, "instead of being an instrument for the suppression or the attenuation of crises, is on the contrary a particularly mighty instrument for the formation of crises."[27]

This was certainly the case in the Great Recession, which was triggered by the massive expansion of debt. It was the availability of cheap credit that fueled the housing bubble. The inflation in housing prices led homeowners to use their home equity to supplement their meager incomes. People borrowed against the values of their homes and maxed out their credit cards, mainly because of falling or stagnating wages and living standards. Overall, workers' wages have stagnated since 1973, and 26.4 percent of workers in the United States work for poverty wages. Essentially, workers had to go into debt in order to maintain their standard of living.[28] Mortgage lenders sold adjustable rate loans with low-interest teaser rates—what is called "subprime" mortgages"—as if they were giving away candy to people who would like to default, once prices dropped, or if they lost their job, or if interest rates shot up. But as long as prices kept shooting up, investors were making money and pretending that everything was fine.

At the top, banks and other financial institutions, taking advantage of deregulation and historically low interest rates, created a "shadow banking system" where investors pooled their money to speculate on various financial "instruments" like currency fluctuations and derivatives, which were "based on an underlying security such as a commodity, bond or currency, but typically representing some kind of gamble about what direction the value of the security would go in."[29] Wall Street banks bought up mortgage debt and bundled them into bonds known as mortgage-backed securities, and selling them to investors at varying levels of risk. The giant investors who bought these bonds expected a steady stream of revenue as the mortgages were paid off. At the same time, a type of derivative called a "credit default swap," a type of insurance against mortgage-backed securities, mushroomed. Companies that sold these swaps were required to cover the losses of those who bought them if mortgage-backed securities declined in value. Everywhere, financial institutions were overextended—their debts massively exceeded the actual value of their assets. In early 2008 it was estimated that credit default swaps were valued at $62.8 trillion—"nearly five times the annual output of the US economy."[30] At the end of 2007, the "theoretical value" of derivatives was estimated at an astronomical $596 trillion![31] Once the housing market collapsed, all this unraveled, the financial industry crashed, and all these artificially inflated prices were brought back down to earth.

Capitalism's Achilles' Heel

Underlying the cyclical crisis of overproduction is a tendency for capitalist growth to produce relatively diminishing returns, a tendency for the rate of profit—how much money is made relative to investment costs—to fall over time. We have already seen that the need to increase market share compels each capitalist to invest in technology that reduces the amount of labor-time necessary to produce a particular commodity, and therefore its cost.

The invention, for example, of the oxygen furnace to replace the open-hearth furnace in the 1960s reduced the time it took to melt iron from ten hours to forty-five minutes. Over the past thirty years, the number of human hours required to produce a ton of steel has dropped by 90 percent among many US manufacturers.[32] The capitalist who is the first to use labor-saving technology is able to undersell his or her competitors—at least until the competitors adopt the same methods. This boosts profits in the short term, but over time it shrinks the role of the very element in the production process that produces profit—labor. How can we explain this?

The working day can be divided into two parts—the paid and unpaid portion, as described earlier. Marx called that portion of the day in which workers produce the equivalent of their own wages "necessary labor," and that portion of the day in which they work for the bosses' profits "surplus labor." In product terms, a portion of the product when sold covers wages, the cost of materials, and the wearing down of machinery, and the other portion is extra, surplus product, that brings surplus value to the capitalist. Marx called the ratio of surplus labor-time to necessary labor-time "the rate of exploitation."

For example, if I work an eight-hour day, and it only takes four hours to make up the cost of my wages for the day, then I am working four hours of unpaid, surplus labor time, which makes for a rate of exploitation of four hours to four hours (4/4), or 100 percent. This rate of exploitation under capitalism is constantly increasing, because with increased productivity, the amount of time necessary to reproduce the necessities of workers goes down (and, what is a result of the same process, the means of subsistence becomes cheaper), leaving a greater portion of the day a grant of free labor to the capitalist. In other words, the time in the workday needed to replace the value of a worker's wage tends to go down, and the amount of unpaid labor as a result tends to go up. As a result, workers can actually receive a higher wage and still be more exploited than a worker who receives a lower wage. This is true because as productivity goes up, and more wealth is produced, a worker may receive more in absolute terms (that is, in terms of purchasing power), but may receive less relative wealth compared to what the boss is raking in, because the total of unpaid labor in relation to paid labor is higher.

Over the past decades, capitalists in the United States have had the best of both worlds: rising productivity (based both on getting workers to work hard and faster, and on investments in new technology) along with barely rising or stagnating wages. As one *New York Times* story reported, "From 1973 to 2011, worker productivity grew 80 percent, while median hourly compensation, after inflation, grew by just one-eighth that amount, according to the Economic Policy Institute, a liberal research group. And since 2000, productivity has risen 23 percent while real hourly pay has essentially stagnated."[33]

As capitalism advances and grows, as it becomes more and more productive, the proportion between what a capitalist spends on technology and machinery ("constant capital") and what a capitalist spends on wages ("variable capital") grows. As productivity increases, living labor becomes a relatively smaller and smaller component of production, and machinery (dead labor) a relatively larger and larger component. As capitalism advances, fewer and fewer workers set greater and greater amounts of machinery into motion—industry as a whole becomes more "capital intensive" and less "labor intensive." Marx calls this the ratio between constant capital and variable capital the "organic composition of capital," and the tendency toward an increasing ratio between constant capital and variable capital the "rising organic composition of capital."[34]

For example, changes in the productivity of printing mean that today a few people operating presses that fill an entire warehouse can print tens of thousands of newspapers in a matter of hours. One result of this is that as capitalism grows and requires less labor to produce more goods, more and more workers become "superfluous."

This poses a problem, however. Since living, unpaid labor is the source of surplus value (machines only transfer their value to the final product, they don't create it), labor's shrinking role in production means that surplus value, as a percentage of the total capital, also shrinks. Capitalists measure their success not by the rate of exploitation, but by the rate of profit—that is, by how much money they're getting back relative to their total expenditure, which includes not only wages but also the costs of machinery and materials. Investing in new machinery leads over time to an increasing ratio of expenditure on machinery compared to labor, and therefore exerts a downward pressure on the rate of profit. But the growth of productivity leads both to an increase in the organic composition *and* an increase in the rate of exploitation. Why can't the rise in the proportion of the working day that is given over to producing surplus value counteract the tendency of the rate of profit to fall? In part, there is no apparent limit to the growth of constant capital, while the working day can only be stretched to a certain point, and the rate of exploitation is a ratio, no matter how it varies, that is limited to the boundaries of the working day. "If the normal working day amounts to eight hours," writes Roman Rosdolsky, "no increase in productive power can squeeze more surplus labor out of the worker than eight minus as many hours as correspond to the production of the wage."[35]

The rate of surplus value rises, which increases profits, but "in an ever smaller relation to the development of the productive forces."[36] As Marx points out, the gain in relative surplus value from increasing productivity becomes smaller and smaller compared to the means of production necessary to advance this process. Increasing the rate of exploitation from 100 percent (half the day unpaid labor) to 200 percent (three-fourths of the day unpaid labor) would lead to a marked increase in profits. But each doubling of productivity after that produces smaller and smaller increments of extra surplus value, to the point where no matter how much productivity increases, and thereby reduces the portion of the day devoted to necessary labor, the relative increase of surplus becomes marginal. "The rate of profit does not fall because the worker is less exploited, but rather because less labor is generally applied in relation to the capital invested."[37]

Ironically, then, the very process that capitalists employ to outbid their competitors and raise their profit rates tends over time to run down the general rate of profit. If this tendency played out to its logical conclusion, the system would simply grind down to a snail's pace and eventually seize up (capitalists would stop investing). But there are counteracting influences on falling profits that prevent it from reaching this point. Wages can be lowered below their value, and workers can be made to work harder. In addition, new inventions that increase labor productivity can reduce the amount of labor a given amount of capital sets in motion as well as cheapen the means of production and therefore reduce the cost of investment. (Over capitalism's history, however, this counteracting tendency cannot overcome the pattern by which the investment in machinery grows in comparison to the growth of wages as a component of the total investment.) Finally, and most importantly, the devaluation of capital brought about by crisis reduces the cost of inputs and therefore raises the rate of profit, permitting a new round of expansion. The deeper and more destructive the crisis, the more value is destroyed and therefore the more the organic composition of capital is lowered, the greater the rebound and the prospects for a robust new wave of expansion, which only perpetuates capitalism's boom-bust cycle.

The decline in the rate of profit can also be offset or slowed down by siphoning off some of the funds that could be used to invest in new machinery to invest instead in luxury goods, financial speculation, or military spending. "The impact of war is self-evident," Marx wrote, "since economically it is exactly the same as if the nation were to drop a part of its capital into the ocean."[38] In the decades following the Second World War, for example, high levels of US government spending on the arms race with the Soviet Union siphoned off money that otherwise would have led to accelerated growth, and by moderating the rate of economic expansion, prolonged the postwar boom. But this "permanent arms economy" could only forestall crisis, not prevent it.[39] At a certain point, the diversion of funds toward military spending acted as a weight dragging down the United States in relation to its European and Japanese competitors, who, under the US-NATO military umbrella, were able to invest in more advanced production techniques and expand in the private sector, without bearing the same cost of military expenditure. What first began as a means to prolong the postwar boom became over time a financial burden that intensified the crisis when it finally came in the 1970s. The massive growth of the financial sector and the siphoning of profits from other, less profitable sectors in the 2000s likewise gave capitalism a new lease on life, only to create massive debt-fueled speculative bubbles that came crashing down in 2007–08.

Like all living systems that go through cycles, the cycles of capitalism's birth are different from the cycles in its old age. This is true for two reasons, the first of which is that competitive capitalism, over time, has turned into its opposite, monopoly capitalism. The relatively freer competition of early capitalism between smaller competing firms has given way to the concentration and centralization of capital into ever-larger units, and the merging of competing firms has in turn created a situation in which a small number of giant firms control entire industries, not just within nations, but internationally. Within international conglomerates, there is greater and greater planning, but anarchy still reigns in the world market as a whole. The character of competition between these giant firms becomes in some ways more regulated, involving greater and greater amounts of state intervention. But this is only because the potential impact of crises under these circumstances is more severe, as giant industrial and financial concerns become "too big to fail," for fear that their collapse—like the collapse of the giant Wall Street firm Lehman Brothers in 2008—will trigger a devastating crisis from which it will be difficult to recover. The mantra of the free market of the last three decades—that markets are "self-regulating" and therefore the state should leave them alone—was geared not so much toward eliminating state intervention so much as all forms of state regulation that interfered with profit. As soon as the economy goes into crisis, as it did in 2008, banks and industries expect the state to bail them out with trillions in tax dollars.

Crises become crises not of one country, but of the world market as a whole, because competition takes place between giant international firms whose operations span the globe. States that only have control of one patch of territory find it harder and harder to affect world economic policy through their manipulation of currency and interest rates, let alone the economy on their own national turf.

The law of the tendency of the rate of profit to fall, for Marx, is "the most important law of modern political economy."[40] The fact that profits—the lifeblood of capitalism—tend to fall is proof of the historical limits of capitalism. "The growing incompatibility between the productive development of society and its hitherto existing relations of production expresses itself in bitter contradictions, crises, spasms," Marx writes.[41] Capitalist production creates its own barrier to further development, one moreover, that "has nothing to do with the production of wealth as such; but this characteristic barrier in fact testifies to the restrictiveness and the solely historical and transitory character to the capitalist mode of production."[42]

But that doesn't mean that capitalism will simply collapse under its own weight as an old house crashes down from rot—an idea some have incorrectly attributed to Marxism. Crises are only temporary disturbances, which give way, often after terrible dislocation causes great human suffering, to new periods of expansion. "Capitalist production constantly strives to overcome these immanent barriers," Marx notes, "but it overcomes them only by means that set up the barriers afresh and on a more powerful scale."[43]

Trotsky, in comparing capitalism in its birth, maturation, and decay to the "the breathing of a human organism," nevertheless reminds us that capitalism, unlike a human being, does not die of "natural" causes, but only if the working class overthrows it: "A man keeps drawing breath until he dies, but a youth, an adult and a dying man each breathe in a different way and the body's health may be judged by the breathing. But nonetheless a human being keeps breathing until death. Similarly with capitalism. The oscillation of these waves, these ups and downs, are inevitable so long as capitalism is not snuffed out by the victorious proletariat."[44]

Chapter Six

No Power Greater—the Working Class

We have discussed two conditions that make socialism both possible and necessary. One is the tremendous abundance that has eliminated the social basis for inequality and want. The other is the yawning contradiction of capitalism that gives rise to periodic, devastating economic crises. Yet another condition is the existence of an exploited class that can, through its own collective action, usher in a new society. "The mystics of the Middle Ages who dreamed of the coming millennium were already conscious of the injustice of class antagonisms," wrote Engels. But the potential for bringing about that millennium lies in the fact that "modern large-scale industry has called into being . . . a proletariat, a class which for the first time in history can demand the abolition, not of this or that particular class organization, or of this or that particular class privilege, but of classes themselves."[1]

The struggle between classes is as old as class society itself. The first recorded strike took place in Egypt around 1158 BC under the reign of Ramses III. Building workers in Thebes who hadn't received their wages (paid in grain and other necessities) walked off the job and staged sit-ins in front of two, and possibly three, funerary temples.[2] According to historian W. W. Tarn, "strikes, an old Egyptian custom, were numerous; not merely riots in which the manager got beaten, but regular withdrawals of labor."[3]

More common in precapitalist societies, where wage labor was less common, were struggles of peasants and slaves. Marx's favorite historical figure was the Thracian gladiator-slave Spartacus, who led seventy thousand slaves against the Roman Empire in 73 BC and destroyed several Roman armies before he was defeated.[4] Peasant rebellions were numerous in ancient China as well as in feudal Europe. Wat Tyler led a great peasant revolt in England in 1381 against attempts by the landlords to push them into serfdom, but it too was crushed.

What all these struggles have in common is that they could not impose their own social order on society because the material conditions did not exist for the elimination of exploitation. As A. L. Morton, author of *A People's History of England*, notes, "The peasants could combine for long enough to terrorize the ruling class but had no means of exercising a permanent control over the policy of government."[5] Sooner or later, the peasants would have to disperse and return to their land, leaving state power to others. The recurring peasant rebellions in China brought power to the peasants' military leaders and, writes Trotsky, "led each time to a redivision of the land and the establishment of a new 'peasant' dynasty, after which history began all over again: new concentrations of lands, a new aristocracy, new usury, new uprisings. So long as the revolution maintained its purely peasant character, society did not emerge from these hopeless rotations."[6]

But the rise of capitalism and modern industry gathered a new class together into sizable workplaces, concentrated in large urban centers. That class is the modern working class, "that class in society which lives entirely from the sale of its labor and does not draw profit from any kind of capital."[7] As we have already noted, the modern working class is "free" from all ownership of means of production—land, tools, and so on—and as such, is forced to sell its ability to work to the capitalists, who have concentrated all the means of production in their hands. The working class has gone through many transformations, but its essential character as the class of wageworkers upon whose labor wealth and profits rest has not.

Work under capitalism becomes a completely alienating experience, in which workers control neither the form, nor the pace of their work, nor the fruits of their own labor. Under capitalism, work dominates the worker, rather than the other way around. Forced to work at the pace of the line, the machine, the stopwatch, or the manager, workers become alienated from their own intellectual and physical potential. Every advance in labor productivity appears to the workers as merely a means to increase the despotism of the workplace over them. In Marx's biting phrase, the worker is degraded to "the level of an appendage to the machine."[8] Work becomes not something fulfilling, "not the satisfaction of a need but a mere *means* to satisfy needs outside itself."[9] Workers come to dread work, doing it only because without it they and their families could not survive. Workers are further degraded by the way in which capitalists force them to compete with each other for work.

But workers are not merely victims. By "throwing great masses in one spot," wrote Engels, capitalism "gives to the proletarians a consciousness of their own strength."[10] The large workplaces—factories, assembly lines, hospitals, warehouses, offices—in which workers form part of an integrated whole, teach workers a collective discipline and cooperation that can be turned to their own advantage. Capitalism brings thousands of workers together into cooperative labor on a scale that was unheard of in previous societies. A single factory today often employs more people that the population of large towns. Hyundai's Ulsan, one of the largest factory complexes in the world, employs more than 34,000 workers producing 6,000 cars a day. Workers learn by their own experience that, in the words of American socialist Eugene Debs, "There is no escape for you from wage slavery by yourself, but while you cannot alone break your fetters," you can bring about change "if you will unite with all other workers who are in the same position that you are."[11]

The potential of the wage working class to organize as a class is quite different from previous exploited classes. Peasants, as we have already noted, are capable of rebellion, but incapable of acting as an organized, independent class. "The small-holding peasants form a vast mass, the members of which live in similar conditions," Marx wrote of the French peasantry in the 1850s, "but without entering into manifold relations with each other. Their mode of production isolates them from one another instead of bringing them into mutual intercourse." As a result, the peasants are "incapable of enforcing their class interests in their own name. . . . They cannot represent themselves, they must be represented."[12] The capitalist mode of production, on the other hand, does bring workers into "mutual intercourse." As a result of their concentration in ever-larger workplaces, and gathered into large cities and towns, workers' interests are collective rather than individual. They are the first exploited class that is capable, therefore, of "representing" themselves—of consciously liberating themselves from the chains of exploitation.

The key weapon of collective action for workers is the strike. Workers may be dependent on the capitalist for a job, but the capitalist is dependent on workers for profit. "Without our brain and muscle, not a single wheel would turn" goes the popular labor song "Solidarity Forever."[13] When labor organizes and refuses to work, the wheels of industry cease to turn, and the bosses' source of profits dries up. Thus, strikes spark fear into capitalists because they are a reminder, to quote Lenin, that "it is the workers and not they who are the real masters."[14]

Workers first engage in strikes because they are the only means to secure immediate redress from their employer. But as an act of collective solidarity, striking helps workers identify their common interests with the whole working class—it helps them to attain class consciousness.

The significance of strikes cannot simply be measured by their immediate results but by the way in which they build workers' confidence in themselves and increase their fighting spirit. Lenin wrote:

> Every strike reminds the workers that their position is not hopeless, that they are not alone. See what a tremendous effect strikes have both on the strikers themselves and on the workers at neighboring or nearby factories or at factories in the same industry. In normal, peaceful times the worker does his job without a murmur, does not contradict the employer, and does not discuss his condition. In times of strikes he states his demands in a loud voice, he reminds the employers of all their abuses, he claims his rights, he does not think of himself and his wages alone, he thinks of

> all his workmates who have downed tools together with him and who stand up for
> the workers' cause, fearing no privations.[15]

As capitalist production becomes more centralized and concentrated, workers become powerful beyond their numbers. If productive power is concentrated, so is the impact on the system when workers withdraw from production. A strike of transport workers can shut down an entire city, even an entire country. A strike of thousands of workers in a factory that produces some essential part can shut down an entire industry. Workers are strategically placed at the heart of production and can therefore have a bigger impact in struggle than previously oppressed classes.

As soon as capitalism began to appear so did the "combination" of workers for the purposes of struggle against the bosses. These struggles, as Marx noted, were often for "maintenance of wages" or other immediate economic concerns. However, bringing workers together in solidarity created a sense that they had a common interest against exploitation. This sense of class consciousness became more developed as workers begin to see that they have a common interest not only with peers in their own workplace or industry but with workers across the entire country, and indeed the entire world. The more organized the struggle, and the more it involved wider layers of workers in struggle, the more this sense of internationalist class consciousness developed. Moreover, as workers organized on a wider scale, they began to see that their interests lie not only in organizing one workplace, or one industry, for the purposes of self-defense, but in organizing *politically*, that is, to secure better laws, and, beyond that, to challenge the power of the state that serves the interests of the employing class. As Marx wrote: "Economic conditions had first transformed the mass of the people of the country into workers. The combination of capital has created for this mass a common situation, common interests. This mass is thus already a class as against capital, but not yet for itself. In the struggle, of which we have noted only a few phases, this mass becomes united, and constitutes itself as a class for itself. The interests it defends become class interests. But the struggle of class against class is a political struggle."[16]

All previous revolutions merely replaced one kind of exploitation with another, one ruling class with another. But by the virtue of its collective social position and weight, the working class is the first exploited class in history with the capacity to reorder society in the interests of the majority—that is, not simply to replace the rule of one class with that of another, but to abolish class society. Workers can't divide up the factories, the hospitals, and the offices and share them out individually as peasants would the land—one person takes a steel furnace, another a lathe, another a heart monitoring machine. You can't parcel out an assembly line. The only way workers can abolish the conditions of exploitation is to collectivize and socialize the means of production and distribution. In doing so, they abolish class exploitation.

Marx and Engels expressed these ideas almost poetically in *The Communist Manifesto*:

All the preceding classes that got the upper hand sought to fortify their already acquired status by subjecting society at large to their conditions of appropriation. The proletarians cannot become masters of the productive forces of society, except by abolishing their own previous mode of appropriation, and thereby also every other previous mode of appropriation. They have nothing of their own to secure and to fortify; their mission is to destroy all previous securities for, and insurances of, individual property.

All previous historical movements were movements of minorities, or in the interest of minorities. The proletarian movement is the self-conscious, independent movement of the immense majority, in the interest of the immense majority. The proletariat, the lowest stratum of our present society, cannot stir, cannot raise itself up, without the whole superincumbent strata of official society being sprung into the air.[17]

But how do workers move from collective workplace action to actually challenging the entire edifice of capitalism? "In depicting the most general phases of the development of the proletariat," summarizes the *Manifesto*, "we traced the more or less veiled civil war, raging within existing society, up to the point where that war breaks out into open revolution, and where the violent overthrow of the bourgeoisie lays the foundation for the sway of the proletariat."[18] Real flesh was put on this passage by the experience of the class struggle itself.

The Importance, and Limits, of Unions

The working class cannot achieve even the most minimal advance without organizing. The bosses have their civic organizations and their manufacturers' associations, and they have at their disposal a centralized state apparatus. Workers must have their own organizations if they are to fight back. Unlike the utopian socialists, who opposed strikes and combinations of workers, Marx understood that the formation of such organizations for the purposes of struggle was an inevitable, and positive, development:

> Large-scale industry concentrates in one place a crowd of people unknown to one another. Competition divides their interests. But the maintenance of wages, this common interest which they have against their boss, unites them in a common thought of resistance—*combination*. Thus combination always has a double aim, that of stopping competition among the workers, so that they can carry on general competition with the capitalist. If the first aim of resistance was merely the maintenance of wages, combinations, at first isolated, constitute themselves into groups as the capitalists in their turn unite for the purpose of repression, and in the face of always united capital, the maintenance of the association becomes more necessary to them than that of wages. This is so true that English economists are amazed to see the workers sacrifice a good part of their wages in favor of associations, which, in the eyes of these economists, are established solely in favor of wages. In this struggle—a veritable civil war—all the elements necessary for a coming battle unite and develop.[19]

These combinations of workers, or unions, are training grounds that give workers confidence in their own collective power of resistance. They are the first line of defense for workers against attempts by capitalists to continually push down wages and conditions to their lowest possible level. Unions, to quote the socialist Eugene Debs, "have been a moral stimulus as well as a material aid to the worker," promoting "the class-conscious solidarity of the working class."[20]

Marx, as we see from the quotation above, sometimes implied that the organizations of workers into unions would naturally develop into a more general challenge to capitalism. But at times he also recognized their limitations. "Trade unions," he wrote, "work well as centers of resistance against the encroachments of capital." However, "they fail generally from limiting themselves to a guerrilla war against the effects of the existing system, instead of simultaneously trying to change it, instead of using their organized forces as a lever for the final emancipation of the working class, the ultimate abolition of the wage system."[21]

Unions seek to change the terms of wage slavery, not to abolish wage slavery. The way unions are organized mirrors this reality. First of all, unions organize workers by their particular workplace, craft, or industry rather than as a class in its entirety. Unions therefore overcome some of the divisions imposed by capitalism—but they also reflect these divisions.

If they are to survive as more or less stable institutions, unions require a full-time officialdom whose job is to maintain the organization and negotiate with employers. These leaders may come from the ranks, but their social position changes with their increased status. Union officials no longer work and experience the same hardships as the workers they represent; their salary is dependent on members' dues and is generally higher (in some cases a lot higher) than the workers they represent. Paradoxically, an organization created to advance workers' interests produces a leadership that can sometimes be a brake on the struggles that are necessary to advance those interests.

The German revolutionary Rosa Luxemburg, writing more than one hundred years ago, summed up the general outlook of union leadership:

> The specialization of professional activity as trade-union leaders, as well as the naturally restricted horizon which is bound up with disconnected economic struggles in a peaceful period, leads only too easily, amongst trade-union officials, to bureaucratism and a certain narrowness of outlook. Both, however, express themselves in a whole series of tendencies which may be fateful in the highest degree for the future of the trade-union movement. There is first of all the overvaluation of the organization, which from a means has gradually been changed into an end in itself, a precious thing, to which the interests of the struggles should be subordinated. From this also comes that openly admitted need for peace which shrinks from great risks and presumed dangers to the stability of the trade-unions.[22]

This explains why workers of different unions experience the same things from their leaders—a reluctance to "risk" the organization in serious confrontations with employers, the tendency to prefer "peaceful" negotiation over a strike, the preference for limited strikes over bigger, more general confrontations. In many cases, union officials become so separated from the rank and file, so bloated with high salaries and so accustomed to hobnobbing with employers, that they are incapable of defending their own members. In this respect, the "maintenance of the association," to use Marx's phrase, reflects workers' solidarity and determination but it also exerts a *conservatizing influence* on the union, especially on its full-time officialdom.

This doesn't mean that union leaders can't or won't fight. Caught between the interests of the rank and file and the employers, union leaders are sometimes forced to lead battles simply to defend their organization. But they lean toward organizational conservatism, trying to harmonize the interests of labor and capital. The US trade union officialdom in the craft-oriented American Federation of Labor, wrote Debs, "are at once the leaders of labor and the lieutenants of capital, and who, in their dual role, find it more and more difficult to harmonize the conflicting interests of the class of whom they are the leaders and the class of whom they are the lieutenants."[23]

Unions more often than not tend to reinforce the separation between economic struggle and political struggle. Particularly in the United States, "pure and simple" unionism, which focuses only on economic issues, is rife. The strongest weapon of the unions—the strike—is reserved for economic issues, and even then is resorted to only reluctantly. Walkouts that make political demands on the government—for a shorter workday, against child labor, to oppose a war—are practically nonexistent. Instead, politics is typically restricted to union leaders mobilizing their members to vote for a bourgeois candidate.

These shortcomings in the US labor movement have weakened and thinned its ranks in the teeth of employer attacks so that in 2011 only 11.8 percent of wage and salaried workers in the United States were members of unions.[24] Several things will be needed to revitalize the union movement in the United States: First, unions will have to link their economic demands with community and social demands, drawing in active public support, as the Chicago Teachers Union did in its 2012 strike. Also, mass unionizing drives from below, a major component of the movement in the 1930s, will be key to rebuilding the size and fighting strength of the unions today. Finally, socialists must play a role in organizing rank-and-file union members independently of the union leaders in order to exert pressure on them to fight for their members' interests, as well as promoting into the ranks of leadership candidates more likely to represent the interests of the rank and file.

Two of the most important questions for the workers' movement therefore are: One, how can it move past the limitations of its own trade union leadership whenever the latter acts against the interests of the rank and file; and two, how can the working class overcome "sectionalism," the splitting up of workers according to differences in wage level, skill, industry, and trade, and develop forms of organization that mobilize and unite the working class as a whole? Unless workers are united as a class, they cannot challenge the system. Unions, therefore, while being crucial organizations of working-class solidarity and defense, are insufficient for the purposes of organizing the working class as a whole to challenge capitalism.

How Parisian Workers Taught Marx

In her book *Marxism and Freedom*, Raya Dunayevskaya reproves those who praise Marx's genius as though it stemmed "from the sheer development of his own thoughts instead of from living workers changing living reality by their actions."[25] Marx and Engels, like the great Marxists who followed them, did not develop their ideas in a vacuum, but always in close contact with the class struggle. It was the emergence of organizing, strikes, and protests in France, Germany, and England that alerted Marx and Engels to its potential power to reshape society. "The first step in the revolution by the working class," Marx and Engels wrote in *The Communist Manifesto*, "is to raise the proletariat to the position of ruling class—to win the battle of democracy."[26] But there hadn't yet been any experience of what a successful workers' revolution would look like when they penned these words.

The revolutions of 1848 in Germany showed Marx and Engels that this new class was powerful enough to frighten the bourgeoisie away from revolution, but not yet capable of providing an *alternative* class leadership in the democratic revolution. "Capitalism had developed sufficiently to render necessary the abolition of the old feudal relations," Trotsky later observed, "but not sufficiently to bring forward the working class, the product of the new industrial relations, as a decisive political force. The antagonism between the proletariat and the bourgeoisie, even within the national framework of Germany, had gone too far to allow the bourgeoisie fearlessly to take up the role of national hegemon, but not sufficiently to allow the working class to take up that role."[27]

Even the Parisian working class—bigger and better organized than its German counterpart, and in a country that had already achieved its bourgeois revolution—was still largely composed of artisans in small workshops and was not yet powerful enough to seize power.

The quick demise of the Paris Commune of 1871 confirmed Marx and Engels's suspicions on this issue. Before then, it might have been possible to argue that "winning the battle of democracy" solely required a worker takeover of the existing state machine—either seizing it by force, or by getting workers' candidates elected to political office and, after gaining a majority, using governmental power to make social and political changes (although it must be added that this was never Marx and Engels's view). But the Paris Commune demonstrated that "the working class cannot simply lay hold of the ready-made state machine and wield it for its own purposes."[28]

Why? We have already noted that the state is a product of class division. So long as society is divided into classes, a state is necessary to keep the exploited in check. In every revolution one exploiting class has replaced the rule of another, but the state remained—the bureaucracy and armed forces simply transferred from the defeated to the victorious classes. Indeed, the bourgeois revolutions of the seventeenth and eighteenth centuries produced even more bureaucratically top-heavy, centralized states than the feudal states, with larger armed forces, too. "At the same pace at which the progress of modern industry developed, widened, intensified the class antagonism between capital and labor," Marx explained, "the state power assumed more and more the character of the national power of capital over labor, of a public force organized for social enslavement, of an engine of class despotism."[29]

In March of 1871, the workers of Paris, organized into the Parisian National Guard, defeated troops sent by France's leader, Louis Thiers, to disarm them. Thiers had just been elected head of France's new republic after Napoleon's Second Empire was disastrously defeated in a war with the Prussian army. The peace terms required France to disarm and allow Prussian troops to march into Paris.

But the Parisian working class refused to give up their arms. The workers rallied heroically around the National Guard militias (themselves made up largely of workers), defeating Thiers's troops and compelling the bourgeoisie, their armed forces, and their political apparatus to flee Paris for Versailles.

The Paris Commune was elected on March 26, 1871, and remained in power for only two months. Fatefully, it didn't follow up its victory by pursuing and disarming Thiers's troops as they were retreating from Paris, nor did it attempt to spread the Commune to other cities in France. This gave Thiers the breathing space to reorganize at Versailles and eventually fight his way back into Paris. The Communards were crushed in an orgy of violence that took thirty thousand workers' lives.

Many socialists looked upon the Commune as a foolhardy exercise. Marx understood the Commune's weaknesses, but he leapt to its support, delivering a series of searing lectures in defense of Parisian workers and outlining the lasting significance of the Commune. It had abolished conscription and the standing army; it decreed the separation of church and state; it began to devise plans to reopen factories under the control of the workers in them; and it abolished night work for bakers. But these achievements were minimal compared to the most important achievement of the Commune. It was, argued Marx, "essentially a working-class government, the product of the struggle of the producing against the appropriating class, the political form at last discovered under which to work out the economical emancipation of labor."[30]

The Communards turned direct suffrage into an instrument of the real rule of society by the majority. "Instead of deciding once in three or six years which member of the ruling class was to misrepresent the people in Parliament," wrote Marx in his brilliant work *The Civil War in France*, "universal suffrage was to serve the people, constituted in Communes."[31] One of the weaknesses of the Commune that Marx failed to note, however, was that suffrage was not universal—women were not given the right to vote. Nevertheless, one of the striking things about the Commune was the leading role played by working women, both in its creation and in its defense. Wrote one reactionary opponent of the Commune, "During the final days [of the Commune], all of those bellicose viragos held out longer than the men did behind the barricades. . . . Many of them were arrested, with powder-blackened hands and shoulders bruised by the recoil of their rifles; they were still palpitating from the over-stimulation of battle."[32]

Marx elaborated on what made the Commune so unique. First, elected delegates to the Commune were workers themselves, "revocable at short terms" and paid at "workman's wages." Moreover, the Commune wasn't set up to be a parliamentary talk shop, but "a working . . . body, executive and legislative at the same time." The police—under the bourgeoisie a special force standing apart from society and en-forcing the interests of the rich—were "turned into the responsible, and at all times revocable, agent of the Commune."[33]

Much has been made about the fact that Marx and Engels used the term "dic-tatorship of the proletariat" to refer to a workers' government—as if they meant rule by an individual or a minority. But they considered all forms of class rule, at bottom, dictatorships of one class over another. Engels answered this charge best when he said: "Of late, the Social-Democratic philistine has once more been filled with whole-some terror at the words: Dictatorship of the Proletariat. Well and good, gentlemen, do you want to know what this dictatorship looks like? Look at the Paris Commune. That was the Dictatorship of the Proletariat."[34]

Though it lasted only two months, the Paris Commune represented the first time workers had ever taken power. A major lesson from the revolt was that because the state exists as a repressive apparatus to maintain the power of the capitalists (a machine for the suppression of one class by another), it cannot simply be "seized" by workers, but must be dismantled and replaced by a system of direct workers' democ-racy based on recallable delegates elected by workers themselves.[35]

In order to prevent the old order from regaining power, and in order to begin to implement a new social and economic program, workers need their *own* state, that is, the organization of the majority to suppress the minority. Only when class antagonisms are completely suppressed can society do away with the state. Thus by setting up a "commune state," workers abolish the basis on which classes—and the state upon which they rely—survive. "The state," Engels concluded, "is nothing but a machine for the oppression of one class by another, and indeed in the democratic republic no less than in the monarchy; and at best an evil inherited by the proletariat after its victorious struggle for class supremacy whose worst sides the victorious proletariat, just like the Commune, cannot avoid having to lop off at once as much as possible until such time as a generation reared in new, free social conditions is able to throw the entire lumber of the state on the scrap-heap."[36]

Workers' Councils: The Modern Form of Workers' Power

Because well-to-do Parisians had fled the city, the Paris Commune ended up being a de facto workers' organization. Its delegates were elected to the Commune out of the Parisian National Guard militias, which were dominated by workers, and by neighborhood. If the Paris of 1871 had a more developed state of industry and thus bigger concentrations of workers, it is likely delegate elections would have been organized by where residents worked rather than where they lived.

In later revolutions, workers would create organs of struggle that were based on delegates elected from workplaces. The workers' council, or soviet (the Russian word for "council"), was first established during the 1905 revolution, as a strike committee in St. Petersburg, made up of elected delegates from the different factories and set up to coordinate a general strike. Though originally an organ of struggle, the soviet soon came to be seen by workers and peasants all over Russia as an alternative center of governmental power. In his description of the 1905 revolution, Leon Trotsky, who was elected president of the Petersburg Soviet, tells a story of how a clerk from an outlying province wrote a letter complaining of his mistreatment by a prince, addressing the envelope to "The Workers' Government, Petersburg"—and it was delivered.[37]

Workers created soviets again during the 1917 revolution—with a ratio of one delegate per one thousand workers. The soviets pulled along behind them all the oppressed and downtrodden. Soviets also spread to soldiers, sailors, and poor peasants. "No political body more sensitive and responsible to the popular will was ever invented," wrote the radical US journalist John Reed of the Russian soviets he witnessed in 1918.[38] This was a superior form of organization to the trade unions because the soviets brought together workers across industries, uniting them nationally as a class, as well as leading all of the oppressed.

But soviets were not some peculiar Russian invention. Similar institutions have sprung up time and time again, in all parts of the world, during periods of mass upheaval. The workers' councils in Germany in 1918, the internal commissions in Italy in 1920, the workers' councils in Hungary in 1956, the *cordones* in Chile in 1973, the workers' *shoras* of the Iranian revolution of 1979, the "inter-factory committees" of Solidarność in Poland in 1980—all these are cases where workers, in the heat of struggle, created mass democratic organizations of struggle embracing the majority of the class.[39] They organized workplaces as centers of workers' power, but they often transcended the workplace by becoming centers of power for all of the oppressed. In every case, these institutions were set up to aid workers in both their political and economic battles. The movements they led did not always become fully conscious of their potential to be an alternative to the old state, but in every case these council organizations represented a "dual power," the incipient power of the working class to reorganize the whole of society on democratic lines.

In Hungary in 1956, after street protests morphed into armed revolutionary street battles, the authority of the bureaucratic state temporarily collapsed. Peter Fryer, a *Daily Worker* correspondent who was in Hungary during that time, wrote of the workers' councils that had sprung up throughout the country in the midst of hostile Soviet troops:

> In their spontaneous origin, in their composition, in their sense of responsibility, in their efficient organization of food supplies and of civil order, in the restraint they exercised over the wilder elements among the youth, in the wisdom with which so many of them handled the problem of Soviet troops, and, not least, in their striking resemblance at so many points to the soviets or councils of workers', peasants' and soldiers' deputies which sprang up in Russia in the 1905 revolution and again in February 1917, these committees, a network of which now extended over the whole of Hungary, were remarkably uniform. They were at once organs of insurrection—the coming together of delegates elected by factories and universities, mine and Army units—and organs of popular self-government, which the armed people trusted. As such they enjoyed tremendous authority, and it is no exaggeration to say that until the Soviet attack of November 4 the real power in the country lay in their hands.
>
> Of course, as in every real revolution "from below," there was "too much" talking, arguing, bickering, coming and going, froth, excitement, agitation, ferment. That is one side of the picture. The other side is the emergence to leading positions of ordinary men, women and youths whom the AVH [Hungary's political police] dominion had kept submerged. The revolution thrust them forward, aroused their civic pride and latent genius for organization, set them to work to build democracy out of the ruins of bureaucracy. "You can see people developing from day to day," I was told.[40]

In the United States, the class struggle has at times been explosive and violent, but workers have never reached a point where council-type organizations have been created on a national scale. But there have been glimpses. In the mid-1930s, during the biggest rank-and-file strike wave in US history, workers throughout the country, following the lead of autoworkers in Flint, Michigan, sat down and occupied their workplaces to demand union recognition. By the end of 1937, almost half a million workers had participated in sit-down strikes.[41]

In Seattle in 1919, almost all the city's workers struck in solidarity with thirty-five thousand longshore workers striking for higher pay. A strike committee was formed of elected representatives from each of the 101 striking union locals. The strike committee discussed not only issues of how to conduct the strike but how to keep basic services running during the strike, like emergency health care and milk delivery. The general strike naturally raised the practical issues of workers' control of production and distribution. An editorial written by Anna Louise Strong on the eve of the strike expressed the potential: "Labor will not only SHUT DOWN the industries, but labor will REOPEN, under the management of the appropriate trades, such activities as are needed to preserve public health and public peace. If the strike continues, Labor may feel led to avoid public suffering by reopening more and more activities, UNDER ITS OWN MANAGEMENT."[42] The strike ended, under pressure from conservative union leaders, in six days. Nevertheless, it posed in embryo the question of who runs society and in what way.

Committees of workers' delegates such as strike committees and workers' councils have demonstrated their potential power to reshape society, particularly workers' councils, which are more democratic and representative than strike committees because they bring together delegates from different workplaces. Nevertheless, the complete trajectory of these worker-led committees—from embryo of a new society to an alternative government—requires not only creating a national form of organization that embraces the majority of workers in cities and towns, but also eradicating the old state structure, as Marx and Engels pointed out in their writings about the Paris Commune. These soviet-type organizations begin as organs of struggle that help coordinate the fight, but they can become the basis of a new way of organizing society. But for this to happen, the revolutionary elements within the movement that seek this outcome must be organized to make a bid for political power—a point we will come back to in chapter 7.

We Want No Condescending Saviors

The 1871 rules of the International Workingman's Association, written by Marx, declared: "The emancipation of the working class must be conquered by the working classes themselves."[43] They cannot be freed by liberal reformers, a heroic band of guerrillas, or a small band of terrorists with dynamite. They cannot be freed by any party or group that stands above or outside their own struggles. The English version of the anthem of the international socialist movement puts the same idea in the negative:

> *No savior from on high delivers*
> *No faith have we in prince or peer*
> *Our own right hand the chains must shiver*
> *Chains of hatred, greed and fear*[44]

Eugene Debs urged workers in his speeches to fight for themselves and not wait for someone to fight for them. "I cannot do it for you, and I want to be frank enough to say that I would not if I could. For if I could do it for you," he stressed, "somebody else could undo it for you."[45]

Marx's phrase underscored an idea that was fundamentally different from a whole number of radical and socialist ideas current then, and which in various forms are still current now. These ideas can be roughly placed under the category "substitutionism." In Marxist terms, any individual, group, class, or party that substitutes its own activity for that of the class it claims to emancipate, that acts as a proxy in the name of and on behalf of the working class and the oppressed, is substitutionist.

In the early days of capitalism, when the working class was still forming, and had yet to systematically assert itself in collective struggle, substitutionism was historically inevitable. The utopian socialists, for example, substituted their own schemes for a better world for workers' own struggles, seeing workers not as the creators of the new world, but merely its beneficiaries.

Marx and Engels also contended with the conspiratorial radicalism of the French socialist Auguste Blanqui and the Russian anarchist Mikhail Bakunin. Engels criticized the Blanquist belief that "a small well-organized minority should attempt a revolutionary uprising at the right moment" that would "carry the mass of the people" with them. Blanqui, Engels noted, "regards every revolution as a coup de main by a small revolutionary minority."[46] Marx and Engels likewise rejected Bakunin's elitist notion that a secret society of (in his words) "a hundred powerfully and seriously allied revolutionaries" acting "like invisible pilots in the thick of the popular tempest" could lead a Europe-wide revolution.[47] Engels criticized these revolutionaries for substituting their urgent desire for immediate revolution with the practical conditions and patient work necessary for its realization. "What childish naiveté," he complained, "to advance impatience as a convincing theoretical argument!"[48] What Marx and Engels took issue with above all in these radical schemes was the way in which the actions of minorities were meant to replace the self-activity of ordinary people acting to free themselves from their chains.

Leon Trotsky made the same case against individual acts of terrorism. Even the smallest strike, sit-in, or street protest can boost the self-confidence of workers, whereas an individual act of violence or terror has the opposite effect. "By its very essence terrorist work demands such concentrated energy for 'the great moment,' such an overestimation of the significance of individual heroism, and finally, such a 'hermetic' conspiracy, that— if not logically, then psychologically—it totally excludes agitational and organizational work among the masses."[49] "In our eyes," wrote Trotsky, "individual terror is inadmissible precisely because it belittles the role of the masses in their own consciousness, reconciles them to their powerlessness, and turns their eyes and hopes towards a great avenger and liberator who some day will come and accomplish his mission."[50]

And, as we shall elaborate in the next chapter, the working class cannot be freed by electing the right people into office, as Rosa Luxemburg, in her last speech, brought home. "Socialism will not be and cannot be inaugurated by decrees; it cannot be established by any government, however admirably socialistic. Socialism must be created by the masses, must be made by every proletarian. Where the chains of capitalism are forged, there must the chains be broken."[51]

Trapped by Their Circumstances?

According to the sixteenth-century French essayist Michel de Montaigne, when three Indians from the coast of Brazil paid a visit to Charles IX of France in 1562, someone asked them "what they thought of all this" and "what they had been the most amazed by" during their stay in France. The Indians, who knew no class division in their own society, "have an idiom in their language which calls all men 'halves' of one another," and they observed that French society was divided into very unequal "halves." They noticed, wrote Montaigne, that "there were among us men fully bloated with all sorts of comforts while their halves were begging at their doors emaciated with poverty and hunger: they found it odd that those destitute halves should put up with such injustice and did not take the others by the throat or set fire to their houses."[52]

Imagine those Native Americans transported to the United States in the twenty-first century. They might have the same question. They would see a society where the richest fifth of Americans have nine times more wealth than the poorest fifth. Why don't the vast majority, whose labor makes such obscene wealth possible, take the 1 percent "by the throat or set fire to their houses"? The answer, of course, is that the oppressed *have* waged rebellions and revolutions throughout history; however, it must be admitted that they have not remained in a permanent state of rebellion—otherwise capitalism would have already been overthrown.

As to why workers have yet to achieve socialism, the answer is usually a very depressing one. In George Orwell's *1984*, the main character, Winston, a low-level government bureaucrat beaten down by the all-seeing, all-knowing dictatorship of "Big Brother," understands that the "proles"—the working class of Oceania—are the only hope if the system is to be overthrown. "They needed only to rise up and shake themselves like a horse shaking off flies," Winston imagines.[53] But Winston is full of despair, because apparently this is completely impossible. As he wanders through the streets of a working-class district, he hears loud shouts in the distance, imagining that it might be a protest—only to find a group of women fighting over a saucepan.

"Heavy physical work," wrote Orwell of the proles, "the care of home and children, petty quarrels with neighbors, films, football, beer, and, above all, gambling filled up the horizon of their minds."[54] In his secret diary, Winston describes the apparent dilemma that makes a workers' revolution impossible: "Until they become conscious they will never rebel, and until after they have rebelled they cannot become conscious."[55] One might wonder how it is that a depressed, low-level bureaucrat can figure out what's wrong with Big Brother but not the "proles."

It is no accident that *1984* is part of practically every high school curriculum. It reinforces what is a widespread prejudice in the United States: that workers are too divided, too distracted by "bread and circuses," and too mentally limited to change the world. This caricature of the working class is widespread. It is an elitist view, to be sure, often argued by educated middle-class professionals who look down upon workers and think of themselves as too "cultured" and "intelligent" to ever be duped or hoodwinked—except when it comes to blindly accepting the idea that the meek cannot inherit the earth.

The truth is that workers hold all sorts of ideas about the world they live in. Some of those ideas express a rejection of the status quo; others express acceptance of it. The capitalist system is buttressed ideologically—on television, radio, in schools, in the newspapers, from the pulpit. Workers are encouraged to accept the ruling ideology—that poverty, greed, racism, inequality, and war are products of immutable human nature; that workers are too uneducated, too stupid to run society; that only the well-born can rule; that revolutions end in tyranny; and that this, as Preceptor Pangloss, the "oracle" of a baron, tells us in Voltaire's *Candide*, is the "best of all possible worlds."[56]

One reason that ruling ideas can take hold at all can be attributed simply to inertia—the inherent conservatism built into a set of human social relations once they are established. "Society does not change its institutions as need arises, the way a mechanic changes his instruments," wrote Trotsky. "On the contrary, society actually takes the institutions which hang upon it as given once for all."[57] The state is always prepared to resort to legal repression and even armed force if it is threatened. But for much of the time, force isn't necessary to maintain order. So long as a majority of people give their passive consent to the status quo, force isn't necessary.

In order to change society, workers must become conscious of their position as the oppressed class and organize themselves as a class to fight for their own interests. According to Orwell's Winston, this is impossible. According to historical experience, it is not. Consciousness is not static or fixed simply because the bosses wish it to be. Workers are not automatons that accept all the ruling ideas of society without question. If that were true, all radical change would be impossible—indeed, even the smallest strike or protest would never happen. Workers accept the everyday "commonsense" ideas—that is, ideas that reinforce existing conditions—as well as ideas that challenge them. To quote the Italian revolutionary Antonio Gramsci, a worker actually carries in his or her head two contradictory consciousnesses: "one which is implicit in his activity and which in reality unites him with all his fellow-workers in the practical transformation of the real world; and one, superficially explicit or verbal, which he has inherited from the past and uncritically absorbed."[58]

This contradiction is a reflection of the fact that capitalism both divides and unites workers, that is, it brings them together in large numbers and at the same time fosters competition among them. "Competition separates individuals from one another, not only the bourgeois but still more the workers," wrote Marx and Engels, "in spite of the fact that it brings them together. Hence it is a long time before these individuals can unite. . . . To demand the opposite would be tantamount to demanding that competition should not exist in this definite epoch of history, or that the individuals should banish from their minds relationships over which *in their isolation* they have no control.[59]

Workers are forced to fight back—to stop a wage or benefit cut, to fight against a draconian labor law, or (for undocumented workers) to fight for amnesty. Hal Draper, an American socialist who wrote an excellent series of books on Marx's ideas, wrote, "To engage in class struggle it is not necessary to 'believe in' the class struggle any more than it is necessary to believe in Newton in order to fall from an airplane. . . . The working class moves toward class struggle insofar as capitalism fails to satisfy its economic and social needs and aspirations, not insofar as it is told about struggle by Marxists."[60]

In the course of struggle, the gap between workers' own experience and the ruling ideas widens to the point where workers begin to reject them—the ruling ideas begin to break down. In big struggles, these ideas break down very quickly. "A strike," wrote Lenin, "opens the eyes of the workers to the nature, not only of the capitalists, but of the government and the laws as well."[61] The important thing is that a group of workers decide to take action. When they do, their experience opens their eyes to reality, which in turn gives them more confidence to fight. Workers who strike quickly learn that the police and courts are set up against them and for the employers—and also that the press defends employers and tries to present workers' interests in a bad light. One struggle gives heart to others to struggle, and one struggle piggybacks on another.

It is the fight against suffering and exploitation, rather than suffering itself, that transforms consciousness. In isolation or defeat, workers are more easily prone to turn their suffering and bitterness on each other, or on scapegoats. But the experience of struggle teaches solidarity to workers, calling into question divisions of race, sex, sexual orientation, language, and nationality that are deliberately fostered among them by the ruling class. They learn that whenever the employers or the state can pit them against each other, they are weak; and when they unite, they are strong. They learn that if any part of the working class or oppressed is held down, it makes it easier for the bosses to hold all workers down.

Socialism cannot come about purely through education, or more precisely, through propaganda about the benefits of socialism. No matter how much propaganda socialists put out, it wouldn't be enough to convince everyone to be socialist. This would of course be preferable—we'd simply send out a series of chain letters (or, perhaps, emails) explaining why we need to reorganize society along rational lines, and eventually we'd reach everyone. Revolution wouldn't be necessary because the vast majority would simply say to the exploiting minority, "Your time is up." Unfortunately, it doesn't work that way. For one thing, the bourgeoisie has control of the mass media and can always reach more people.

In fact, it is primarily struggle that teaches. As Lenin noted:

> When bourgeois gentry and their uncritical echoers, the social reformists, talk about the "education of the masses," they usually mean something schoolmasterly, pedantic. . . .
>
> The real education of the masses can never be separated from their independent political, and especially revolutionary, struggle. Only struggle educates the exploited class. Only struggle discloses to it the magnitude of its own power, widens its horizon, enhances its abilities, clarifies its mind, forges its will.[62]

It was this concept that prompted Marx to remark, "Every step of real movement is more important than a dozen programs."[63] That is why in periods of relative calm, when there is little struggle, the possibility of fundamental change seems remote. But beneath the inertia are molecular processes that are creating the dry conditions in which a spark can ignite the tinder and cause a conflagration. It is in fact partly the natural conservatism of the mind—the way in which people cling to old ideas long after they make sense—that gives rise to social explosions. As Trotsky concluded from his participation in the Russian Revolution, "The swift changes of mass views and moods in an epoch of revolution . . . derive not from the flexibility and mobility of man's mind, but just the opposite, from its deep conservatism. The chronic lag of ideas and relations behind new objective conditions, right up to the moment when the latter crash over people in the form of a catastrophe, is what creates in a period of revolution that leaping movement of ideas and passions which seems to the police mind a mere result of the activities of 'demagogues.'"[64]

A statement issued by the founding meeting of the united shoras (Iranian workers' councils) in March 1979, after the fall of the shah, shows the way in which revolutionary struggle raises up the working class and makes it the natural leader of all the oppressed. "We the workers of Iran," the statement began, "through our strikes, sit-ins and demonstrations, overthrew the Shah." Workers of Iran put up with privation and death "in order to create an Iran free from repression, free of exploitation. We made the revolution in order to end unemployment and homelessness, to replace the SAVAK [the Shah's secret police]-oriented Syndicate with independent workers' Shoras, formed by the workers of each factory for their own economic and political needs." Among the statement's demands were free health care, housing benefits, an end to the intervention of armed forces to break up strikes, and free nursery services at work.[65]

Farrell Dobbs was a Trotskyist worker who played a leading role in the 1934 Minneapolis Teamsters' strike, one of the most important rank-and-file–led strikes of the era. Answering the naysayers who claimed workers lacked the capacity for struggle, he wrote:

Wiseacres of the day spoke pontifically about the "passivity" of the working class, never understanding that the seeming docility of the workers at a given time is a relative thing. If workers are more or less holding their own in daily life and expecting that they can get ahead slowly, they won't tend to radicalize. Things are different when they are losing ground and the future looks precarious to them. Then a change begins to occur in their attitude, which is not always immediately apparent. The tinder of discontent begins to pile up. Any spark can light it, and once lit, the fire can spread rapidly.[66]

We're All Middle Class?

The Marxist conception of class is not widely accepted in the United States. Our textbooks offer up deliberately fuzzy terms that blur and cover up extreme class and wealth inequality. Terms such as "the American people," the "average American," and "middle class" are far more common than any mention of "workers" or "the working class." The historian James W. Loewen examined twelve US high school textbooks and found that

> six of them contain no index listing at all for "social class," "social stratification," "class structure," "income distribution," "inequality," or any conceivably related topic. Not one book lists "upper class," "working class," or "lower class." Two of the textbooks list "middle class," but only to assure students that America is a middle-class country. . . . Talking about the middle class is hardly equivalent to discussing social stratification, however; in fact, as Gregory Mantsios has pointed out, "such references appear to be acceptable precisely because they mute class differences."[67]

The use of the term "middle class" conveniently lumps together everyone who is neither extremely poor nor extremely rich. Even a 1999 book titled *The Coming Class War in America* can argue that the middle class in the United States is 60 percent of the population, a neat trick accomplished by simply taking the 60 percent of the population whose income lies between that of the 40 percent falling below or above them, and slapping the label "middle class" on it.[68] One could just as easily divide incomes into six categories and say there are six classes in the United States: lowest, low, lower-middle, middle, upper-middle, and wealthy. There's no end to the creative but arbitrary subdivisions we could come up with, but they wouldn't help us much, because they don't get beyond the surface.

Income doesn't necessarily tell us about a person's place in the economic system—for example, whether someone *worked* for their wealth or not. Even the concept of "haves" versus "have-nots," or "rich" versus "poor," and 1 percent versus 99 percent, while an improvement, are still only *descriptive* devices that tell us nothing about why some have and others have not.

Calibrating class by income can actually be very misleading. For example, a small business owner who exploits ten employees might have a smaller income in a given year than a skilled carpenter who works for a construction company. If we were to determine class by income, the carpenter would be "above" the businessperson, obscuring the fact that the carpenter's labor is exploited for the profit of the builder, whereas the businessperson is in fact a small-scale *exploiter*.

Classes are defined by their relationship to the production process in any given society; in particular, the production and control of the *surplus* is key. What this means is that a skilled auto mechanic who works for Firestone might make a great deal more money than a strawberry picker—but both are part of the working class because both perform surplus labor for capitalists. By this definition, workers are a majority of society. The ruling class "could easily be seated in Yankee stadium, which holds 57,000 people."[69] The middle class are those that are neither simply wage laborers nor capitalists, but fall somewhere in between the two. More accurately defined as managing and supervisory staff, high-paid professionals, small businesspeople, and farmers, the middle class constitutes at most 25 percent of the working population.[70]

Between Labor and Capital

Workers and bosses are not the only classes under capitalism. There are the chronically destitute—people who live in abject poverty who cannot find steady work, or any work at all, and turn to activities like selling trinkets or petty crime to survive. In addition, between labor and capital there is a middle class that consists of professionals, managers, and small businesspeople—sometimes referred to as the petite, or petty, bourgeoisie. The upper end of this layer shares more in common in its lifestyle and outlook with the capitalist class. The lower end, in terms of salary and working conditions, has more in common with the working class. As a whole, the middle class vacillates between the two main classes. Strictly speaking, the middle class is not a class in the sense that is used in reference to workers and bosses. Its conditions are too heterogeneous. Loosely speaking, it is all those who are either small-scale exploiters, control the labor of others, or rely on their professional skills and education to draw a large salary.

As a small businessperson, a shopkeeper tends to identify with the capitalists; however, as someone who labors long hours to make ends meet, the shop owner has more in common with wageworkers. If the class outlook of the working class is collectivist, the class outlook of the middle class is individualist. Its whole class position reinforces not collective interest and collective action but advancement through individual pluck and ability. This isn't only true of small businesspeople, whose material conditions tend to reinforce the idea of individual merit, but is especially true of the "intelligentsia"—academics, artists, writers, and professionals such as lawyers and doctors. Their whole educational and life experience reinforces individualism. It is this very sense of individualism that ties the middle classes to capitalism.

"The writer does not have to get up when the alarm sounds," wrote Trotsky, "behind the doctor's back stands no supervisor, the lawyer's pockets are not searched when he leaves the court. But in return, he is compelled to sell not his mere labor power, not just the tension of his muscles, but his entire personality as a human being—and not through fear but through conscientiousness. As a result, these people don't want to see and cannot see that their professional frock-coat is nothing but a prisoner's uniform of better cut than ordinary."[71]

This individualist ideology is encouraged also among certain types of white-collar workers—teachers and civil servants, for example—to convince them that they are "professionals" rather than workers. But these workers find that they must do all the same things other workers do—organize, strike, fight back—in order to protect their job conditions and living standards. And so their own experience tends to contradict the myth of their "professionalism" and individualism.

When well-educated academics muse about how workers are too "well off" to want real change, they are oblivious to the fact that their assessment is a more apt description of their own class position. The working class, though bombarded with propaganda about the sacredness of the individual, has a different class experience. "A worker," contrasts Trotsky, "comes to socialism as a part of a whole, along with his class, from which he has no prospect of escaping. He is even pleased with the feeling of his moral unity with the mass, which makes him more confident and stronger."[72]

Middle-class radicalism, whatever particular form it takes, tends toward a rejection of class conflict, replacing it with a sense of commitment to improving humanity in general on the basis of moral imperatives, which often translates into moral preaching. The middle-class German "True Socialists," contemporaries of Marx, in rejecting French-style class struggle, "felt conscious of having overcome 'French one-sidedness.'" Their defanged brand of socialism, commented Marx and Engels, represented "not true requirements, but the requirements of Truth; not the interests of the proletariat, but the interests of Human Nature, of Man in general, who belongs to no class, has no reality, who exists only in the misty realm of philosophical fantasy."[73] The petty bourgeoisie is an in-between class, "a class shading off into the bourgeoisie or the proletariat," writes Hal Draper, citing Engels. "One 'in which the interests of the two classes are simultaneously mutually blunted.' In consequence the petty-bourgeois 'imagines himself elevated above class antagonism generally.'"[74]

The middle class is incapable of offering its own solution to the problems of capitalism. In the battle for socialism, it can only play an auxiliary role. It can be drawn into struggle in times of deep-seated crisis. At times, anger or despair draws sections of the middle class to the right—as in Germany in the 1930s, or in Europe today, where sections of the middle class are drawn to the far right. In Greece, European-imposed austerity measures to force repayment on Greece's government debt has meant massive cuts in social spending and pensions and an unemployment rate of 25 percent. This has led to a growth in support not only for the left coalition Syriza (which almost won the 2012 presidential elections for standing up against the austerity packages) but also for the openly fascist Golden Dawn party. The middle classes can also be drawn to the left—as in Argentina in 2001 when sections of the middle class joined workers and the unemployed to bring down the government. But it is also more volatile, and quicker to abandon the fight. While the working class and sections of the middle class can together bring down a government, only working-class leadership in the movement can lead the struggle to a new society.

Why Workers Must Lead

Workers have time and again brought their concentrated power to bear in bringing down unpopular, oppressive regimes. The tremendous power of Black workers in South Africa was the most important factor in the downfall of apartheid—the system of racial separation and white supremacy. Strikes by Iranian oil workers were key to bringing down the shah of Iran in 1979; in 2003, miners in Bolivia played an important role in bringing down hated neoliberal president Gonzalo Sánchez de Lozada. In Egypt, the entrance of workers into the struggle against Mubarak tipped the balance against his rule in February 2011. Yet in all these cases, while workers may have plowed the ground, others gathered the fruits of victory, or succeeded in limiting the horizons of change. The struggle in most cases united a variety of different social and class forces that were agreed on what they opposed, but not on what they were for.

In South Africa, a combination of armed struggle, mass protest, and strikes—under the leadership of the African National Congress (ANC)—was able to finally bring an end to apartheid. The ANC's 1955 Freedom Charter stated, "South Africa belongs to all who live in it—Black and White." But the ANC was not prepared to go beyond this basic democratic goal. The charter, insisted the ANC's chief leader Nelson Mandela, aimed not at socialism but rather "the transfer of power . . . to all the people of this country, be they workers, peasants, professional men or petty bourgeoisie." As for capitalism—the ANC sought to "open fresh fields for the development of a prosperous non-European bourgeois class" with the end of apartheid.[75] Its commitment to the continuation of capitalism in South Africa meant that many of the issues that brought the masses of Black South Africans to rebel—lack of housing and basic services, unemployment, landlessness, and severe exploitation at the hands of multinationals—continue today under a Black majority government.

Ashwin Desai describes how Mandela, some two months after his election as South Africa's first Black president, emphasized his government's commitment to job security, accessible health care, and affordable education. Ten years later, ANC stalwart and South African president Thabo Mbeki was singing a different tune, pushing a program promoting free-market deregulation and "fiscal discipline." The new program, whose acronym was GEAR, "operated as a homegrown structural adjustment program. Markets were opened, taxes to the rich were cut, state assets were privatized, services were commodified, and social spending was reduced." Small wonder that Pamela Cox, head of the South Africa division of the World Bank, enthused: "What they [the ANC] have done to put South Africa on a right footing, is, I think, almost miraculous."[76]

Workers have an interest in taking the fight for a better society further than middle-class forces that want to restrict the struggle to a set of more or less limited reforms that leave the economic system of exploitation intact. To avoid playing an auxiliary role—providing the muscle while other classes reap most of the rewards—workers must be organized politically as a class capable of asserting themselves as an independent class. But in doing so, workers must be able to present a social and political program of change capable of leading all the exploited and oppressed in society.

Writing a few months after the outbreak of the 1905 revolution, Lenin warned: "The outcome of the revolution depends on whether the working class will play the part of a subsidiary to the bourgeoisie, a subsidiary that is powerful in the force of its onslaught against the autocracy, but impotent politically, or whether it will play the part of leader of the people's revolution."[77] Though feudal autocracy has long since disappeared, Lenin's formula still applies to the struggle against tyranny today. Are workers to play a "subsidiary" role or a leading role in struggles against national oppression, the fight against military dictatorship, or any other fight that brings disparate class elements together against some aspect of the status quo? Is the struggle, in other words, to end in limited reforms or in complete emancipation?

Liberals and reformists who look to limit demands to what is possible within the framework of capitalism turn this question on its head, claiming that workers' interests are narrowly economic, while the movement must be broad and encompass the interests of all social "sectors." There is nothing wrong with broad forces uniting to fight for particular demands they are all agreed upon. The problem comes when, in the name of broad unity, the moderates try to prevent anyone from taking the struggle further. In the name of broadening the movement its aims are then narrowed, and further progress is truncated, or even abandoned.

Revolutionaries, on the other hand, have always sought to build a workers' movement in which the working class takes the lead not only in fighting for better wages and conditions but in fighting against all forms of tyranny and oppression, from racism to women's inequality. When socialists talk about workers' power, we aren't talking simply about the impact of a well-placed strike (that is, the relative social weight that workers hold in the process of production). We're talking about the need for the working class to play an independent and leading role in the struggle of all the oppressed and exploited if we're to turn the fight into one against the system in its entirety. Rather than restricting itself to economic demands for the betterment of its conditions, the working class must present itself as the only class capable of leading the whole of society, minus the minority of exploiters and its defenders, toward total human emancipation in all its forms.

Socialism doesn't arise automatically from the class struggle. Workers can play the crucial role in a revolution, but without political organization, they can find their interests sidelined. Unless workers organize as an independent force that fights for their aims, the struggle can only go so far. And they cannot play this role unless they are organized as a class—that is, into their own political party—and thus capable of using their concerted power in the interests of all the exploited and oppressed.

Marx learned this during the revolutions that swept Europe in 1848. "The democratic petty bourgeois," he wrote, "far from wanting to transform the whole society in the interests of the revolutionary proletarians, only aspire to a change in social conditions which will make the existing society as tolerable and comfortable for themselves as possible." The working class therefore had to be organized into an independent political party that would march with the petty-bourgeois democrats against the old autocratic regimes, but would "oppose them in everything whereby they seek to consolidate their position in their own interests."[78]

"It is our interest and our task," Marx and Engels concluded,

> to make the revolution permanent, until all more or less possessing classes have been forced out of their position of dominance, the proletariat has conquered state power, and the association of proletarians, not only in one country but in all the dominant countries of the world, has advanced so far that competition among the proletarians in these countries has ceased and that at least the decisive productive forces are concentrated in the hands of the proletariat. For us the issue cannot be the alteration of private property but only its annihilation, not the smoothing over of class antagonisms but the abolition of classes, not the improvement of existing society but the foundation of a new one.[79]

Chapter Seven

Democracy, Reform, and Revolution

Earlier we discussed the Hobbesian idea that the state is there to prevent a war of each against all. The "Hobbes lite" view, appropriate to modern liberal theories about democracy, is that the state's role is to balance various competing interests—business, labor, women, minorities, immigrants, farmers, consumers, and so on. In this view, sometimes called *pluralism*, the role of the state is to reconcile various competing interests so that "all the active and legitimate groups in the population can make themselves heard at some crucial stage in the process of decision."[1] The state in this view is a neutral body standing above society and arbitrating between competing interests. The US government, our history books tell us, has a system of "checks and balances" that guarantees this fairness.

But does this view correspond to reality? For things to really work this way, the various groups would need to have more or less equal clout. But this view of power obscures the fact that in a capitalist society some interest groups are more "legitimate" than others. Pluralism disguises the fact that society contains a fundamental class divide, and that the basis of political power is economic rather than geographic or territorial. The fact that most people over eighteen can vote in this country does not mean that we all have an equal say or equal power. "One man, one vote is, apparently, the be-all and end-all of democracy," observed the late British socialist journalist Paul Foot. "One man may own six newspapers, two television stations and six factories. Another may earn 20 pounds a week, 7 pounds of which goes in rent and 13 of which has to make do for his family. Each has one vote. But are they equally represented in society?"[2]

In the United States, wealth is concentrated at the top. The top 1 percent of households in 2010 had three times more wealth than the bottom 80 percent, and 9.5 times more financial (non-house) wealth. The bottom 40 percent of the US population owns a pitiful 0.3 percent of the wealth. "The top 0.1%—that's one-tenth of one percent—

had more combined pre-tax income than the poorest 120 million people."[3] The "Forbes 400," the wealthiest individuals in the United States, each with net worth of more than $1.1 billion, saw their wealth increase by $200 billion in 2011, while median household income dropped 4 percent.[4] In a society based upon massive concentrations of wealth on the one end, and poverty and low wages on the other, one billionaire has more political clout than even millions of workers. The economic pecking order determines the political pecking order.

Marx developed a far more accurate theory of the state than the pluralists, arguing in *The Communist Manifesto* that, "the executive of the modern state is but a committee for managing the common affairs of the whole bourgeoisie."[5] That doesn't mean that the state directly represents the interests of each individual capitalist. Sometimes it sacrifices the interests of some businesses over others. But overall, it manages the "common affairs" of the wealthiest class.

Of all the various groups that seek "access" to government, therefore, the ones that get the biggest hearing are the wealthiest. And here we are speaking not only of individuals but of colossal institutions—banking conglomerates, investment firms, and giant corporations—that control the US economy. "Parliamentarism," (and in the United States, representative democracy) wrote the socialist Paul Lafargue, "is a system of government in which the people acquires the illusion that it is controlling the forces of the country itself, when, in reality, the actual power is concentrated in the hands of the bourgeoisie."[6]

The capitalist class exercises its dominance over the state in a number of ways. First of all, as is fitting of a society based upon the market, politicians are bought and sold to the highest bidder—hence the billion-dollar corporate lobbying industry in Washington, the international capital of influence peddling. In 2011, corporations and other institutions spent $3.33 billion on lobbying efforts. (Of this, $50 million, or 0.015 percent, came from labor unions.)[7] Secondly, the entire system is set up so that it is impossible to run even a local candidacy without enormous sums of money. At the presidential level, the price of the ticket has become astronomical. The two main candidates in the 2012 presidential election, Mitt Romney and incumbent Barack Obama, each spent more than $1 billion on their campaigns—up from half a billion dollars in 2000 and $171 million in 1976.[8]

The notorious revolving door—where business leaders and former corporate lobbyists take congressional or government jobs, and vice versa, where officeholders and politicians move into the corporate or corporate lobbying world to cash in on their governmental "expertise"—ensures a seamless connection between the economic and political power of the ruling class. Opensecrets.org has identified thirty-six Goldman Sachs employees who moved either from that company to government posts or the reverse, including Bush treasury secretary Henry Paulson, who had been CEO of Goldman Sachs, and Robert Rubin, Clinton's treasury secretary, who had been

Goldman Sach's cochairman.[9] The same revolving door applies to regulatory agencies that are ostensibly set up to regulate industries. "Many of the agrichemical industry's former executives, lawyers, and scientists," according to the Pesticide Action Network, "serve in the government agencies that are charged with keeping watch over their industries."[10] After the 2010 Deepwater Horizon disaster, which produced the worst oil spill in history, the Minerals Management Service, the department that regulates oil drilling, was exposed as a cesspool of corruption whose "staffers were both literally and figuratively in bed with the oil industry." Obama's interior secretary Ken Salazar promised top-to-bottom reform—but after referring a few employees for prosecution, he did little else. Rather than putting the brakes on offshore drilling, "Salazar immediately throttled it up to record levels."[11]

Capitalists, however, don't need direct control of the state for it to act in their interests. As Michael Parenti, in his book *Democracy for the Few*, notes:

> Because business controls the very economy of the nation, government perforce enters into a unique and intimate relationship with it. The health of the capitalist economy is treated by policymakers as a necessary condition for the health for the nation, and since it happens that the economy is in the hands of large investors, then presumably government's service to the public is best accomplished by service to the investors. The goals of business (rapid growth, high profits, and secure markets) become the goals of government, and the "national interest" becomes identified with the dominant capitalist interests.[12]

What capitalists want most is a government that creates the optimum conditions for them to make money. They are more or less content with any state that can guarantee the conditions necessary for them to accumulate wealth unhindered, whether it is a democratic republic, a constitutional monarchy, or—if necessary to holding popular resistance in check—a military dictatorship. Our side vastly prefers democracy over military dictatorship or a police state, because bourgeois democracy, however limited, creates freer conditions to organize and fight against capitalism.

But capitalists will even put up with a fascist dictatorship, like Hitler's, if such a state promises to prevent revolution and crush all resistance. Even the most democratic government sets up legal loopholes that permit it to suspend democratic rights when "national security" is threatened. In 1851, Karl Marx noted that the French Constitution "guarantees liberty," save for "exceptions made by law." "For each paragraph of the constitution contains its own antithesis, its own Upper and Lower House, namely, liberty in the general phrase, abrogation of liberty in the marginal note."[13] The marginal note comes in handy during periods of civil unrest or wartime, as a means to suppress dissent.

The Patriot Act, passed by the administration of George W. Bush not long after the September 11 attacks, ushered in a period of increasing curtailment of democratic rights. Though Obama supporters had great hope that his policies would be different,

Obama expanded and institutionalized many of the new Bush-era practices. The National Defense Authorization Act of 2012, for example, authorizes the military to arrest and indefinitely detain anyone, including citizens, suspected of "assisting terrorists." Obama's administration has also granted itself the right to order assassination of citizens, punish whistle-blowers, expand its domestic surveillance operations; and it has presided over an increasing militarization of local and federal police agencies, which have engaged in "increasingly punitive treatment of protesters" and undocumented immigrants.[14]

These sorts of policies have plenty of antecedents in US history. The Alien and Sedition Acts of 1798 gave the government the right to imprison or deport any "alien" considered a threat to the US government, and made any spoken or printed criticism of the government, or opposition to any of its laws, punishable by two years in prison. The Espionage Act of 1917 "made it a felony to make 'false statements' or statements that might cause 'insubordination' or 'disloyalty' in the armed services or statements that could 'obstruct' enlistment into the armed services."[15] The Sedition Act of 1918 made it a crime in wartime to use "disloyal, profane, scurrilous, or abusive language" about the US government, its flag, or its armed forces.[16] The Smith Act of 1940— used in 1941 to prosecute and imprison eighteen members of the Socialist Workers Party—made advocating or organizing for the overthrow of the government punishable by up to twenty years in prison.[17]

Thousands of socialists and anarchists—including both native-born and immigrant workers—were spied on, imprisoned, deported, beaten, tortured, and otherwise abused during the First World War. Montana's Sedition Law, which became the prototype of the national law, imprisoned dozens of Montanans under its statutes, which included making it a crime to speak German. One of the biggest backers of the law was Anaconda Copper Mining Company, which saw the law as a means to quell labor unrest.[18] The ruling class's contempt for genuine freedom of speech was summed up by the Mexican anarchist Enrique Flores Magón, who served three years in US prisons between 1918 and 1920 for publishing a radical newspaper: "This ill-called Country of Liberty has now converted into a crime punishable by twenty years in the Penitentiary anyone who preaches free thought and free speech." This statement earned him deportation back to Mexico.[19] Eugene Debs, in his 1918 antiwar speech in Canton, Ohio (which also landed him in jail), sarcastically remarked, "It is extremely dangerous to exercise the constitutional right of free speech in a country fighting to make democracy free for the world."[20]

Ordinary workers have had to fight every step of the way for what limited democracy capitalism is willing to concede. In Britain, the working class had to organize mass protests in order to win complete universal male suffrage without property restrictions—and women didn't win the right to vote in the United States and Britain until the twentieth century. Many ruling classes were at first fearful that complete universal suffrage might threaten their rule. Long after slavery was abolished in the

United States, millions of Blacks in the South—and many poor whites—were denied the right to vote. Today, Republicans in the United States are pushing through various state voter ID laws that are aimed at restricting the ability of poor people to cast votes.

Freedom of the press comes most readily to those who have the millions of dollars necessary to own one. There is formal legal equality in many societies, but the poor are the law's most common victims. The nineteenth-century French writer Anatole France has a character in one of his books, the poet Choulette, who mocks the "the majestic quality of the law which prohibits the wealthy as well as the poor from sleeping under the bridges, from begging in the streets, and from stealing bread."[21] Debs joked that in the United States, the "judicial nets are so adjusted as to catch the minnows and let the whales slip through."[22] A socialist who was a shoe fitter and a participant in the 1877 St. Louis General Strike put a fine point on this double standard: "A man who stole a single rail is called a thief, while he who stole a railway is a gentleman."[23]

The formal equality of the law hides extreme inequality—the most egregious modern example being the 1986 law establishing a hundred-to-one sentencing disparity (changed in 2010 to 18 to 1) between convictions for crack versus cocaine possession, crack being the drug of the poor, cocaine of the more affluent.[24] But there are plenty of other examples. In California and twenty-two other states where there are "three strikes" laws in place, there are thousands of people serving life sentences for having committed a third felony offense, which can be as trivial as stealing pizza from a grocery store. In one notorious case, a hungry and homeless ex-convict was given a life sentence for attempting to break into a church kitchen, where he had been fed in the past, to get food.[25]

True, capitalists who get caught defrauding other capitalists are sometimes punished by the state, as were the heads of WorldCom and Enron, in order to placate other capitalists but also to demonstrate that the judicial system "works." But often the punishment is just ineffectual wrist slapping. As of fall 2012, there has not been a single criminal prosecution of an executive in the wake of the 2008 financial meltdown, despite "abundant evidence of widespread . . . criminal behavior in the financial sector."[26]

When a conglomerate of companies, including General Motors, Standard Oil, and Firestone, conspired to rip up the electric trolley system across the nation in the mid-1930s and get cities to convert to GM buses and cars, a judge fined each company five thousand dollars, and a handful of executives a dollar each. By 1955, the corporations had destroyed 88 percent of the country's electric trolley system. In the words of one former executive, this example "suggests that the larger the crime, the more the boundaries between 'crime' and 'business as usual' begin to blur. As former Atlanta mayor and UN ambassador Andrew Young once said, 'Nothing is illegal if 100 businessmen decide to do it.'"[27]

The greatest portion of the state—the military, police, and intelligence agencies, the state bureaucracy, and much of the judiciary—isn't even subject to elections. This tremendous apparatus is not accessible, even indirectly, to the pressures of popular voting. Those who run these institutions have close ties to private business interests outside of government, and, as Parenti notes, are in every way predisposed to consider a "good business climate," that is, the interests of capitalists, foremost in their functioning. Voters don't make crucial decisions like whether or not to go to war, make treaties, or conclude trade agreements. We don't get to vote on military spending or what kind of health care system we have.

And of course there is no workplace democracy. At work, the employer is a despot, setting the nature and pace of work, and hiring and firing at will (especially if there is no union). If we don't like our pay, benefits, or working conditions, we can't fire our boss or vote to change anything. We're told instead, "If you don't like it, go someplace else and work." This is the limit of our "freedom" as workers, even though we spend at the very least half of our waking life at work.

Virtually every important decision that affects our lives is set beyond the reach of the majority. Modern-day representative democracy—in which we choose unaccountable (mis)representatives every two, four, or six years—has been very successful in providing the illusion of real democracy in a society where a small number of very wealthy people and the bureaucrats who serve them make all the important decisions. Workers have an interest in fighting for the freest and most complete democracy; whereas the employing class aims to stunt and curtail democracy, and, when necessary, even eliminates it.

The Democratic Party and the Limits of Reformism in the United States

Illusions in the Democratic Party as a "party of the people" have been the great Achilles' heel of the left in the United States. Throughout much of the country's history, the Democratic Party has positioned itself as a popular alternative to the more conservative, blatantly pro-capitalist Republican Party. Both parties, however, are intimately tied and committed to capitalism. "Part of the reason that the US 'survival of the fittest' periods of economic restructuring are so relentless rests on the performance of the Democrats as history's second-most enthusiastic capitalist party," writes former right-wing pundit Kevin Phillips. "They do not interfere much with capitalism's momentum, but wait for the excesses and the inevitable populist reaction."[28] The game of political musical chairs between the two parties cannot be played properly if it appears to the electorate that both teams are wearing the same jerseys and are serving the same owners. The system is designed so that when voters are dissatisfied with one party, there is always the other one waiting in the wings that can take over with minimal disruption to the system as a whole.

The two-party system has been tremendously successful in preventing the emergence of any successful third-party challenges, from the left or the right. As far back as 1893, Engels astutely observed that the formation of a workers' party in the United States was hindered by a "Constitution . . . which makes it appear as though every vote were lost that is cast for a candidate not put up by one of the two governing parties."[29] His description of the US political system—one consisting of "two great gangs of speculators, who alternately take possession of the state power and exploit it by the most corrupt means and for the most corrupt ends"—reads like it was written yesterday.[30]

Both parties have always been funded by big business, both are supporters of overseas conquest, and both have used troops to quell strikes. Before the civil rights movement, moreover, the Democratic Party was the party of Jim Crow segregation. In his Socialist Party campaign speeches Debs constantly hammered on these truths. "If the Democratic Party is the 'friend of labor' any more than the Republican Party," he said in 1900, "why is its platform dumb in the presence of Coeur d'Alene?" Debs was referring to an 1892 strike of Idaho miners where, after company guards killed five strikers, the miners marched the guards and strikebreakers out of town. The strike was broken when the governor sent in fifteen hundred troops and locked up six hundred strikers in a stockade prison. "What has the Democratic Party to say about the 'property and educational qualifications' in North Carolina and Louisiana, and the proposed general disfranchisement of the negro race in the southern states?" asked Debs. "The differences between the Republican and Democratic parties involve no issue, no principle in which the working class have any interest."[31]

The New Deal and civil rights eras are the touchstones today for those who argue that the Democrats are the party of the people. In the 1930s, the Democrat Franklin Delano Roosevelt, warily eyeing the mass working-class upsurge that led to the formation of the Congress of Industrial Unions (CIO), presented himself as both a friend of labor and a savior of capitalism. "Those who have property fail to realize," he wrote to Supreme Court justice Felix Frankfurter, "that I am the best friend the profit system ever had."[32] During the course of the civil rights movement, Southern Democrats deserted the party. Northern liberal Democrats were always one step *behind* the civil rights movement, eager to wind down the struggle (which they feared) and win the voting allegiance of enfranchised Blacks (which they coveted).

The populist rhetoric of the Democrats is designed to take the fire out of any move to form a radical third party. Alarmed by the growth of the Populist Party, for example, which received 1.4 million votes in the 1894 midterm elections, the Democratic Party fielded William Jennings Bryan as its presidential candidate in 1896. Bryan breathed populist rhetoric in order to win over Populist Party supporters. Democratic leaders also diligently cultivated the "fusionist" wing of the Populists, which proposed merging the two parties.

At its 1896 convention, the Populists voted to endorse Bryan as their candidate. Populist leader Tom Watson knew this signaled the end of Populism, writing, "Populists cannot denounce the sins of the two old parties and yet go into political co-partnership with them. The moment we make a treaty the war must cease . . . and when we cease our war upon the two old parties, we have no longer any excuse for living."[33] Watson warned, "Fusion means the Populist Party will play Jonah, and they [the Democrats] will play the whale."[34] Watson was right. The decision to back Bryan effectively killed the Populist Party.

The absence of any radical working-class or left political parties is one of the secrets of the relative stability of bourgeois politics in the United States historically, narrowing at election time the choice, for workers and the poor, to one between two evils. The history of the two-party system shows that electing the lesser evil demobilizes mass struggle by putting the masses' faith in the actions of bourgeois politicians. It lowers the political level of the movement, too, because it compels activists to become apologists for a party that does not represent their interests.

If the lesser evil wins, his (so far there have been no women presidents) policies in office are glaringly different from his campaign rhetoric. The most famous case of this was Lyndon Johnson, who won the presidential race in 1964 on a promise to end the war, but then sent five hundred thousand troops to Vietnam. This was a particularly egregious case because it turns out Johnson had secret plans to send more troops to Vietnam before he won the election.[35]

The Democrats' populist paint began to peel after Ronald Reagan's election, when the Democrats shifted rightward and began backing the employers' neoliberal agenda and pandering to the neoconservative ideology of small government and "personal responsibility." It is only by comparison to the GOP, which moved even further rightward, that the party can still present itself as liberal, though the Democrats' policies today are politically indistinguishable from the GOP in its past incarnations.

Obama's election as president in 2008 was historic in that he was the first African American to be elected president in US history. He entered office, moreover, with the largest Democratic House majority since 1992 and the largest Senate majority since 1978. His campaign and election coincided with the Great Recession. Millions were fed up with politics as usual. To win, he positioned himself rhetorically as the friend of Main Street over Wall Street, a critic of the Iraq War (though he said he supported the Afghan war), a promoter of alternative energy, and a supporter of universal health care. Many thought that he'd usher in a new New Deal. In one of his campaign speeches he evoked the civil rights movement and union struggles, saying that change "happens from the bottom up. Dr. King understood that."[36] But there were early indicators of whose class interests he was preparing to serve: he raked in more money from Wall Street donors than did John McCain, his GOP opponent.[37] A post-election analysis concluded that Obama got about a quarter of his money from individuals contributing $200 or less.[38] And Wall Street got its money's worth. The new president's economic team consisted of former Clinton administration officials who were committed to financial deregulation and free trade. Obama's response to the financial crisis in 2008 was largely focused on bailing out the bankers and far less focused on ordinary people, millions of whom suffered chronic unemployment or lost their homes. As Lance Selfa writes, "Obama and the Democrats legitimized massive government spending without changing any of their neoliberal assumptions. Instead, the administration pursued a kind of 'neoliberal Keynesianism'—putting trillions of taxpayer dollars at the disposal of private business and trying to 'incentivize' business to carry out social policy. It didn't work. The banks and big corporations were happy to take the money, but they didn't commit to lending it, saving homes, or hiring workers."[39]

In a meeting with financial CEOs in 2009, Obama explained, "My administration is the only thing between you and pitchforks." A grateful CEO who attended the meeting explained his relief that Obama "mostly wanted to help us out, to quell the mob."[40] Instead of pitchforks, big business got profits, which grew on average by 77.9 percent per year (admittedly from an abysmally low rate) between 2009 and the end of 2012, based largely on holding down wages, ratcheting up productivity, and feeding at the public financial trough.[41] Obama promised to pass the Employee Free Choice Act, a bill that would have made it easier for workers to organize into unions. He reneged on that promise—a betrayal that hasn't prompted unions to stop pouring funds into Democratic campaigns. The Obama administration's 2009 bailout and restructuring of the auto industry led to tens of thousands of layoffs, a freeze on wages, and other concessions—including the UAW giving up the right to strike when its contract expired in 2011—amounting to more than a billion dollars per year.

The bailout represented an enormous transfer of wealth from taxpayers to the financial sector. To pay for the ensuing debt crisis, business looked to austerity measures—slashing government spending—to pay the debt down. Despite pre-election promises to restore the Bush-era tax cuts on the rich, Obama acquiesced to GOP demands to maintain them in his first term, and embraced austerity, saying, "Everything must be on the table."

Banks were "too big to fail," but ordinary people were not. One of the Obama administration's first acts was to create a special commission (Bowles-Simpson) to recommend ways to cut Social Security, Medicaid, and Medicare benefits in order to reduce the deficit. In 2010, Obama proposed even steeper cuts than those recommended by his commission. It failed only because Republican House Speaker John Boehner walked away from the deal. On the eve of his second term, Obama expressed his intent to achieve a "grand bargain" with Republicans to cut the federal deficit by four trillion dollars over ten years—including plans to squeeze Social Security and slash Medicare—in return for minor tax increases on the wealthy, a proposal he sold as "shared sacrifice." Again, a stalemate produced something called the "fiscal cliff," an agreement to let the Bush-era tax cuts expire and to impose a 10 percent, across-the-board cut in government spending if Congress took no action by December 31, 2012. Bush-era tax cuts were lifted on all but the very wealthy, and the automatic, across-the-board cuts, called "sequestration," were pushed off until March 1. Among the $85 billion in cuts set to take effect for the year meant fewer food safety inspections, more cuts to national parks, a 10 percent cut in unemployment benefits, the loss of Section 8 housing vouchers for 125,000 poor people, 10,000 teacher layoffs, and the cancellation of after-school programs at schools already suffering from cuts.

Throughout this fiasco, the Democrats positioned themselves not as opponents of destroying the social safety net but as the party that would kill it more slowly. As Lee Sustar wrote in *Socialist Worker*, "The discussion about sweeping and indiscriminate budget cuts . . . serves an important purpose for the political class as a whole, regardless of party—to convince the rest of us that there is no alternative to accepting some level of budget cuts, with Democrats representing austerity on a somewhat less catastrophic scale compared to Republicans." Sustar continued: "The staged conflict between Democrats who supposedly want to 'preserve vital government programs' and Republicans who want to 'reduce the deficit' is false. The truth is that both parties are committed to austerity—and that neither would propose the obvious ways to 'preserve vital programs' and 'reduce the deficit' at the same time: by raising taxes on corporations and the rich and massively cutting the Pentagon budget."[42]

Obama's "crowning" achievement, the 2010 Patient Protection and Affordable Care Act, was in its broad outlines the GOP alternative to Clinton's failed health care proposal in 1993. Ruling out from the start a government-sponsored single-payer plan, the only plan that could cut runaway health costs and improve benefits and coverage to all Americans, Obama crafted a plan mandating that citizens buy private health insurance. The plan was welcomed by the pharmaceutical and insurance industries for the windfall they expected the expanded coverage would bring.

The GOP, its base reenergized and mobilized under the banner of the "Tea Party," made big gains in the 2010 midterm elections. But most voters were not reacting to Obama's alleged "liberalism," but to him not really delivering to his popular base, who stayed at home in droves. It was the extreme conservative lunacy of the GOP, rather than Obama's great record in office, that won him a second term. Despite the absurd claims by his Republican opponents that Obama was a "socialist," he himself remarked in 2012 that two decades ago he would have been considered a "moderate Republican."[43] He not only ratcheted up domestic surveillance and repression against dissent, he implemented harsh measures toward immigrants, deporting more undocumented immigrants than Bush did.[44]

Breaking from the Two-Party Straightjacket

The logical conclusion from the historical experience is that the working class and the oppressed must build a political alternative independent of the twin parties of US capitalism. Marx and Engels had much to teach on the value of the left and progressives running their own candidates. In 1886, the Central Labor Union in New York formed the Independent Labor Party of New York and Vicinity in order to participate in New York City's mayoral race. The new party chose single-tax advocate Henry George as its candidate. George himself was not from the labor movement, but was a middle-class populist. He had recently written a popular book, *Progress and Poverty*, which advocated a single tax on landed property as a panacea to solve society's ills. In a hotly contested race in which the ruling class pulled out all the stops to prevent a Labor Party victory, George came in second in a three-way race, with 31 percent of the vote. Writing from Europe, Engels was positive about the election:

> In a country that has newly entered the movement, the first really crucial step is the formation by the workers of an independent political party, no matter how, so long as it is distinguishable as a labor party. . . . That the first program of this party should still be muddle-headed and extremely inadequate, that it should have picked Henry George for its figurehead, are unavoidable if merely transitory evils. The masses must have time and opportunity to evolve; and they will not get that opportunity unless they have a movement of their own—no matter what its form, providing it is their own movement—in which they are impelled onwards by their own mistakes and learn by bitter experience.[45]

The working class must have an independent political party of its own—a lesson we still need to learn in the United States today. Unions spend huge sums of money to get Democrats elected—one-quarter of election contributions to Democrats in 2010, for example, came from labor unions—and year after year the investment has proven to be one that yields no returns. "Since 1973," writes Lance Selfa, "when the median wage in real terms peaked, the Democrats have held the White House for half as long as the Republicans have, but they have held the majority in Congress and the state legislatures for most of that time. Yet they did little to reverse the conservative-inspired offensive against working people's living standards."[46]

What about the oft-repeated argument that voting for left candidates "steals" votes from liberals and helps the right wing into power? According to this logic, there is no good time to break from the Democratic Party. We are doomed in perpetuity to vote for a party that does not truly represent our interests. During every election we hear the argument that it is the "most important election of our lifetime," and that the only way to defeat the right wing is to elect liberals. "The ultimate intention of all such phrases," wrote Marx, "is to dupe the working class."[47]

If I tie a rope to the fender of a car sinking into a muddy lake to pull it out, but the car pulls me into the muck instead, it is clear who is doing the pulling and who is being pulled. The repeated attempts by the left in the United States to capture or move the Democratic Party leftward follows this pattern. Misplaced support on the left for the Democratic Party has meant that our side is unable to use elections to count our forces. Worse, presidential elections disorient and disorganize our side. Liberals spend a great deal of time convincing activists to tone down the criticism, to refrain from struggle in the lead-up to the election, so as not to embarrass or undermine the Democratic candidate. Depending on the state of the class struggle, some more liberal Democrats may even offer verbal support for some of the demands of the social movements. But in the end their purpose is to bring anyone leaning away from the Democrats back into the fold. On Election Day, they will be asked to vote for the more conservative Democratic candidate who has been chosen for his or her "electability."

Dennis Kucinich ran a long-shot primary campaign in the 2004 presidential election that raised opposition to the occupation of Iraq and the Patriot Act and support for universal health care. When it came time to choose the Democratic presidential candidate, he pressured all his supporters to vote for John Kerry, a pro-occupation, pro–Patriot Act, anti–universal health care centrist. "The Democratic Party created third parties by running to the middle," explained Kucinich during his campaign. "What I'm trying to do is to go back to the big tent so that everyone who felt alienated could come back through my candidacy."[48] He ran not to win, but to corral leftists and progressives into the party. Kucinich played a similar role channeling support toward Obama's health care plan by withdrawing his and Representative John Conyers's single-payer bill, saying, "This is not the right time."[49] Of course, the right time never comes.

The practical result of not presenting a real left pole at election time is to permit a rightward drift of the general political climate in which both the liberal and conservative bourgeois candidates feel absolutely no pressure from the left. This "politics of realism" or of "the possible," therefore, makes the prospects for building an independent movement capable of achieving real radical change more remote. University of Pennsylvania professor Adolph Reed, in a 2014 *Harper's* piece, examines this process of rightward accommodation that flows from this approach:

> But if the left is tied to a Democratic strategy that, at least since the Clinton Administration, tries to win elections by absorbing much of the right's social vision and agenda, before long the notion of a political left will have no meaning. For all intents and purposes, that is what has occurred. If the right sets the terms of debate for the Democrats, and the Democrats set the terms of debate for the left, then what can it mean to be on the political left? The terms "left" and "progressive"— and in practical usage the latter is only a milquetoast version of the former—now signify a cultural sensibility rather than a reasoned critique of the existing social order. Because only the right proceeds from a clear, practical utopian vision, "left" has come to mean little more than "not right."[50]

The logic of lesser evilism, both in the electoral sphere and in the realm of struggle, is always to narrow, constrict, and moderate demands, to accept anything so long as it is not the worst alternative. "You can't fight the victory of the rightmost forces," argued Hal Draper, "by sacrificing your own independent strength to support elements just the next step away from them."[51] But that is precisely the logic that the two-party system imposes on the left.

Eugene Wagner, a Michigan attorney who served on the board of the National Coalition to Abolish the Death Penalty, makes a typical argument. Death penalty opponents shouldn't support "illegal" civil disobedience protests, he insists, because it might drive away important affiliates, expose the organization to criminal proceedings, and give "aid and comfort to many of our opponents in spreading the false and pernicious idea that abolition of the death penalty is based on radical left-wing principles."[52] This is miles away from any idea that abolishing the death penalty is a struggle that must be taken to the streets, or that it is a class issue, part of a general attack on the poor and working class. On the contrary, many abolitionist lawyers believe that demonstrations actually hurt a prisoner's chance of finding justice: "You'll anger the prosecutor or judge." The ultimate logic of this argument is that the best way to fight for reforms is not to fight at all—you'll anger those in power and there will be a backlash.

This was the message of the "paper of record" toward the immigrant rights protests that swept the country, culminating in boycotts, walkouts, and marches involving a few million people across the country on May 1, 2006. "Sleeping giants can, and should, get moving," the *New York Times* editorial graciously granted to a movement it had no power to stop, "but they should tread carefully." The *Times* editors warned that the protests were a "perilous business," suggesting "delicate consensus building" instead of boycotts and strikes to avoid antagonizing the immigrant-bashing right or sending "students the wrong message about the importance of education."[53] As if mass action to achieve social reform were not educational or effective! Liberals have a long history of preaching to mass movements to tread delicately so as not to "provoke" reaction. Naturally, there is no danger of a backlash if the oppressed never fight back. To those who cautioned the civil rights movement to "wait," Martin Luther King Jr. replied, "We know through painful experience that freedom is never voluntarily given by the oppressor; it must be demanded by the oppressed."[54]

Revolution: Political and Social

Revolution is the ultimate social leap—a period when the gradual accumulation of mass bitterness and anger of the exploited and oppressed coalesces and bursts forth into a mass movement to overturn existing social relations and replace them with new ones. A few days of revolutionary upheaval bring more change than decades of "normal" development. Rulers and systems that seemed invincible and immovable are suddenly unceremoniously toppled. One need only think of the five days of mass protest and strikes that toppled the tsar in February 1917, or more recently, the Tunisian and Egyptian revolutions of 2011, where long-standing dictators were toppled in a matter of a few weeks.

The last three centuries have been filled not only with wars but also with revolutions and near-revolutions. A list of only some of these gives us an idea of the scope of revolutionary upheaval since the dawn of modern capitalism—the American Revolution (1776–87), the French Revolution (1789–94), the US Civil War (1861–65), the European revolutions of 1848, the Russian revolutions (1905 and 1917), the German Revolution (1918–23), China (1925–27), the Spanish Civil War (1936–39), the Hungarian Revolution (1956), Chile (1973), Portugal (1974–75), Iran (1979), Poland's Solidarność uprising (1980–81), and the Egyptian and Tunisian revolutions in 2011. This partial list is enough to put to rest the notion that such social upheavals are rare or unusual occurrences. Revolution, therefore, is not an aberration in an otherwise smoothly functioning society, any more than crisis is an aberration in an otherwise smoothly functioning economy. But what, to be more exact, is a revolution? More precisely, what did Marx mean by it?

Like the terms "democracy" and "freedom," what revolution means is not always clear, and it can be abused, as in when it is used in commercials to discuss the latest hair-care breakthrough. But even when the term isn't abused, its meaning can be quite elastic.[55] Revolution, broadly speaking, is used to refer to sweeping social, political, and economic transformations that happen over a period of time. Hence we talk about the "industrial revolution," the decades-long rise in factory production in Britain that ushered in the era of modern capitalism. More commonly, revolution is used to refer to a forceful transfer of governmental power.

This type of revolution can be purely political—in the sense that it simply transfers power from one section of the ruling class to another, or from a military to a democratic form of government (or the reverse), while leaving the social structure of society intact. When a political revolution transfers power to a new rising class and puts it in a position to begin a social restructuring of society, it then becomes a *social* revolution. "Every real revolution is a social one, in that it brings a new class to power and allows it to remodel society in its own image," Engels wrote.[56]

A social revolution is thus not a military coup by a handful of plotters, nor is it simply a change of personnel at the top as a result of mass protests. The mass protests in the Ukraine in 2014, for example, toppled the existing government, but politicians beholden to similar interests—the powerful corporate oligarchs who had been running society before the protests—filled the power vacuum. Mass protest can overthrow a government in a political revolution—as we've seen many times in Latin America, and most recently, in Egypt and Tunisia. But often the overthrow has only put another leader in power without changing the fundamental class relations in society, or, more substantially, has resulted in the transfer from military to civilian rule. Or, as in Egypt, has gone backwards after only a partial political transformation, moving back to military rule. So long as the social transformation fails to burst the bounds of existing capitalist social relations, it remains, in its essence, a political revolution.

Sometimes revolutions are equated with the use of violence. But though all major revolutions involve violent clashes between contending social forces, revolution is not equal to violence, which is merely a means to an end, and an end that is not always aimed at the social transformation of society.

Nevertheless, when harnessed to social aims, and employed as a means by a mass social movement, revolution can play a crucial role, as Engels explains. "Force," he wrote, can play "a revolutionary role. . . . In the words of Marx, it is the midwife of a very old society pregnant with a new one, it is the instrument with the aid of which social movement forces its way through and shatters the dead, fossilized political forms." In this regard, Engels was scornful of those pacifists who looked askance at all forms of violence "because all use of force demoralizes the person who uses it." Engels recognized that "the immense moral and spiritual impetus which has been given by every victorious revolution" was proof enough of the falsity of absolute pacifism.[57]

There is not a wall between political and social revolutions. On the contrary, political revolutions often involve a social element, or are transitional to a more thoroughgoing social revolution. As Hal Draper notes, one should not "make a hard-and-fast distinction between political revolutions and social revolutions, but, if anything, the reverse: to recognize how often they are mingled in given revolutionary situations, so that the two elements must be distinguished by analysis. For, especially in modern times, revolutionary events tend to blend both in varying proportions."[58]

This is true because in any mass upheaval, the oppressed classes that are mobilized have social and economic aspirations that tend to extend beyond the interests of those classes who, though they may seek political, and even social, change, have interests that place them ultimately in opposition to those aspirations. This has always been true in bourgeois revolutions, where the strivings of the masses that are mobilized to topple the old regime do not coincide with the bourgeois elements that, rather than abolishing exploitation, seek to replace one form with another. But it is also true of modern social upheavals, where often the genie of social revolution—which is inherent in any mobilization involving the mass of workers and the oppressed—is latent but fails to find direct expression because the struggles are led by class forces that wish to contain the struggle within the bounds of capitalism.

Marxism does not counterpose political and social revolution. In fact, the latter cannot take place without the former. That is, workers cannot initiate a social revolution without it also being first a political revolution—one that replaces the political power of the capitalists with that of the workers.

In bourgeois revolutions, the class that assumed power and replaced the old feudal class—the bourgeoisie—had already developed its economic power within the womb of the old order. The gradual development of new capitalist social relations allowed this new ruling class to "attain effective control of economic power within the framework of the old society, before it was able to take political power and change the class nature of the state. . . . The bourgeois could use this position of strength as a fortress from which to press further toward the acquisition of decisive political power."[59] Once in power, the bourgeoisie was able to push through a social transformation that accelerated processes that were already taking place. In fact, in many cases, this economic power was developed enough that a revolutionary struggle was not even necessary for capitalism to emerge victorious over the old feudal relations. In Germany and Japan, for example, society was transformed from above, through the intervention of the state, not from below.

The pattern of workers' revolution is entirely different. Why? Because workers own no property, and have no means to build up any economic power, or to establish different social relations, within the womb of capitalism. They must as a result first achieve, through mass revolutionary struggle, their own political power by displacing the political power of the capitalists. As Draper writes,

> In sum: for Marx, the working class (unlike the bourgeoisie) cannot inseminate its own system of economic power within the old one, thereby establishing a plateau of power from which to gain the political heights. The order necessarily is the reverse. The proletariat, through the organization of its political movement, like every other aspiring class—must first conquer political power and then begin the process of socioeconomic transformation. For the bourgeoisie, political power was finally plucked as the ripe or overripe fruit of its socioeconomic power, its power as a possessing class. For the proletariat, political power is needed as the engine with which to bring a new social order into existence.[60]

You Can't Skin a Tiger Paw by Paw

There have always been moderates in the socialist movement who have made the case for peaceful reform, rather than revolution, as the most "realistic" way to achieve socialism. The German Social Democratic moderate "revisionists" in the early twentieth century (social democracy was the name given to socialist parties at the time) are the best known. Their leading spokesperson, Eduard Bernstein, argued that capitalism, no longer crisis prone, was softening class antagonisms by slowly improving workers' living standards. The growth of trade unions and cooperatives, and above all the rise of a socialist majority in parliament, were all that was needed—and if they didn't frighten away businesses by moving in too radical a direction, German Social

Democrats could slowly but surely bring about socialism. Socialism was no longer an economic, but rather a moral, imperative, and as such could also be an idea appealing to the well-to-do.

Bernstein's famous dictum was that "the ultimate aim of socialism is nothing, but the movement is everything."[61] But "revisionism"—named for its revising of Marx's revolutionary doctrine into a moderate one—also had a peculiar conception of just what the "movement" was. It denigrated the importance of struggle, embodied in such activities as strikes and street protests. These were seen as too disruptive, too threatening to the bourgeoisie, whom the reformists hoped to placate by only demanding incremental change. (For the record, Bernstein also supported colonialism, defending the right of "civilized peoples to act" as "the guardians of the uncivilized.")[62]

There are two problems with this view of socialism. The first is that in this scenario, workers do not liberate themselves. They depend on others to make changes on their behalf. Class struggle plays no role, except as a means to exert pressure on the top. Workers do not learn through their own action how to construct a new world. They are at best a mere stage army, or, worse, a passive voting bloc. But the second—and most important—problem with reformism is that it doesn't work, for the simple reason that those who hold power won't give it up voluntarily or peacefully. "No privileged class," wrote Albert Rhys Williams, a witness to the 1917 revolution in Russia, "voluntarily resigns any of its privileges. No class steeped in tradition discards the old and gladly embraces the new."[63] If socialism is really to be the expropriation of wealth and the socialization of production, that means depriving the bosses of their power and taking away their wealth and their ability to extort any more wealth. Whether you propose to do this in small installments or all at once, the ruling class will resist with all their might. Or as the British historian R. H. Tawney put it, "Onions can be eaten leaf by leaf, but you cannot skin a live tiger paw by paw."[64]

When Southern US slaveholders found their monopoly of political power undermined in Washington as a result of the creation of non–slave states in the 1850s, they resorted to secession and war to protect their economic and political power. Even assuming socialists could gain a majority of elected positions in government, they would still face a pro-slavery rebellion—an all-out effort by the capitalist class to ensure that such a government either acquiesced to their interests or was swept aside. That is why capitalist states have police, armies, and prisons. The purpose of armed force is to act as a last line of defense against any attempt to challenge capitalism.

There are times when even formal democracy becomes too threatening to the powers that be—as the many military coups around the world show. Rosa Luxemburg pointed this out at the turn of the twentieth century: "In this society, the representative institutions, democratic in form, are in content the instruments of the interests of the ruling class. This manifests itself in a tangible fashion in the fact that as soon as democracy shows the tendency to negate its class character and become transformed into an instrument of the real interests of the population, the democratic forms are sacrificed by the bourgeoisie and its state representatives."[65]

This is certainly what happened in Chile in 1973. The electoral victory of the Popular Unity socialist government gave encouragement to a series of mass strikes, along with factory and land takeovers. President Salvador Allende preached a peaceful, constitutional "Chilean road" to socialism, attempting at every turn to restrain the mass movement in order to prove his commitment to "constitutionalism." He brought military generals into his cabinet (including Pinochet, the man who would soon lead the coup against him), assuring the populace that the officers respected the constitution. He signed a "statute of guarantees" not to touch the armed forces, or the legal and educational systems, and authorized the army to conduct searches of factories to confiscate arms that workers were stockpiling to defend themselves against fascist gangs.

Unfortunately, Chile's wealthy (and their friends in Washington) were committed to the constitution only insofar as it guaranteed their rule. Fearing the growing working-class movement, they threw their support behind a brutal military coup, which was backed by the United States. "I don't see why we need to stand by and watch a country go communist because of the irresponsibility of its own people," US secretary of state Henry Kissinger had remarked in 1970. "The issues are much too important for the Chilean voters to be left to decide for themselves."[66] Under the command of General Augusto Pinochet, the army murdered Allende in the presidential palace and drowned the workers' movement in blood. Tens of thousands were rounded up and imprisoned in the Santiago stadium, and thousands were murdered. Though Allende's behavior was heroic—he insisted on staying at his post at the presidential palace and was murdered by Pinochet's forces—his constitutionalism at any price disoriented the mass movement, allowing General Pinochet the breathing room he needed to destroy it.[67]

Communist Parties (CPs) throughout the world at that time, who long before had abandoned revolutionary Marxism under the tutelage of Stalinist Russia in the 1930s and 1940s, drew deeply conservative conclusions from Allende's defeat. The problem in their assessment was not that Allende disarmed the workers' movement and opened the door to defeat, but that the class struggle had gone too far and had thereby provoked the reaction. "The tragic Chilean experience has demonstrated," fretted Italian CP leader Enrico Berlinguer, "how the anti-democratic reaction tends to become more violent and ferocious when popular forces begin to conquer the fundamental levers of power in society and the state."[68] Berlinguer's conclusion was that the working class should compromise with capitalism rather than try to conquer power. "Liberalism has always said to the workers that by their class struggle they 'provoke' the reaction," wrote Trotsky. "The reformists repeated this accusation against the Marxists. . . . These accusations reduced themselves, in the final analysis, to the profound thought that if the oppressed . . . balk, the oppressors will not be obliged to beat them."[69]

Marx and Engels were sharply critical of what they called "parliamentary cretinism," the tendency to place all hopes for social change on parliamentary institutions.[70] They ridiculed Social Democrats who, while putting off socialism "as an heirloom for their children," focus attention on "all sorts of trifles, tinkering away at the capitalist social order so that at least something should appear to be done without at the same time alarming the bourgeoisie."[71] Marx and Engels were not opposed to electoral campaigns. For them, elections were good opportunities for revolutionaries to "bring before the public their revolutionary attitude."[72] But they heaped scorn on socialists who saw their task as getting "educated" men elected in order to represent workers' interests from above. "We cannot co-operate," they snapped in an angry circular to German socialist leaders, "with men who say openly that the workers are too uneducated to emancipate themselves, and must first be emancipated from above by philanthropic members of the upper and lower middle classes."[73] The whole process of seeking electoral victory at all costs created a trend among the socialists committed above all else to winning elections to broaden their mass appeal by toning down their politics. Instead of politics being guided by principles, reformism fell into opportunism—what Rosa Luxemburg described as "sacrificing the basic principles of class struggle for momentary advantage."[74]

This has certainly been the experience of socialist parties that have been elected to office throughout history. Instead of challenging capitalism, they have ended up as its apologists, adapting to it rather than transforming it. During the First World War, the leaders of the German Social Democratic Party—along with the leaders of the other main socialist parties in Europe—cast their support for their "own" government's war effort, completely abandoning the principle of working-class internationalism laid down in *The Communist Manifesto*. "For this system, not one man, not one penny," had been the party's slogan.[75] Reformists had degraded Marxism from a movement of revolutionary internationalism into one of national reformism. The German socialist Karl Kautsky offered as an excuse for European socialism's collapse into opportunism that the Socialist International "is essentially an instrument of peace," and therefore ineffective in wartime.[76] "The global historical appeal of the *Communist Manifesto* undergoes a fundamental revision," wrote Luxemburg in 1915, "and, as amended . . . now reads: proletarians of all countries, unite in peace-time and cut each other's throats in war!"[77] There are more recent examples. French socialists François Mitterrand in the 1980s and Lionel Jospin in the 1990s implemented policies that helped to gut France's social safety net—and enabled the French bosses' system to stay profitable.[78]

Mitterrand's election to the presidency in 1981 initially struck fear into French capitalists, who mobilized all their financial clout to put pressure to bear on him. He quickly allayed their fears by embarking on a series of austerity measures that included a wage freeze and a plan for restructuring French industry designed to weaken the unions and, in the words of Daniel Singer, "sacrifice many of their conquests on the altar of flexibility."[79] Mitterrand, like Bill Clinton in the 1990s, was able to push through a series of conservative measures without provoking the same level of working-class resistance that would have resulted had a right-wing government attempted to impose them. Along with this reformism went a new ultra-moderate image. "To say that French socialism had mellowed is an understatement," wrote Singer. "The concepts of class and capitalism, even the very word *socialism*, had disappeared from their vocabulary."[80] For this, capital was eternally grateful. The French stock exchange, the Bourse, rose at twice the rate of the New York Stock Exchange during Mitterrand's presidency. "When Mitterrand was elected," according to Singer, "he was viewed with suspicion. Five years later, when the defeated socialists were leaving the government, the lonely president was being hailed unanimously by the *Economist*, the *Financial Times*, and the *Wall Street Journal* as a wise statesmen, having done yeoman service for the left, for France, and for the Western world."[81]

If the old social democrats shared with Stalinism an identification of socialism with the state, modern socialist parties in Europe have even dropped the pretense of being for any kind of socialism. After the Second World War, European social democratic parties were advocates of a "mixed economy," somewhere between the market and state ownership of the means of production. In the era of neoliberalism, they abandoned a commitment even to state "socialism." Instead, they now argue for a "third way," and have become open supporters of neoliberal austerity policies aimed at cutting the social wage and eroding labor rights.[82] In this way they have cut themselves off more and more from their former working-class supporters.

Reformism would only work if the state were a neutral body, an empty vessel to be filled up by whichever party gets into office. Luxemburg, in her epitaph on the failure of reformism, noted that those who favor legislative reform over social revolution "do not really choose a more tranquil, calmer and slower road to the same goal, but a different goal. Instead of a stand for the establishment of a new society they take a stand for the surface modifications of the old society."[83]

It is important to remember, however, that rejecting reformism is not the same as rejecting *reforms*, and in particular, the fight for reforms. As Lenin argued, "Unlike the anarchists, the Marxists recognize struggle for reforms, i.e., for measures that improve the conditions of the working people without destroying the power of the ruling class." He continued:

> At the same time, however, the Marxists wage a most resolute struggle against the reformists, who, directly or indirectly, restrict the aims and activities of the working class to the winning of reforms. Reformism is bourgeois deception of the workers, who, despite individual improvements, will always remain wage-slaves, as long as there is the domination of capital. . . .
>
> The stronger reformist influence is among the workers the weaker they are, the greater their dependence on the bourgeoisie, and the easier it is for the bourgeoisie

to nullify reforms by various subterfuges. The more independent the working-class movement, the deeper and broader its aims, and the freer it is from reformist narrowness the easier it is for the workers to retain and utilize improvements.[84]

It is precisely through struggles for immediate demands—over wages, working conditions, and for political and social improvements—that workers are able to develop consciousness of their own power, as well as the confidence born of collective action, to move toward revolutionary action. Struggle changes consciousness. That is why the fight for reforms has the potential to go further; because once in struggle, the horizons of workers expand beyond their immediate conditions. The possibility of another world looms more closely on the horizon. But the struggle for reforms cannot be equated with revolution. In a revolution, that is, in a period of mass upheaval and social convulsion, consciousness is transformed on a mass scale. This transformation is both a condition and a result of revolution. As Marx and Engels wrote:

> Both for the production on a mass scale of this communist consciousness, and for the success of the cause itself, the alteration of men on a mass scale is necessary, an alteration which can only take place in a practical movement, a revolution; this revolution is necessary, therefore, not only because the ruling class cannot be overthrown in any other way, but also because the class overthrowing it can only in a revolution succeed in ridding itself of all the muck of ages and become fitted to found society anew.[85]

What Does a Revolution Look Like?

Trotsky described socialist revolution as "the direct interference of the masses in historic events . . . the forcible entrance of the masses into the realm of rulership over their own destiny."[86] The question of revolution always boils down to a contest for power in which a new class imposes a new order on the ruins of the old by deposing the old ruling class. We know that the state often resorts to violence even when the struggle is not revolutionary—witness the way police in the United States come out in full riot gear every time a peaceful antiwar protest is organized. Imagine what they might do if millions of workers attempted to seize control of the factories, hospitals, and schools to run them democratically. Perhaps that's why socialists are often confronted with the question, isn't the state too powerful to challenge?

This seems to be an unsolvable paradox. Piecemeal reforms are incapable of transforming society, and yet revolution will be met with superior force—and defeated. Perhaps the best we can hope for are minor changes that don't threaten the power of bosses. This is wrong on two counts. First of all, the more militant and united the struggle, the greater the chances that even minor reforms will be successful. Second, there are plenty of examples of powerful regimes falling under the weight of mass revolt that before their fall seemed impregnable. No one predicted the fall of the shah of Iran—protected by his dreaded secret police—in 1978. The Western press treated the Eastern European states as impregnable fortresses of Stalinist tyranny before they fell in 1989. Mubarak's thirty-five-year dictatorship in Egypt, which fell in seventeen days, seemed fully entrenched.

The view that the state is all-powerful is based on a misconception of what revolutions are and the conditions that give rise to them. Revolutions succeed not because those who are rebelling have superior arms. If that were a requirement, a revolution could never win. Revolutionary situations arise only when millions of ordinary people become convinced that society can't continue in the old way, and when there are splits and confusion at the top over how to restore order and overcome the crisis. As Lenin wrote,

> To the Marxist it is indisputable that a revolution is impossible without a revolutionary situation; furthermore, it is not every revolutionary situation that leads to revolution. What, generally speaking, are the symptoms of a revolutionary situation? . . . (1) when it is impossible for the ruling classes to maintain their rule without any change; when there is a crisis, in one form or another, among the "upper classes," a crisis in the policy of the ruling class, leading to a fissure through which the discontent and indignation of the oppressed classes burst forth. For a revolution to take place, it is usually insufficient for "the lower classes not to want" to live in the old way; it is also necessary that "the upper classes should be unable" to live in the old way; (2) when the suffering and want of the oppressed classes have grown more acute than usual; (3) when, as a consequence of the above causes, there is a considerable increase in the activity of the masses, who uncomplainingly allow themselves to be robbed in "peace time," but, in turbulent times, are drawn both by all the circumstances of the crisis *and by the "upper classes" themselves* into independent historical action.[87]

For a period, a rising movement can throw the state and the ruling class it represents onto the defensive. Divisions develop at the top over how to restore order—should reforms be granted to mollify the movement, or should repression be used, or both? Reforms are granted. Instead of stopping the movement, placating it, the reforms embolden the movement, which draws into its train all of the oppressed and exploited—women, national minorities, and others.

Sections of the ruling class and the military begin to debate the possibility of restoring order by force, that is, by physically crushing the rising. Reactionary forces begin testing the defenses of the movement, probing for its weakest spots. Society balances on a knife's edge. Will the old order reimpose itself, or will new social forces seize power? This is the essence of all revolutionary situations. Of course, if those leading the movement are able to channel the struggle into reforms that do not fundamentally challenge the status quo, then it is possible that the movement can be defused before it reaches revolutionary proportions. When this happens, as it did after the May 1968 general strike in France, for example, the movement subsides and the old order is able to restore itself without counterrevolutionary violence. But if workers are convinced that they can and must move forward, then the only two choices are: the dispersal of the old state power by the united working class, leading millions behind it, or the suppression of the movement.

A necessary feature of every revolutionary situation is "dual power," the existence of popular forms of power—workers' councils or similar institutions—alongside the old state. But "dual power" cannot last. In all revolutionary situations, either society moves forward to the establishment of a new state based upon workers' councils or some similar form of direct democracy, or backward to the destruction of the workers' organizations and the reestablishment of capitalist order.

A precondition for socialism is the formation of organs of working-class self-organization that can be both the means to organize the struggle and the potential institutions of revolutionary state power. But the working class can only become the new power if it disperses the old power. For that to happen, the working class must not only be organized but also have behind it the majority of the oppressed and whole sections of the middle class. And it must also be armed and ready to defend its control of workplaces and the streets. Force must be the deciding factor in the end because as we've already pointed out, the ruling class will use the utmost force to stay in power.

Trotsky wrote after his experience as president of the main workers' council in Petrograd in the 1905 Russian Revolution:

> In struggle it is extremely important to weaken the enemy. That is what a strike does. At the same time a strike brings the army of the revolution to its feet. But neither the one nor the other, in itself, creates a state revolution. The power still has to be snatched from the old rulers and handed over to the revolution. That is the fundamental task. A general strike only creates the necessary preconditions; it is quite inadequate for achieving the task itself. At a certain moment in revolution the crucial question becomes: on which side are the soldiers—their sympathies and their bayonets?[88]

In mass upheavals, the weakest link of the ruling class is the armed forces. Repression can only work if soldiers are disciplined to carry out their orders. But in circumstances of great social upheaval, this isn't a foregone conclusion—because most soldiers are themselves workers. If this were not true, revolutions could never win.

"The fate of every revolution at a certain point is decided by a break in the disposition of the disposition of the army," writes Trotsky in his history of the 1917 revolution. "Against a numerous, disciplined, well-armed and ably led military force, unarmed or almost unarmed masses of the people cannot possibly gain a victory. But no deep national crisis can fail to affect the army to some extent. Thus along with the conditions of a truly popular revolution there develops a possibility—not, of course, a guarantee—of its victory."[89] A mass movement can fight for the hearts and minds of soldiers, thereby splitting the military and winning soldiers to the side of revolution. But the movement can only succeed if it really convinces the soldiers that it is fighting for power. The "all-powerful" state then becomes temporarily paralyzed because it cannot rely on its own armed forces. But the movement must be strong enough and provide a clear program that convinces the soldiers that the movement can win. Trotsky explains further:

> The more the soldiers in their mass are convinced that the rebels are really re-
> belling—that this is not a demonstration after which they will have to go back to
> the barracks and report, that this is a struggle to the death, that the people may win
> if they join them, and that this winning will not only guarantee impunity, but al-
> leviate the lot of all—the more they realize this, the more willing they are to turn
> aside their bayonets, or go over with them to the people. In other words, the revo-
> lutionaries can create a break in the soldiers' mood only if they themselves are ac-
> tually ready to seize the victory at any price whatever, even the price of blood.[90]

This is what happened in the 1917 revolution in Russia. Trotsky describes how in the midst of mass street demonstrations, even the Cossacks sent to suppress protests winked as workers dived under their horses, and regular soldiers turned their guns on the police when they attacked the crowds.[91] There are countless examples of this throughout the history of class struggle.

During the 1877 great railroad rebellion in the United States, the first mass na-
tional strike wave in US history, many of the local militias refused to attack striking railroad workers. A local Pennsylvania militia was sent out to crush a strike on the Philadelphia and Reading Railroad after workers seized control of company property. The militiamen made it clear that they would report for duty, but "if ordered to fire, they will lay down their arms; that they are workingmen and do not desire to kill other workingmen."[92]

The late Marxist Tony Cliff described a similar process during the 1975 Por-
tuguese Revolution:

> The families living in the shantytown of Bairro da Boavista in the outskirts of Lisbon
> took over a housing estate that had stood empty for three years. . . . An army com-
> pany . . . was deployed to force the families back to the corrugated lean-tos of the
> shantytown. The officer in charge . . . went straight to what he thought was the
> weakest link, an old widow who had just moved with her six sons to a two-bedroom
> flat with electricity. She replied: "You better shoot me right here. All my life I have
> had the earth for a floor. At least I will die on a proper floor." The officer stood
> there for a moment. Outside, the men, women and children who had assembled
> to resist any eviction were speaking to the soldiers: "This could be your shantytown!
> Remember that you, too, are the people! Turn the guns on the speculators and not
> on your brothers and sisters!" The officer understood, and, taking the company
> with him, left the estate.[93]

Chapter Eight

From Marx to Lenin: Marxism and Political Organization

For Marx and Engels, socialism wasn't something that would come automatically, that would just "happen" because all the conditions within capitalism have ripened, like fruit falling from a tree. If it were that simple, capitalism would have fallen long ago. As they wrote very early on in their political development: "History does nothing, it 'possesses no immense wealth,' it 'wages no battles.' It is man, real, living man who does all that, who possesses and fights; 'history' is not, as it were, a person apart, using man as a means to achieve its own aims; history is nothing but the activity of man pursuing his aims."[1]

Capitalism creates the objective material conditions that make socialism possible: the abundance born of its mad drive to accumulate, its tendency toward periodic crises, and the existence of a class with "radical chains" whose own emancipation entails the end of all class domination.[2] Capitalism itself organizes the working class, and the working class is the only oppressed class in history whose collective struggle points to a society without class oppression. For socialism to come about, this class must be organized in such a way as to effect that change.

To change society, new ideas are necessary, but for these ideas to exert any force on society they must be embodied in real people organized to achieve them. "Ideas cannot carry out anything at all," Marx and Engels wrote. "In order to carry out ideas men are needed who can exert a practical force."[3] With the development of modern industry and a modern wage-earning working class, Engels noted, "Communism now no longer meant the concoction, by means of the imagination, of an ideal society as perfect as possible, but insight into the nature, the conditions and the consequent general aims of the struggle waged by the proletariat."[4]

But the working class is both united by the conditions of modern production and divided by competition, and by myriad oppressions within its ranks. These divisions are deliberately fostered by those at the top who benefit from the labor of the many, and are able not only to prevent revolt this way, but by pitting sections of workers and the oppressed against each other, they also can drive down the conditions of all. The "ruling ideas of society" mentioned in *The Communist Manifesto* are precisely directed at those at the bottom whose rebellion might threaten the system.

To say, then, that the working class is a revolutionary class is to describe its *potential*. As Hal Draper notes, "It is a label for a social drive; it is not a description of current events. The revolutionary class begins, like everybody else, by being filled with 'reactionary cravings' and prejudices: otherwise the proletarian revolution would always be around the corner."[5] The question for Marx was this: how do workers move from being a class "in itself"—that is, a class by virtue of its position in the production of society's wealth (those who sell their labor power and upon whose labor profits depend) to becoming a class "for itself"—a class that is conscious of its historical mission to seize control of production and convert it to serve human need, and organize in such a way to achieve its mission?

The contradiction between workers' own experience and the "ruling ideas" opens up the space for workers to change their consciousness—to adapt new ideas contrary to those that reinforce the prevailing order. In the tug of war between what we are told to believe and what we experience in practice—through what we observe, but especially in the struggles that the system forces upon us—some workers (but not all) begin to draw anticapitalist conclusions. Struggle promotes this burgeoning consciousness. Organization makes the struggle more effective, and in turn helps to widen the number of workers who draw the same conclusions. Organization is both a precondition and a result of struggle.

There is no such thing as pure spontaneity. In order to act collectively, the collective (however small or large) must be organized in some way: that is, some individuals or groups must take it upon themselves to initiate action. Once in motion, more permanent and effective forms of organizing suggest themselves to the movement's participants. As the Italian Marxist Antonio Gramsci wrote from a fascist prison, "Every 'spontaneous' movement contains rudimentary elements of conscious leadership" and "of discipline."[6] In most cases, though, those who took the initiative to kick things off don't bother to write down what they did and how they did it.

Only the most individualistic middle-class anarchist would deny the necessity of organization. The owners have their own think tanks, their managers and pundits, as well as their own public and private armies that, when consent fails, are able and ready to intervene to protect their system. Our side must also be organized if we want to change the world. The question is: What kind of organization? That question, however, is meaningless unless we also ask whom we are organizing (what social classes or forces?), and what it is we are organizing *for*. Obviously, a great deal more consciousness and organization is necessary to fight for socialism than to fight for a longer lunch break.

In bourgeois revolutionary movements, the exploited classes were mobilized to achieve the goals of another class or classes. In essence, the masses in these revolutions were used as a battering ram against the old order. In playing this role, they did not need to be fully conscious of their aims and goals. Indeed, a certain degree of deliberate deception on the part of the revolution's leaders was necessary to win mass support, by presenting the revolution ultimately benefitting a new set of exploiters as one that was in the interest of all the oppressed and downtrodden.

The transition to capitalism, moreover, from feudal society was aided by the fact that capitalist economic relations grew up within the womb of feudalism, and the capitalists built up their economic and financial power before they won political power. "The bourgeois could use this position of strength," writes Draper, "as a fortress from which to press further toward the acquisition of decisive political power."[7] In many instances the strong economic position of the bourgeoisie allowed it to achieve political power by the gradual transformation of the state (which could be described as a revolution "from above").

The working class cannot achieve power this way. By definition, it is a property-less class that must sell its labor power piecemeal to survive. It cannot build up its economic power within the womb of capitalism and use that economic leverage to get political power. For the working class, the situation is reversed compared to that of the bourgeoisie. Only by winning political power can it implement its own program of economic and social transformation of society. Of course, it can use its collective power to bring production to a halt: but without winning political power it cannot proceed to reorganize production to suit human need.

To achieve this, it must not only be organized economically but also *politically*. To be a leading class—a class capable of leading other exploited and oppressed people in society and positioning itself as a class around whose emancipation a new society could be constructed—it needs to do more than fight for its interests in the workplace or for economic reforms; it must take up the fight against all forms of social and political tyranny and oppression, thereby drawing around itself all sectors of society oppressed by capitalism. Marx began to develop this idea quite early on. He wrote, for example, in 1843, that no class is able to play a leading revolutionary role "without arousing a moment of enthusiasm in itself and in the masses, a moment in which it fraternizes and merges with society in general, becomes confused with it and is perceived and acknowledged as its *general representative*."[8] Unions, for example, cannot fulfill this function, because they limit themselves to fighting the effects of capitalism rather than capitalism itself. For the working class to organize itself *as a class* against capitalists as a class, something more is needed—an organization aimed at combining the economic and political struggle of the working class—a political party.

The Communist Manifesto mentions only briefly how the "organization of the proletarians into a class, and, consequently into a political party, is continually being upset again by the competition between the workers themselves. But it ever rises up again, stronger, firmer, mightier."[9] At the 1871 London conference of the International Workingmen's Association, Marx and Engels drafted the following resolution that gave their idea greater shape:

> [A]gainst this collective power of the propertied classes the working class cannot act, as a class, except by constituting itself into a political party, distinct from, and opposed to, all old parties formed by the propertied classes;
>
> . . . [T]his constitution of the working class into a political party is indispensable in order to ensure the triumph of the social revolution and its ultimate end— the abolition of classes;
>
> . . . [T]he combination of forces which the working class has already effected by its economical struggles ought at the same time to serve as a lever for its struggles against the political power of landlords and capitalists.[10]

Without its own political party—one that combines both the economic and political struggles—the working class would be taken in tow by other classes and their own aims subordinated to the interests of other classes.

That is why Marx and Engels were quite critical of the Bakuninists, for example, for urging the working class to abstain from politics. "Whether for political or social goals," government oppression would "force the workers to concern themselves with politics, whether they like it or not," wrote Engels. If the workers are robbed of free speech, a free press, and the right of assembly, is the working class simply to sit back and do nothing in the name of political abstention? Preaching abstention merely makes it easier, Engels argued, for bourgeois parties to capture the allegiance of the working class. How is it possible for them not to engage in politics when the only means by which workers can abolish class society is through their own "political domination"? Therefore: "Especially in the aftermath of the Paris Commune, which placed the political action of the proletariat on the agenda, abstention is quite impossible." He continued: "Revolution is the supreme act of politics; whoever wants it must also want the means, political action, which prepares for it, which gives the workers the education for revolution. . . . But the politics which are needed are working class politics; the workers' party must be constituted not as the tail of some bourgeois party, but as an independent party with its own objectives, its own politics."[11]

This conception of a political party for the working class, as can be seen here, was not limited to parliamentary activity. Marx and Engels thought that elections were an effective means to reach a large number of people who otherwise could not be reached by socialist propaganda, and socialist deputies could help to organize and broaden the struggle outside the walls of parliament or congress. However, as Engels was later to argue, universal suffrage cannot be "anything more" than "the gauge of the maturity of the working class."[12]

For Marx and Engels, the question of politics was primarily one of class power—replacing the class rule of the bourgeoisie with the democratic class rule of workers. As Engels wrote in a letter in 1889: "We are agreed on this: that the proletariat cannot conquer political power, the only door to the new society, without violent revolution. For the proletariat to be strong enough to win on the decisive day it must—and Marx and I have advocated this ever since 1847—form a separate party distinct from all others and opposed to them, a conscious class party."[13]

What type of organization did this imply? Marx and Engels laid out their *general* approach in *The Communist Manifesto*. The communists, they argued, were "*the most advanced and resolute section of the working-class parties of every country*, that section which pushes forward all others; on the other hand, theoretically, they have over the great mass of the proletariat the advantage of clearly understanding the lines of march, the conditions, and the ultimate general results of the proletarian movement."[14] [my emphasis]

This section of the class, however, to exert influence over others and to win over the rest of the class, must engage in day-to-day struggle and find a way to connect struggles for immediate demands with the final aim. Hence, the *Manifesto* argues, "The Communists fight for the attainment of the immediate aims, for the enforcement of the momentary interests of the working class; but in the movement of the present, they also represent and take care of the future of that movement."

The job of Communists isn't only to involve themselves in workers' struggles, moreover, but to "support every revolutionary movement against the existing social and political order of things," including struggles for Irish and Polish independence, against feudalism, for women's equality, and so on. But in actively supporting every manifestation of struggle, "they never cease, for a single instant, to instill into the working class the clearest possible recognition of the hostile antagonism between bourgeoisie and proletariat." No matter what the state of development of the workers' movement, and in all types of movements, "they bring to the front, as the leading question in each, the property question," that is, the question of the transformation of capitalist property relations by the common action of the working class.[15]

In the early stages of the development of mass workers' movements in various countries, Marx and Engels favored the development of broad workers' parties, no matter their state of development or clarity of their politics. It was on these grounds that Marx stated, "*Every step of real movement is more important than a dozen programs.*"[16] Engels, for example, criticized the German socialist émigrés in the United States who valued programmatic purity over participation in the real unfolding workers' movement—in particular the Knights of Labor. The movement, he argued, "ought not to be pooh-poohed from without but to be revolutionized from within."[17] This did not mean, Engels argued, dissolving into the movement. "I think all our practice has shown that it is possible to work along with the general movement of the working class at every one of its stages without giving up or hiding our own distinct position and even organization."[18]

The alternative was sectarianism—staying "pure" (and therefore sterile and irrelevant) by standing outside the real movement. "The sect," Marx wrote, "sees the justification for its existence and its 'point of honor'—not in what it has in *common* with the class movement but in the *particular shibboleth* which *distinguishes* it from it."[19] But once such workers' parties had been formed, for example in Germany, Marx and Engels placed much more emphasis on the importance of theoretical and political clarification, debates, and splits, if necessary, to ensure the revolutionary and proletarian character of the party—that is, to "revolutionize it from within." They were highly critical of those unity criers in the movement "who want to stir everything up together into one nondescript brew." In an 1874 letter to German socialist leader August Bebel, Engels explained: "A party proves itself a victorious party by the fact that it splits and can stand the split. The movement of the proletariat necessarily passes through different stages of development; at every stage one section of people lags behind and does not join in the further advance; and this alone explains why it is that actually the 'solidarity of the proletariat' is everywhere realized in different party groupings which carry on life and death feuds with one another."[20]

Marx and Engels were not organizational fetishists; in fact, their view on organization changed with the circumstances, and they believed that different situations required different methods of organizing. But there are some general conclusions that can be gleaned from their writings.

Wherever possible (conditioned by the degree of state repression), they opposed secret, conspiratorial, top-down organizations and favored open, democratic organizations. They opposed sectarianism (pooh-poohing movements from without). They always and everywhere emphasized the political *independence* of the working class. They emphasized mass struggle as opposed to the actions of small groups substituting themselves for the working class. And finally, they opposed hero worship, or any idea that workers must be led by members of the "educated" classes or by a self-selected elite.

For example, one of the first things they did when they joined the League of the Just in Germany in 1847 was to convince their fellow members to move away from its hitherto highly secretive and conspiratorial character and to adopt democratic forms of organization and leadership. Marx later said that he and Engels joined the organization "only on conditions that anything conducive to a superstitious belief in authority be eliminated from the rules."[21]

The Social-Democratic Detour

Marx and Engels, especially Engels, lived to see the formation of the first mass socialist workers' party in Germany. However, as much as they came to consider the newly formed Socialist Workers Party of Germany their party (which became the Social Democratic Party, or SPD, in 1891), Marx and Engels were critical of what they considered its political shortcomings and always fought any attempt to dilute its working-class character.

Engels lived long enough to witness the growing electoral success of the German party—in 1884, the year after Marx's death, the SPD got more than a half a million votes, and before Engels's death in 1895 it won two million votes. Though impressed by this success, Engels was also alarmed by the growing opportunism brought about by that success. The more or less smooth growth of its electoral support from year to year, the expansion of the German economy, along with the slow and steady growth of trade union membership—at a time when the class struggle remained at a relatively low ebb—tended to reinforce opportunist tendencies inside the party, particularly among the upper strata of party members who were trade union leaders, parliamentary representatives, and party administrators. This had two effects. One was to encourage the practice of watering down the party's political message for the sake of popularity in electoral campaigns. The second was to reinforce support for peaceful gradualism in the party's leaders, who saw in "precipitate" action the possibility of state repression that might jeopardize the organization they had so painstakingly built. "The interest of the proletariat today more than ever before demands that everything should be avoided," warned Karl Kautsky, the party's theoretical leader in 1893, "that would tend to provoke the ruling class to a purposeless policy of violence."[22] When the time came, this approach, justifiable at first given the party's successes, would become an argument against strikes, mass protests, and ultimately, against insurrections.

The SPD had a "maximum program" and a "minimum program." The maximum program set forth the final goals of the movement—the conquest of state power and the socialist transformation of society; the minimum program elucidated the immediate goals of the movement, including reforms such as the eight-hour workday, freedom of assembly, and progressive taxation. But increasingly the maximum program was something proclaimed in May Day speeches, while the practical work of the party focused solely on the minimum program—various social reforms compatible with the existence of capitalism.

The discovery that Marx and Engels made from the experience of the Paris Commune, that the working class cannot simply "lay hold of the ready-made state machinery and wield it for its own purposes," was gradually replaced in the social-democratic movement by the idea that socialism could be achieved by winning a majority in parliamentary institutions. In 1912, when the SPD had achieved a million members, received four million votes, and had won 110 seats in the German Reichstag (twenty-four seats in 1884), Kautsky wrote: "The objective of our political struggle remains . . . the conquest of state power through the conquest of a majority in parliament and the elevation of parliament to a commanding position within the state. Certainly not the destruction of state power."[23]

It should be noted that prior to the Russian Revolution and the publication of Lenin's *State and Revolution* in 1918 (written in 1917), which revived Marx's and Engels's writings on the state, almost all European revolutionary Marxists—though they rejected the idea of a parliamentary road to socialism—held a conception of the state and state power that departed from Marx and Engels. Even for Lenin, Luxemburg, and Trotsky, the role of revolution was to seize state control, not destroy the bourgeois state machine and replace it with a new "commune"-type state.

The SPD's conception of the political party followed from this: it should embrace not the "most advanced and resolute section" of the working class, but all of the organized sections of the class. In the social-democratic conception, the party and the working class are, or should be, identical. "The ideal organization," Kautsky wrote in 1909, "is the unification of all proletarian parties, the political societies, the trade unions, the co-operatives, as equal members . . . of a class-conscious, all-embracing Social-Democracy."[24] This model of an all-embracing party that united all tendencies within the working class movement became the model for all the Socialist parties of the Socialist International. Indeed, in direct response to the factional divisions in the Russian Socialist movement—whose revolutionary wing (Bolsheviks) and moderate wing (Mensheviks) had divided in 1912 into two separate and competing parties—Kautsky signed an open letter quoting the 1913 Amsterdam resolution of the Second International, which stated that "it is necessary that in every country there exist only *one* Socialist party, as there exists only *one* proletariat."[25]

The SPD was as a result a very heterogeneous organization. It had its reformists like Eduard Bernstein, who remarked at the 1907 Stuttgart congress, "Socialists too should acknowledge the need for civilized peoples to act somewhat like guardians of the uncivilized."[26] But it also had its revolutionaries like Rosa Luxemburg, who pushed for mass strikes and was a principled opponent of imperialism. In between, it had self-proclaimed "centrists" like Kautsky who tried to hold all the pieces together by straddling.

The SPD's structures, in fact, institutionalized a situation where the party leadership could use the least radical members of the party to outvote the most class-conscious workers. Its conferences gave much more weight to small-town delegates than the more radical delegates from Germany's large industrial centers. At the SPD's 1911 national congress, smaller party units in less populated areas were given one delegate per fifty-seven members, whereas in the big industrial centers the ratio was one delegate per fifty-seven hundred members.[27]

The SPD did not openly proclaim its departure from revolution and internationalism. The international congress of the Second International, the gathering of all the mass Socialists parties, on more than one occasion defeated the right wing on paper, passing resolutions such as one put forward by Lenin and Luxemburg, that in the event of the outbreak of world war, it was the duty of Socialists everywhere to use all means to oppose the outbreak, and once war came, to utilize the crisis brought about by the war to hasten the downfall of capitalism.[28]

The left wing of the German party formally defeated Bernstein's ethical and gradualist version of Socialism in 1899, but he remained a member of the party—as did many like him. The SPD may have formally rejected Bernstein's gradualist views, but in practice it did not.

Leftists inside the party like Rosa Luxemburg sharply attacked the growing conservatism of the SPD. In 1907, after her return to Germany from Russia and having experienced the tumultuous mass strikes and protests of the 1905 Revolution, she lamented in a letter to German revolutionary Clara Zetkin the "irresolution and the pettiness" of the SPD leaders. "Whenever anything happens which transcends the limits of parliamentarism," they "try their best to force everything back into the parliamentary mold, and they will furiously attack as an 'enemy of the people' anyone who wants to go beyond these limits." She described the party's "upper stratum" of editors, trade union leaders, and party officials as a "dead weight."[29]

Despite this trenchant critique, Luxemburg never insisted on expelling the right wing, nor did she (at least before 1914) try to organize her own left faction as a counterweight to the reformists inside the SPD until after the outbreak of the First World War. While there were important local groupings of the left wing, there was no identifiable, coherent national left-wing faction in the party. Luxemburg fully accepted that the party should encompass all political tendencies in the working-class movement. In a 1906 party debate, for example, she attacked the right wing for wanting to expel anarcho-syndicalists from the party by saying: "At least remain faithful to our old principle: nobody is evicted from the party for his views. Since we have never kicked out anyone on the far right, we do not now have the right to evict the far left."[30]

Luxemburg held the same position toward the Russian Socialist movement. After attending a joint congress of Bolsheviks and Mensheviks in 1907, she wrote in a letter to Clara Zetkin that the Mensheviks leaders at the conference were "the most pathetic things the Russian revolution has to offer," and praised the Bolsheviks for "having a sense of principled politics."[31] Yet right up to the outbreak of world war she persisted in supporting official efforts by the International to unite the two wings of the Russian Socialist movement in a single party.

Luxemburg's chief motivation for not splitting away from the SPD was her desire to maintain contact with the German working-class movement, which she could not conceive of doing outside the party. "A split among Marxists—which is not to be confused with differences of opinion—is fatal," she wrote to her Dutch comrade Henrietta Roland-Holst in 1908. "Your resignation from the SDAP [Holland's social-democratic party] would mean simply that you are leaving the social-democratic movement. . . . The worst of workers' parties is better than nothing!"[32]

As her alarm over the entrenched opportunism in the party's leading bodies grew, she believed that the only possible means to overcome the party's conservatism was through the "maximum development of mass action . . . which brings into play the broadest masses of the proletariat." She wrote, "Only in this way can the clinging mists of parliamentary cretinism . . . be got rid of."[33] If Kautsky's view of the incremental and inevitable, slow and steady parliamentary progress of Socialism was fatalist, Rosa Luxemburg's idea that mass struggle would by itself force the party into revolutionary channels was also fatalist. There were for her no organizational means to combat the party's drift toward reformism.[34]

It was not until the war and the capitulation of the SPD to its "own" government's war aims (the SPD parliamentary deputies voted for the German government to issue war credits, or bonds), that she and others began to see the necessity of solidifying the left wing; it became obvious what the problems were with an organization that embraces all "Socialists," regardless of where they stood on such key questions as imperialist war, revolution, colonialism, the role of mass strikes, and parliamentarianism. The revolutionaries who remained inside these parties became prisoners of organizations that backed their own governments' war machine.

When put to the test of major events, the social-democratic parties could not stand. The right wing acted as firemen to put out revolutionary sparks in the name of gradualism; the "centrists" vacillated between the right and the left. The left wing was compelled to split away in order to uphold the revolutionary and internationalist principles of Marxism. These profound differences became most clear when revolution broke out in Germany.

When in November 1918 mass protests and strikes brought down the Kaiser, SPD leaders Ebert and Noske collaborated with the German military high command to head off further radicalization by agreeing to a democratic republic. As head of the new republic, Noske used right-wing paramilitary units to crush a mass workers' uprising in Berlin in January 1919 and kill members of the German Communist Party, which had only formed *ten days* before the uprising. Part leaders Rosa Luxemburg and Karl Liebknecht were murdered, along with several hundred others.

More than mass action was necessary for revolution to succeed in Germany; what was needed was a sizable, organized nucleus of revolutionaries, rooted in various workplaces and localities, active in the day-to-day struggle, possessed of a degree of experience, sharing the confidence of their fellow workers, and capable of both learning from and exerting a concerted influence on the broader movement.

Such a party, however, did not exist, and could not be created overnight. Less than a month before Germany's November 1918 revolution, Lenin could write, "Europe's greatest misfortune and danger is that it has no revolutionary party."[35] When the German Left finally declared itself a party, it only had only a few thousand members—largely hot-headed youth—yet to secure solid contacts among the best-organized workers, sailors, and soldiers with whom to navigate in the revolutionary storms unfolding around them.

The Russian Experience

In 1916, Lenin wrote a commentary on a German antiwar tract called *The Junius Pamphlet*, written by Rosa Luxemburg under a pseudonym. At the end of his analysis, Lenin observed: "Junius' pamphlet conjures up in our mind the picture of a lone man who has no comrades in an illegal organization accustomed to thinking out revolutionary slogans to their conclusion and systematically educating the masses in their spirit."[36]

This assessment sums up the sharp difference between the experience of revolutionaries in Germany and in Russia. In Russia, Lenin and other revolutionaries maintained their own factional organization (the Bolsheviks) from 1903 on, with its own newspaper, committees, and so on, independently of the moderate or reformist Socialists (Mensheviks), which finally formally split from the latter in 1912. As a result, they were "accustomed to thinking out revolutionary slogans to their conclusion and systematically educating the masses in their spirit."

In his 1920 pamphlet, "*Left-Wing" Communism: An Infantile Disorder*, written in an effort to educate Western Marxists on how the Bolsheviks were able to play a successful role leading the working class of Russia to power, Lenin remarked on the concentrated, rich, and varied history of the workers' movement and of Marxism in Russia. Bolshevism "went through fifteen years of practical history (1903–17) unequalled anywhere in the world in its wealth of experience." He went further:

> During those fifteen years, no other country knew anything even approximating to that revolutionary experience, that rapid and varied succession of different forms of the movement—legal and illegal, peaceful and stormy, underground and open, local circles and mass movements, and parliamentary and terrorist forms. In no other country has there been concentrated, in so brief a period, such a wealth of forms, shades, and methods of struggle of all classes of modern society, a struggle which, owing to the backwardness of the country and the severity of the tsarist yoke, matured with exceptional rapidity, and assimilated most eagerly and successfully the appropriate "last word" of American and European political experience.[37]

Lenin the Elitist?

The widespread, almost completely unchallenged, view of Lenin, no matter what part of the political spectrum expresses it, is that he was a power-hungry elitist. His unique contribution to, or for some, departure from, Marxism, lay in his conception of the "vanguard" revolutionary party as consisting of a small, top-down, tightly centralist, and highly conspiratorial party of professional revolutionaries.[38] Such a party was necessary supposedly because Lenin "lost faith" in the working class. Western historians have created an echo chamber in which a few Lenin quotes, torn out of context, have become proof of all these theories. The truth is quite different.

In fact, the whole Russian Socialist movement was forced by illegal conditions to operate clandestinely. This prevented, for example, open elections, which require publicity. And whenever more open conditions permitted, the movement was uniformly in favor of more democratic and open forms of operation. "Any attempt to practice 'the broad democratic principle' will simply facilitate the work of the police in carrying out large-scale raids," Lenin noted in his famous work, *What Is to Be Done?* In contrast, when the outbreak of mass protests and strikes in 1905 opened up a larger space for free assembly and organization, Lenin called for "the full application of the democratic principle in Party organization."[39]

Lenin's emphasis on centralism was in the first instance part of an effort to create a single party uniting all the disparate local committees that were operating separately, without any central publications or central leadership. In the context of the time, his emphasis on creating a core of revolutionaries engaged full time in the difficult work of organizing (whether these "professional revolutionaries" came from the working class or the intelligentsia) in conditions of harsh police repression was entirely necessary and practical.

With the outbreak of the 1905 revolution he changed gears and emphasized the necessity of drawing in masses of young, radicalizing workers into the ranks of the party as quickly as possible and moving as many workers as possible into leadership roles in the party committees. He hammered away against the party "committeemen"—its dedicated professional revolutionaries, who were resistant to "diluting" the party's ranks with inexperienced recruits—in a letter to two party leaders inside Russia. "All we have to do," he urged, "is to recruit young people more widely and boldly, more boldly and widely, and again more widely and again more boldly, *without fearing them*. . . . Either you create *new*, young, fresh, energetic battle organizations everywhere for revolutionary Social-Democratic work of all varieties among all strata, or you will go under, wearing the aureole of 'committee' bureaucrats."[40]

Lenin's argument in favor of "democratic centralism" (a term he did not coin, by the way)—not to be confused with the bureaucratic centralism of Stalinism that came later—was that a party must be able to act as one after it has had the opportunity to fully debate a question. He wrote in 1906, for example, "The principle of democratic centralism and autonomy for local Party organizations implies universal and full *freedom to criticize*, so long as this does not disturb the unity of *a definite action*; it rules out *all* criticism which disrupts or makes difficult the *unity* of an action decided on by the Party."[41]

As for the question of democracy more broadly within society, Lenin was uncompromisingly in favor of fighting for the fullest, freest democracy, and for the complete fulfillment of all democratic rights. His argument, one formulated in the early years of the Russian Socialist movement by Plekhanov when Lenin was still a child, was that the Russian working class must be the spearhead of this all-round democratic struggle against tsarist oppression. He wrote, for example, in 1915:

> The proletariat cannot be victorious except through democracy, i.e., by giving full effect to democracy and by linking with each step of its struggle democratic demands formulated in the most resolute terms. . . . We must *combine* the revolutionary struggle against capitalism with a revolutionary program and tactics on all democratic demands: a republic, a militia, the popular election of officials, equal rights for women, the self-determination of nations, etc. While capitalism exists, these demands—all of them—can only be accomplished as an exception, and even then in an incomplete and distorted form. Basing ourselves on the democracy already achieved, and exposing its incompleteness under capitalism, we demand the overthrow of capitalism, the expropriation of the bourgeoisie, as a necessary basis both for the abolition of the poverty of the masses and for the *complete* and *all-round* institution of *all* democratic reforms. Some of these reforms will be started before the overthrow of the bourgeoisie, others *in the course* of that overthrow, and still others after it. The social revolution is not a single battle, but a period covering a series of battles over all sorts of problems of economic and democratic reform, which are consummated only by the expropriation of the bourgeoisie. It is for the sake of this final aim that we must formulate *every one* of our democratic demands in a consistently revolutionary way.[42]

What about Lenin's alleged loss of faith in the capacity of workers to become Socialists? If anything, Lenin's whole being was infused with a firm belief in the capacity of ordinary workers to change society. He wrote, for example, in 1900:

> Not a single class in history has achieved power without producing its political leaders, its prominent representatives able to organize a movement and lead it. And the Russian working class has already shown that it can produce such men and women. The struggle which has developed so widely during the past five or six years has revealed the great potential revolutionary power of the working class; it has shown that the most ruthless government persecution does not diminish, but, on the contrary, increases the number of workers who strive towards Socialism, towards political consciousness, and towards the political struggle.[43]

There were important factors that contributed to the differences between the Socialist movement in Western Europe and in Russia. The conditions of tsarist repression meant that no Socialist in Russia could have illusions in parliaments or trade unions, for the simple fact that neither of these institutions existed to any significant extent. Trade unions were illegal and the Duma, Russia's legislative assembly formed after the 1905 revolution, was an entirely toothless body with a highly restricted electorate. Though revolutionaries in Russia looked to the German SPD as their guiding model, tsarist repression *compelled* them to organize clandestinely; even then, the average period of active political life for a revolutionary committee before being arrested could be counted in months. An open, public, mass working-class party simply could not exist.

If in the West the Socialist movement tended to separate trade union and political (electoral) work, in Russia conditions impelled Socialists to take an active and direct interest in workers' struggles and to link their economic struggle with political demands against the autocracy. "I did not fully appreciate how efficacious this method was," wrote the underground activist and Lenin's wife, Krupskaya, discussing the Russian Socialists' agitation among factory workers in the late 1890s, "until years later, when, living in France as a political emigrant, I observed how, during the great strike of the postal workers in Paris, the French Socialist Party stood completely aloof from it. It was the business of the trade unions, they said. In their opinion, the business of a party was only political struggle. They had no clear idea whatever about the necessity of combining the economic and the political struggle."[44]

The Russian revolutionaries considered their methods of operation to be adaptations to the peculiarities of building a socialist movement under conditions of a repressive autocratic state, holding their ideal model to be the German SPD. Lenin "let slip no occasion to pay homage to German Social Democracy," writes historian Pierre Broué, "the model of that 'revolutionary social democracy' which he wished to construct in Russia, in opposition to those he regarded as opportunists, whom he wished to exclude from the Party only because they denied the necessity for its existence and wished to 'liquidate' it."[45]

From its inception, the Marxist movement in Russia was founded on the idea that, though workers were yet a minority of Russian society, they were the only class capable of leading a consistent revolutionary struggle against the autocracy, since the peasantry was too scattered and the capitalists feared workers' revolt more than they hated tsarist restrictions. This guided all of Lenin's practice. What was fundamentally different in Lenin's approach compared to other revolutionaries of his day is that he paid much closer attention to organizational questions.

Despite Lenin's strong identification with Kautsky and German social democracy, there *was* something different about Lenin compared to his European Socialist contemporaries. What was unique was the way in which Lenin explored the organizational implications of political questions. "Lenin," writes historian Moira Donald, "succeeded in elevating the question of party organization to the plane of Marxist theory in a way which was not understood by Kautsky or by other contemporary theoreticians."[46]

We find in Lenin a desire not only to uphold *politically* the central ideas of Russian Marxism against its critics—something that Rosa Luxemburg also did against the moderates in the SPD. We also find in Lenin a desire to create at each moment the best organizational forms to move the struggle forward, and to organizationally demarcate the movement from trends that pulled the movement away from its goals.

For example, in 1899 there emerged in the Russian Socialist movement a new trend, heralded by a document called "the credo," that argued that Socialists should follow the "line of least resistance" and confine their activity to assisting workers' economic struggles. The credo associated itself with Eduard Bernstein's revisionist trend in Germany. It chastised "intolerant Marxism," and argued that in its place must come a social-democratic organization that "will recognize society" and transform "its striving to seize power" into a "striving to reform present-day society."[47]

Lenin denounced this new "retrograde" trend as "an attempt to . . . convert the revolutionary workers' party into a reformist party."[48] If the economists had their way, workers would become an appendage of the liberals, rather than the leaders of the movement against absolutism. "The motto of Social-Democracy must be: aid to the workers, not only in their economic, but also in their political struggle; agitation, not only in connection with immediate economic needs, but also in connection with all manifestations of political oppression; propaganda, not only of the ideas of scientific Socialism, but also of democratic ideas."[49]

But Lenin was not content to condemn this reformist trend, which emerged at a time when the movement consisted of scattered, isolated committees and no nationally organized party. He, along with other young revolutionaries, made a compact with the older veteran Marxists Georgi Plekhanov, Pavel Axelrod, and Vera Zasulich to produce the newspaper *Iskra* and the journal *Zarya* in an effort to decisively defeat economism and win a majority of the Russian Socialist movement to create a united national party.

The aim was to unite the movement, but on the basis of firm principles, sorted out by rigorous debate, not simply the effecting of a formal unity. "Before we can unite," wrote Lenin in an article announcing the publication of *Iskra*, "and in order that we may unite, we must first of all draw firm and definite lines of demarcation. Otherwise, our unity will be purely fictitious, it will conceal the prevailing confusion."[50]

Lenin's Emphasis on the Organizational Question

The Russian Marxist movement's first serious attempt, in 1903, to create a unified national political party along the lines of the Social Democratic parties in Europe produced a more or less permanent split into two main factions, "Bolsheviks" (majority) and "Mensheviks" (minority)—which more often than not operated as independent organizations. The result was that in Russia, unlike in Western Europe, what were in effect the reformist and revolutionary wings of the Socialist movement, though nominally in the same party until 1912 when the split became permanent, operated with their own committees, newspapers, electoral candidates, programs, strategies, and tactics. It was not until after the outbreak of the world war, and even more so the success of the 1917 Revolution, that it became clear that the experience of the Bolsheviks in this regard had international significance.

The issues that brought about the split seemed quite small. One of them was a disagreement about membership. Arguing against Lenin's definition of a party member, Pavel Axelrod (a founder of the Russian Socialist movement) wanted to include in the ranks of the party "people who consciously, though perhaps not very actively, associate themselves with that party."[51] Julius Martov followed with the remark that, "The more widespread the title of party member the better. We could only rejoice if every striker, every demonstrator . . . could proclaim himself a party member."[52]

Lenin wanted to distinguish "those who chatter from those who do the work."[53] To Axelrod's complaint that Lenin's concept of membership would "throw overboard" people who should be considered party members, Lenin responded:

> Are we to build the Party on the basis of that already formed and welded core of *Social-Democrats* which brought about the Party Congress, for instance, and which should enlarge and multiply Party organizations of all kinds; or are we to content ourselves with the soothing *phrase* that all who help *are* Party members? . . . What is the meaning of the phrase "throwing over board," which at first glance seems so terrible? [T]here can be no talk of throwing anyone overboard in the sense of preventing them from working, from taking part in the movement. On the contrary, the stronger our Party organizations, consisting of real social democrats, the less wavering and instability there is within the party, the broader, more varied, richer and more fruitful will be the party's influence on the elements of the working-class masses surrounding it and guided by it. The party, as the vanguard of the working class, must not be confused, after all, with the entire class.[54]

Lenin's conception of the workers' party already departed from Kautsky's in practice. German social democracy in fact identified the party with the class, or at least the organized parts of the class. Lenin returns to Marx's formulation, that the party must be the working class's most "advanced and resolute section."

Because there are "differences in degree of consciousness and degree of activity," Lenin insisted, "a distinction must be made in degree of proximity to the party."[55] We can only accept someone as a party member, argued Lenin, when the title corresponds to fact—that is, if that person is genuinely class-conscious and is ready to work. "We should be indulging in complacent daydreaming if we tried to assure ourselves and others that every striker can be a social democrat and a member of the Social-Democratic Party, in face of that infinite disunity, oppression, and stultification which under capitalism is bound to weigh down upon such very wide sections of the 'untrained,' unskilled workers," Lenin wrote.[56]

The revolutionary party embraces, not the entire class—whose consciousness is mixed and divided as a result of the "infinite disunity, oppression and stultification" that weighs down upon it—but its most conscious and active minority that seeks to raise the consciousness and combativeness of the class as a whole. But this "vanguard" is constantly in flux. In a period of reaction, where the level of class struggle is low and the prospects for revolution seem remote, fewer workers are prepared to embrace socialist ideas. But in a period of radicalization and heightened class struggle, when revolutionary possibilities seem more immediate, a larger number of workers will begin to draw radical conclusions. Under these circumstances, a workers' party can become a mass organization.

It should be clear by now that Lenin's conception of a "vanguard," so maligned on the left today, was not elitist. As the late British Marxist Duncan Hallas noted, "The essence of elitism is the assertion that the observable differences in abilities, consciousness and experience are rooted in unalterable genetic or social conditions and that the mass of the people are incapable of self-government now or in the future. Rejection of the elitist position implies that the observed differences are wholly or partly attributable to causes that can be changed. It does not mean denial of the differences themselves."[57]

And in fact it was these "observable differences in abilities, consciousness and experience" that in Lenin's view the party should strive to overcome, by raising the consciousness of the class as a whole, by organizing and fighting alongside workers in struggle. "Vanguard," in its use by Lenin and others, merely meant that part of the class that was the best organized and most politically conscious, not something standing apart and opposed to the working class. As such, it was something that had to be actively coalesced and tested in practice, not declared. "It is not enough to call ourselves the 'vanguard,' the advanced contingent." Lenin wrote in *What Is to Be Done?* "We must act in such a way that all the other contingents recognize and are obliged to admit that we are marching in the vanguard. And we ask the reader: Are the representatives of the other 'contingents' such fools as to take our word for it when we say that we are the 'vanguard'?"[58]

Lenin emphasized the way in which during revolutionary periods the revolutionary energy of the working classes and oppressed becomes hundreds of times higher than in periods of "hum-drum" existence; and, resulting from this struggle, their class consciousness grows in great leaps, sometimes in a matter of weeks or even days. A week after "Bloody Sunday," the massacre of a workers' procession to the tsar's palace in 1905 that kicked off an abortive revolution, he wrote from exile:

> In the history of revolutions there come to light contradictions that have ripened for decades and centuries. Life becomes unusually eventful. The masses, which have always stood in the shade and have therefore often been ignored and even despised by superficial observers, enter the political arena as active combatants. These masses are learning in practice, and before the eyes of the world are taking their first tentative steps, feeling their way, defining their objectives, testing themselves and the theories of all their ideologists. These masses are making heroic efforts to rise to the occasion and cope with the gigantic tasks of world significance imposed upon them by history; and however great individual defeats may be, however shattering to us the rivers of blood and the thousands of victims, nothing will ever compare in importance with this direct training that the masses and the classes receive in the course of the revolutionary struggle itself.[59]

This profound faith in the creative capacity of oppressed peoples once moved into action wasn't, for Lenin, a passive admiration. Revolutionary periods were schools of training not only for the masses; they also demanded more from revolutionaries:

> Revolutions are the locomotives of history, said Marx. Revolutions are the festivals of the oppressed and the exploited. At no other time are the masses of the people in a position to come forward so actively as creators of a new social order as at a time of revolution. At such times the people are capable of performing miracles, if judged by the narrow, philistine scale of gradual progress. But the leaders of the revolutionary parties must also make their aims more comprehensive and bold at such a time, so that their slogans shall always be in advance of the revolutionary initiative of the masses, serve as a beacon, reveal to them our democratic and Socialist ideal in all its magnitude and splendor and show them the shortest and most direct route to complete, absolute and decisive victory. . . . We shall be traitors to and betrayers of the revolution if we do not use this festive energy of the masses and their revolutionary ardor to wage a ruthless and self-sacrificing struggle for the direct and decisive path.[60]

Revolutions put theory to the test of events. Perhaps more than any other Marxist, Lenin was concerned with the relationship between theory and practice. He took time to study the nature of Russian capitalism, the relations between classes, the nature of imperialism, and so on. And he was not in the least dogmatic. For him, theory was a guide to action. If events in the world presented him with evidence that the theory was incomplete or incorrect, he was not at all averse to reexamining the theory. "There is no better critic of an erroneous doctrine," he wrote during 1905, "than the course of revolutionary events."[61]

Moreover, even with a correct theory, there always had to be a *translation* of the theory into the practical question of what had to be done next in any given moment.

"A line of conduct can *and should* be grounded in theory, in historical references, in an analysis of the entire political situation," he wrote. "But in all these discussions the party of a class engaged in a struggle should never lose sight of the need for absolutely clear answers—which *do not permit of a double interpretation*—to concrete questions of our political conduct: "yes" or "no"? Should this or that be done right now, at the given moment, or should it not be done?"[62] In this passage is all of Lenin the revolutionary politician. More than any other Marxist, he was the most practically and directly engaged in attempting to fuse theory and practice, and to find the precise organizational and tactical measures necessary at every moment to move the struggle to the next level.

One could have perfect theory, but if you do not have a way to translate that theory into practice—through real people, real organizations, able and willing to test those ideas in the hurly-burly of everyday events, the theory becomes sterile and lifeless. On more than one occasion Lenin would shift tact, or discard an old argument he considered relevant to a given period, and adopt a new position based on new conditions. Thinking through new tasks as conditions change—the level of class struggle, the degree of repression, the confidence or lack thereof of the regime, and so on—is, Lenin argued, the most difficult task, "because it requires of people not a simple repetition of slogans learned by heart . . . but a certain amount of initiative, flexibility of mind, resourcefulness and independent work on a *novel* historical task."[63]

To give one example: During the 1905 revolution, when the tsar agreed to form the Duma, the Bolsheviks called for a boycott. So long as the revolution still had momentum and it was possible to overthrow the tsar, it had been justifiable, Lenin argued, to boycott the Duma. But when it became clear that the revolutionary moment was ebbing away, Lenin changed his position (to the chagrin of many other Bolsheviks, who called him an opportunist) and argued that the Bolsheviks should run their own candidates. "We were obliged to do—and did—everything in our power to prevent the convocation of a sham representative body," Lenin wrote. "But since it has been convened in spite of all our efforts, we cannot shirk the task of utilizing it."[64] We should not, however, "exaggerate its modest importance." "We shall," he emphasized, "subordinate the struggle we wage in the Duma to another form of struggle, namely strikes, uprisings, etc."[65]

While the revolutionary wave had temporarily brought the Bolsheviks and Mensheviks together, the aftermath drove them further apart. The revolution confirmed the Bolsheviks' commitment to working-class leadership in a worker-peasant alliance directed at the overthrow of autocracy, the Mensheviks drew conservative conclusions, denouncing a December 1905 workers' uprising in Moscow as premature, and placing emphasis on the need to moderate the militancy of the working class in order to cement alliances with the liberal bourgeoisie. As the Menshevik leader Alexander Martynov wrote:

The coming revolution will be a revolution of the bourgeoisie; and that means that . . .
it will only, to a greater or lesser extent, secure the rule of all or some of the bourgeois
classes. . . . If this is so, it is clear that the coming revolution can on no account assume
political forms *against the will of the whole* of the bourgeoisie, as the latter will be the
master of tomorrow. If so, then to follow the path of simply *frightening* the majority
of the bourgeois elements would mean that the revolutionary struggle of the proletariat
could lead to only one result—the restoration of absolutism in its original form.[66]

The Mensheviks believed that the liberal Russian bourgeoisie would have to lead the
revolution, in the same way that the French bourgeoisie had led the revolution in
1789.[67] The role of the Socialists, in their view, was to mobilize the working class to
put pressure on the bourgeoisie to fulfill this task. Consequently, they cautioned the
working class not to do anything that might frighten the capitalist class into the arms
of reaction.

The Bolsheviks, however, argued that the Russian capitalists were far too tied
up with the landowning classes to lead a revolt against the autocracy. "The bourgeoisie
as a whole is incapable of waging a determined struggle against the autocracy." Lenin
continued: "It fears to lose in this struggle its property which binds it to the existing
order; it fears an all-too-revolutionary action of the workers, who will not stop at the
democratic revolution but will aspire to the Socialist revolution. It fears a complete
break with officialdom, with the bureaucracy, whose interests are bound up by a
thousand ties with the interests of the propertied classes. For this reason the bourgeois
struggle for liberty is notoriously timorous, inconsistent, and half-hearted."[68]

As reaction set in and the radical organizations were smashed apart and driven
back into a hunted, underground existence, leading Mensheviks renounced underground party work, and called for the formation of a legal organization dedicated to
improving the conditions of the working class. Lenin systematically denounced this
trend—which he observed had close affinities to the old "economist" trend—as "liq-
uidationism," which he defined as "an attempt on the part of some of the Party intelligentsia to liquidate the existing organization of the Russian Social Democratic
Labor Party and to substitute for it an amorphous federation acting at all cost within
the limits of legality, even at the cost of openly abandoning the program, tactics and
traditions of the Party."[69] These Socialists wanted a broad, open, "European"-style
labor movement in Russia. Not only was this idea a practical pipe dream in conditions
of police reaction, it was also tantamount to abandoning the revolution. As historian
Neil Harding points out, "Insistence on the need to overthrow the autocracy was
obviously incompatible with being granted a legal status by it."[70]

That didn't meant the Bolsheviks repudiated the struggle for reforms and the
utilization of legal forms of opposition. "We make use of every reform . . . and of
every legal society," Lenin insisted. The Bolsheviks excelled at taking advantage of
the slightest legal opening —for example, working in workers' insurance organiza-

tions, to promote their cause. "But we use them to develop the revolutionary consciousness and the revolutionary struggle of the masses."[71]

Lenin not only fought the reformism of the Mensheviks. In his own Bolshevik faction, he fought against a left-wing faction called the Otzovists, led by Alexander Bogdanov, which demanded the recall of the social-democratic deputies from the Duma and refused to work in the trade unions or other legal organizations. This faction essentially drew the conclusion that tactics appropriate to revolution were appropriate for nonrevolutionary times. New conditions, Lenin argued, required a return to more "humdrum" tactics—utilizing every legal opportunity to put forward the party's views and organize its supporters. In 1908 he maneuvered to expel this faction—whose policies threatened to lead to the party's increased isolation and irrelevance—from the Bolsheviks.

The Bolsheviks were denounced by many on the left as sectarian hairsplitters. But during this period the Bolsheviks were able to maintain the strongest organization, and were quickest to recover and avail themselves of new opportunities for legal and illegal work in Russia when the class struggle began to revive in 1912. Their daily newspaper, *Pravda*, became the most widely supported, distributed, and read newspaper among Russia's most active workers.

Like Marx, Lenin did not believe in a one-size-fits-all approach to organization. Yet in all this, there is an important thread that is drawn out and developed more clearly after the collapse of the Second International, and particularly after the success of the Russian Revolution in 1917: the idea of the party not as representing the class or embracing the working class as a whole, but the party as the most advanced, most class-conscious and revolutionary section of the working class. It was not until the Socialist parties in Germany and elsewhere betrayed their principles and backed their own governments' war ambitions in World War I that Lenin drew the conclusion that what the Bolsheviks had done in Russia had *international* significance, that is, that revolutionaries outside of Russia must break organizationally with reformism.

That idea could not come to full fruition in the international socialist movement without Lenin's work *State and Revolution*, which revived the ideas of Marx and Engels that workers must dismantle the old state and replace it with a *council* state (that is, a state of the Paris Commune–type, with directly elected, revocable delegates) or without the Russian Revolution, which showed in practice how such a revolution could be achieved. As the late British Marxist Chris Harman writes, just as the revolutionary party does not substitute itself for, or *represent* the class as a whole, it also is not to be *identified* with the future socialist state, as the Second International Marxists had done. "For Lenin the party is not the embryo of the workers' state—the Workers' Council is." The party leads the class, but the working-class as a whole must create its new state, which must represent "all the diverse interests of all the sections—geographical, industrial, etc.—of the workers."[72]

Lenin's Unique Contribution

Rosa Luxemburg once pointed out the contradictory process facing the working class in the course of its struggle to end capitalism:

> The international movement of the proletariat toward its complete emancipation is a process peculiar in the following respect. For the first time in the history of civilization, the people are expressing their will consciously and in opposition to all ruling classes. But this will can only be satisfied beyond the limits of the existing system.
>
> Now the mass can only acquire and strengthen this will in the course of day-to-day struggle against the existing social order—that is, within the limits of capitalist society. On the one hand, we have the mass; on the other, its historic goal, located outside of existing society. On one hand, we have the day-to-day struggle; on the other, the social revolution. Such are the terms of the dialectic contradiction through which the Socialist movement makes its way.
>
> It follows that this movement can best advance by tacking betwixt and between the two dangers by which it is constantly being threatened. One is the loss of its mass character; the other, the abandonment of its goal. One is the danger of sinking back to the condition of a sect; the other, the danger of becoming a movement of bourgeois social reform.[73]

In the fight for reforms, Socialists can either adapt to "what exists," merging into movements and disappearing in them; or on the other hand they can separate themselves and become an isolated sect. Before the Russian Revolution and the outbreak of revolution in Germany convinced her of the need to make an organizational break with reformism, Luxemburg was unable to conceive of the separate organization of revolutionaries as anything but an isolated sect. Observing the German experience, she could only see rising class struggle as a corrective against the organizational conservatism of social democracy. Lenin, on the other hand, showed practically how organizational forms could be adapted that allowed revolutionaries to tack "betwixt and between the twin dangers" to which Luxemburg so eloquently referred.

Lenin's conception of a "vanguard" is best understood simply as a "leading body." To really be a leading body, it cannot be proclaimed or imposed from above, and it cannot be built by standing apart from the working class and holding up revolutionary ideas to which it expects the working class, at the right moment, to suddenly flock. It has to be built in practice, in the course of struggles over partial economic and political demands, and in alliance with organizations and forces that are not revolutionary.

We are a long way away from building mass revolutionary parties in the world today. But on the way toward creating them—whatever tactical and organizational twists and turns we may go through—the theoretical and practical legacy of Lenin and the Bolsheviks, as much as Marx and Engels, is indispensable. Sadly, these lessons and insights were quickly appropriated and distorted beyond recognition by the Stalinists in the 1920s, who portrayed the "Leninist vanguard party" as a top-down, bureaucratic, commandist organization that seeks one-party rule and stratification of the economy. This conception has little to do with the actual experience of the Bolsheviks.

The Bolshevik experience should teach us that Socialists should operate as comrades in struggle who, in participating in today's movements, try to move the struggle as far as it can go, introducing to wider layers of workers the need for the socialist alternative along the way. It doesn't offer utopian blueprints of the socialist future, but rather gathers together and distills the most important historical lessons of past struggles, in order that those experiences can provide lessons for future struggles. In that sense, the revolutionary party also serves as the memory of the working class in a world where such lessons are rarely preserved in any other way.

The dreaded "democratic centralism" is a concept whose meaning should be clear to anyone in any democratically run activist organization that is attempting to implement a decision—first debate, then vote, and then act in unison to put that decision into effect. Democracy is necessary, as Lenin explained, because "the success of mass action requires the conscious and voluntary participation of every individual worker." A strike, for example, "cannot be conducted with the necessary solidarity . . . unless every worker consciously and voluntarily decides for himself the question: to strike or not to strike?" Lenin insisted that "firm and intelligent" decisions, not those based on "clannishness, friendship, or force of habit," could be made only on the basis of open debate and discussion.[74] But socialist organizations are not talk shops that value discussion for its own sake. Once debate is had, a decision must be made that the collective is disciplined enough to act on. That is the "centralism" part of democratic centralism.

If all workers moved to socialism uniformly and simultaneously, organization and leadership would not be necessary. But they do not. As Trotsky wrote in 1932, "The class itself is not homogeneous. Its different sections arrive at class consciousness by different paths and at different times. The bourgeoisie participates actively in this process. Within the working class it creates its own institutions, or utilizes those already existing, in order to oppose certain strata of workers against others."[75] The differences in degrees of consciousness and activism means that all social struggles produce some kind of leadership—that is, groups of people who exert influence over the movement. In reality, even those anarchists who are "anti-leadership" are in fact promoting their own politics about how the movement should be formed, that is, attempting to assert their leadership.

Workers do not exist in a vacuum, but are in reality influenced, and deliberately so, by bourgeois, pro-capitalist ideas that seek to divide them and convince them that they are powerless. With these facts in mind it becomes clear how necessary it is to organize the best elements, the most conscious, the most self-sacrificing, the most committed to changing the world, into a common organization so as to be able to exert a counter-influence. The question, then, is not leadership versus no leadership, but what *kind* of leadership, fighting for what purposes, will emerge and will predominate. In denying the need for leaders, anarchist forms of organization often produce *unaccountable* leaders, not leaderless movements.

Every mass movement gives rise to debates about the way forward. The trade union officialdom, the old reformist leaders, and liberal organizations step to the fore and attempt to corral the movement, to lead it and to contain it. In such a situation, a distinction always needs to be made between the reformism of the masses being drawn into activism for the first time—ordinary people who do not yet believe they have the power to run society and therefore look to *better* rulers than the old ones, or look for improvements that benefit them without thinking of going beyond the framework of capitalism—as opposed to more entrenched political forces that are *consciously committed* to reforming capitalism in order to save it. In every revolutionary movement, the need for an organization of revolutionaries that can fight inside the movement to break past the constraints of reformism, and win the majority of workers to the idea that they must pose a new alternative to capitalism, becomes pressing.

Such an organization has to be built up *before* the outbreak of revolutionary developments, or it will not have sufficient influence and experience to help guide the struggle. Again, to quote Trotsky, "[D]uring a revolution, i.e., when events move more swiftly, a weak party can quickly grow into a mighty one provided it lucidly understands the course of the revolution and possesses staunch cadres that do not become intoxicated with phrases and are not terrorized by persecution." Trotsky continues: "But such a party must be available prior to the revolution inasmuch as the process of educating the cadres requires a considerable period of time and the revolution does not afford this time."[76] This is certainly the lesson of the German Revolution. All the conditions existed, as in Russia, for a successful workers' revolution. The missing ingredient was a revolutionary party of sufficient size and depth of experience to play the kind of leading role played by the Bolsheviks in 1917.

In periods of mass struggles, the barrier between economic and political struggle breaks down. Workers who not long before believed they had no power suddenly find themselves engaging in mass action, finding confidence and demanding respect. Every manifestation of injustice becomes a target of action. Each struggle inspires the next, and no issue or grievance is beyond action. For example, a strike wave in the summer of 1981 in Poland, during the heyday of Solidarność (the mass democratic independent trade union movement that emerged in Poland in 1980), involved a strike by airline workers demanding the right to choose their own manager, a dock strike to stop the export of food (people were starving in Poland), a protest by newspaper print shop workers against anti-Solidarność propaganda in the news, a strike of transport workers against corruption, a strike of workers in one town demanding those responsible for repression against an earlier strike movement be fired, and hunger marches by thousands of women demanding food.

In a mass upsurge of struggle, an increasing number of militants begin to grasp the possibility that the movement, if it is to move forward, must seize power. Things must either go forward or backward, but can't stagnate. If these militants are not organized and united around a common campaign to win over the rest of the class to a program of revolutionary action, their sentiments, ideas, and partial insights will dissipate without real effect. Reformist leaders will retain dominance in the movement, and, in the name of unity and realism, will encourage the working class to curb its enthusiasm.

In Poland many of the leaders of Solidarność, such as Lech Walesa, accepted the idea of a "self-limiting revolution."[77] Though many militants were aware of the fact that Solidarność— a mass movement of almost ten million workers that sprang from mass strikes—had the potential to be far more than a trade union fighting for reforms, there was no organized or coherent attempt to challenge its leaders from the left. The fact that the Polish state capitalist regime had claimed the mantle of Socialism, and had appropriated phrases like "class struggle" did not help; the working class was reinventing workers' power against a ruling class that had appropriated their traditional symbols and terms of revolt.

But this experience highlights the key role a genuine socialist organization of militants could have played in Poland at the time. "Solidarnosc's 'self-limitation,'" writes Colin Barker in his account, "was a disastrous strategy. . . . Time and time again, the leaders of Solidarnosc found themselves urging their members not to 'go too far,' not to 'frighten the authorities.' Time and time again, they reined the movement in, rather than encouraging it forward. Their members' militancy was a 'problem' for them, rather than the key to a solution."[78]

The alternative was a revolutionary strategy aimed at seizing control of workplaces, winning over the rank and file of the armed forces, and replacing the bureaucratic state apparatus with workers' democracy. Only a strong organization united around such a program could have even posed this alternative as a possibility in Poland. Sadly, none existed.

Without a revolutionary party, the revolutionary moment is lost and the movement either goes into decline or is defeated. Either way, society begins to flow back into its old channels and "order" is restored once again. "Without a guiding organization, the energy of the masses would dissipate like steam not enclosed in a piston-box," wrote Trotsky. "But nevertheless what moves things is not the piston or the box, but the steam."[79]

The type of organization socialists should strive to build was described perfectly by the late British Socialist Duncan Hallas in 1971:

> The events of the last 40 years largely isolated the revolutionary Socialist tradition from the working classes of the West. The first problem is to reintegrate them. The many partial and localized struggles on wages, conditions, housing, rents, education,

health and so on have to be coordinated and unified into a coherent forward movement based on a strategy for the transformation of society. In human terms, an organized layer of thousands of workers, by hand and by brain, firmly rooted amongst their fellow workers and with a shared consciousness of the necessity for Socialism and the way to achieve it, has to be created.[80]

A number of factors that there isn't space here to explore—the rise of Stalinism and the bureaucratic degeneration of "actually existing Socialism," the unprecedented revival of capitalist growth after the Second World War, and the repression against the Left during the Cold War—largely severed socialism from the working class. The connection, under new conditions, has to be reestablished. That is the chief tasks of socialists today.

Chapter Nine

Russia: The God That Failed?

The Russian Revolution of 1917 was a historical watershed. The overthrow of tsarism and the erection for the first time of a society with workers on top and bosses on the bottom, gave inspiration to workers and the oppressed the world over. It sparked revolutionary upheavals from Europe to the Middle East to Asia. For the world's national ruling classes, Russia's "red specter" cast a dark shadow, striking fear into their hearts. The revolution's victory over the forces of reaction convinced millions that ordinary people could rise up and seize control of society in their own interests. Socialists the world over strove to emulate what Russia had done. In his 1918 speech against the war, Eugene Debs expressed the enthusiasm for the Russian Revolution and the outbreak of revolution in Germany, that was felt by millions:

> Like a raging conflagration it leaps from shore to shore. The reign of capitalism and militarism has made of all peoples flammable material. They are ripe and ready for the change, the great change which means the rise and triumph of the workers, the end of exploitation, of war and plunder, and the emancipation of the race. Let it come! Let us all help its coming and pave the way for it by organizing the workers industrially and politically to conquer capitalism and usher in the day of the people.
>
> In Russia and Germany our valiant comrades are leading the proletarian revolution, which knows no race, no color, no sex, and no boundary lines. They are setting the heroic example for world-wide emulation. . . .
>
> From the crown of my head to the soles of my feet I am a Bolshevik, and proud of it.
>
> "The Day of the People has arrived!"[1]

The revolution's isolation, degeneration, and defeat at the hands of the Stalinist bureaucracy in the 1920s presented a devastating blow to the international socialist movement. All defeats are a blow, but this one was particularly damaging. In Russia, Marxism came to be associated with an ideology that represented a complete distortion—or rather inversion—of Marxism. Socialism came to be identified not with workers' democratic control of society, but with a dictatorial, one-party state and the gulag. Working-class internationalism was replaced with "socialism in one country."

Ideologues in both the East and West, for their own reasons, agreed that Stalin was the natural heir of Lenin, and that the rise of his rule represented not the revolution's failure, but its logical culmination. The only difference was that supporters of Stalin's Russia put a plus by this conclusion and its critics a minus. Official Marxism in Russia became not a guide to action or a theory of workers' power, but a state ideology out of which all genuine Marxist content had been wrung—an ideology justifying not workers' control over production, but the exploitation of, and rule over, the working class. In the West, reports of militarized regimentation of society, the cult of personality around Stalin, and forced labor camps became extremely effective tools in the hands of defenders of capitalism against socialism.

Both the Stalinist defenders of Lenin and anticommunist historians in the West held to the view that Stalin was the natural heir of Lenin—the one group to claim Lenin's heritage, the other to demonstrate that all revolutions lead to tyranny. Yet toward the end of his life, in 1922, Lenin wrote a testament demanding Stalin's removal from power in a desperate attempt to stop the growing state bureaucracy. A few years later, Trotsky took up the same theme, organizing a faction within the Bolshevik Party in a last-ditch effort to defend workers' power in the Soviet Union against its bureaucratic degeneration.

There was another interpretation of the reasons for the degeneration of the Russian Revolution—a Marxist one. The Russian Revolution was not a coup and its leaders were not master manipulators. The defeat of the revolution was due not to Lenin or any other Russian revolutionary's hankering for power, or because socialism goes against human nature, but because the harsh conditions of an embattled, isolated post-revolutionary Russia were too undeveloped, too backward, for the building of a socialist society. To understand what's being argued here, we need to examine both how the Russian Revolution was won and how it was lost.

How the Revolution Was Won

The Bolshevik Party was composed of activists and had a mass base among Russia's three million industrial workers. On the eve of the October Revolution in 1917, its membership stood at 240,000. The party was neither perfect nor the monolith that Stalinist hacks later made it out to be, but there can be no doubt that it was a mass party consisting in the majority of industrial workers, not a clique of professional revolutionaries, when it led the Russian Revolution to victory.[2]

Manchester Guardian correspondent Morgan Phillips Price, by no means a supporter of the Bolsheviks (whom he called "Maximalists"), offered this observation on the eve of the revolution: "The Maximalist fanatics, who still dream of the social revolution throughout all Europe, have, according to my observations in the provinces, recently acquired an immense, if not amorphous following." He notes with a tone of disdain:

> The majority of their followers, however, have no idea of what the Maximalist means when he talks of "all power to the councils." . . . The peasant, furious with the delay in the land reform, hears promises of immediate seizure of the landlord's land and goes with him. The worker hears talk about State control over the banks and goes with him. . . . All the recent provincial elections have given immense majorities to this wing of the revolutionary democracy.[3]

The revolution came in two installments. On February 23, 1917—International Women's Day—hundreds of thousands of Russian workers took to the streets of Russia's capital, Petrograd, inaugurating a series of mass protests and strikes that would in a matter of days bring down a monarchy that had ruled Russia for centuries.[4]

Eight months later, in a second installment, armed workers—led by the Bolshevik Party—brought down the capitalist "provisional" government that had rushed in to reestablish order after the tsar's fall. In its place ruled the soviets—the democratic councils of workers, soldiers, sailors, and poor peasants—that had been hastily erected throughout Russia during and after the February Revolution.

The revolution combined two revolts—that of peasants in the countryside and of workers in the towns, the result of Russian economic development combining the old with the new. In his *History of the Russian Revolution*, Trotsky quoted Marx's statement that "the country that is more developed industrially only shows, to the less developed, the image of its own future." This idea, however, "has become less applicable in proportion as capitalist evolution has embraced all countries," wrote Trotsky. "England in her day revealed the future of France, considerably less of Germany, but not in the least of Russia and not of India."[5]

Newcomers to capitalism after Britain did not simply repeat the same gradual stages English economic development went through but combined and even skipped some. In Russia, more backward forms of economic life combined with the most modern forms, which were simply grafted on top of the old. Capitalism did not develop in late-nineteenth-century Russia gradually out of its own village handicrafts. On the contrary, with the aid of state intervention and an influx of foreign capital, modern factories were built alongside "villages of wood and straw." Peasants were "thrown into the factory cauldron snatched directly from the plow," wrote Trotsky.[6]

Russia in 1917 was a country made up overwhelmingly of peasants, scratching out a meager existence under the sway of big landowners. But it was also a country where state intervention and foreign investment had superimposed the world's most modern factories on top of Russia's old feudal structure. This peculiar mode of development gave rise to a weak capitalist class, dependent on the state and foreign capital, fearful of its own shadow. One sign of its weakness was the fact that the party most identified with the liberal bourgeoisie, the Constitutional Democrats, or Cadets, wasn't formed until 1905. On the other hand, Russia's industrial working class, though numerically a minority, were tremendously concentrated in a few urban centers like Petrograd and Moscow, giving them a relative power that far exceeded their numbers. Precisely because of the late arrival of capitalism to Russia, the most advanced factories, employing in many cases thousands of workers, arose alongside the most primitive agricultural techniques in the countryside. The famous Putilov metal factory in Petrograd, for example, employed more than 24,000 workers.[7] The workers had already begun to take collective strike action as early as 1896.

As explained in the previous chapter, the two wings of the Russian Social Democratic Labor Party (RSDLP)—Menshevik and Bolshevik—had very different views of Russia's revolution, which affected their approach to it. While both agreed there would be two distinct revolutions: one bourgeois, which would overthrow tsarism, establish Western-style democracy, and distribute land to the peasants; and later a second, working class–led revolution, which would bring about socialism, they differed significantly about what that meant. The Mensheviks' desire to become allies of Russian liberals meant that they turned their backs on the peasantry and tried to moderate the demands of the working class. The Bolsheviks considered the liberal bourgeoisie a weak, wavering class that would in the end prefer the autocracy over workers' power and therefore looked to an alliance between the urban working class and the rebellious peasantry to carry out the revolution.

The Bolsheviks' assessment that the bourgeoisie would recoil in fear from revolution, and in the event of its success, seek to channel it into acceptable limits was amply confirmed during the revolution. Amid the mass protests of February 1917 that brought down the tsar, Rodzianko, the liberal president of the Duma, whined, "I do not want to revolt. I am no rebel, I have made no revolution and do not intend to make one. . . . But there is not government any longer. Everything falls to me. . . . All the phones are ringing. Everybody asks me what to do. What shall I say? Shall I step aside?"[8] The less panicked Kadet leader Pavel Miliukov called on the Duma to take power "to curb growing anarchy."[9]

The practical difference between the two positions was that while the Mensheviks sought to hold back workers' militancy so as not to provoke the liberals into bolting from the role Menshevism had allotted them, the Bolsheviks criticized the liberals and sought to organize the working class independently of them. Only the working class, they argued, could spearhead the movement, uniting behind it the oppressed peasants. Incidentally, the Menshevik line became the basis, later, for the Stalinist conception that revolutions must of necessity go through two stages, the democratic and then the socialist one.

Trotsky took the Bolsheviks' line of reasoning a step further. If the town leads the country, and the capitalists cannot lead "their" revolution—then workers must lead it, in alliance with the peasantry. In this his views coincided with Lenin's. But if the workers led, then they would not be able to stop at the democratic or bourgeois stage. After a successful revolution, workers would be compelled to retain power in their own hands and begin to push through socialist measures. Trotsky did not disagree with the argument that Russia was not economically ripe for socialism on its own, but he placed Russia's fate in its international context. Workers could begin the fight for socialism, but could not complete it without the revolution spreading and taking hold in other, more economically advanced countries. Trotsky viewed the revolution as a link in an international chain of struggle, not as an isolated national event.

Trotsky called this theory, which he first formulated in 1905, "permanent revolution." Marx and Engels used the term "permanent revolution" long before Trotsky adopted it, and in their analysis after the 1848 bourgeois revolutions in Europe, they foreshadowed the theory by arguing that in future revolutions in Germany, due to the unwillingness of the bourgeois liberals to press their democratic demands, the working class would have to take the lead and carry through the democratic revolution as an immediate prelude to a workers' revolution. "It is our interest and our task to make the revolution permanent until all the more or less propertied classes have been forced out of their position of dominance," they wrote in 1850.[10] By permanent, then, Trotsky did not mean endless revolution, but rather a revolution that would not stop halfway, and would proceed until all exploiting classes had been driven from power. He also meant a revolution that did not stop at national borders.

The First World War brought disaster to Russia. Food shortages, disease, and the slaughter of troops at the front—all these factors came to a head in 1917. At the top, the ruling circles became utterly paralyzed, the tsar and tsarina retreated into mysticism, their ministers unable to act; corruption and graft became rampant. The fanatical cruelty of the ruling couple was best expressed in a letter to the tsar by the tsarina, in which she exclaimed, "Russia loves to feel the whip. That is *their* nature."[11] Trotsky described how the tsar praised as "fine fellows" a certain regiment for shooting down workers, and how he "'read with satisfaction' how they flogged with whips the bob-haired girl students, or cracked the heads of defenseless people during Jewish pogroms."[12]

As the war wore on, soldiers deserted in droves. After a short patriotic lull, workers began to go back out into the streets—renewing the fervor they had exhibited through mass strikes before the war broke out in 1914. Hundreds of thousands of workers struck and demonstrated, confronting the tsar's police and troops. Discipline in the armed forces cracked, and whole regiments joined the revolution, turning against the police who stayed loyal to the tsar. The tsar completely lost his grip on power in a matter of days.

Lenin in 1905 described revolution as the "festival of the oppressed," and Trotsky, in his famous *History of the Russian Revolution*, as "the forcible entrance of the masses into the realm of rulership over their own destiny."[13] This description, taken from Trotsky's chapter on the fall of the tsar in February, gives a sense of this process during the mass demonstrations:

> A worker-Bolshevik, Kayurov, one of the authentic leaders in those days, relates how at one place, within sight of a detachment of Cossacks, the demonstrators scattered under the whips of the mounted police, and how he, Kayurov, and several workers with him, instead of following the fugitives, took off their caps and approached the Cossacks with the words: "Brothers-Cossacks, help the workers in a struggle for their peaceable demands; you see how the Pharaohs [slang for police] treat us, hungry workers. Help us!" This consciously humble manner, those caps in their hands—what an accurate psychological calculation! Inimitable gesture! The whole history of street fights and revolutionary victories swarms with such improvisations. But they are drowned without a trace in the abyss of great events. . . . "The Cossacks glanced at each other in some special way," Kayurov continues, "and we were hardly out of the way before they rushed into the fight." And a few minutes later, near the station gate, the crowd were tossing in their arms a Cossack who before their eyes had slaughtered a police inspector with his sabre.[14]

The outcome of the tsar's overthrow was "dual power."[15] On the one side, workers and soldiers—carrying over their experience of 1905—created the Soviet of Workers' and Soldiers' Deputies, based on a structure of one delegate for every thousand workers or soldiers. On the other side, the liberal landowners and bourgeois representatives formed—after some prodding and begging from the Menshevik leaders—the provisional government, formed by liberal members of the old Duma. This was in fact a counterrevolutionary government. It fully recommitted Russia to the imperialist war; it abhorred workers' control in the factories, and it opposed land seizures by the peasants—all the while promising at some future date, always put off, a constituent assembly that would solve Russia's problems.

The soviet had at this point far more power and prestige than the provisional government. However, the delegates of the first soviet meeting elected Mensheviks and Socialist-Revolutionary (SR) leaders who were not committed to taking power. Though the peasantry formed its mass base, the SR Party balked at immediate land redistribution, appealing to the peasantry to wait for elections to a promised constituent assembly rather than take action into its own hands. "Those socialists who stood at the head of the soviet," wrote Trotsky, "were already looking around with alarm to see if they could find a real 'boss.' They took it for granted that the power ought to pass to the bourgeoisie."[16] Consequently, they insisted that the provisional government take power into its hands, even though the liberals who comprised it feared the revolution and expected the soviet to arrest them. As the situation unfolded, the moderate Mensheviks and SRs not only supported the provisional government but also entered it as cabinet members.

Though no single political party initiated the February revolution, many of its leaders on the ground, once it got under way, were Bolsheviks and other militants.[17] Although the Bolsheviks were sizable, they were not yet a mass party outside of Petrograd and were concentrated in the biggest factories of Petrograd and other towns, with a mass-circulation daily—*Pravda*, or "truth" in Russian—that regularly sold forty thousand copies in the factory districts. They were thus in no position immediately to lead a revolt against the provisional government. In these initial stages of the revolution they were still scattered and disorganized by months of intense police repression. They began with only a small minority of delegates in the Petrograd Soviet—forty of sixteen hundred; however, by April they had already achieved majority support in the delegation committees organized inside the factories.

What accounted for this paradox? "The elections to the organs and institutions of the victorious revolution attract and challenge the infinitely broader masses than those who battled with arms in hands," wrote Trotsky.[18] In this early phase, the majority of workers did not make a distinction among the different socialist parties, and the influence of the intellectuals and of the petty officers in the army impressed their moderating stamp on the public's consciousness. "In giving their confidence to the socialists the workers and soldiers found themselves, quite unexpectedly, expropriated politically."[19] A period of struggle was necessary to clarify where matters stood, who was for workers' power and who was not. "The country," argued Lenin from exile, "is passing from the first stage of the revolution—which, owing to the insufficient class consciousness and organization of the proletariat, is in the hands of the bourgeoisie—to its second stage, which must place power in the hands of the proletariat and the poorest sections of the peasants."[20]All power, Lenin argued, must pass from the provisional government to the soviets, a step that could only be accomplished by patiently convincing the masses of its necessity.

> The masses must be made to see that the Soviets of Workers' Deputies are the *only possible* form of revolutionary government, and that therefore our task is, as long as *this* government yields to the influence of the bourgeoisie, to present a patient, systematic, and persistent explanation of the errors of their tactics, an *explanation* especially adapted to the practical needs of the masses.
>
> As long as we are in the minority we carry on the work of criticizing and exposing errors and at the same time we preach the necessity of transferring the entire state power to the Soviets of Workers' Deputies, so that the people may overcome their mistakes by experience.
>
> . . . Not a parliamentary republic—to return to a parliamentary republic from the Soviets of Workers' Deputies would be a retrograde step—but a republic of Soviets of Workers', Agricultural Laborers' and Peasants' Deputies throughout the country, from top to bottom.[21]

Lenin was explicit that the old Bolshevik formula—that a socialist revolution could only follow after a successful bourgeois revolution—must be rejected. "The only way out," he wrote bluntly in April 1917, "is through a proletarian revolution." He also rejected—after an intense reexamination of Marx and Engels's view of the state— the old social-democratic formula that the socialists must seize control of the existing state machine. He now argued that what was needed was a new kind of state based on *soviet* democracy.

> Marxism differs from anarchism in that it recognizes *the need for a state* for the purpose of the transition to socialism; but (and here is where we differ from Kautsky and Co.) *not a state of the type* of the usual parliamentary bourgeois-democratic republic, but a state like the Paris Commune of 1871 and the Soviets of Workers' Deputies of 1905 and 1917. . . .
>
> *Living reality,* the revolution, has *already actually* established in our country, albeit in a weak and embryonic form, precisely this new type of "state," which is not a state in the proper sense of the word.[22]

Other Bolshevik leaders did not at first embrace Lenin's views. Clinging to the old formula that Russia must first pass through a bourgeois phase, many (Lev Kamenev and Stalin, for example) called for critical support for the provisional government, seeing in it not a counterrevolutionary institution, but the fulfillment of Russia's "bourgeois" revolution. Freed from prison after February and as the new editors of *Pravda,* Kamenev and Stalin pledged support for the provisional government "insofar as it struggles against reaction or counter-revolution."[23] The problem was that with the fall of the tsar, the provisional government had become a center of counterrevolution.

But the essence of party policy had in fact been to stress the leading role of the working class in the revolution. Entire party committees, including the famous industrial Vyborg district of Petrograd, had already come to the conclusion that the provisional government should be replaced by soviet power. After some hard debate—in which he was able to appeal to the rank and file of the party that had in many cases independently drawn similar conclusions—Lenin was able to convince the party leaders of a strategy aimed at transferring all power to the soviets. Thus, in practice, Lenin adopted Trotsky's theory of permanent revolution.

The Bolsheviks were not interested in a putsch by a minority, let alone a rising by the working class without support among the soldiers and peasantry. The task of the Bolsheviks, Lenin wrote, was to "patiently explain" to the as-yet-unconvinced masses the need for the movement to transfer all power to the soviets, that only a soviet government would end the war, give land to the peasants, and create a full democracy in Russia. Once they secured a majority for this position in the soviets—which served as a barometer of mass feeling—the provisional government could be replaced by soviet power.

The Bolshevik line struck a chord with a growing number of workers, and thousands of them joined the party. Already by April, workers in Petrograd were demonstrating in support of Bolshevik demands. Here the Bolsheviks played a crucial role in the struggle, actually restraining a premature insurrection. By June, a majority of workers in Petrograd supported the Bolsheviks and were ready to overthrow the provisional government. The danger, as the Bolshevik leaders saw it, was that a revolt in Petrograd would be isolated and easily crushed. More time was needed to win over Moscow and other towns. In what became known as the "July Days," Lenin and other leaders appeared at the head of an armed demonstration and, much to the chagrin of the protesters, urged calm.

After a series of desultory armed clashes with police, the protests disintegrated, and for a few weeks the Bolsheviks were driven underground. Lenin, framed on trumped-up charges that he was a German agent, and vilified by the other socialist parties, was forced to flee to Finland to avoid arrest and possible execution. Trotsky and some other Bolshevik leaders were arrested. But the movement was not crushed, and the Bolsheviks quickly bounced back. Trotsky was released, and in a new upsurge of revolutionary ferment was elected president of the Petrograd Soviet (as he had been in 1905, when he was only twenty-five). He was also elected head of the "military-revolutionary committee," which was set up to mobilize workers' militias and troops loyal to the soviet to defend it against counterrevolutionary forces that were stirring.

In August, a right-wing general, Lavr Kornilov, began mobilizing a coup to march on Petrograd and smash both the soviets and the provisional government—which was headed by the right-wing Socialist-Revolutionary leader Alexander Kerensky. Kerensky, who had been toying with the idea of making common cause with Kornilov against the Soviets, now realized that his political life was also on the line. The ruling class had decided, in a last-ditch effort, that Kerensky could not be depended on to repress the revolution, and so he had to go.

The soviet executive committee formed a Committee for Struggle Against the Counterrevolution on August 28. According to the Menshevik memoirist Nikolai Sukhanov, "The committee, making defense preparations, had to mobilize the worker-soldier masses. But the masses, insofar as they were organized, were organized by the Bolsheviks and followed them."[24]

The Bolsheviks were the only left party untainted by support for or participation in the provisional government. They could easily have turned their backs on it, but they realized that the real target of the coup was the soviet power behind which stood the workers, sailors, and soldiers of Russia. Though not relinquishing their criticisms of the provisional government or their plans to overthrow it, they agreed to join forces with the soviet executive to jointly defend the revolution. The provisional government, the Bolsheviks decided, could be dealt with more easily once the immediate threat of a coup was defeated. The Bolshevik position regarding how to fight Kornilov is best summed up by the advice given to sailors by Trotsky and

Bolsheviks still imprisoned after the July Days: "Use Kerensky as a gun-rest to shoot Kornilov. Afterward we will settle with Kerensky."[25]

"It is no wonder that the masses led by the Bolsheviks in fighting against Kornilov did not place a moment of trust in Kerensky," writes Trotsky. "For them it was not a case of defending the government, but of defending the revolution. So much the more resolute and devoted was their struggle. The resistance to the rebels grew out of the very road beds, out of the stones, out of the air."[26]

In the factories, workers immediately reinforced security and formed armed Red Guard units. At the request of the soviet executive committee, pro-soviet troops, mostly Bolsheviks according to Trotsky, were summoned to defend the city. Sailors and soldiers committees and soviets immediately denounced the coup plot and began preparing to resist the counterrevolution. The three thousand well-armed sailors of the Kronstadt naval fortress declared themselves ready to defend the revolution.

But Kornilov's forces were never able to reach Petrograd. Historian Alexander Rabinowitch explains how a unit from the army's "Savage Division" was stopped on August 28, thirty-seven miles from the capital:

> Rail workers there had blocked the right of way with lumber-filled railway cars and had torn up the track for miles beyond. Not only were the troops unable to progress further by rail, it was impossible for them to communicate effectively with other elements of the division or with General Krymov [in charge of the troops], Stavka [the army high command], or Petrograd. While the division's officers fumed helplessly, the soldiers were harangued by a stream of agitators, among whom were emissaries from the Committee for Struggle, several Petrograd district soviets, and a number of Petrograd factories, as well as from garrison military units. . . . Also on hand were a team of nearly a hundred agitators selected by Tsentroflot (the Central Executive Committee of the Navy) from among sailors in the Second Baltic Fleet Crew who previously had been attached to the Savage Division and machine gunners, and a smaller, all-Moslem, delegation, dispatched by the Executive Committee of the Union of Moslem Soviets. . . .
>
> At times, echelons of the Savage Division were encircled by local workers and peasants who berated them for betraying the revolution. The troops had not been told the real reason for their movement northward, and, as it turned out, most had little sympathy for Kornilov's objectives and no desire to oppose the Provisional Government and the Soviet. On August 30 the troops hoisted a red flag inscribed "Land and Freedom" over the headquarters and arrested the head commandant when he protested. They then formed a revolutionary committee to prevent any further movement toward Petrograd, to inform other units in the division about how they were being "used" by the counterrevolution, and to organize a meeting of representatives of all units in the division.[27]

The Bolsheviks acquitted themselves as the best and most consistent defenders of the revolution. As a result, after August 1917, they won a majority of delegates in the soviets. Lenin, Trotsky, and a handful of other leaders argued that the time for talk had passed, and that workers now expected the Bolsheviks to organize an insurrection to disperse the provisional government and transfer all power to the soviets. Lenin came up against resistance from some Bolshevik leaders, like Kamenev and Zinoviev, who feared that the time wasn't ripe (Lenin for a brief time called for the latters' expulsion for openly opposing insurrection in a non-party publication). But Lenin, Trotsky, and others were able to overcome this hesitancy and win the Bolshevik leadership to insurrection. So the party in the end played four crucial roles: First, it outlined a clear strategic policy aimed at winning a majority of workers to the idea that they should take power into their own hands. Second, it was able to tactically restrain sections of the class when it was clear that other sections were not ready to go forward. Third, it was able to win a majority of workers to its side by demonstrating in practice its superior leadership in the struggle, informed by a clear set of politics that corresponded to workers' own experience as the revolution unfolded. Finally, its cadre, well placed in the workplaces, the streets, and the military garrisons, were able to decisively mobilize the insurrection when it became clear that the time was ripe.

It should be noted here that, even in the heat of the mass movement, the Bolsheviks made major decisions on the basis of open and democratic debate and discussion. There were countless times when Lenin was in fact a minority in the leadership and had to fight to convince the others of his views. The myth of the Bolshevik Party as a conspiratorial dictatorship derives from a misreading of the party's history. Historian of the revolution Rabinowitch partially attributes the success of the Bolshevik Party to the "magnetic attraction" of its slogans, "Peace, Land, and Bread," and "All Power to the Soviets," as well as its systematic work among soldiers to win them over to its side. But he gives as much credit to the party's democratic give and take:

> Perhaps even more fundamentally, the phenomenal Bolshevik success can be attributed in no small measure to the nature of the party in 1917. Here I have in mind neither Lenin's bold and determined leadership, the immense historical significance of which cannot be denied, nor the Bolsheviks' proverbial, though vastly exaggerated, organizational unity and discipline. Rather, I would emphasize the party's internally relatively democratic, tolerant, and decentralized structure and method of operation, as well as its essentially open and mass character—in striking contrast to the traditional Leninist model.
>
> As we have seen, within the Bolshevik Petrograd organization at all levels in 1917 there was continuing free and lively discussion and debate over the most basic theoretical and tactical issues. Leaders who differed with the majority were at liberty to fight for their views, and not infrequently Lenin was the loser in these struggles.[28]

On October 25, the Bolshevik Party and its allies organized a successful armed insurrection. The timing was meant to coincide with the opening of the Congress of

Soviets, and Trotsky, who had recently been elected president of the Petrograd soviet, provided capable leadership of the uprising. Workers easily dispersed the provisional government and transferred power to the soviets. Though the subsequent civil war and isolation of the revolution eventually robbed Russian workers of their victory, the Russian Revolution shows us not only that ordinary people can change society, but that to win, we must build a network of organized, conscious revolutionaries committed to that change. "Not by compromise with the propertied classes," wrote the revolution's able chronicler, American leftist and journalist John Reed,

> or with the other political leaders; not by conciliating the old Government mechanism, did the Bolsheviki conquer power. Nor by the organized violence of a small clique. If the masses all over Russia had not been ready for insurrection it must have failed. The only reason for Bolshevik success lay in their accomplishing the vast and simple desires of the most profound strata of people, calling them to the work of tearing down and destroying the old, and afterward, in the smoke of falling ruins, cooperating with them to erect the framework of the new.[29]

How the Revolution Was Lost

The Russian Revolution initiated changes unheard of even in the most advanced capitalist countries. It granted freedom to the oppressed nationalities, established workers' control in the factories, and distributed land to the peasantry. It established the right of immediate recall for all elected officials. It legalized divorce and decriminalized homosexuality. It initiated mass literacy campaigns and began producing cheap editions of great Russian books. It opened up free nurseries for children and communal kitchens and laundries in order to free women from the drudgery of housework, and formed a special women's department in order to increase the active participation of women in the revolutionary process. Lenin and the other revolutionaries reiterated over and over again that the success of all these changes depended on the initiative of ordinary workers, struggling to reorganize society. Sadly, these first seeds of socialist construction, through no fault of the revolutionaries themselves, failed to flower into a new society.

The Russian Marxists were clear that economic conditions were ripe for socialism on a *world* scale, but an isolated Russia could not possibly survive as a workers' state. "We always staked our play," wrote Lenin, "upon an international revolution. . . . In one country it is impossible to accomplish such a work as a socialist revolution."[30] The Russian Revolution could not succeed ultimately unless it spread. "Without the direct governmental support of the European proletariat," Trotsky had written in 1906, "the working class of Russia will not be able to maintain itself in power."[31] Revolutionaries saw backward Russia with its militant working class as the weak link in a great chain of revolutionary developments on a world scale. Russia could initiate the process, but it would be up to the working class of Europe, and particularly Germany, to consolidate success in Russia by ushering in an unstoppable process of world revolution. "It would . . . be erroneous," Lenin wrote in 1920, "to lose sight of the fact that, soon after the victory of the proletarian revolution in at least one of the advanced countries, a sharp change will probably come about: Russia will cease to be the model and will once again become a backward country (in the 'Soviet' and the socialist sense)."[32]

This internationalism was as much a practical as a moral imperative. In isolation, Russia did not possess the material or cultural basis for building a socialist society. Eighty percent of the population still lived off the land, and the average income per head in 1913 was, according to one calculation, somewhat below what it was for people in 1688 in England.[33] Socialism must be based upon material abundance. This is, Marx and Engels wrote, "an absolute practical premise [of communism], because without it, privation, *want* is merely made general, and with *want* the struggle for necessities would begin again, and all the old filthy business would necessarily be restored."[34]

Engels warned what might happen if the leader of an extreme party were "compelled to take over a government in an epoch when the movement is not yet ripe for the domination of the class which he represents." That leader, he argued, would be "compelled to represent not his party nor his class, but the class for whom conditions are ripe for domination. . . . What he *can* do contradicts all his previous actions and principles and the immediate interests of his party, and what he *ought* to do cannot be done."[35]

A revolutionary wave swept Europe in the wake of the Russian Revolution. But nowhere were workers' parties able to take power. The Russian Revolution was forced to fight a tough civil war without the support of any other revolutionary governments. In isolation, the revolutionary leaders of the new workers' government were compelled to behave in contradiction to their principles. Temporary measures of coercion necessitated by the extraordinary conditions of civil war became permanent. Leaders made a virtue of necessity, mistaking "War Communism," an enforced equality born of extreme scarcity, for the real thing.

Trotsky and other Russian revolutionaries had expected defeat, if it came, through the physical destruction of the workers' state by counterrevolutionary armies. But the Bolsheviks triumphed in the civil war. The failure of the German Revolution of 1918–23 sealed the revolution's doom by reinforcing its isolation.[36] The revolution—besieged, blockaded, and starved—degenerated from within.

In 1918, Germany occupied the Ukraine, Russia's breadbasket. With arms and money from Western powers, the former generals of the Russian Army formed counterrevolutionary "white armies" to attack the new regime. They were aided by the initial leniency of the workers' state, which let former tsarist officers, military students, and others who took up arms against the revolution out of detention on the written promise that they not take up arms against the revolution. These promptly "dispersed themselves throughout the length and breadth of Russia, and there organized the civil war."[37] Japanese and US troops also invaded, and Czech troops along the trans-Siberian railway rose up in arms against the Soviet government. Britain, France, Italy, Romania, Serbia, Poland, and Canada also intervened militarily against soviet power.

The results of the civil war and blockade were catastrophic. If socialism is founded on workers' control of production, by 1919 in Russia there were neither workers nor production. The most militant Bolshevik workers left the factories to fight at the front against the white armies or to work for the new government. The personnel of the old state worked to sabotage basic administrative functions. Fuel became scarce, and railroad transportation—the country's lifeblood—was reduced to a sliver of its prewar capacity. What meager resources there were went toward fighting the war. By the end of 1920, factory production had declined to 12.9 percent of its 1913 level, iron ore to 1.6 percent. There was a mass exodus of workers from the towns to the country in search of food. The number of industrial workers in 1921–22 was less than half of what it was in 1917. In three years, Petrograd lost 57.5 percent of its population, and Moscow 44.5 percent.[38]

"Owing to the war and to the desperate poverty and ruin," Lenin admitted in 1921, the working class "has become declassed, i.e., dislodged from its class groove, and has ceased to exist as a proletariat. The proletariat is the class which is engaged in the production of material values in large-scale capitalist industry. Since large-scale capitalist industry has been destroyed, since the factories are at a standstill, the proletariat has disappeared. It has sometimes figured in statistics, but it has not been held together economically."[39]

To make matters worse, the Bolsheviks were forced to requisition grain from the countryside in order to feed the troops and the towns because they had nothing to trade for it. This drove a wedge between the soviet government and the peasantry. The worker-peasant alliance continued to hold together precariously during the civil war, but when the war ended, the peasantry turned against the Bolsheviks. The revolution was like a furious wooden train, tearing off pieces of itself to feed the engine—consuming itself in an effort to keep moving. Faced with these conditions, as Duncan Hallas wrote, "the Bolshevik party came to substitute itself for a decimated, exhausted working class that was itself a small fraction of the population."[40]

Holding on to power in a vast country with pinched resources and violent counterrevolution bearing down upon them, the Bolsheviks ruled increasingly by centralized force from above rather than creative reconstruction from below. The plough may be necessary to churn up the soil for planting wheat, writes Lenin's biographer Tony Cliff. The use of centralized violence may be necessary to fight counterrevolution, but it in no way does it prefigure a future socialist society.

> Unfortunately the plow alone will not produce wheat. The liberation of the working class can be achieved only through the action of the working class. Hence one can have a revolution with more or less violence, with more or less suppression of civil rights of the bourgeoisie and its hangers on, with more or less political freedom, but one *cannot* have a revolution, as the history of Russian conclusively demonstrates, without workers' democracy—even if restricted and distorted.[41]

Increasingly, as Soviet democracy atrophied and desperate wartime conditions persisted, democratic control from below was replaced by control of the party, and society, by an apparatus of functionaries that drew heavily on the engineers, technicians, and bureaucrats of the old tsarist state. What began as a multiparty workers' democracy, albeit led by the Bolsheviks, quickly evolved into a one-party state, as different left parties—the left Social-Revolutionaries and the Mensheviks, for example—were banned by the Bolsheviks after they began mobilizing against the government.

Lenin was forced to admit in 1922 that a thin veneer of Bolsheviks stood at the head of a vast layer of old tsarist administrators.[42] The party was forced to see itself as the trustee of workers' power whenever the international working class could aid Russia in reviving its industry and reestablish direct workers' rule once again. But as that possibility faded, the bureaucracy began to settle in as a new ruling caste with its own interests. It was on this foundation that the bureaucracy, led by Joseph Stalin, grew in importance. Stalin was at that time the party's general secretary—a post that in previous times wasn't powerful, but became more so as Soviet democracy withered and a centralized authority grew in order to prosecute the civil war. In his analysis of the revolution's degeneration, Trotsky explained:

> The revolution got no direct help from the West. Instead of expected prosperity of the country an ominous destitution reigned. . . . Moreover, the outstanding representatives of the working class either died in the civil war, or rose a few steps higher and broke away from the masses. And thus after an unexampled tension of forces, hopes and illusions, there came a long period of weariness, decline and sheer disappointment in the results of the revolution. The ebb of the "plebian pride" made room for a flood of pusillanimity and careerism. The new commanding caste rose to its place upon this wave.[43]

In the twelve years following Lenin's death in 1924, Stalin, the personification of the new party bureaucrat, pushed through a complete counterrevolution, obliterating all traces of 1917. The soviets ceased to be organs of democratic control and became rubber stamps. Bureaucratic managers ran the factories, not workers' committees, and workers were deprived of legal rights. Stalin promoted anti-Marxist ideas under the guise of Marxism. His theory of "socialism in one country" justified the new bureaucratic caste that ruled society. He physically liquidated the leaders of the revolution. According to his successor, Nikita Khrushchev, Stalin was responsible for the murders of 70 percent of the members and candidates of the party's central committee elected in 1934, 80 percent of whom had joined the party before 1921.[44] Trotsky was exiled, and later murdered by a Stalinist agent in Mexico in 1940.

Returning to Engels's warning at the beginning of this section, the Bolshevik leadership was "compelled to represent not [its] party nor [its] class, but the class for whom conditions are ripe for domination." That class was the bourgeoisie—the capitalists. But in Russia the revolution had economically destroyed the capitalist class. The bureaucrats became a kind of collective capitalist. If the Bolshevik Party was forced to substitute itself for the working class, the bureaucracy in turn substituted itself for a nonexistent capitalist class.

What worried Stalin most was Russia's international position. How could Russia survive without heavy industry? The turning point of Stalin's counterrevolution came in 1928 with the announcement of the first Five-Year Plan, which set drastically high goals for industrial growth. The plan was accompanied by the beginning of the forced collectivization of the peasantry, aimed at squeezing maximum surplus from agricultural production. Russia's workers and peasants were dragooned into the service of breakneck industrialization, superexploited for the sake of Russia's industrial development. Prior to this period, economic growth was accompanied by improvements in living standards. Now, wages and social spending were entirely subordinated to the siphoning of the maximum amount of surplus wealth into expanding heavy industry. Forced labor was employed on a mass scale, entire populations were uprooted, and millions died in the state terror used to carry it all through. It was as if the period of primitive accumulation—the expropriation of the peasantry, chattel slavery, and so on—prior to the takeoff of industrialization in Britain was condensed into a period of several years instead of a few centuries. "We are fifty or a hundred years behind the advanced countries," Stalin declared in 1931. "We must make good this distance in ten years. Either we do so, or we shall go under."[45] The real meaning of socialism was distorted beyond recognition, and used not as a guide to human liberation but as an ideology to justify a program of accumulation on the backs of the Russian workers and peasants.

The success of the Russian Revolution remains the high point of working-class power, and stands as proof that the working class is capable of overturning capitalism and starting on the path toward the reconstruction of society for the good of humanity. Its defeat, however, reminds us that people make history, but not in conditions of their own choosing. No matter how heroic their actions, even the strongest-willed revolutionaries cannot alter circumstances that are overwhelmingly stacked against them. Russia gave us only a brief but brilliant glimpse of workers' power. Sadly, the Stalinist bureaucracy that rose on its ruin for decades gave real socialism a bad name—one it does not deserve. Rosa Luxemburg's beautiful defense of the Russian Revolution written in 1918 reads in retrospect as the best epitaph on the revolution's enduring significance:

Everything that happens in Russia is comprehensible and represents an inevitable chain of causes and effects, the starting point and end term of which are: the failure of the German proletariat and the occupation of Russia by German imperialism. It would be demanding something superhuman from Lenin and his comrades if we should expect of them that under such circumstances they should conjure forth the finest democracy, the most exemplary dictatorship of the proletariat and a flourishing socialist economy. By their determined revolutionary stand, their exemplary strength in action, and their unbreakable loyalty to international socialism, they have contributed whatever could possibly be contributed under such devilishly hard conditions. . . .

Lenin and Trotsky and their friends were the *first*, those who went ahead as an example to the proletariat of the world; they are still the *only ones* up to now who can cry with Hutten: "I have dared!"

This is the essential and *enduring* in Bolshevik policy. In *this* sense theirs is the immortal historical service of having marched at the head of the international proletariat with the conquest of political power and the practical placing of the problem of the realization of socialism, and of having advanced mightily the settlement of the score between capital and labor in the entire world. In Russia, the problem could only be posed. It could not be solved in Russia. And in *this* sense, the future everywhere belongs to "Bolshevism."[46]

The Myth of "State" Socialism

The single worst legacy of Stalinism was to reinforce the mistaken notion that socialism can be measured by the degree of state control of the economy. Capitalist societies with relatively strong social spending programs (at least in the past) and some state-run industries were considered moderately socialist—like Sweden. (I can't count how many times I have been asked, "When you say socialism, do you mean Sweden?") Societies with more complete state control of the economy—like the Stalinist Soviet Union before it fell, or Cuba today—were considered fully socialist, or "communist."

The existence of a more or less expansive social safety net may indicate a strong history of class struggle and strong unions that at some point were able to extract important concessions from the employers. But concessions wrested from a capitalist state do not render that society socialist. Nor is the degree of state ownership a measure of socialism. State-run industries under capitalism do not operate as islands of socialism, but on the same principles of profit and loss as in the private sector. "A kind of spurious socialism has arisen . . . that . . . declares *all* state ownership . . . to be socialistic," Frederick Engels wrote more than one hundred years ago. "Certainly, if the taking over by the state of the tobacco industry is socialistic, then Napoleon . . . must be numbered among the founders of socialism."[47]

Even complete state ownership, Engels argued, is not socialism:

The transformation—either into joint-stock companies and trusts, or into State-ownership—does not do away with the capitalistic nature of the productive forces. In the joint-stock companies and trusts, this is obvious. And the modern State, again, is only the organization that bourgeois society takes on in order to support the external conditions of the capitalist mode of production against the encroachments as well of the workers as of individual capitalists. The modern state, no matter what its form, is essentially a capitalist machine—the state of the capitalists, the ideal personification of the total national capital. The more it proceeds to the taking over of productive forces, the more does it actually become the national capitalist, the more citizens does it exploit. The workers remain wageworkers—proletarians.[48]

Before Stalin expelled him from Russia in 1928, Trotsky waged a fight against the rising bureaucracy. But he clung to the idea that since nationalized property in Russia had been established as a result of a workers' revolution, Russia could not be "state capitalist," that is, a nation where the state exercised the same control over industry as the capitalists in other countries. Nevertheless, he could still say about the nationalized industries in Mexico in the 1930s that "the nationalization of railways and oilfields in Mexico has of course nothing in common with socialism. It is a measure of state capitalism." Trotsky noted that in Mexico, union leaders were involved in the management of these state-run industries. This had nothing to do with workers' control. The union leaders' were expected to play the role of "disciplining the working class, making it more industrious in the service of the common interests of the state, which appears on the surface to merge with the interests of the working class itself."[49] This is certainly the role that unions played in Stalin's Russia.

In 1980, a workers' newspaper, *Jednosc,* published by Solidarność activists in Szczecin, Poland, made the same point, arguing that a distinction must be made between state ownership and social ownership, because the Polish state "apparatus" represented the "denial" and "negation" of the "world of labor."[50]

With state ownership of production, "the capitalist relation is not done away with," wrote Engels, "it is rather brought to a head."[51] Countries where most of the means of production are concentrated in the hands of a state bureaucracy, but where workers have no control over that production, have nothing to do with socialism. Workers' revolts in Eastern Europe—including the forming of workers' councils in Hungary in 1956, similar to the 1917 soviets—were the practical proof that these societies, which had been erected after Soviet invasion and based on the Stalinist model, were socialist in name only.

The Cuban Revolution overthrew a corrupt regime, stood up to the colossus to the north, and implemented a series of sweeping social reforms benefiting Cuba's poor, making it one of the most remarkable revolutions in the Western Hemisphere. But Cuba's workers played hardly any role at all in its victory, nor did they exercise any control over the state in its aftermath. Fidel Castro, Ernesto "Che" Guevara, and a relatively small group of several hundred guerrillas toppled the brutal and corrupt regime of Fulgencia Batista in 1959. Facing a US embargo, they began to nationalize US-owned property. Castro only retroactively declared the Cuban Revolution "socialist" some two years later, modeling Cuba's one-party state (based on Fidel's personal rule) on Russian-style state capitalist–led development. Supporters of Cuba (that is, who support the regime itself rather than its defense against the United States) claim that various reforms such as improved health care, better education, and so on, are indications of Cuba's socialist character. These were no doubt important gains of the revolution. But then again, a number of important democratic and social gains issued also from the French Revolution, and it was not socialist. If free secondary education and national health care are to be deemed socialist, then Canada too must be included on the list.[52]

The claim is also made that the Cuban people exercise democratic control over the government. But this is to confuse mass participation and popularity with democratic decision-making and control. Popular organizations in Cuba are transmission belts for directives from the top, rather than institutions of control from below. Bureaucratic planning is geared toward figuring out how to develop and diversify the Cuban economy, of which labor is merely another input that is exploited in the same way workers are exploited in a GM factory in Detroit. Raúl Castro, Fidel's brother, described the role of unions in Cuba in the 1970s as something akin to the role of managers in a capitalist enterprise: "One of the principal functions of the trade unions under socialism is to serve as a vehicle for the orientation, directives, and goals which the revolutionary power must convey to the working masses. . . . The principal tasks [in which the unions should be involved] are productivity and work discipline; [and] more efficient utilization of the work day."[53] Minister of Labor Jorge Risquet was careful that same year to inform Cuba's workers that "the fact that Fidel and I have suggested that the workers should be consulted does not mean that we are going to negate the vanguard role that the Party must play. . . . The decision and responsibility [in the enterprise]," he insisted, "fall to the management," which must have, "and does have, all the authority to act."[54]

The same holds true for planning. A socialist society seeks to end the anarchy of the market by introducing conscious planning. But planning alone doesn't equal socialism. There are already elements of planning under capitalism. There is planning within firms, within the Pentagon, in the post office, and so on. But none of these forms of planning eliminate the anarchy of the market. Instead, they are driven by it. There is state planning in Cuba, but the plan is shaped by Cuba's need for survival and the negotiation of its precarious position within the world economy, of which it is a small, isolated patch. The planning isn't democratic, or fully under the planners' control. In all of these examples, the planning is designed to maximize output and profit at the expense of the worker, not to meet human need. Imagine the tremendous organization and planning involved in executing a major US-led war, and you get some idea of what might be possible if all that energy were used to adequately feed, house, clothe, and educate everyone on the planet.

The question of nationalization is not unimportant, as for example when Bolivian workers and peasants demand that the country's natural gas industry be nationalized in order that the wealth it yields doesn't end up siphoned off by global capital. But so long as nationalization is based upon production and competition in a world market, it will be *capitalist* nationalization.

For Marxists, nationalization can only be a weapon in the transformation of society in a socialist direction if the working class has first placed itself in power. Is it doing the planning or is it being planned? The question of whether socialism exists therefore does not depend on this or that form of property (private ownership or nationalization), but on whether the society is in the hands of the associated producers—the working class. In fact, the aim of workers' power is to implement a series of economic and social transformations that do away with all class distinctions and create a society whereby the state—an instrument of class domination—gradually fades away. As Engels wrote, "The proletariat seizes the public power, and by means of this transforms the socialized means of production, slipping from the hands of the bourgeoisie, into public property." The economy, now under workers' control, socializes the means of production so that production and distribution can be carried out according to a rational plan that meets human need. "In proportion as anarchy in social production vanishes," Engels continued, "the political authority of the state dies out."[55] To be successful, this process requires that socialism be international. All talk of there being long-standing islands of socialism—socialist states—floating for years on a sea of capitalist competition is simply absurd. Socialism in one cooperative, one city, one island, or one country, is a contradiction in terms.

Chapter Ten

Imperialism, Nationalism, and War

The late historian Eric Hobsbawm calculated that 187 million people died from wars in the twentieth century—more than the total world population in AD 1000 and a tenth of the total world population in 1913.[1] This century—with the US wars and occupations in Iraq and Afghanistan, its drone attacks, and its military interventions in several other countries—promises similar, if not worse, barbarism.

Given this grim picture, it is tempting to see war as something that is inherent in human nature—something we are "hard-wired" to do. In this view, war comes from the fact that people naturally divide into groups—racial, ethnic, linguistic—and develop hostility to those who are "different." This concept has been reinforced by various pseudo-scientific studies that compare humans to other animals—though they are careful to choose only the aggressive ones—in order to show that we relish war.

In *The Dark Side of Man*, Michael Ghiglieri, a protégé of primatologist Jane Goodall, argues that men are biologically programmed to commit rape, murder, war, and genocide, and that this tendency derives from our closest primate, the chimpanzee.[2] "Chimpanzee-like violence," write primatologists Dale Peterson and Richard Wrangham in another book, *Demonic Males*, "preceded and paved the way for human war, making modern humans the dazed survivors of a continuous, 5-million-year habit of lethal aggression."[3]

The reference to primate behavior to explain human behavior is highly selective. Some experts argue that the chimp example itself exaggerates the level of violence among them—for example, the famous researcher Jane Goodall noted that violence among chimpanzees increased considerably when she and her fellows began providing bananas to them, thus altering their natural patterns of behavior.

Instead of choosing allegedly violence-prone, hierarchically organized chimps, why not use the equally genetically close to human primates, the bonobos? "Had

Bonobos been known earlier," writes authors Frans de Waal and Frans Lanting, "reconstructions of human evolution might have emphasized sexual relations, equality between males and females, and the origin of the family, instead of war, hunting, tool technology, and other masculine fortes. Bonobo society seems ruled by the 'Make Love, Not War' slogan of the 1960s rather than the myth of a bloodthirsty killer ape that has dominated textbooks for at least three decades."[4]

But the real point is that human behavior cannot be understood by studying nonhumans. It may be true that human beings have the capacity for aggression, submission, and a host of other behavioral traits. But for every example of aggression in human behavior, we can also find peaceful cooperation and sharing. Moreover, it is a big step from aggressive behavior and systematic, armed conflict, that is, warfare. If human beings are naturally warlike, one wonders why it is necessary for governments to take young men at a very early age and put them through a rigorous retraining to make them capable of systematically killing other humans.

As noted in a previous chapter, our ability to change culturally—mediated through cooperation, tool use, and language—makes human beings adaptable to different environments—and capable of exhibiting, depending on the context, a wide range of potential behaviors. In short, we are not hard-wired for little else but cooperative behavior.

One of the most popular anthropology books—still used in many introductory classes—is the 1968 *Yanomamö: The Fierce People* by Napoleon A. Chagnon. The book examined a group of Amazonian hunters who were gripped by constant warfare. Chagnon claimed that the violent lifeways of the Yanomami represented "a truly primitive cultural adaptation . . . before it was altered by or destroyed by our culture."[5] Chagnon's account has been used repeatedly to bolster the idea that warring was the normal state of tribal peoples before contact with Europeans.

But the Yanomami were far from being a pristine culture. The Yanomami had begun contact with Europeans beginning in the mid-1700s, when slave-catchers invaded their territory. Anthropologist R. Brian Ferguson argues convincingly that there was a big spike in warfare among the Yanomami beginning in the 1950s as a result of game depletion, disruption of the culture caused by the introduction of devastating European diseases, and, most importantly, "antagonistic interests regarding access to or control over trade in Western manufactured goods."[6]

For the majority of our time on the planet, as noted earlier in this book, we have lived largely in foraging bands with no formal hierarchy, no standing armies, no class divisions, and no state structures. Food and other resources were shared. In these societies, warfare was far less frequent, and its character far less severe, than today's warfare. "Under conditions where portable wealth does not exist," wrote anthropologist Bronislaw Malinowski, "where food is too perishable and too clumsy to be accumulated and transported; where slavery is of no value because every individual consumes exactly as much as he produces—force is a useless implement for the transfer of wealth."[7]

Modern-day and recently existing hunter-gatherer societies cannot be said to be living or to have lived in a state unaffected by the impact of global capitalism over the past couple of centuries. Yet studies reveal that many of these societies either have no war at all or are considered "unwarlike." An extensive 1940s study of existing anthropological data, *The Study of War*, found that among 590 different societies reviewed, 64 percent were either found to have no war or to be unwarlike—and half of those relatively peaceful societies were nomadic foraging societies.[8] They were not nonviolent societies—but feuds and the occasional revenge killing can hardly be compared to the massive slaughterhouse that is modern-day warfare.

The character of war in pre-class and pre-state societies of which we have any record was vastly different from modern warfare. There were no professional groups of fighters. Men (and sometimes women) were hunters or fighters, as conditions demanded. Often, war consisted of skirmishes that broke off as soon as anyone was killed or injured. Among Plains Indians, war parties tried to avoid combat that resulted in death, and "counting coup," touching an enemy's body with the hand or a special stick, ranked as a higher feat than killing.[9] Renegade Rhode Island colonist Roger Williams noted that the fighting between the Indian nations he observed was "farre lesse bloudy and devouring than the cruell Warres of Europe."[10] According to Captain John Underhill, a leader of a massacre on an undefended Pequot village in 1637, a group of Narragansett Indians allied with the English withdrew from the attack, complaining that the English style of warfare "slays too many men."[11]

Only with the rise of agriculture and the production of a surplus—which in turn produced the first ruling classes (the keepers of the surplus)—did warfare become a systematic practice, engaged in by specially armed subjects of a ruler in order to gain wealth and slaves. The rulers in turn created loyalty among their armed retainers by giving out the spoils of conquest—land, slaves, and goods.

But the struggle for the surplus didn't just produce wars between rival kingdoms. Class society also gave rise, inevitably, to violent conflict between social classes over how the surplus was used. Systematic warfare came with the emergence of the state—of special armed bodies whose purpose was both to protect the position of the minority who controlled the surplus (from the majority who produced it), as well as pillage the wealth produced by other groups.

Modern warfare has economic rather than biological roots. "In the modern world undoubtedly the most potent cause of war is economic rivalry—a purely cultural phenomenon having no biological basis whatsoever," wrote anthropologist Ashley Montagu.[12] But even the wars of conquest and plunder by Alexander the Great and the Roman Empire pale in comparison to war as it developed under capitalism.

White Man's Burden

The idea of peaceful competition is an invention of economics professors. War, conquest, and plunder accompanied capitalism from its inception. With the emergence of the world's first commercial powers in Europe in the fifteenth and sixteenth centuries, violence was the rule rather than the exception. As the merchant capitalists became powerful, they depended upon their "home" governments to extend their markets and sources of raw materials and goods by force. What we know as freewheeling pirates on the open seas were often employees of one state, hired to capture and plunder the booty stolen, extracted, or extorted from some part of the world by another state. The market and the state intertwined, producing a system of competing states, fighting in Europe, North America, and Asia for control of the world's trade and the creation of colonies that could be exploited for raw materials and labor.

In the European powers' struggle for supremacy in North America, Native American peoples were deliberately pitted against each other. European encroachment on their farmlands and hunting grounds, and the introduction of European diseases decimated their ranks, pushing them westward and forcing them to cling to survival in tiny enclaves. Massacres were common. Marx described in *Capital* how

> in 1703 those sober exponents of Protestantism, the Puritans of New England, by decrees of their assembly set a premium of 40 pounds on every Indian scalp and every captured redskin; in 1720, a premium of 100 pounds was set on every scalp; in 1744, after Massachusetts bay had proclaimed a certain tribe as rebels, the following prices were laid down: for a male scalp of 12 years and upwards, 100 pounds in new currency, for a male prisoner 105 pounds, for women and children prisoners 50 pounds, for the scalps of women and children 50 pounds.[13]

This earlier, commercial, and colonial form of imperialism—which as we've seen also involved the slave trade and forced labor—gave way later to a new form of imperialism based on the rise of industrial power.

At the time Marx cowrote *The Communist Manifesto*, industrial capitalism had developed only in Britain and a few European countries. But as the twentieth century approached, capitalism became a truly global system. The relatively small capitalist enterprises of the early phase of industrial capitalism gave way, in the process of competition and crisis, to monopoly—the dominance of one or a handful of giant conglomerates over a single market. With the growth of monopoly capitalism, capitalist production burst the bounds of the nation-state.

The period of the 1890s found the most powerful new industrialized states—Britain and France, and soon the United States, Germany, and Japan—scrambling to divide the world between themselves into colonies or "spheres of influence." The new imperialism was marked off from its predecessors by the sheer scale of the conquest. In 1876, for example, Africans controlled almost 90 percent of African territory. By

1900, Europeans controlled 90 percent of African territory. Indeed, the entire surface of the globe was conquered and divvied up between a tiny number of powers.[14]

The great powers sought colonies and semi-colonies in order to secure sources of raw materials (produced with cheap, sometimes forced, labor) and investments, as well as to keep out competing empires. In southern Africa, Black Africans were forced off their land and compelled to work in gold and diamond mines, making a handful of men like Cecil Rhodes and J. B. Robinson extremely rich. (Knowing this, I wince every time I turned on the radio to hear a bouncy advertisement for J. B. Robinson jewelry.) When gold was discovered in Matabeleland in the 1880s, Lobengula, chief of the Matabele people, refused to accept a treaty he had been tricked into signing that gave Rhodes and his associates the right to mine for gold anywhere they wanted. Rhodes, who was already rich from mining diamonds, organized an army and invaded Matabeleland, massacring thousands using the Maxim gun. Each of the 672 soldiers in Rhodes's army was promised six thousand acres of land and twenty gold claims.[15] This is how Britain brought "enlightened" rule to Africa. The massacre prompted the poet Hillaire Belloc to write: "Whatever happens we have got / The Maxim gun and they have not."[16]

The case of the Belgian Congo is the most horrific example of how the effort to extract maximum profit could lead to mass murder. King Leopold of Belgium formed a society called the International Association of the Congo, whose "noble aim" was to render "lasting and disinterested services to the cause of progress."[17] The association's lasting service was, in reality, to provide a humanitarian cover for naked plunder. Leopold established a system to force Africans in the Congo River Basin to collect ivory and rubber. In order to force Africans to work, the colonizers sent armed militias to exterminate selected villages to compel other villages to submit. "To gather rubber in the district," wrote a former district commissioner in the Congo, "one must cut off hands, noses, and ears."[18] Historians estimate that Leopold's "humanitarian" enterprise resulted in the deaths of roughly six to ten million people between 1885 and 1908. This genocidal treatment of Africans was extremely profitable. The Anglo-Belgian India Rubber and Exploration Company made a profit of more than 700 percent in the Congo.[19]

The impact of British rule in India was no less atrocious. India on the eve of its conquest by the British in the 1750s was economically as wealthy as Europe. But forced labor, the wrecking of India's textile industry with cheap British manufactures, and the destruction of India's traditional irrigation and granary systems all combined to drain India's economy for many decades. Tens of millions of people died of starvation in a series of devastating famines. In Britain, criticism of the stinginess of its famine relief in India was brushed aside on social Darwinist grounds: "Every benevolent attempt made to mitigate the effects of famine and defective sanitation," finance minister Evelyn Baring assured his colleagues, only "serves but to enhance the evils resulting from overpopulation."[20] Aside from the construction of railroads—which in any case the British set up only in order to transport troops and move India's wealth out of the country—India was for a long period underdeveloped by British imperialism. "If the history of British rule in India," concluded historian Mike Davis, "were to be condensed to a single fact, it is this: there was no increase in India's per-capita income from 1757 to 1947."[21]

The Eagle and Its Talons

There is a peculiar national myth told in this country that the United States is neither an empire nor imperialist. We are, so the tale goes, a freedom-loving nation that goes to war only for noble causes like spreading freedom and democracy or defending the weak against the strong. "America the benevolent," wrote historian Sidney Lens,

> does not exist and never has existed. The United States has pilfered large territories from helpless or near-helpless peoples; it has forced its will on scores of nations, against their wishes and against their interests; it has violated hundreds of treaties and understandings; it has committed war crimes as shocking as most; it has wielded a military stick and a dollar carrot to forge an imperialist empire such as man has never known before; it has intervened ruthlessly in the internal life of dozens of nations to prevent them from choosing the leaders they did want or from overthrowing, by revolution, ones they didn't.[22]

This shouldn't surprise us, since the nation was founded on continental conquest based on the dispossession of lands occupied by the indigenous people who already inhabited it, as well as the carveout of a large part of Mexican territory in the West.

The United States emerged as a world power in the late 1800s, and quickly became the biggest economic power in the world. But it emerged as a power after the scramble for colonies was mostly completed. As a result of this, the United States found it congenial to develop a more informal empire. Where it was unable to establish its own exclusive sphere, for example in China, Washington advanced the "open door" policy in order to push its way in. But in its own "backyard," the Caribbean and the Pacific, the United States established a "closed door" policy, using its military power to establish absolute hegemony. When the United States went to war with Spain in 1898, it claimed that it was motivated by a desire to free Spanish colonies—Cuba, Puerto Rico, and the Philippines, from Spanish tyranny. As payment for this benevolent service, the United States made colonies or protectorates out of all of them.

Politicians in Washington were not above justifying conquest on racist grounds, either. President William McKinley explained to a group of Methodist Church leaders in 1899 that granting the Filipinos "self-government" would undoubtedly create "anarchy and misrule." Therefore, the only choice for the United States was to "take them all and to educate the Filipinos, and uplift and civilize and Christianize them."[23] But first the United States had to send seventy thousand troops to the Philippines to crush the independence movement there, which had first developed in opposition to Spanish rule, but had since turned against the Americans. One historian describes how by 1901 the war had degenerated into a mass slaughter. After Filipino nationalist guerrillas attacked a town in Samar under US occupation and killed fifty-four US soldiers, the American military instigated a reign of terror on the island:

> General ["Howlin' Jake"] Smith, fresh from his "victories" in northern Luzon and Panay, was chosen to lead the American mission of revenge. Smith's order to his men embarking upon the Samar campaign could not have been more explicit: "Kill and burn, kill and burn, the more you kill and the more you burn the more you please me." . . . When asked to define the age limit for killing, Smith gave his infamous reply: "Everything over ten." Smith ordered Samar to be turned into a "howling wilderness" so that "even the birds could not live there."[24]

In the end, the US Army's murderous scorched-earth policy wiped out upwards of a million Filipinos.[25]

The barbarism of the United States in the Philippines prompted the great satirist Mark Twain to become a staunch opponent of imperialism. "I left these shores . . . a red-hot imperialist. I wanted the American eagle to go screaming into the Pacific," Twain told a *New York Herald* reporter in 1900. However, he explained, "I have seen that we do not intend to free, but to subjugate the people of the Philippines. We have gone there to conquer, not to redeem." He concluded, "I am an anti-imperialist. I am opposed to having the eagle put its talons on any other land."[26]

Even where the United States shunned formal colonies, its practices were almost identical. In the Caribbean, the United States made a practice of demanding that countries hand over control of their customs houses to US officials and banks, in order to ensure repayment of loans. When a country refused, the United States invaded. Marines occupied Haiti and stayed there from 1915 to 1934, for example. They imposed a new constitution that opened up Haiti to foreign land ownership and handed the country's customs houses and banking system over to the National City Bank of New York, and crushed all resistance.[27]

Woodrow Wilson in 1907 clarified how, for the United States, the "open door" policy was a strategy to maximize US dominance: "Since trade ignores national boundaries, and the manufacturer insists on having the world as a market, the flag of his nation must follow him, and the doors of the nations which are closed against him must be battered down. Concessions obtained by financiers must be safeguarded by ministers of state, even if the sovereignty of unwilling nations be outraged in the process."[28]

Imperialist Rivalry and War

As the earth became completely carved up into "spheres of influence" between the great powers, competition between them intensified. A "balance of power" was maintained by each state arming itself to the teeth. But the balance was continually in danger of being upset by the emergence of a new power eager for a slice of the imperial pie.

Lenin, writing at the time of the First World War, described this new period of capitalism as *imperialism*—in a nutshell, capitalism in its monopoly stage, the world market dominated by giant capitalist trusts, backed up by powerful states fighting to carve up the world amongst themselves. He called monopoly capitalism "the economic essence of imperialism," noting its main features as "monopolies, oligarchy, the striving for domination and not for freedom, the exploitation of an increasing number of small or weak nations by a handful of the richest or most powerful nations."[29]

Lenin's analysis, written in 1916 in the midst of the slaughter of the First World War, pointed to how imperialism was not a policy, but a new stage in the development of capitalism that grew out of earlier conditions. Just as "free" competition gave way to monopoly, so "free trade" gave way to trade wars and armed conflict. The logic of imperialism was grounded in international economic competition between states, leading to war.

There were people at the time, like German socialist Karl Kautsky, who argued that the creation of a world market and economic interdependence between nations would make war obsolete, creating a new system of "ultra-imperialism."[30] Unfortunately, the fact that there is economic interdependence does not lead to peaceful relations between states, much less their disappearance. Two tendencies always have to be kept in mind, as Lenin noted, in capitalism's development: on the one hand, "the awakening of national life . . . and the creation of nation states" and, on the other hand, "the development and growing frequency of international intercourse" and "the break-down of national barriers."[31] These two contradictory tendencies—toward interdependence on the one hand, and toward consolidation of national states on the other—have been constant features of capitalism throughout its history. The balance between the two tendencies, and the way the contradiction has expressed itself, has shifted. But the contradiction remains, even today, at the heart of world capitalism.

In addition to its role in maintaining class rule, capitalists needed a centralized state as a means of creating a single, unified market that could facilitate commerce. But the state is also crucial in providing necessary infrastructure, and sometimes the pooling of capital resources needed for national capitalists to operate and compete effectively. As capitalism burst the bounds of the nation-state, the coercive military function of the state took on a new dimension—that of protecting (and projecting) the interests of the capitalists of one country over those of another. The role of the state increased, the size of the state bureaucracy increased, and the size of its coercive apparatus increased.

"The development of world capitalism leads," wrote Russian revolutionary Nikolai Bukharin, "on the one hand, to an internationalization of economic life and, on the other, to the leveling of economic differences—and to an infinitely greater degree, the same process of economic development intensifies the tendency to 'nationalize' capitalist interests, to form narrow 'national' groups armed to the teeth and ready to hurl themselves at one another at any moment."[32]

It is true that, as Trotsky wrote during the First World War, "the natural tendency of our economic system . . . is to seek to break through the state boundaries. The whole globe, the land and the sea, the surface as well as the interior, has become one economic workshop, the different parts of which are inseparably connected with each other."[33] But this process, rather than leading to peaceful competition, leads to a struggle for dominance: "The way the governments propose to solve this problem of imperialism is not through the intelligent, organized cooperation of all of humanity's producers, but through the exploitation of the world's economic system by the capitalist class of the victorious country; which country is by this War to be transformed from a great power into a world power."[34]

Two devastating world wars that consumed millions of lives underscored the truth of Trotsky's observation. The whole history of world conflict up to the present day consists of the continual rejigging of power relations between a handful of states and their allies. The economic relations between different states continually change (think of the recent rise of China and India), compelling new trade and diplomatic intrigues, as "upstarts" try to assert their power and the established powers try to hang on, or expand, what power they have. Ultimately, force decides who is to be top dog. But since the economic balance of forces keeps changing, new conflicts always emerge and the game begins anew.

Today, we no longer have a world divided between many contending colonial powers, as in the early twentieth century. A series of anticolonial movements and revolutions, combined with the declining economic value of the colonies, put an end to this era in the years following the Second World War. The United States emerged as the world's dominant power, both economically and militarily. Instead of a world divided between several centers of world power, imperial rivalry took the form of a Cold War between two superpowers, the United States and the Soviet Union. Each had enough nuclear weapons to destroy the world several times over, in a balance of terror appropriately called "MAD"—mutually assured destruction.

Much of the conflict of the Cold War took the form not of direct military conflict between Soviet Union and the United States, but of smaller conflicts on the system's periphery, such as the wars in Korea and Vietnam. Russia was never economically strong enough to challenge US hegemony over major parts of the globe. Ideologically, though, the United States used the Russian threat as an excuse for whatever interventions it undertook, such as when it destabilized and overthrew nationalist regimes it opposed. Fighting communism was used as the excuse to overthrow the Mossadegh government in Iran in 1953, the Arbenz government in Guatemala in 1954, the Allende government in Chile in 1973, and many others.[35]

The end of the Cold War did not mean the end of imperialism or military conflict, but it has changed the playing field. The United States emerged as the sole superpower, more than twice the size of its nearest economic rival and several times bigger militarily. Even today, the United States accounts for half the world's military spending.[36] It is the only state with a truly global military reach, boasting 725 military bases around the globe, not including the United States.[37] The logic of imperialist rivalry compels America's rulers to continually demonstrate and reinforce this dominance, lest its relative position in the world pecking order slips or any potential challengers detect any weakening.

After the fall of the Soviet Union, the United States cast around for a new rationale for its role as global hegemon. It found it in the "war on terror." The Bush administration saw in the September 11, 2001, tragedy a unique window of opportunity—a modern-day Pearl Harbor—that created ideal conditions for advancing its agenda. Some months after September 11, Secretary of State Condoleezza Rice described the attacks as an "enormous opportunity," and that the United States "must move to take advantage of these new opportunities."[38]

The invasion of Afghanistan was first and foremost a warm-up for the invasion of Iraq, and was secondarily about establishing a strategic military presence in Central Asia. Overthrowing the Taliban and going after al-Qaeda was merely a pretext. Likewise, the invasion and occupation of Iraq had nothing to do with the character of the Iraqi regime. The United States has always supported "friendly" dictators—and continues to do so. The US invasion of Iraq in 2003, in the extremely accurate preinvasion prediction of Jay Bookman of the *Atlanta Journal-Constitution*, was "not really about Iraq. It is not about weapons of mass destruction, or terrorism, or Saddam, or U.N. resolutions." Rather, the war was intended "to mark the official emergence of the United States as a full-fledged global empire, seizing sole responsibility and authority as planetary policeman." They never had an "exit strategy," argued Bookman, not out of incompetence, but because the United States was interested in creating "permanent military bases in that country from which to dominate the Middle East, including neighboring Iran."[39]

It is tempting to see the movement of American imperialism into overdrive after September 11 as the product of temporary insanity. Some of the pronouncements of the Bush administration would have come off as almost Monty Pythonesque if it weren't for the terrible bloodletting they justified. "The generals in Iraq must understand clearly there will be consequences for their behavior," Bush smugly warned on the eve of the US invasion. "Should they choose . . . to behave in a way that endangers the lives of their own citizens, as well as citizens in the neighborhood, there will be a consequence. They will be held to account."[40] This is reminiscent of the Spanish *requerimiento*, an official document that sixteenth-century conquistadors were meant to read out loud to their victims (in Spanish, a language those about to be attacked could not understand) before they conquered them. The document insisted that its listeners bow down to the Church and the Spanish Crown, warning:

> But if you do not do this, and maliciously make delay in it . . . we shall powerfully enter into your country, and shall make war against you in all ways and manners that we can, and shall subject you to the yoke and obedience of the Church and of their highnesses. We shall take you, and your wives, and your children, and shall make slaves of them, and as such shall sell and dispose of them as their highnesses may command; and we shall take away your goods, and shall do you all the mischief and damage that we can, as to vassals who do not obey. . . . And we protest that the deaths and losses which shall accrue from this are your fault, and not that of their highnesses, or ours, nor of these cavaliers who come with us.[41]

The text may be arcane, but its twisted logic is utterly modern. Obey the United States, and if you refuse, you will be to blame for the destruction we visit on you. Only now a twist is added: Since we are here to give you "freedom," you have no reason to resist. "We're here to give you your fucking freedom," a US Marine shouted at a crowd of Iraqis protesting the occupation in Baghdad. "Now back off."[42]

The insanity thesis ignores the essential continuity in US foreign policy. The disagreements between different administrations and parties in Washington have not been over *whether* the United States should militarily and economically dominate the world, but *how* (unilaterally or with subordinate allies?). Democrat Bill Clinton, it should be recalled, ratcheted up the military budget by $112 billion, rehabilitated Reagan's "Star Wars" missile defense program, and sent troops into other countries more times than all four previous presidents combined. He enforced devastating sanctions against Iraq that resulted in a dramatic increase in child mortality rates.[43] Indeed, the Clinton administration made the case for intervening in "failed states" to impose "regime change," setting the table for what was to come.[44]

Three of the chief goals of US imperialism today, according to Chalmers Johnson, are: to "maintain absolute military preponderance over the rest of the world, a task that includes imperial policing to ensure that no part of the empire slips the leash"; "attempting to control as many sources of petroleum as possible, both to service America's insatiable demand for fossil fuels and to use it as a bargaining chip with even more oil-dependent regions"; and "providing work and income for the military-industrial complex (as, for example, in the exorbitant profits Halliburton has extracted for building and operating Camps Bondsteel and Monteith)."[45] This comprehensive framework has the advantage of explaining not only why the United States invaded Iraq (oil) but why it meddles in Africa, Asia, and every other corner of the globe.

Obama's presidency has not diverted from Washington's goal of maintaining US military and economic hegemony. The style may have changed—as a necessary part of rehabilitating the tarnished image of the United States resulting from Bush's disastrous overreach in the wake of 9/11—but the substance of US foreign policy remains.

Obama signaled the essential continuity between his and Bush's foreign policy by reappointing Bush's defense secretary Robert Gates. "Contrary to popular misperception," writes Ashley Smith, "Obama was never a 'peace candidate' nor did he ever intend to be a 'peace president.' He has increased military spending, which surpassed $700 billion in 2011, deployed 30,000 troops in his surge into Afghanistan, expanded that war into Pakistan, tried to bully Iraq into allowing an extension of the American occupation, increased drone and black operations in Yemen and Somalia, and launched the NATO air war to topple Washington's one-time ally Muammar Gaddafi."[46]

In his Nobel Peace Prize Address in December 2009, Obama offered standard boilerplate arguments about how the United States "has helped underwrite global security for more than six decades with the blood of our citizens and the strength of our arms."[47] (One can only marvel that this sentence could be part of an acceptance speech for a "peace" prize.) Several Republicans notables praised Obama's remarks. "The irony is that George W. Bush could have delivered the very same speech. It was truly an American president's message to the world," said Bradley A. Blakeman, a businessman and former Bush White House strategist.[48]

Obama's message involved more than speeches. He refused to investigate torture under Bush's watch, failed to come through on his promise to close down the prison at Guantánamo where the United States indefinitely holds "terror" suspects without trial, and, as already noted, gave himself the authority to assassinate US citizens suspected of engaging in terrorism.

The domestic component of the ongoing "war on terror," which, despite rhetorical alterations, continued under Obama, has actually intensified since the passage of the USA PATRIOT Act. During his first election campaign, Obama criticized the Bush administration for being "one of the most secretive administrations in our nation's history." He promised to protect whistle-blowers, calling their acts courageous and patriotic. Once elected, he continued to promise "unprecedented levels of openness."[49] Obama subsequently has proven to be more committed to secrecy and Orwellian levels of state surveillance than any previous president. He prosecuted PFC Chelsea Manning and sent her to prison for thirty-five years for leaking information exposing war crimes committed by the United States in the Middle East—war crimes for which no one was held accountable. He is also seeking to prosecute Edward Snowden, a former defense contractor employee for the CIA, for leaking National Security Agency documents exposing the US government's two hitherto secret surveillance plans to vacuum up, in collusion with the telecommunications industry, massive amounts of electronic data from US citizens, including records of phone calls, as well as online communication between people inside and outside the United States.[50] Alongside the shadow banking system that brought down the world economy in 2008 has grown a secret, shadow government dedicated to protecting US power.

In response to the failed efforts by the United States to leverage large-scale invasions to its own advantage in Iraq and Afghanistan, Obama has increasingly relied on unmanned drone attacks in Afghanistan, Pakistan, and North Africa, which have resulted in the killing of hundreds of noncombatants, including many children. According to a 2012 study by Stanford Law School and New York University's School of Law, "drone strikes killed 2,562–3,325 people in Pakistan, of whom 474–881 were civilians, including 176 children."[51]

The United States has been an imperialist power now for more than a century, cloaking its predatory aims with claims to be spreading democracy, removing tyrants, fighting communism, bringing humanitarian help, and now defending the "homeland" against terrorism. The most significant innovation after September 11 was the brazenness with which pundits proclaimed America's God-given right to police the world. It is now fashionable to accept that the United States is an empire that has the right and duty to be, in the words of international relations professor and former army colonel Andrew Bacevich, "the world's sole military superpower until the end of time."[52]

That does not mean that everything has gone Washington's way. The defeat in Vietnam was a clear reminder that the beast is not invulnerable. The way in which the occupations of Iraq and Afghanistan, which were meant to be cakewalks, turned into quagmires, thanks primarily to the stiff resistance Iraqis and Afghans put up to the destruction of their respective countries, is another reminder.

The "National Interest"

Politicians from both sides of the aisle are fond of making pronouncements about "national interests," or what's good or bad for "America" and its "national security." It is a time-honored practice to present the interests of the dominant class as those of the nation as a whole. An appeal to nationalism justifies all sorts of nefarious practices, from government surveillance and repression to building up large military arsenals and bombing other countries.

The idea of the nation has some basis in reality—everyone on the planet belongs to some nationality and lives in a territory ruled over by a state. But everyone also belongs to a social class, and national policy serves the interests of the dominant one. "Beware of people who make a sacred idol of the State," writes international studies professor Benedict Anderson, "and beware of those who talk a lot about 'our splendid ancestors.' Your pocket is about to be picked."[53]

Whenever phrases like "national interests" are thrown around to defend some government action—whether it is a spending cut or a declaration of war—it is necessary to ask, in Lenin's words, "who stands to gain?" "It is not important," wrote

Lenin, "*who* directly advocates a particular policy, since under the present noble system of capitalism, any money-bag can always 'hire,' buy, or enlist any number of lawyers, writers, and even parliamentary deputies, professors, parsons, and the like to defend any views. We live in an age of commerce, when the bourgeoisie have no scruples about trading in honor or conscience."[54]

In every war the United States has fought, the country's rulers have claimed it was fought in the "national interest." Yet in each case the beneficiaries were a minority at the top. Every extension of empire benefited not the majority, whose conditions of life always had more in common with the majority of the people being conquered, but bankers, industrialists, military contractors, and so on. This truth, in wartime, can be a dangerous one for those expressing it. "Wars throughout history have been waged for conquest and plunder," Eugene Debs told a crowd in 1918. "The master class has always declared the wars; the subject class has always fought the battles."[55] For that speech, Debs was imprisoned at age sixty-two.

Globalization: The New Frontier-Less Frontier?

Capitalism has always been a global system. But the term "globalization," as used by politicians and the media, seems to mean something more. What are they referring to? Globalization (sometimes called *neoliberalism*) is "shorthand for an aggressive program," first developed in the late 1970s, "that involves government deregulation of industry, privatization of government services and liberalization of barriers to international finance and trade."[56] These policies, pushed by international financial and trade institutions like the World Trade Organization, the International Monetary Fund (IMF), and the World Bank over the last twenty-five years, are designed to pry open national markets to US and European capitalist interests. As an ideology, globalization has been used to justify the necessity of domestic austerity measures, job cuts, and social service cuts. "Each national ruling class and government can wash their hands of responsibility, saying essentially, 'Globalization made me do it,'" writes journalist Lee Sustar.[57]

Some writers see globalization as more than neoliberal economic policies—instead, it is a new stage of world economic development. Capitalist production, trade, and investment are so footloose, the argument goes, that national states have become irrelevant. "This emerging new stage in world capitalism," writes one left-wing economist, "points to a supersession through transnational integration of 'national' economies. Fundamentally, there has been a progressive dismantling of autonomous . . . national production systems and their reactivation as constituent elements of an integral world production system."[58]

The changes over the past three decades are certainly impressive. State capitalism has disappeared in Russia and Eastern Europe, as part of a steady worldwide trend away from directly state-owned economic economies, industries, or enterprises. World trade, foreign investment, and international financial transactions have increased astronomically over the past few decades. Foreign direct investment increased between 1982 and 2000 from $57 billion to $1.3 trillion.[59] The volume and value of world exports have grown tremendously since the 1980s, consistently higher than the world GDP growth rate. World merchandise exports increased from $1.84 trillion in 1983 to $7.4 trillion in 2003 Exports really took off after that, rising to $15.7 trillion in 2008, before dropping 15 percent for two years in a row after the onset of the Great Recession.[60] As of 2009, some 78,000 transnational corporations (TNCs) with about 780,000 foreign affiliates dominated world trade and production, employing 73 million people (up from 25 million in 1990), whose sales quadrupled from $6 to $25 trillion between 1990 and 2006.[61] According to researchers at the Swiss Federal Institute of Technology, of the 43,060 transnational corporations they examined in 2011, 147 interlocking corporations—many of them financial sector firms—control 40 percent of the wealth among them, and 737 control 80 percent.[62]

These facts have led some to revive the arguments made by Karl Kautsky in 1914 that economic integration signals the end of imperialism, that is, of competition between states for world domination. "The United States does not, and indeed no nation-state can today, form the center of an imperialist project," argue Michael Hardt and Antonio Negri in their influential tome *Empire*. "Imperialism is over. No nation will be world leader in the way modern European states were."[63]

The Hardt and Negri thesis is especially strange given the scale and number of military interventions by the United States in recent decades. If anything, the United States is far more dominant in the world today than any European power was in the era of classical imperialism. Moreover, it is committed to maintaining, in the words of neoconservative Paul Wolfowitz in a draft policy statement written in 1992, "the mechanisms for deterring potential competitors from even aspiring to a larger regional or global role."[64]

International economic institutions that are meant to reflect capitalism's global integration are actually controlled by a handful of nations. The IMF and the World Bank are not located in Washington, DC, by coincidence. The United States established these institutions after the Second World War, and they, along with the World Trade Organization, have been largely under its control. IMF "structural adjustment policies"—under which loans are advanced to poor countries on condition that they privatize, cut public spending, and open up their economy to foreign investment—are examples not of stateless globalization, but of economic imperialism.

There is a great deal of sense to the argument that capital is footloose and global. Transnational corporations are constantly shifting their finances and investments around the world in search of the best return, offering their "allegiance" to those states that give them the best tax breaks and other financial incentives, always looking

to park their money in offshore tax havens to avoid having to pay for the infrastructure—or other state provisions that provide some kind of safety net for workers and
the poor—without which their businesses could not operate.

But the argument that TNCs are completely stateless is exaggerated. Big corporations like Walmart, General Motors, and Monsanto may have a global reach, but
they still rely on their "home" state to provide the proper infrastructure—transportation, communication systems, and so on—necessary for their businesses to run profitably; not to mention the same infrastructure funded and guaranteed by other
countries within which they operate. Governments spend a great deal of their revenue
helping grease the wheels of big business. As one book noted,

> Up to half the total money spent each year by governments on various public poli-
> cies is used to ensure that business can do business. Denmark spends almost as
> much on direct business subsidies as it does on defense, policing, and housing and
> communities combined. The UK government provides more to businesses through
> various tax benefits and subsidies each year than it extracts in total corporate taxa-
> tion. It also spends over a quarter of its entire budget purchasing goods and services
> directly from the private sector. In Sweden, one-quarter of the costs of social pro-
> tection expenditure are directed towards employers. . . . [B]usinesses' share of total
> public expenditure—the amount of public expenditure dedicated to meeting the
> needs of business—accounts for at least 40 percent of total public expenditure in
> the major economies, with the highest corporate welfare bill, as a percentage of
> total expenditure, being recorded in the US.[65]

US multinationals receive enormous amounts of government help in the form of direct subsidies, tax breaks, government-funded university research and development,
and a host of other forms of corporate welfare. Walmart, the world's largest retailer,
with more than thirty-five hundred stores nationwide and eighteen hundred overseas,
has received state and local subsidies amounting to a billion dollars, according to a
2004 report.[66] Between 2011 and 2015, the oil and gas industry is expected to receive
$80 billion in tax breaks.[67] (This is particularly ironic, given that oil magnates the
Koch brothers, whose Koch Industries has received tens of millions in state subsidies,
are founders of the libertarian think tank CATO Institute that rails against corporate
welfare.)[68] A 2012 *New York Times* study found that states, counties, and cities "are
giving up more than $80 billion each year to companies," and that these companies
deliberately pit different locations against each other to extract the maximum concessions.[69] A 1996 *Boston Globe* study on government handouts to corporations concluded: "The $150 billion for corporate subsidies and tax benefits eclipses the annual
budget deficit of $130 billion. It's more than the $145 billion paid out annually for
the core programs of the social welfare state: Aid to Families with Dependent Children (AFDC), student aid, housing, food and nutrition, and all direct public assistance (excluding Social Security and medical care)."[70]

A stateless corporation is at a disadvantage compared to one backed by an economically and militarily powerful state that can provide various services to give it an edge over its rivals. The United States Export-Import Bank, for example, spends a billion dollars a year to promote the sale of US products overseas, mostly as subsidies to Fortune 500 companies.[71] The member countries of the Organization of Economic Cooperation and Development (OECD)—that is, the world's richest countries—impose high tariffs on food imports and give generous subsidies to domestic agricultural interests, without which they would not be profitable.[72] Foreign aid is notoriously employed to pry open foreign markets for the donor country's products.[73] "There are many companies with worldwide operations," writes one analyst. "Some even have multinational boards and executive teams. But, almost without exception, the world's most successful companies remain clearly identified with their countries of origin."[74]

Perhaps most importantly, business depends on state funds to bail it out in times of crisis; it was the aggressive actions of states—chiefly their central banks—that prevented the 2008 crisis from becoming even worse and reestablished the solvency and profitability of the financial system.

It would also be a mistake to think that the last several decades have been marked solely by a drive toward privatization. Much of the success of those developing or formerly developing nations that have become industrial nations with industries capable of competing with the United States, Europe, and Japan—South Korea, for example—is attributable not to state deregulation and privatization, but to conscious state-led economic planning and coordination. Even in China, which decided to open itself to the world market in the late 1970s, the state continues to play an outsized role in economic ownership and planning. In 2008, state-owned enterprises, though comprising only 3.1 percent of the total number of enterprises, accounted for 30 percent of total assets for all enterprises in China.[75]

Corporations also depend on other states when they operate overseas, requiring domestic and foreign governments to maintain a "good business climate." Whatever country they are operating in, corporations rely on the local police and other armed forces in order to keep the class struggle in check, and they depend on borders to manipulate the flow of migrant labor.

Economic integration does not equal peaceful coexistence between nations. The Russian Marxist Nikolai Bukharin's thoughts on the matter are still very relevant today. It doesn't follow from the internationalization of economic life, he argued,

> that social progress has already reached a stage where "national" states can coexist harmoniously. For the process of the internationalization of economic life is by no means identical with the process of the internationalization of capital interests. . . . Only those who do not see the contradictions in capitalist development, who good-naturedly assume . . . anarchic internationalization to be organized internationalization—can hope for the possibility of reconciling the "national" capitalist groups in the "higher unity" of peaceful capitalism.

The process of the internationalization of economic life can and does sharpen, to a high degree, the conflict of interests among the various "national" groups of the bourgeoisie. Indeed, the growth of international commodity exchange is by no means connected with the growth of "solidarity" between the exchanging groups. On the contrary, it can be accompanied by the growth of the most desperate competition, by a life and death struggle.[76]

Thomas Friedman formulated the relationship between the "free market" and armed force most famously: "The hidden hand of the market will never work without a hidden fist."[77] So long as there is no international (or supranational) state, backed by its own armed forces that represent the world capitalist class, capitalists will need the armed forces of their own national territory.

The economies of Asia are highly integrated and depend on trade with each other. That, however, does not prevent extreme tension from developing between China and Japan, for example, over control of strategic islands. Nor does it prevent the United States, as it witnesses the rise of China as a major world player, from attempting to "pivot" toward Asia as a means to shore up its regional alliances and contain China's aspirations to become a global power that might challenge US global hegemony. But even short of conflict between big powers, the United States, in order to demonstrate its dominance, routinely engages in armed intervention around the world. It does this not only because it needs, however disturbing this may seem, "practice." Failing to do so will give other nations and powers the idea that it isn't willing to back up its claims to hegemony with the appropriate force. How often have we heard the argument from politicians that failure to intervene in some particular region of the world will lead the United States to "lose credibility"?

Ultimately, the established international pecking order of power is a more or less unstable equilibrium that will eventually be shattered and replaced by new arrangements based on the relation of military force and the uneven development of the world economy, in which some states will emerge stronger and others decline. Lenin made this observation in 1916, when formal colonies still existed. Nevertheless, his point is still relevant:

> The only conceivable basis under capitalism for the division of spheres of influence, interests, colonies, etc., is a calculation of the *strength* of those participating, their general economic, financial, military strength, etc. And the strength of these participants in the division does not change to an equal degree, for the *even* development of different undertakings, trusts, branches of industry, or countries is impossible under capitalism. Half a century ago Germany was a miserable, insignificant country, if her capitalist strength is compared with that of the Britain of that time; Japan compared with Russia in the same way. Is it "conceivable" that in ten or twenty years' time the relative strength of the imperialist powers will have remained unchanged? It is out of the question.[78]

The prolonged period, dating back to the Second World War, in which the United States has been the dominant world power may seem to contradict what Lenin is saying here. With the collapse of the Soviet Union, the United States hoped to become the world's sole superpower—and indeed, it continues to pursue that goal. It largely compels the rest of the world—through its superior arms as well as the consensus among other nations that its commanding role internationally should be accepted as the best and only current alternative—to follow its lead. However, beneath this reality, significant molecular economic shifts have taken place that have changed the "relative strength" of the world's leading economies, so that some years down the road, barring major social transformations, we may face a kind of barbarism on a world scale, given the existence of nuclear weapons, far worse than that of the Second World War.

The End of War

War isn't hard-wired into our brains, but it is "hard-wired" into capitalism. Its continued existence is bound up with the existence of capitalism itself. War cannot be abolished unless the class interests upon which it rests are abolished. But most solutions for ending war assume mistakenly that war can be gotten rid of without getting rid of the system that breeds it. "Politics must continue; war cannot," explains war historian John Keegan. "That is not to say that the role of the warrior is over. The world community needs, more than it has ever done, skillful and disciplined warriors who are ready to put themselves at the service of its authority. Such warriors must properly be seen as the protectors of civilization, not its enemies."[79]

But it is not possible to separate war and politics. Lenin was fond of quoting the nineteenth-century theorist of war, Carl von Clausewitz: "War is a mere continuation of policy by other means."[80] Keegan's idea of ending war, perhaps expressed unconsciously, is for the world's dominant powers—for they control the "world community"—to come together and militarily impose peace. His answer to imperialist war is the answer every aspiring power strives for: a peace based on its own dominance, a "Pax Romana," or a "Pax Britannica," or a "Pax Americana." Implicitly, though he states otherwise, he accepts the fact that war and politics are inseparable.

The same confusion surrounds the belief that the United Nations can be an instrument of peaceful conflict resolution. Also established after the Second World War, the UN's only decision-making body with enforcement power, the Security Council, is dominated by five permanent members—the United States, Russia, Britain, France, and China. Each member has veto power over council decisions, ensuring that US interests can never be threatened. It is not an international parliament, but a committee of the most powerful states. When they all agree, the council acts;

when they disagree, the big states simply ignore it. John Bolton, US ambassador to the UN as of 2006, gave the clearest description of the organization's international role: "There is no United Nations. There is an international community that occasionally can be led by the only real power left in the world, and that is the United States, when it suits our interest, and when we can get others to go along. . . . When the United States leads, the United Nations will follow. When it suits our interest to do so, we will do so. When it does not suit our interests we will not."[81]

Marx likened the international capitalist class to warring brothers, ready to join forces against threats from below, but also in competition with each other, and therefore able to form only temporary agreements and alliances. One state may possess the power to impose some kind of peace based on its own ability to wield superior force—like a mafia don whose gangs have cleaned out all competitors and created the conditions for "peaceful" commerce in a particular city. This is the peace of the victor; a peace that lasts only until a rival gang emerges to oust the old boss.

Though socialists look to a world without war, no socialist can condemn all wars. Wars of conquest and imperial rivalry are reactionary, but wars are also waged by the oppressed against their subjection. A million mostly working-class men died in the Battle of the Somme (during the First World War) for the sake of profits for the British, French, and German empires. That war was reactionary to the core, even though each side in the dispute claimed to be defending itself against the other. The Civil War in the United States—a bloody affair—was fought to destroy the institution of slavery. That war was progressive and justified.

We live in a world of abundance in which there is no longer any justification for war. Given a different social order, one based upon planned production and distribution for human need, it would be possible to provide everyone with a healthy existence without recourse to exploitation of one by another, or of warfare.

But unlike pacifists, who believe that simply an appeal to reason or moral suasion can convince those who rule today to act differently, Marxists understand that war is built into the very fabric of capitalism, and that it can only be abolished when the weapons of the world's ruling classes are wrested from their hands. We want the end of war, but we also understand that those who hold power in the world will not relinquish it peacefully. Marxists understand that the violence of the oppressor cannot be equated with the violence of the oppressed. As Trotsky explained in his defense of the use of violence by the Russian working class against the counterrevolution in 1919:

> When a murderer raises his knife over a child, may one kill the murderer to save the child? Will not thereby the principle of the "sacredness of human life" be infringed? May one kill the murderer to save oneself? Is an insurrection of oppressed slaves against their masters permissible? . . .
>
> Does life cease to be sacred when it is a question of people talking another language, or does Kautsky consider that mass murders organized on principles of

strategy and tactics are not murders at all? Truly it is difficult to put forward in our age a principle more hypocritical and more stupid. As long as human labor power and, consequently, life itself, remain articles of sale and purchase, of exploitation and robbery, the principle of the "sacredness of human life" remains a shameful lie, uttered with the object of keeping the oppressed slaves in their chains. . . . To make the individual sacred we must destroy the social order which crucifies him.[82]

In its war against the people of Vietnam, the United States inflicted unimaginable devastation with its use of carpet bombing, toxic defoliation, and systematic massacres of civilians. Though accurate figures are impossible, one more recent estimate concluded that there were 3.8 million violent war deaths of Vietnamese people, combat and civilian, during the war.[83] The war ended in a victory for the national liberation movement in Vietnam because of a combination of mass protests at home, armed resistance to the US occupation in Vietnam proper, and the disintegration of the US Army as soldiers increasingly refused to fight in an unjust war. During the first Christmas of the First World War, German and British soldiers, disobeying their officers, laid down their weapons and fraternized in "no man's land."[84] The Russian Revolution of 1917 forced Russia out of the First World War and sparked revolts of workers in Germany and other countries, including mass fraternization between soldiers of opposing countries. This kind of international struggle and solidarity is the key to ending war.

Internationalism

The Communist Manifesto ends with the resounding phrase, "Workers of the world, unite." This was not simply a moral appeal. Capitalism has created a world working class in the hundreds of millions from whose labor the profits of the world's multinationals derive. Workers face the same essential conditions the world over. Whether their pay is high or low, all workers are exploited. They therefore have a common interest that spans national borders, in spite of their national differences.

Some argue that the plunder of one nation by another precludes working-class solidarity, because the workers in the plundering nation benefit from the plunder. The steady decline of living standards for American workers, the growing gap between rich and poor and the diversion of social spending toward military spending and corporate welfare make this argument today seem out of touch with reality.

Workers in Europe and the United States, so the argument goes, are better paid because they are somehow benefiting from the comparatively lower pay of workers in Mexico. It is true that an autoworker in the United States and an autoworker in Mexico working at the same level of productivity receive different wages, but they are both exploited, and by the same masters. Indeed, in many cases, well-paid workers are as exploited—in terms of how much surplus work they perform for the bosses—as low-paid workers, if not more. The lowest pay is usually associated with industries that are the most "labor intensive," that is, where the rate of exploitation is lowest because less labor-saving machinery is employed. The inequality of wages worldwide acts to the detriment of the world working class because it permits capitalists to pit lower-paid workers against higher-paid ones. A rise in the standard of living for any section of the working class, on the other hand, cannot but benefit all.

Capitalism's economic crises are also increasingly global in scope. That means that struggle also takes on an increasingly international character. In the mid-1840s, when industrial capitalism was limited to Britain and parts of mainland Europe, a series of revolutions spread across Europe. They were bourgeois revolutions, and they ended in defeat, but in each country the working class emerged for the first time as a social force to be reckoned with.

Again, in 1917, the Russian Revolution sparked international revolution. Coming on the heels of world war and economic hardship, it set off a world conflagration. German workers rose up and overthrew the Kaiser, setting up workers' councils similar to the Russian soviets. There were soviets in Hungary and Finland before the revolution was crushed. Workers in Italy formed factory councils, and in 1920 came to the brink of revolution before they were undercut by moderate socialists. "The whole of Europe," fretted British prime minister Lloyd George, "is filled with the spirit of revolution."[85] The war and the Russian Revolution also set off anticolonial revolts in India, Ireland, and elsewhere. Victor Serge described the atmosphere of both bourgeois panic and revolutionary hope in 1918:

> The newspapers of the period are astonishing. Each day, in large type with headlines across the page, they carry last-minute dispatches, vague rumors picked up in Stockholm by anxious ears: riots in Paris, riots in Lyon, revolution in Belgium, revolution in Constantinople, victory of the Soviets in Bulgaria, rioting in Copenhagen. In fact, the whole of Europe is in movement; clandestine or open Soviets are appearing everywhere, even in the Allied armies; everything is possible, everything. On 15 October, Vorovsky telegraphs Zinoviev from Stockholm: *Revolution builds up in France* (so runs the headline of his dispatch in the newspapers); "a workers' popular movement began two days ago, and is spreading energetically in Paris. . . . The workers are demanding the immediate release of all political prisoners. . . . A Soviet of Allied soldiers has made contact at the front with the Soviet of German soldiers."[86]

The division of the world into national states means that struggles in each country have a certain tempo and dynamic that is not identical in timing or character. Revolution starts in one or a few states and then spreads. But as the experience of the Russian Revolution shows, any revolution that remains in isolation cannot survive. Engels made this conclusion as early as 1847, in a question-and-answer piece he wrote that was scrapped for *The Communist Manifesto*: "Will it be possible for this revolution to take place in one country alone? No. By creating the world market, big industry has already brought all the peoples of the Earth . . . into such close relation with one another that none is independent of what happens to the others."[87]

The call for workers to unite across national boundaries, then, is not merely a moral appeal. The material condition for socialism—abundance—exists on a world scale, but not within the confines of national borders. This is true because economic development is extremely uneven, with enormous wealth and productive power concentrated in some regions far more than others. Any country that attempts to fall back on its own resources quickly finds that its production system is too lopsided and incomplete to pull itself up by its own bootstraps. Having been shaped in connection with the world economy, one country finds it doesn't produce enough agricultural products and must import them; another, not enough machinery and spare parts. The problem, moreover, is most acute for countries that were colonies in the past, because their economies were distorted by the needs of the country that exploited them, which usually meant turning them into sources of cheap labor and raw materials, and retarding their industrial development. Cuba, for example, remained dependent on sugar exports for 80 percent of its capital needs for decades. First dependent on the United States, it later depended on Russia for substantial support. But even then, it has never been able to create a fully diversified industrialized economy. This is the reason why the Marxist movement always argued—until Stalinism distorted and inverted the message—that there cannot be isolated pockets of socialist development.

Chapter Eleven

Marxism and Oppression

W e live in a society rife not only with economic inequality but with myriad forms of oppression—unequal treatment of various groups based on perceived racial, sexual, national, and other differences.

As a result of decades of mass struggle, legally sanctioned racial discrimination has been eliminated in the United States since the successful civil rights movement of the 1960s. But contrary to claims that we live in a "post-racial society" (often advanced to cover up and deny the existence of racism by racists themselves) racial oppression is still very much with us, whether we are discussing the systematic profiling, police brutalization, and imprisonment of Black men by the US legal system, the substantially higher unemployment rates and lower pay of African Americans compared to whites, or the daily humiliations suffered by Blacks such as being followed around by store clerks, having trouble hailing a cab, or being denied a loan or a place to live in certain neighborhoods.

There have been important struggles for women's freedom, from the women's movement of the late 1960s to the "Slutwalks" of 2011 where young women marched against sexual double standards that still blame women for inviting sexual assault by the way they dress. But women still make on average less pay than men, and are still vastly underrepresented at certain fields and income levels. They face sexual harassment and rape at disturbing levels, and still carry the major burden of domestic work in the home. Since the 1980s, they have faced increasing restrictions on their right to control their own reproductive health, and sexist imagery and commentary that denigrate women are more and more a part of the mainstream.

The level of acceptance in society toward lesbian, gay, bisexual, transgender, and intersex (LGBTI) people has increased over the past few decades (at least for gays and lesbians), especially over the past several years. In particular, there are more positive portrayals of gay characters in film and television, and a marked shift toward support for gay marriage, including successful initiatives to legalize gay marriage in seventeen states between 2008 and 2013. Nevertheless, LGBTI people still face systematic legal and social discrimination, as well as bigoted violence and police brutality. According to the National Coalition of Anti-Violence Programs, gay men were 3.03 times more likely to report hate crimes to the police than those who were not gay men, and transgender people were 3.32 times as likely to experience police violence than non-transgender people.[1]

Immigrants, especially poor and working-class immigrants of color, and in particular undocumented immigrants, are forced by their situation to work for low wages in terrible conditions, under the constant threat of deportation. The Obama administration is on track to deport more than 3 million immigrants; it's already deported 1.5 million, more than any other previous administration.[2]

Native Americans in the United States were first systematically enslaved, murdered, pushed aside, and devastated by European diseases; then forced onto small reservations, usually in areas deemed "useless" by European settlers (and then, later, when the land was again deemed useful in some way, removed again); their rights and sovereignty denied, their children stolen from them and forced into schools to scrub away their language and culture. Today, rates of poverty, suicide, and imprisonment among Native Americans is far higher than the national average. On the Lakota Pine Ridge Reservation in North Dakota, for example, 97 percent of the people live below the poverty line; the average life expectancy is forty-five; the teenage suicide rate is 150 percent higher than the national average, and the infant mortality rate is 300 percent higher than the national average.[3]

People with disabilities are often treated as burdens to be excluded from the labor force, segregated, institutionalized, and managed at a minimum cost. When employed, they are superexploited; and in the public sphere, they are often denied necessary facilities.

While some activists and academics in the past might have been tempted to argue that these different forms of oppression have no connection to one another, the argument is hard to maintain in the face of the politics of the Republican Right in the United States. For these hard-core conservatives, bashing gays, scapegoating Blacks and immigrants, restricting women's reproductive freedom, and opposing social spending (as well as staunchly opposing unions and workers' rights) are all part of an integrated web of oppression and exploitation.

It is not a coincidence that the theories of "scientific racism" in the late nineteenth and early twentieth century targeted as genetically and socially inferior not only Blacks, Mexicans, and Asians, but poor people in general. As Allan Chase, author of an exhaustive study of "scientific racism" in the United States, argues, "To the scientific racists, the poor and the near poor of all nations were—and still are—held to be a race apart, 'a definite race of chronic pauper stocks.'"[4] At the Third International Congress of Eugenics, Dr. Russell Robie of the Essex County Mental Hygiene Clinic in New Jersey noted that the millions of workers unemployed that year, the major portion of which he deemed "social inadequates" and "mental defectives," would have been spared their misery, he suggested, "if they had never been born." Speaker after speaker stood up to agree, calling for the compulsory sterilization of millions of unemployed people.[5]

Capitalism needs oppression. "Ye are many, they are few," the poet Percy Shelley wrote in a poem dedicated to English workers, in which he invited them to "Rise like lions after slumber, in unvanquishable number."[6] In order to prevent such an unpleasant scenario, the ruling powers split the working class and set it against itself, by means of race, sex, nationality, sexual preference, language, disability, pay differentials, and many other characteristics. Without these divisions, capitalism could not survive. At the moment they are overcome, and all the oppressed and exploited united against the common oppressor, the system's days are numbered.

In 1892, Engels wrote to a German socialist in the United States about one of the principle obstacles to working-class unity there, how "your bourgeoisie knows much better even than the Austrian Government how to play off one nationality against the other."[7] The nineteenth-century US robber baron Jay Gould bluntly confirmed Engels's assessment, stating, "I can hire one half of the working class to kill the other half."[8] The historian John R. Commons visited a Chicago employment office in 1904 and described the following scene: "I saw, seated on benches around the office, a sturdy group of blond-haired Nordics. I asked the employment agent, 'How comes it you are employing only Swedes?' He answered, 'Well, you see, it is only this week. Last week we employed Slovaks. We change about among different nationalities and languages. It prevents them from getting together. We have the thing systematized.'"[9]

The ability of bosses to pit workers against each other this way is reinforced by something we discussed in an earlier chapter—that the labor market forces workers into competition with each other for jobs. The economic conditions of labor and work under capitalism both unite and divide workers. As Sharon Smith writes,

> While capitalism propels workers toward collective forms of struggle, it also forces them into competition. The unremitting pressure from a layer of unemployed workers, which exists in most economies even in times of "full employment," is a deterrent to struggle—a constant reminder that workers compete for limited jobs which afford a decent standard of living. Without the counterweight of the class struggle this competition can act as an obstacle to the development of class consciousness, and encourage the growth of what Marx called "false consciousness"—part of which is the ideas which scapegoat other sections of society. The growth of such ideas divides workers, and impedes their ability to focus on the real enemy.[10]

Similar to how they view the economic relations of exploitation, Marxists do not believe that the social relations of oppression in society, and the formation of various identities (national, racial, gender, and so on), are based on "human nature," or are somehow "natural," but that they are historically and socially created. There is, for example, no scientifically (that is, biologically based) acceptable definition of "race"—which is in fact a set of outward (and imprecisely defined) physical characteristics that society labels as such. Moreover, what appears natural, fixed, and unchanging is in fact not. As historian Barbara Fields writes, "All human societies, whether tacitly or overtly, assume that nature has ordained their social arrangements. Or, to put it another way, part of what human beings understand by the word 'nature' is the sense of inevitability that gradually becomes attached to a predictable, repetitive social routine: 'custom, so immemorial that it looks like nature,' as Nathaniel Hawthorne wrote."[11]

And indeed the dominant classes of any society encourage and reinforce this idea of a "natural order" of things—things that are in fact historically created and conditioned. One of the most insidious forms this takes is presenting gender—the socially created expectations of what constitutes a "man" and a "woman"—as somehow a direct and natural result of what kind of genitalia one possesses. "The female brain is predominantly hard-wired for empathy," writes Cambridge psychologist Simon-Baron Cohen. "The male brain is predominantly hard-wired for understanding and building systems."[12]

This kind of argument has been used for centuries, in various forms, to explain the allegedly innate inferiority of women, when in fact the argument has merely justified social inequality using the dubious claims of science—and used this fake science to reinforce in the minds of the oppressed that they are trapped within the bounds society has set for them. To quote one seventeenth-century feminist: "A man ought no more to value himself upon being Wiser than a Woman, if he owe his Advantage to a better Education, and greater means of Information, then he ought to boast of his Courage, for beating a Man, when his Hands were bound."[13]

Capitalism needs oppression, but it did not invent it. It has appropriated older forms, and it has reshaped and remolded them to its own needs, as well as creating new oppressions. The divide-and-rule strategy no doubt predates capitalism, because class society predates capitalism; but capitalism has perfected it. Nevertheless, simply saying that capitalism needs oppression for its survival doesn't tell us the origins and nature of different oppressions, each of which has its own distinctive characteristics and function that must be examined. But before we do that, we must dispel some myths about how Marxism treats the question of oppression.

Class and Oppression

Marx and Engels argued that the foundation of society is its relations of production and its corresponding class relations. But society is not reducible to these relations.

On their basis arise the legal and political superstructure and corresponding forms of beliefs, morals, and consciousness—as well as family relations, relations of ethnicity, race, and nationality, and many other features.

Yet Marxism is often presented as concerning itself solely with economic questions. As ZNet's Michael Albert summarized it in an Internet debate, "Marxism . . . tends to exaggerate the centrality of economics and gives insufficient attention to gender, race, polity, and the environment."[14] This view remains dominant in academia on whole sections of the left. Exaggerated or not, the emphasis on economic relations has not prevented Marxists from dealing with questions of race and gender, or anything else. On the contrary, it has provided a powerful tool to unlock answers to issues that have more commonly been presented as having nothing at all to do with economic relations and more with innate "human nature," "bad ideas," or both. Marxism seeks not to separate exploitation and oppression, but to show how they are interconnected and condition each other, and how the solution to one cannot be separated from the solution to the other.

Marx and Engels were lifelong staunch defenders of the Polish national struggle against Russian domination and of the Irish struggle against British colonization. "No nation can be free," Marx wrote, "if it oppresses other nations."[15] "The modern individual family is founded on the open or concealed domestic slavery of the wife," wrote Engels in his work *The Origin of the Family, Private Property, and the State*. To the argument that it was woman's "natural calling" to be a home-based "wife and mother," August Bebel, a leading German socialist wrote, "There can be no emancipation of humanity without the social independence and equality of the sexes."[16]

To say that class exploitation is at the heart of capitalism is not to reduce oppression, or other features of capitalist reality, to economics, any more than saying that the heart is the center of the system of circulation of blood in the body denies the absolute importance to a living body of veins and capillaries as complementary components of that system.

The origins of capitalism are deeply intertwined with the system of racial slavery in the 1700s and 1800s. As Marx writes in *Capital*, the primitive accumulation of wealth that allowed capitalism to emerge was based upon the enslavement and mass murder of indigenous people and "the conversion of Africa into a preserve for the commercial hunting of black skins."[17] He wrote that, "The treasures captured outside Europe by undisguised looting, enslavement and murder flowed back to the mother-country and were turned into capital there."[18] Slavery was "as much the pivot upon which our present-day industrialism turns as are machinery, credit, etc. Without slavery there would be no cotton, without cotton there would be no modern industry. It is slavery which has given value to the colonies, it is the colonies which have created world trade, and world trade is the necessary condition of large-scale machine industry."[19] In a morbidly poetic passage, he wrote, "The veiled slavery of the wage laborers in Europe needed the unqualified slavery of the New World as its pedestal."[20]

Wage slavery became the pivot around which all other inequalities and oppressions turn. Marx noted, for example, how the brutal exploitation of English textile workers in England in the nineteenth century was facilitated by the conquest of Ireland and the dispossession and starvation of the Irish peasant. "Every time Ireland was about to develop industrially, she was crushed and reconverted into a purely agricultural land," Marx wrote. The result—the "despairing flight of starving Irish to England filled basements, hovels, workhouses in Liverpool, Manchester, Birmingham, Glasgow with men, women, children in a state almost of starvation." He concluded: "All their accumulations were sent therefore to England for investment . . . and thus was Ireland forced to contribute cheap labor and cheap capital to building up 'the great works of Britain.'"[21]

Marx and Engels did not fully theorize oppression (in all its myriad forms) and its relationship to exploitation under capitalism. As Sharon Smith has noted, "Although they were often able to anticipate future sites of struggle, they were also constrained in other respects by the historical limits of the social relations of their time." However, crucial insights can be gathered from their writings on, for example, national or women's oppression, and what they said was far in advance of most of their contemporaries. It took further social and historical developments, as well as new social struggles, for subsequent Marxists to develop and extend them—for example, with regard to the question of LGBTI oppression. This should not detract from how Marxism provides us with the best analytical tools and method by which we can come to grips with these questions.

It is not Marxism but its critics who tend to put the working class over on one side and the oppressed over on the other. This is an artificial separation. Wageworkers (the majority of the working population in most parts of the world today) are men, women, gay, straight, Black, white, brown, speak many different languages, and comprise many nationalities. If the working class is to successfully challenge capitalism, it must surmount these divisions. If it is to surmount these divisions, then it must challenge each and every manifestation of oppression. And if the working class is to devise a strategy to overcome oppression, it must discover the root sources of division and inequality. Indeed, as I shall argue, workers are the best-positioned class in society to mount the most far-reaching challenge to oppression.

The Right to Self-Determination

As explained in the previous chapter, the development of modern nation-states on the one hand, and the creation of a world market on the other hand, are both features of the rise of capitalism. Capitalism both breaks down national divisions and reinforces them in new ways. The contradiction between these two factors produces a struggle over what national ruling class will be dominant. The unevenness of capitalist development produces a pecking order of states in which the weaker are dominated by the stronger, in a perpetual struggle of each ruling class to not only maintain its own national patch, but to extend its own realm of control and dominance. The shape of imperialist conflict changes, but its main feature—competition between the biggest powers over hegemony and the subordination of weaker nations to stronger nations—will continue as long as world capitalism survives. It is this that underlies national oppression.

The ruling classes of every country play upon nationalist sentiments to solidify their rule. National chauvinism is a corrosive ideology that poisons workers' minds and turns them against their natural allies—workers of other countries. One of the goals of socialists is to challenge attempts to set workers of one nation against those of another, or to elevate in workers' minds the claimed superiority of "their" nation, language, or culture over those of another. Socialists aim to break down national divisions and foster solidarity between workers of different countries based on their common class interests. This is, incidentally, not an argument for the obliteration or homogenization of cultures (music, language, food, customs), but against the elevation of any one culture over another, or the suppression or forced "assimilation" of any nation or culture by another. Cultural interchange, in language, food, music, and all other forms of free human interaction, has always been the wellspring of human development and creativity, and the deliberate segregation between cultures impoverishes them all.

Genuine internationalism requires full equality between nations, that is, that no nation or culture is privileged over another. It follows that Marxism does not lump all nationalisms together. In a phrase, it makes a distinction between the nationalism of the oppressor and the nationalism of the oppressed. The distinction can sometimes be confusing, because all nations in wartime claim that they are the aggrieved party, defending themselves against aggression.

When the thirteen colonies fought for independence from the British Empire, it was a case of an oppressed nation fighting an oppressor nation. However, when the United States wrenched away half of Mexico in the 1847 war, it was a war of conquest, and Mexico was the aggrieved party. Every overseas military intervention conducted by the United States since then has placed it in the same position as the British Empire when it fought the Boston Minutemen. And yet when it oppresses other nations, the United States cloaks its actions in the garb of 1776. It was a complete inversion of reality, for example, for Bush the younger to call the Iraqi resistance "terrorists" and the occupying US Army "liberators."[22] The British used the same jargon during the American Revolution. In his failed 1777 military campaign in northern New England and Canada, General John Burgoyne claimed that he was fighting an "unnatural Rebellion" whose aim was to establish "the compleated system of Tyranny."[23] Burgoyne quickly moved from appeals to threats, promising "devastation, famine and every concomitant horror that a reluctant but indispensable prosecution of military duty must occasion."[24]

National equality can only be established if oppressed nations have the right to self-determination—not to be colonized, annexed, occupied, or otherwise denied their own sovereignty. "If we were to forget about [self-determination] or were afraid to put it forward for fear of impinging on the national prejudices of our compatriots of Great-Russian origin," wrote the Russian Marxist Plekhanov, "the battle-cry of world Social-Democracy, 'Workers of all countries, unite!' would be a shameful lie on our lips."[25] Eugene Debs made a similar argument in a Socialist Party debate about the rights of immigrant workers. "If Socialism, international, revolutionary Socialism, does not stand staunchly, unflinchingly, and uncompromisingly for the working class and for the exploited and oppressed masses of all lands, then it stands for none and its claim is a false pretense and its profession a delusion and a snare."[26]

Karl Marx made a similar argument in relation to Britain's oppression of its first colony, Ireland. "It is a precondition of the emancipation of the English working class," Marx argued, "to transform the present forced union (i.e., the enslavement of Ireland) into an equal and free confederation if possible, into complete separation if need be."[27] Working-class liberation in England was impossible, Marx contended, without Irish liberation. Marx applied the same methodology to the question of slavery in the American South, arguing that working-class emancipation could not be accomplished without destroying slavery. "Labor in a white skin cannot emancipate itself where it is branded in a Black skin," he argued in *Capital*.[28]

In the era of imperialism, the questions of national oppression and national liberation became of pressing general importance to the socialist movement worldwide. Everywhere, workers in the oppressor nations were being encouraged to support colonial oppression by "their own" governments. Lenin argued that working-class internationalism was impossible unless workers in the oppressor countries—the dominant nations that forcibly held colonies all over the world—were broken from any allegiance to their own ruling class. That meant socialists in countries that oppressed other nations had to support the oppressed nation's right to be free and independent. Only then could there be unity between workers of both nations on the basis of equality.

But Lenin made a sharp distinction between the Marxist position for self-determination and the concern that the statesmen for the great powers mouthed about the rights of nations—a concern that never extended to the nations they themselves ruled over. When President Woodrow Wilson touted the self-determination of nations in his 1918 "Fourteen Points" speech, for example, the United States was three years into a brutal Marine Corps occupation of Haiti that had handed that country's customs house and banking system over to the National City Bank of New York.[29]

Lenin compared the right of self-determination to the right of divorce. Marxists support the right of women to dissolve a marriage not because all marriages must break up, he argued, but because equality of the sexes cannot exist where women are legally bound to their husbands.[30] Likewise, equality between nations cannot exist where one is not free to secede from another. The increasing interdependence of nations, as well as the breakdown of national boundaries between peoples, is a good thing—so long as it is based on voluntary association—because it increases the international solidarity of the working class.

But socialists adamantly oppose any forced unity. For example, in the United States, socialists oppose efforts to make English the nation's official language, or to prevent people from being able to seek education in their native tongue. Socialists stand strongly in favor of the right of people to be provided with instruction in their own language. On the other hand, we are not in favor of the breakup of student populations on the basis of sex, language, nationality, race, ethnicity, or religion. Capitalism works hard to keep people of different races and nationalities divided, because it is then easier to pit them against each other. Our job is to combat that separation, rather than reinforce it.

To be consistent internationalists, socialists must oppose all efforts by the United States to impose its will on other countries and peoples—whether in Iraq, Puerto Rico, Cuba, Afghanistan, or Venezuela. Puerto Ricans must have the right to separate from the United States and form an independent nation if they so choose. Venezuelans and Cubans have the right to be free of US meddling in their affairs, as do the peoples struggling for freedom in the Middle East.

Lenin's last political fight before his death demonstrated the vehemence with which he insisted that socialists unconditionally champion the rights of oppressed nations, and of doing everything in their power to prove their commitment to equality. In December 1922 he dictated an angry statement regarding efforts by Stalin, who was then consolidating his control over the Soviet state bureaucracy, to subordinate Georgia and other republics to Great Russian control, as had been done in tsarist times. The note stated:

> A distinction must necessarily be made between the nationalism of an oppressor nation and that of an oppressed nation, the nationalism of a big nation and that of a small nation. In respect of the second kind of nationalism we, nationals of a big nation, have nearly always been guilty, in historic practice, of an infinite number of cases of violence; furthermore, we commit violence and insult an infinite number of times without noticing it.
>
> That is why internationalism on the part of oppressors or "great" nations, as they are called (though they are great only in their violence, only great as bullies), must consist not only in the observance of the formal equality of nations but even in an inequality of the oppressor nation, the great nation, that must make up for the inequality which obtains in actual practice. Anybody who does not understand this has not grasped the real proletarian attitude to the national question, he is still

essentially petty bourgeois in his point of view and is, therefore, sure to descend to the bourgeois point of view.[31]

This does not mean a positive support for nationalism in its own right. For in these national struggles, there are different class interests involved. Every national struggle involves different classes, and each class strives, beyond national independence, for very different things. The wealthy classes in the oppressed nation try to limit the scope of the national struggle, to elevate the nation over the class interests of workers, and to stifle the aspirations of the most oppressed for complete liberation, lest their struggles threaten their own rule. Indeed, in some cases, fear of mass mobilization from below has often rendered bourgeois nationalists half-hearted and vacillating in the fight for independence, and willing to make deals with bigger powers to secure some advantage or another. They also have their own national aspirations as a ruling class that involve oppression of other groups—for example, Indonesia's bloody seizure of East Timor after it achieved independence, or the conquest of the West at the expense of Mexicans and Native Americans by the newly independent United States. As Lenin argued, "The bourgeois nationalism of any oppressed nation has a general democratic content that is directed against oppression, and it is this content that we unconditionally support. At the same time we strictly distinguish it from the tendency towards national exclusiveness; [for example,] we fight against the tendency of the Polish bourgeois to oppress the Jews."[32]

It is for the very reason Lenin cites here that Marxists have looked upon Zionism as a form of reactionary rather than progressive nationalism. Zionism as a movement never defined itself as a national liberation movement. On the contrary, from very early on Zionism identified strongly with racist white South Africa. But instead of exploiting native-born labor, as white colonial societies did in South Africa, the purpose of Jewish colonization was to build an exclusively Jewish state based on the removal of the native Palestinian population. To accomplish its goals, the Zionist movement required the backing of a major imperial power. Zionist leader Theodor Herzl sold the Zionist project to great powers as an "outpost of civilization as opposed to barbarism."[33]

There was of course the propaganda for public consumption that Palestine was "a land without a people for a people without a land." But to each other the Zionists were more sanguine. "All colonization," wrote revisionist Zionist leader Vladimir Jabotinsky, "must continue in defiance of the will of the native population."[34]

The Zionist movement's aim was not to liberate Jews from oppression, but to accept the impossibility of their "assimilation." Herzl, for example, thought anti-Semitism to be natural and inevitable wherever Jews lived alongside non-Jews, and considered it futile to "combat" anti-Semitism.[35] After Hitler came to power, the leading German Zionist organization wrote a memo to Hitler that expressed Zionism's hope for the "collaboration even of a government hostile to Jews," on the assumption that its aims (separation of Jews from gentiles) were similar to theirs. Hitler shut down socialist, labor, and Jewish resistance organizations, but permitted the Zionists to continue to operate. An agent of Haganah, the Zionist militia operating in Palestine seeking Nazi assistance, told SS leader Adolf Eichmann in 1937 that Zionists were pleased with Germany persecution of the Jews because it increased the strength of the "Jewish population." When asked in 1938 if he was interested in saving all Jewish children in Germany, Zionist leader David Ben-Gurion remarked that if it were possible to save them all by sending them to Britain, or only half by sending them to Israel, he would prefer the latter.[36]

Israel was established in 1948 after a series of military assaults on the Palestinians, including several massacres designed to terrorize people into fleeing their homes and farms. Most Israeli towns today are built on older towns in Palestine forcibly emptied of Palestinians in 1948 and since.

To this day, the United States looks upon Israel, which it backs to the hilt financially and militarily, as, in the words of Noam Chomsky, a "Middle-East Sparta in the service of American power."[37] In the popular press, Zionism is presented as the nationalism of an oppressed nation, an argument that has always been bolstered by the historical oppression of Jews, culminating in the Nazi Holocaust. The truth, however, is exactly reversed. The horrors of the Holocaust were manipulated by Zionist leaders to justify the establishment of a national state based on the oppression of another people.

While socialists in the oppressed country must wholeheartedly support the national struggle against imperialism, the working class should retain its own independent organization to ensure that its own class aims, which always go further than the bourgeois nationalist leaders, are not sidelined. Form alliances, Lenin argued, but do not merge uncritically with the nationalists. "A resolute struggle must be waged," he wrote in 1920, "against the attempt to clothe the revolutionary liberation movements in the backward countries, which are not genuinely communist, in communist colors."[38]

The rise of Stalinism led precisely to this tendency Lenin warned against—to paint what were essentially nationalist movements in "communist colors." A number of national liberations movements in the last century—from China to Cuba to various African nations—were led by middle-class nationalist forces rather than the working class. These were heroic, earth-shaking struggles that successfully removed the yoke of colonial oppression. They drew inspiration from the Russian model of state development, and thus often proclaimed their national revolutions "socialist." These movements were not led by the working class, nor did they put the working class in power. "Socialism" was identified with state-directed development, not workers' power. Unfortunately, many see the reproduction of all the forms of exploitation and oppression that exist in the countries that once colonized them as proof of the failure of one form of "socialism" or another. In reality, what we have witnessed is the limits of a purely national solution to the problems of imperialism.

The twentieth century witnessed an era of colonization, decolonization, and the rise of national liberations movements throughout the world. This era may be over, but not the era of national and ethnic oppression, imperialism, and military conquest. It still remains an important job for socialists in the dominant countries like the United States to stand firmly against efforts to dominate the world.

The Roots of Women's Oppression

All societies require both production (the labor processes that create the things we need to survive) and reproduction. Reproduction entails the continual renewal, or re-creation, of the conditions necessary for production in any given society. Therefore, reproduction does not only include making sure there are enough machines, tools, raw materials, and labor for another round of production. Reproduction also requires that the people who labor themselves be reproduced, not just in terms of the propagation of the species but also the rearing, maintenance, and training of the current and next generation of workers. While the essential biological aspects of reproduction have not changed, the same cannot be said of the social and cultural arrangements that surround human reproduction. The forms in which this reproduction takes place are conditioned by the given relations of production of a particular society, and therefore are subject to change historically. In the words of Marxist-feminist Martha Gimenez, "the mode of production determines the mode of reproduction."[39]

Much of what passes as "analysis" of the relations between the sexes really just involves projecting an unchanging family unit—consisting of a man, a woman, a few children, and a dog—into the past. This "nuclear" family, it is often assumed, constitutes the "natural" order of things. And yet the way that people are raised and cared for in our society—with families as "private" sites that are separate from the public world of production and exchange, would seem entirely foreign, for example, to a farm household in eighteenth-century New England, where the labor involved in raising children, cooking, and cleaning was mixed in with the labor of farming, making clothing, and other things that today are produced and purchased from the market outside the family.

The truth is that the family is an institution, not a biological fact, and it has changed historically from one mode of production to the next. As a result the status of women in society has also changed considerably, and that status has also been strongly impacted by a woman's race and her class location in society.

The popular idea is that relations between the sexes are shaped by the unchanging nature of men as providers and women as nurturers—thus it has been and thus it always will be. Yet these gender stereotypes are not supported by historical evidence. In many pre-class societies, women engaged in other work besides childrearing and other "household" tasks. In these societies, though there was a sexual division of labor—men tended to do the jobs that took them further afield: hunting, for example. Women, as child-bearers, tended to do those jobs that kept them nearer to the home base: gathering roots and berries, preparing hides and clothes, and cooking. Later, in the first horticultural societies, women moved naturally from gathering to planting and harvesting. In both cases, with the exception of societies living in very cold climates where hunting was the primary source of food, women's role as gatherers and agriculturalists was more important for the survival of the group than men's hunting.[40]

Both because women's work was central to the survival of the band, and also because relations of economic coercion did not yet exist, the sexual division of labor did not automatically mean male domination, or that men (or their role in society) were considered superior to women. In many reported cases, women held a high social status. Perhaps more importantly, they were not subject to coercion or exploitation. These facts undermine the least-supported argument as to why women are oppressed—because men are stronger. What this questionable idea boils down to is that men oppress women because they can. The argument doesn't stand up to the evidence. In North America, for example, sexual coercion was rare or nonexistent in native societies. As John D'Emilio and Estelle B. Freedman explain in their history of sexuality in the United States,

> Perhaps the most striking contrast between English and Indian sexual systems was the relative absence of sexual conflict among Native Americans, due in part to their different cultural attitudes toward both property and sexuality. Indians easily resolved marital discord by simply separating and forming new unions, without penalty, stigma, or property settlements. In cultures in which one could not "own" another person's sexuality, prostitution—the sale of sex—did not exist prior to the arrival of European settlers. Rape—the theft of sex—only rarely occurred, and it was one of the few sexual acts forbidden by Indian cultures. Contrary to their fears about suffering sexual brutality at the hands of savages, English women captured during the colonial-era Indian wars noted with relief that native American men did not assault them sexually. "I have been in the midst of those roaring lions and savage bears," wrote Mary Rowlandson about her captivity by New England Indians. "[B]y night and day, alone & in company, sleeping all sorts together, and yet not one of them every offered me the least abuse of unchastity to me in word or action." In contrast, the Spanish settlers justified the rape of Indian women as a right of conquest and expected sexual service from female captives of war. In the South, only in the nineteenth century, after a period of close contact with white settlers, did the Cherokee Nation find it necessary to enact laws punishing rapists.[41]

In many pre-class societies, sexual relations were treated more freely, often without the jealousy, possessiveness, and objectification that is today associated with sexual relations. In most matrilocal or matrilineal societies—where descent was reckoned through the female rather than the male line—women and men were free to engage in unrestricted sexual activity before marriage without any fear of stigma. Women were able to combine both reproductive and productive work because such societies did not make much of a distinction between them. The ethnographer Bronislaw Malinowski, who studied the Trobriand Islanders of northwest Melanesia in 1929, noted that in this matrilineal society, "women have a considerable share in tribal life, even to the taking of a leading part in economic, ceremonial, and magical activities—a fact which deeply influences all the customs of erotic life as well as the institution of marriage."[42] Malinowski noticed that children were raised without adult coercion, which the Trobrianders considered "unnatural and immoral." Children were allowed to explore their sexual curiosity without fear or shame: "There is no interference by older persons," he wrote, "in the sexual life of children."[43]

Gender categories, too, and the relative status of people who fit into those categories, have also been historically conditioned and variable. "Native Americans have often held intersex, androgynous people, feminine males and masculine females in high respect," writes Walter L. Williams, a professor of anthropology, history, and gender studies at the University of California. "They are honored for having two spirits, and are seen as more spiritually gifted than the typical masculine male or feminine female. Therefore, many Native American religions, rather than stigmatizing such persons, often looked to them as religious leaders and teachers."[44]

With the rise of class society, women's status changed. As gatherers, women played a key role in the discovery and development of plant domestication, and in many horticultural societies, where land was held in common by the whole tribe, such as the Iroquois in upstate New York, women's status remained high. Though men hunted and did the heavy work of clearing fields for planting, women not only planted and tended the crops but they also controlled the storage and distribution of the harvest as well as the distribution of meat after a hunt. Women controlled the longhouse: the center of Iroquois family and social life. Women inherited whatever individual property existed. Their centrality to the production and distribution of the nation's subsistence requirements also accorded them high social status. Women could decide the life or death of prisoners, had an equal voice in the management of religious festivities, chose and deposed "chiefs," and could decide whether to initiate or end a war.[45]

The same sexual relations have been recorded in Europe, Asia, Africa, and Latin America in societies sharing similar social relations. Changes in the character of production associated with the development of sedentary agriculture seems to have changed the status of men and women in society. There is evidence, for example, that with the invention of the heavy plough, the domestication of animals, and the development of an agricultural surplus, men became the primary agricultural laborers, and, because of their traditional role as hunters, were also in charge of animal domestication. Men—or at least a minority of men—came to dominate in the sphere of production, and became therefore the owners of society's surplus wealth, whereas women, because of the heavy burden of childbirth and child rearing, were deprived of their key role in the production of food. The rise of class society and the state, as Engels pointed out, did not only mean the subordination of the majority to a tiny minority of male exploiters, it meant the "world historic defeat of the female sex."[46]

With the development of sedentary agriculture and animal domestication came private property. The family as a patriarchal setup in which descent was reckoned through the male head of the household developed as a way to ensure that a father passed his wealth to his male offspring. In the new monogamous family, men expected strict chastity from women, but not from themselves. Engels wrote that, "The man seized the reins in the house too, the woman was degraded, enthralled, became the slave of the man's lust, a mere instrument for breeding children."[47]

The sexual division of labor thus only took on an oppressive dimension with the rise of class society, when a handful of men became the controllers of the agricultural surplus. Women—and most men unlucky enough to be slaves or serfs—became subordinated to a new ruling class. In the patriarchal household, women were expected to rear children as well as engage in various kinds of labor for the family's survival (sowing, milking, bread-making, and so on). But capitalist development creates technological changes that render the sexual division of labor more or less obsolete, and creates, as we shall see, the conditions for women's full emancipation.

Capitalism and Social Reproduction

Capitalism has developed commodity exchange to the point where almost everything that we depend on for our lives is produced for sale and profit on the market. Our clothes, our food, our tools, our means of transportation—most things that we consume we must first buy. In this sense, much of the labor that was once performed directly in the household for its own consumption is no longer necessary. More than in precapitalist societies, families under capitalism are units of consumption rather than production (though not exclusively).

A condition for capitalist production is, on the one hand, the concentration of the principal means of production (machinery, tools, raw materials) into the hands of a relatively small group of owners; a second condition, which is shaped by the first, is the existence of people who can subsist only by selling their capacity to work: their labor power, to those who have monopolized the principal means of production. The must have, in Marx's words, "no other commodity" other than labor power to sell on the market.

The capitalists' source of labor power must be continually replenished for capitalism to reproduce itself year in and year out; and, as capitals compete for market share, they must do so on an ever-expanding scale. This requires an expanding supply of cheap and plentiful labor. The capitalist pays for labor power according to its value, and its value, like other commodities, Marx noted, is determined by the labor necessary for its production—the cost of replacing the laborer's means of subsistence, of ensuring the workers' perpetuation. This perpetuation not only involves covering the cost of food, clothing, and shelter, but also the cost of "special education or training" necessary for the work to be adequately performed. And that is not all: "the means of subsistence necessary for the production of labor-power must [also] include the means necessary for the laborer's substitutes, i.e., his children, in order that this race of peculiar commodity-owners may perpetuate its appearance in the market."[48] In short the constant supply of labor requires maintenance not only of the laborers themselves but also the reproduction and rearing of their offspring, future laborers.

Marx did not fully draw out the implications of this insight, but others have since.[49] Labor to maintain the functioning and replenishment of labor power extends beyond working for the wages necessary for the subsistence of workers and their families. Necessities of life must not only be purchased from wages; they involve the use of additional labor in the home, that is, work performed outside the relations of commodity production. This domestic component of the labor of reproduction, performed by women (and to a lesser extent, men and older children) in the home, consists of childrearing, cooking, cleaning, intellectual and psychological nurturing, and so on.

Of course, not all the labor necessary to reproduce labor power takes place in the home. Some services, such as prepared meals, child care, education, laundry service, and so on, could in theory be purchased entirely as commodities on the market. The state, to varying degrees, has taken on some of these functions too.

After the initial phases of industrialism, which tended to destroy family life, the needs for trained and compliant wage labor necessitated a certain minimum of education above and beyond family life. Along with laws curtailing child labor came a prolongation of adolescence, and with it, of public education. The state came to play an increasing role in the reproduction of labor power (the training of new workers) as a complement to privatized reproduction in the family, not as a substitute for it. Public education ideologically reinforced thriftiness, punctuality, and obedience to authority and also ideas about gender and family norms.

The creation of a social safety net—what later became known as the welfare state after the Second World War—was partly a response to struggle from below by workers themselves and partly a response to the needs of capitalism. Such programs were not designed as public replacements for the family, but as means to reinforce it, and to sustain at poverty levels a reserve army of the poor prepared to work when required.

Capitalism continues to depend on unpaid domestic labor, performed predominantly by women, to ensure its own lifeblood—cheap and plentiful labor power—because this remains the most cost-effective means (from the standpoint of capitalist interests) to accomplish it. It is this that explains women's continued oppressed condition under capitalism. As Susan Ferguson and David McNally write, the reproduction of labor power "overwhelmingly is a private, domestic affair undertaken according to the bio-physical fact that procreation and nursing require female-sexed bodies." This, they argue,

> explains why the pressures on the household to conform to unequal gender norms exist in the first place. That is, women are oppressed in capitalist society not because their labor in the home produces value for capital, nor because of a transhistorical patriarchal impulse pitting men against women. . . . The socio-material roots of women's oppression under capitalism have to do instead with the structural relationship of the household to the reproduction of capital: capital and the state need to be able to regulate their biological capacity to produce the next generation of laborers so that labor-power is available for exploitation.[50]

Socialized reproduction—the creation of publicly funded and freely provided kitchens, baths, child care centers, and so on—are not considered feasible options because the ruling class is not willing to foot the bill or to consider a system of reproduction that appears to challenge the idea of the private exploitation of labor and appropriation of wealth. This is especially true in the neoliberal era when even social services necessary for the maintenance of capitalism that were once considered the natural domain of the state are being privatized—like education, for example.

With capitalism came the separation of the realm of production from reproduction; work and home became separate spheres. In the families of the wealthy and of the middle classes, men were public providers, and women were expected to be polite ornaments and let the servants take care of household duties. Men, who were considered naturally inclined toward sexual activity, could engage in sexual dalliances and prostitution outside marriage, but women were expected to observe the strictest loyalty to their husbands. Whereas prior to the rise of capitalism women were considered sexual beings, the ideal "bourgeois" woman was asexual but monogamously procreative. In a certain way, this helped to shield lesbians from prosecution at a time when male homosexuality was publicly under attack.

Initially, capitalism wrecked family relations for workers. The development of markets for consumer goods rendered women's work in the home, like spinning and weaving, obsolete. In the early phases of industrialization, factory owners coveted the nimble fingers of children and women, and hours were impossibly long. The result was that family life almost ceased to exist. Marx and Engels saw the entry of women into the workforce, however horrific its implementation and effects on the working-class family, as an important starting point for women's freedom, because it created the conditions necessary for women to assert themselves as the equals of men.

But even capitalists at some point realized that for a steady supply of labor they needed some way for workers to reproduce themselves. Under real pressure from below, laws were passed restricting the labor of children and women. In the Victorian era, the middle-class ideology of the nuclear family, of the man at work supporting the wife at home who cleaned and took care of the kids, was adopted by the working class. In exchange for some relief from the horrors of endless factory labor, working-class women became subordinate to men, and were almost solely responsible for rearing children in the home. Men were expected to make a wage that could support a family. The invasion of the market into virtually every sphere of life also transformed sex into a commodity, reinforcing the idea of women as sexual objects to be "possessed" by men.

But women were never completely shut out of the public sphere and relegated purely to domestic labor. The demands of capitalism for cheap and plentiful labor acted as too strong a pull, as did women's interest in leading lives beyond the cramped confines of the home. Whereas only 5.6 percent of married women were counted in the workforce in 1900, by 2002, 56.1 percent of mothers with children and 70 percent of childbearing-age women were in the labor force.[51]

This change has not by itself freed women by any means. Instead, it has imposed a double burden on women, who are expected to cook, clean, and raise children, as well as work outside the home. Moreover, owing to the dominant ideology of women as "housewives" first, women working for wages outside the home could be "treated as alien visitors within the masculine world of the public economy. Having stepped outside their 'natural' sphere, women were not to be treated as full-fledged wageworkers. The price they paid involved long hours, substandard working conditions and grossly inadequate wages."[52]

Engels took note of this contradiction, writing that while "modern large-scale industry" opened up the possibility again of women engaging in social production outside the domestic sphere, "it was opened in such a manner that, if she carries out her duties in the private service of her family, she remains excluded from public production and unable to earn; and if she wants to take part in public production and earn independently, she cannot carry out family duties."[53] As a result, "although women play a productive role in advanced capitalism," writes Sharon Smith, "this alone hasn't translated into equality with men as it did in pre-class societies."[54]

In the United States African American women never experienced the gilded oppression of bourgeois white women; and they were never expected, ideologically or practically, to be stay-at-home moms. They have always experienced the double burden of family and work. Under slavery they worked alongside men doing the same work for the plantation masters in a system of severe exploitation that left little space for real family life. Plantation life placed them under the ever-present threat of sexual assault by their masters. After slavery they became agricultural and domestic workers—cooking and cleaning for middle-class and rich white women. But they also worked in factories and mills. Writes Angela Davis,

> The unorthodox feminine qualities of assertiveness and self-reliance—for which Black women have been frequently praised but more often rebuked—are reflections of their labor and their struggles outside the home. But like their white sisters called "housewives," they have cooked and cleaned and have nurtured and reared untold numbers of children. But unlike white housewives, who learned to lean on their husbands for economic security, Black wives and mothers, usually workers as well, have rarely been offered the time and energy to become experts at domesticity. Like their white working-class sisters, who also carry the double burden of working for a living and servicing husbands and children, Black women have needed relief from this oppressive predicament for a long, long time.[55]

The mythology of the stay-at-home mom keeping house and raising children was only true for a very limited period even for white working-class women, namely during the economic boom after the Second World War. As author Stephanie Coontz notes, in the nineteenth century, without the modern technology and availability of prepackaged food we take for granted today, household cleaning and food preparation was a "mammoth task." Middle-class women therefore could only engage in child-rearing by employing domestic help. "For every nineteenth-century middle-class family that protected its wife and child within the family circle," Coontz writes, "there was an Irish or German girl scrubbing floors . . . [and] . . . a black girl doing the family laundry." Meanwhile, working-class women of all backgrounds in the North were, in addition to raising their own children, finding work as domestics, sweatshop workers, and factory hands.[56]

Today, too, there is an "uncomfortable mismatch between cultural norms and images and the ways in which people are actually living their lives."[57] The "ideal" family portrayed in old television shows like *Leave It to Beaver* were never very close to the truth, even in the 1950s. They are even less true today, though this fantasy family is still the ideal of the Christian right. In fact, over half the workforce in the United States is made up of women. Single parents head many families. Rather than being a haven in a heartless world, in many cases the family acts as a breeding ground for frustration and violence, focusing the frustrations that workers feel outside the home. While relations between men and women have changed a lot over the past few decades, women's status is still one of inequality with men. "Women have gained the freedom both to have children and to pursue careers," writes author Arlene Skolnick, "but society and institutions have not adapted to a world where women are in the workplace to stay."[58]

Women are still paid less than men—averaging 77 cents for every dollar a man makes.[59] They still perform more childrearing and housework than men—though today as a result of the woman's movement and the entry of so many women into the paid workforce men share some, but by no means all, of the burden of housework. Women are portrayed in various media as physical objects of sexual desire rather than as full human beings. Sexual abuse, from verbal harassment to more severe forms of domestic violence and rape, is widespread. In a 2000 US Department of Justice report, 17.6 percent of women surveyed reported having experienced rape or an attempted rape—the assaults occurring in more than half the cases when they were younger than eighteen.[60] Women's reproductive rights (both to bear children and to terminate pregnancies) are circumscribed—one product of the backlash of the past few decades against women—through restricted access to health care and abortion, especially for working-class women. In 2013 alone, for example, thirty-nine states passed 141 provisions restricting women's reproductive health and rights.[61]

Why are women still oppressed? This question is usually answered in two unsatisfactory ways: male biology (men are stronger) or male psychology (men *need* to dominate women), or a combination of the two. According to this view, held often by both conservatives *and some feminists*, women's oppression isn't going to disappear as long as there are men around.

If physical or biological differences between men and women were ever very significant, modern technology has rendered those differences largely irrelevant. Women's oppression persists because of the way in which capitalism benefits from women's unpaid labor in the home. As long as the task of raising the next generation of workers falls to the private family, rather than being taken on by society as a whole, the basis for completely freeing women from their oppression will not exist. Women's entry into the workforce, the public sphere, has not resulted in her liberation, though it has given her more economic independence and more confidence to fight back, which helps in part to explain the succeeding waves of women's movements over the past hundred years.

Women's complete liberation from oppression is inseparably bound up with the fight to socialize the process of childrearing and other household tasks that are now left entirely up to family members. Today, it means fighting for equal pay, free and available health care and access to abortion, and more daycare centers. It also requires a fight against sexist ideas held by men—and also internalized by women themselves. Such a fight is possible because these changes would benefit working-class men as well as women.

Sexist ideas can and do break down, however, as the women's movement in the 1960s and 1970s definitively showed. Attitudes about everything from a woman's proper role in society to interracial relationships have shifted dramatically since the 1960s. The film *Salt of the Earth*, about a strike of copper miners in Arizona in the 1950s, is brilliant in showing how struggle can challenge and break down sexist ideas. In the film a legal injunction against men picketing during the strike prompts the women to insist that they take over the picket lines. The men violently reject this idea but in the end relent because it's their only chance of success. In the process, gender roles are completely reversed. The women go to the picket line every day and the men take care of the kids. The experience gives women confidence to speak in public, and to assert themselves with their husbands.

The willingness of men to share housework is a product of struggles such as those of the women's movement, and reflect the way in which struggle can break down old ideas about what is natural and what is not. These changes are important because they improve our chances for a successful struggle to achieve more far-reaching changes. But the solution to women's oppression cannot be solved solely by getting men to share more housework. The fact that the family remains privatized and that men are typically paid more than women in the workforce creates an economic incentive for women, rather than men, to take time off to care for children and elderly relatives. Those who can afford it deal with the problem of juggling work and family by hiring maids and servants. Wealthy bourgeois women, in other words, don't experience the burdens of women's inequality in the same way that working-class and poor women do. In working-class families, equal sharing of housework "would mean . . . that working-class men would share the burden for the reproduction of labor power along with working-class women—to the continued benefit of the capitalist class."[62]

As with other forms of oppression, women's oppression cuts across class lines, a fact that has led some feminists to claim that women and men do not share any common interests. Liberal feminism pursues a strategy of improving the lot of middle-class women within the confines of capitalism, whereas separatists look for the complete separation of women from men as the only solution to their oppression. The former strategy is limited, the second unrealistic, and neither will end women's unequal status in society. "However apparently radical the demands of the feminists," wrote the Russian revolutionary Alexandra Kollontai of the bourgeois women's movement of her day, "one must not lose sight of the fact that the feminists cannot, on account of their class position, fight for that fundamental transformation of the contemporary economic and social structure of society without which the liberation of women cannot be complete."[63]

Women of the ruling class face sexism, but their conception of how to confront it is shaped by their class position. Yahoo CEO Marissa Mayer, whose monetary worth tops $300 million, built a state-of-the-art nursery at work—for *herself*—so that she could juggle motherhood and her work life. Mayer banned Yahoo employees from working at home, but she didn't build company nurseries for Yahoo's women employees so they could similarly manage work and childrearing. Nor did she or provide women employees with paid maternity leave or the extra pay necessary to cover exorbitant child care costs. It is directly counter to Marissa Mayer's interests as a capitalist to do for workers what she has done for herself.[64]

Working-class women require a more thorough social transformation, one that takes into account the family burden that they primarily bear. The working-class solution to women's oppression requires a society in which the means of production *and* reproduction are socialized, where sex is no longer debased as a commodity that can be bought and sold, and where women have full control of their own bodies. Communal laundries, kitchens, and child-care centers would free women from the double burden of work and housework and provide them with the means to become fully free and equal members of society. In a 1923 speech Trotsky said: "The problem of women's emancipation, both material and spiritual, is closely tied to that of the transformation of family life. It is necessary to remove the bars from those confining and suffocating cages into which the present family structure drives woman, turning her into a slave, if not a beast of burden. This can be accomplished only through the organization of communal methods of feeding and childrearing."[65]

Heroic attempts were made in Russia to build a new society of freedom after the revolution. Homosexuality was decriminalized, and abortion was also legalized. Laws denying recognition of children born out of wedlock were wiped away. The Bolshevik government established communal laundries, kindergartens, nurseries, and kitchens. Alexandra Kollontai was put in charge of a special women's department devoted to organizing women, increasing their social and political participation in public life, and promoting their interests. Special efforts were made to provide literacy and education, especially to women. "Not a single bourgeois republic," said Lenin, "had done in decades so much as a hundredth part of what we did [for women] in our first year in power."[66]

Lenin, Trotsky, and others believed that it was impossible to talk of real communism until women had been completely emancipated. But the material resources did not exist in Russia to create an alternative to the old family and free woman from her status as a domestic slave. "It proved impossible to take the old family by storm," wrote Trotsky,

> not because the will was lacking, and not because the family was so firmly rooted in men's hearts. On the contrary, after a short period of distrust of the government and its creches, kindergartens and like institutions, the working women, and after them the more advanced peasants, appreciated the immeasurable advantages of the collective care of children as well as the socialization of the whole family economy. Unfortunately society proved too poor and little cultured. The real resources of the state did not correspond to the plans and intentions of the Communist Party.

The impoverished condition of Russia meant that the social services provided by the revolutionary government were of such a poor quality that workers chose to return to reliance on the private family. As a result, "Back to the family hearth! But home cooking and the home washtub, which are now half shamefacedly celebrated by orators and journalists, mean the return of the workers' wives to their pots and pans that is, to the old slavery." Material conditions made the establishment of new communal forms untenable. "You cannot 'abolish' the family," Trotsky concluded. "You have to replace it. The actual liberation of women is unrealizable on a basis of 'generalized want.' Experience soon proved this austere truth which Marx had formulated eighty years before."[67] The Russian Revolution could pose a solution to women's oppression, but it could not solve it.

The family, and the forms it has taken over time, is not determined genetically, but by society's changing social relations. Neither a sexual division of labor nor women's subordination has any justification in today's world of abundance and technological advancements. "The past of the family does not limit its future," writes Kathleen Gough.[68]

Gender and LGBTI Oppression

Human beings have engaged in all kinds of sexual behavior since the dawn of humankind, including sex between people of the same sex. However, the way sex, sexual behavior, and gender roles have been treated have been quite variable. As historian David Greenberg notes, "Some societies are comparatively hostile to homosexuality, while others tolerate or even fully accept and institutionalize it"—for example the ancient Greeks. Not only that, but the very concepts and definitions that are attached to various sexual behaviors is historically conditioned. "It is not merely that some societies are more accepting than others," writes Greenberg. "It is that the kinds of sexual acts it is thought possible to perform, and the social identities that come to be attached to those who perform them, vary from one society to another. There are societies, including some where homosexual acts are frequent, that lack any concept of a homosexual person."[69]

There have been many tribal societies in which boys who reached puberty were placed in the company of men with whom they were expected to form sexual bonds in preparation for their transition to manhood. In many highly militarized societies the raising and training of boys involved sexual relations as part of the creation of close-knit bonds between fighting men.

There are also many examples of egalitarian same-sex relations in various cultures. Writes Greenberg:

> Lesbian affairs were virtually universal among unmarried Akan women of the Gold Coast (now Ghana), sometimes continuing after marriage. Whenever possible, the women purchased extra-large beds to accommodate group sex sessions involving perhaps half-a-dozen women. Hottentot men who enter into a compact of mutual assistance often become lovers. Frequently, though, relationships of this kind develop among children and adolescents. Observers usually describe them as casual

or as involving "exploration," "experimentation," or play, though the participants may take them seriously.[70]

The association of a particular sexual activity or preference to gender—as well as the concept of gender itself—is something that is determined historically and socially. Among the Tahitians, for example, traits like aggressiveness and gentleness were not sex linked, and the language "has no grammatical categories based on gender."[71]

Gender and sex are not identical, though they are closely related concepts in our society. Gender refers to a set of cultural and behavioral traits associated with being "male" and "female," whereas sex refers to a person's reproductive organs. Gender is something that individuals acquire through cultural cues, not something they are born with. These cues begin immediately for children and they are strongly visual, but also behavioral; they quickly funnel those who are defined as girls to act like girls, and those who are defined as boys to act like boys.

The stereotypes become so ingrained that we think they are natural, and we forget how malleable human behavior is. In one study, four boy and four girl preschoolers were read stories that subverted gender stereotypes, after which two of the boys began to play with toys traditionally considered for girls that they had previously ignored, and the four girls "abandoned stroller, baby doll, and ironing board to experiment with fire trucks, blocks, and helicopters. By the last few days of the experiment these girls were playing almost exclusively with the boyish toys."[72]

As we get older, we learn that men can be affectionate, nurturing, and emotional, and women can be the opposite. We see around us a great deal of information that challenges gender stereotypes—athletic, muscular women whose ability far exceeds the majority of men, for example. Often, that does not lead us to jettison the stereotypes completely. There is just too much "evidence" around us—isn't it mostly the women who are home taking care of the kids?—which shows us that men and women are different. Individual families may try to buck the stereotypes by creating a "gender-neutral" environment for their kids. But the barrage of cultural cues kids receive outside the home, and the limited time and resources of working-class households even to create a home environment along these lines, makes this almost impossible.

The idea, still prevalent in our society, that gay men are "effeminate" or less "masculine" and that lesbians are more "masculine" is "almost certainly the result of antipathy to homosexuality rather than empirical observation." Indeed, the existence of stereotyped conceptions of gender-based behavior as well as antigay bigotry creates the conditions in which the observance of "feminine" or "masculine" traits in some percentage of people identified as gays or lesbians becomes corroboration of the stereotype, and the many examples of gays and lesbians who exhibit different traits are simply ignored.[73]

Ironically, while children get endless "education" about gender, they get only the haziest instruction on the actual biological and anatomical facts about sex. Indeed, before children are aware of male and female sex organs and the difference between them, they are already clear (according to the norms they witness around them) that boys don't wear dresses and only girls wear barrettes in their hair. There are many people who are anatomically male or female (or, for a tiny portion of the population, exhibit biological and physical traits that place them somewhere in between and are termed "intersex") but "discover" at some point in their lives that they belong to a different gender than the one their parents and society assigned to them—a clear indication that gender is a malleable concept and does not bear a one-to-one relationship with our biological makeup. People whose behavior "bends" gender concepts have existed for centuries; however, only in the latter half of the twentieth century "did some gender variant people begin to identify themselves as transgender."[74]

In the period of the rise of the world market prior to the rise of industrial capitalism, sexual behavior came to be considered acceptable only when it was linked to procreation in families. The patriarchal household shaped the parameters of what was considered acceptable sexual behavior. One engaged in sex to have children. Sexual relations that happened outside that relationship, which were considered "crimes against nature," were punished to one degree or another. Homosexual acts were considered unnatural, but so were heterosexual anal and oral sex, and even masturbation—and fell under the more broadly defined category of "sodomy." In this period, same-sex acts were sometimes proscribed and sometimes punished, but there was no conception of homosexuality as an attribute of a particular type of person.

It was not until the 1870s that there began to develop, in Europe and the United States, the concept of the "homosexual" as a distinct type. The medical profession pioneered the idea of the homosexual as a person or people who, by their very nature, deviated from societal and biological norms of sexuality. Writes author Jeffrey Weeks,

> The latter part of the nineteenth century . . . saw the clear emergence of new conceptualisations of homosexuality although the elements of the new definitions and practices can be traced to earlier periods. The sodomite, as Foucault has put it, was a temporary aberration. The "homosexual," on the other hand, belonged to a species, and it is this new concern with the homosexual person, both in legal practice and in psychological and medical categorization, that marks the crucial change, both because it provided a new subject of social observation and speculation, and because it opened up the possibility of new modes of self-articulation.[75]

The same pseudo-scientific ideology that defined gays as sick, degenerate, or mentally defective ironically also contributed to establishing the basis of a gay identity among people who preferred sexual relations with the same sex.

With capitalism came the dissolution of fixed relations and its replacement by the free interconnection of individuals regulated only by the market. As Marx writes in the *Manifesto*, the modern bourgeoisie "has put an end to all feudal, patriarchal, idyllic relations. It has pitilessly torn asunder the motley feudal ties that bound man to his 'natural superiors,' and has left remaining no other nexus between man and man than naked self-interest, than callous 'cash payment.'" The "fixed, fast-frozen relations" of feudalism were "swept away," replaced by market social relations in which individuals appear to be "detached from natural bonds."[76]

The growing dominance of market relations, the emergence of wage labor and the growth of cities created conditions in which people with different sexual orientations and preferences could find ways to link up outside the traditional family setting and explore their sexuality. It was for the first time possible for adults to live outside of family relationships and, in the anonymity of city life, explore different ways of living. These possibilities were opened up further by the experience of the two world wars, which segregated the sexes, herded large numbers of men together, and accelerated the entry of women into the paid workforce. Contradictorily, imperialism and militarism both reinforced reactionary gender stereotypes while it also opened up greater space for sexual experimentation and set the stage for the growth of movements for sexual liberation.

With the rise of capitalism, however, the family, as we have seen, moved further away from being a site of production to one of reproduction; it increasingly came to be seen as the setting of "'personal life,' sharply distinguished and disconnected from the public world of work and production."[77] Thus at the same time as capitalism has torn asunder old social ties and arrangements, it continues to depend on the family for cheaply raising the next generation of workers—and upon an ideology that emphasizes gender roles that stigmatize same-sex and other sexual identities that threaten the "traditional" family. As John D'Emilio, in his essay "Capitalism and Gay Identity," writes:

> On the one hand, capitalism continually weakens the material foundation of family life, making it possible for individuals to live outside the family, and for a lesbian and gay male identity to develop. On the other, it needs to push men and women into families, at least long enough to reproduce the next generation of workers. The elevation of the family to ideological preeminence guarantees that a capitalist society will reproduce not just children, but heterosexism and homophobia. In the most profound sense, capitalism is the problem.[78]

There have been significant changes in the treatment and social status of people who choose alternative sexualities under capitalism—including legal changes permitting same-sex marriage in a growing number of states, and along with that, changing social attitudes towards same-sex relationships. These changes are largely the product of social movements of the past several decades. But so long as capitalism depends on the family, it will be difficult, if not impossible, to completely eliminate the oppression of lesbian, gay, bisexual, and transgender people. To create a society in which human beings are free to explore their sexuality and to mold their personal relationships and identities as they see fit, and women are liberated from their second-class status, will require the elimination of the social relations of capitalism that commodify sexuality and depend upon privatized reproduction.

Origins of Racism

Modern racism—the singling out of one group for second-class citizenship or differential treatment on the basis of imputed physical attributes such as skin color—has its origins in the period of the creation of a world market, the expansion of European colonial empires, and the rise of plantation slavery in the Americas. Prior to the rise of Nazism, biological theories about the superiority of "the white race" were widespread, along with various other arguments used to justify colonial slavery, conquest, and violence.

In our era, when most *legal* forms of racial discrimination and exclusion have been eradicated, and where the persistence of racial oppression is papered over with coded messaging and claims of racial "colorblindness," it is easy to forget how recently theories of racial hierarchy—which purported to show that white "Anglo-Saxons" were the superior race, Black Africans were at the bottom, and non-Anglo and non-"Teutonic" brown and white people somewhere in between—were entirely acceptable in public discourse in the United States and Britain.

These pseudo-scientific racist ideas have been pushed more to the margins, but they have not disappeared. More recent bestsellers like *The Bell Curve*, which purport to show innate racial differences in intelligence, reveal the extent to which such ideas have made a comeback among conservatives.[79]

Clear evidence never got in the way of this kind of spurious pseudoscience. Arguments like those in *The Bell Curve* are used to justify cuts in funding for social programs and affirmative action, not to serve the truth. Racists were pleased by studies of Black draftees during the Second World War that found they had lower IQs than those of white draftees. But as genetic biologist Theodosius Dobzhansky points out, the average IQ of Northern African American draftees "was higher, not lower, than that of white draftees from southern states."[80] Not surprisingly, this evidence was not offered as proof that whites were genetically inferior to Blacks, or that the tests measured something other than innate intelligence. While French psychologist Alfred Binet designed the IQ test in the early 1900s originally as a diagnostic tool to determine if children needed remedial education, social Darwinists in the United States appropriated the test and claimed it was a way to measure someone's inherited level of intelligence. Differences in performance on the test that were obviously attributable to economic deprivation, culture, and educational level were, a priori, attributed to someone's alleged "racial" or "inferior" social origin.[81]

Racism is not innate—it is a historical invention. Indeed, the concept of race itself is a historical invention rather than scientific fact. There is no biological or genetic foundation for singling out groups of people according to some superficial physical characteristic (or set of characteristics) and treating that group as a separate race. In the words of historian Barbara J. Fields, "Anyone who continues to believe in race as a physical attribute of individuals, despite the now commonplace disclaimers of biologists and geneticists, might as well also believe that Santa Claus, the Easter Bunny and the tooth fairy are real, and that the earth stands still while the sun moves."[82]

Nevertheless, race as a social construct is very real, and has a very real impact on people. "Blacks in America," writes anthropologist Ashley Montagu, "have . . . been deprived, oppressed, discriminated against, impoverished, ghettoized, and generally excluded from the brotherhood of man. Hence it should not be surprising that there have been and continue to be significant differences in the achievements of Blacks and whites as 'measured' by tests which have been arbitrarily standardized on middle-class Whites."[83]

As historian Thomas F. Gossett in his classic *Race: The History of an Idea in America* notes, "The fact that race has no precise meaning has made it a powerful tool for the most diverse purposes."[84]

In the New World, British colonists opted for a plantation system to produce lucrative cash crops like tobacco, rice, and sugar. Once the native people were forcibly dispossessed, there was plenty of land, but not enough labor to work it. Indians escaped too easily, and with disease their numbers dwindled. European indentured servants were used commonly for some time, but they expected land after serving five to seven years for a master. When indentured servants became less viable as a steady cheap source of workers, planters turned to enslaving Africans. According to Caribbean historian Eric Williams, the reason for the enslavement of Black Africans was "economic, not racial." The African slave's so-called subhuman characteristics "were only the later rationalizations to justify a simple economic fact." Therefore, argues Williams, "slavery was not born of racism; rather, racism was the consequence of slavery."[85] In order to justify the enslavement of Africans, writes one historian, "their very humanity had to be denied."[86]

Racialized slavery performed a number of functions. It provided the planters with a steady stream of laborers from Africa that could be branded as their property for life. The differences in appearance between Africans and Europeans, and the enslaved's lack of acculturation, would make it difficult for them to resist or run away. Racial laws could be enacted that ensured that the African's slave status—or that of her children—could never be altered. Finally, racial ideology helped the planters to build a sense of solidarity with poor whites who might otherwise seek common cause with slaves against the rich—something that had happened, for example, in Virginia in the mid- to late 1600s.

What this system added up to was fabulous profits both for the ruling planter classes in the colonies, and for the merchants, manufacturers, and state treasuries of the "mother" countries in Europe. "Rising British capitalism had a magic money machine," writes historian Peter Fryer, "an endless chain with three links: sugar cultivation; manufacturing industry; and the slave trade. And the slave trade was the 'essential link.'"[87]

The basis for adopting race-based chattel slavery did not emerge from nowhere. Already ruling classes in Europe saw the poor and dispossessed as inherently inferior beings who rightly lived in various states of bondage and unfreedom. "Brutal repression of 'rowdy' elements in Britain as well as savage colonization of Ireland preceded the English assault on Native Americans and enslavement of Africans," writes historian Peter Kolchin. "If the English regarded the Africans inferior by nature, members of the English gentry regarded their own lower classes—and the Irish—in much the same way: they were ignorant and 'brutish' and required physical repression to keep them in line."[88]

In the South, during slavery and after, racism was fostered among poor whites to prevent them from seeing that they shared with Blacks the same exploiters—the white planter class. "The slaveholders," wrote Black abolitionist Frederick Douglass, "by encouraging the enmity of the poor, laboring white man against the Blacks, succeeded in making the said white man almost as much of a slave as the Black himself. . . . Both are plundered by the same plunderer."[89]

The ideology of white supremacy justified not only continental conquest (over Indians and Mexicans) and slavery but also overseas expansion in the Pacific and the Caribbean that characterized modern imperialism. Social Darwinism—the theory that there is a genetic hierarchy of humans, with white conquerors at the top—became widespread. In the struggle for markets and colonies, "survival of the fittest" operated—and put the "fittest," that is, whites, at the top. "Slavery disappeared," writes Lance Selfa, "but racism remained as a means to justify the enslavement of millions of people by the United States, various European powers, and later Japan."[90] In 1893, when the United States was first entering the arena of colonial expansion into the Caribbean and the Pacific, historian and Indiana senator Albert J. Beveridge called white Anglo-Saxons "the most masterful race in history."[91]

Professors, anthropologists, and scientists endeavored to prove that there was a natural hierarchy of racial superiority and inferiority. A branch of "scientific racism" called eugenics was used to justify the forced sterilization of tens of thousands of indigent and poor Black, Puerto Rican, Indian, and white women and men, as well as disabled and ill people in the United States throughout the twentieth century. In a landmark 1974 case, a federal judge found that 100,000–150,000 poor, mostly African American women, were sterilized annually under federally funded programs without giving their informed consent, and that countless others were coerced into accepting sterilization to avoid having their welfare benefits cut off.[92]

Racism, therefore, is not simply a holdover from slavery, but a feature of capitalism. In his discussion of England's oppression of Ireland, Marx got to the root of why capitalism fosters and depends on racism:

> In *all the big industrial centers in England*, there is a profound antagonism between the Irish proletarian and the English proletarian. The average English worker hates

the Irish worker as a competitor who lowers wages and the standard of life. He feels national and religious antipathies for him.

He regards him somewhat like the poor whites in the southern states of North America regarded black slaves. This antagonism among the proletarians of England is artificially nourished and kept up by the bourgeoisie. It knows that this scission is the *true secret of maintaining its power*.[93]

The same logic is at work today. One has only to think of the deliberate racism fostered against Mexican immigrants. If native-born workers can be made to believe that immigrant workers threaten their jobs; if white workers can be made to hate or resent Blacks; or if Americans can be made to think that Arabs and Muslims are the enemy, it makes it more difficult for workers and the oppressed to unite against their common enemy. Racist and xenophobic ideas do not benefit workers and the poor, whatever their race, sex, or ethnicity. But they do benefit the exploiters—by making sections of the exploited believe they have common interests with their exploiters because they share the same language or skin color. For example, certain industries view illegal immigrant labor as ideal because illegal immigrants cannot organize unions and live in constant fear of deportation, so it's easy to pay them next to nothing. The solution is not to restrict immigration, but to organize immigrant workers alongside native-born workers to fight the common enemy.

Historically, unions have been weakest in the South. This has kept wages lower than in the rest of the country. But the reason unions have been weak in the South is primarily because of racism. The antagonism of whites toward Blacks has been the secret by which employers in the South have kept workers from organizing successfully. The fight against racism, therefore, cannot be separated from the class struggle as a whole. As the old labor slogan tells us, an injury to one is an injury to all. The special oppression faced by one part of the working class drags down the rest. Conversely, the elimination of that oppression, the liberation of the oppressed, is the condition for lifting up all.

One can see the logic of oppression under capitalism at work if we look at the impact of both the rise and fall of the civil rights and Black struggles in the United States. These movements inspired and gave impetus to many other struggles—of women, gays and lesbians, workers, and antiwar activists. As Brian Jones notes, "African Americans, a historically denigrated and despised group, suddenly enjoyed tremendous moral and political prestige and authority."[94] In the decades that followed, the ruling class looked to roll back the gains of all the social movements of the 1960s and push through an attack on working-class living standards. To put the genie of struggle back in the bottle, it had to get people to accept the idea that the government had the right to cut social programs, to privatize public services and utilities, and to transfer a greater portion of the value workers produce, and the public wealth that comes largely from our tax dollars, to the rich.

Destroying the influence and prestige of the Black movement was paramount to this process. The right-wing ideological backlash that began in the Reagan era targeted "crime" and "welfare queens"—code words for young Black men and women—and blamed Black poverty on the individual failings of African Americans. The highly charged racist climate of this campaign was used to justify rolling back many of the social gains of the civil rights and antiracist movements, and also of the women's movement and the union movement. The policies and programs that have gone on the chopping block under both Republican and Democratic administrations benefitted white workers, too. Whites in fact make up the majority of recipients of Aid to Families with Dependent Children, Medicaid, and food stamps (now called SNAP). The ideology of "individual responsibility" has been used to break up the solidarity of all the poor and working class and convince ordinary people that they, rather than the system, are to blame for their problems. In this climate, it has been easier for governments, politicians, and pundits to begin openly discussing cutting what was once considered a "third rail" of US politics—Social Security, a program that traditionally *underserves* Black people.[95]

As part of the backlash against the civil rights movement, the US political and economic elite embarked on a campaign beginning in the 1970s centered on the criminalization of Black youth through the mantra of fighting "street crime" and later the "war on drugs." The United States has the dubious distinction of imprisoning a greater portion of its population than any other country on the planet. Since 1970, incarceration rates in the United States have skyrocketed, increasing more than sixfold. Between 1980 and 2008, the prison population went from half a million to 2.3 million, largely fueled by a "tough on crime" political climate and the so-called war on drugs. Of that number, a million are African Americans; and, together with Latinos, they make up 58 percent of prisoners. Blacks are incarcerated at six times the rate of whites. According to the NAACP, "African Americans represent 12 percent of the total population of drug users, but 38 percent of those arrested for drug offenses, and 59 percent of those in state prison for a drug offense."[96] Blacks are sent to prison for drug offenses at ten times the rate of whites, even though five times as many whites as Blacks use illicit drugs. As of 2001, one in six Black men has been incarcerated in the United States.

Writer Michelle Alexander describes the way in which millions of Blacks are relegated to second-class citizenship by the criminal justice system as the "new Jim Crow," the title of her timely 2011 book. The impact of mass incarceration goes far beyond the degradation of prison life. Millions find that a criminal record makes it near to impossible to find paid work. Almost six million people, many of them African Americans, are permanently barred from exercising their right to vote.[97] Writes Alexander, "More [Blacks] are disenfranchised today than in 1870, the year the Fifteenth Amendment was ratified, prohibiting laws that explicitly deny the right to vote on the basis of race."[98] Of course, the prison population boom has also meant the stratospheric growth of the number of Latino, white, Native American, Asian, and other people in prison.

The Great Recession has had a devastating impact on all workers, but it has disproportionately hurt African Americans, whose average net wealth was already far lower than that of their white counterparts, and was concentrated in their homes. The subprime loan peddlers deliberately targeted Black communities, so the 2007 housing collapse dramatically reduced Black homeownership. That, combined with persistently high unemployment rates and the decline of public-sector jobs traditionally depended on by Blacks for steady work and benefits, has led to a drastic reduction in Black income. According to the Economic Policy Institute, "By 2009, the median net worth for white households had fallen 24 percent to $97,860; the median black net worth had fallen 83 percent to $2,170."[99]

The crisis also had a devastating impact on white workers. A study conducted by the Associated Press found, for example, that as a result of the higher levels of unemployment, "more than 19 million whites fall below the poverty line of $23,021 for a family of four, accounting for more than 41 percent of the nation's destitute, nearly double the number of poor blacks."[100]

The degradation of one group of people as a means to degrade the conditions of *all* workers is a key function of racism. It is not simply a system of prejudice that arbitrarily singles out groups of people for bad treatment because they look different. It does not persist because of some "innate" tendency for human beings to treat those deemed to be "other" badly. There are too many historical examples of people considered to be the same "race" slaughtering each other (think of the two world wars, or of the Rwandan genocide), as well as other examples of people with various differences of physical appearance, language, religion, and culture getting along perfectly well without any urge to hurt or degrade each other. Racial categorization is a purposeful system designed to keep all of us down and looking for scapegoats while the real culprits at the top can pick the pockets of *everyone at the bottom* without disruption. The point was made by Lyndon Johnson to an aide in 1960: "If you can convince the lowest white man that he's better than the best colored man, he won't notice you picking his pocket. Hell, give him somebody to look down on, and he'll empty his pockets for you."[101]

If the struggle for Black freedom and its decline since the 1970s teaches us anything, it is that to the degree that freedom is achieved for one group of oppressed people, it is achieved by others; and to the degree that it is not achieved by one group, it hurts all the oppressed and exploited.

Can There Be Multiracial Unity?

After losing the Civil War, the old Southern planter class aimed at "getting things back as near to slavery as possible."[102] But they were temporarily stymied during the period of Radical Reconstruction. Blacks were granted the right to vote. In some cities, laws restricting the rights of Black people were thrown out. Biracial public education was established where there had never before been any public education. Fourteen Blacks were elected to Congress from the South. These changes also benefited poor whites who had had no public education and few rights under slavery. The importance of this period is that it showed how quickly racist ideas could break down in periods of rapid change. But by the 1870s, the Northern capitalists joined the Southern planter class in being eager to put an end to Radical Reconstruction. They feared the possibility that a population of poor whites and Blacks, "if combined for any political purpose, would sweep away all opposition the intelligent class might make," as the *New York Tribune* opined in 1871.[103]

The Southern ruling class successfully defeated Reconstruction by using racism, Klan terror, and fraud. The biggest threat to their rule came with the Populist movement in the 1890s. A national movement of farmers and sharecroppers who were losing their farms to bankers and speculators, the populists vowed to "raise less corn and more hell."[104] Populism's most radical wing was in the South. The Georgia Populist Tom Watson said of the government, "There is no remedy for it but destruction."[105]

The movement began to break down the divisions between Blacks and whites. The Southern Alliance, a multistate league of Populist farmers, claimed three million members—1.3 million of them Black—in 1890. Watson appealed to Black and white tenant farmers, saying: "You are made to hate each other because upon that hatred is rested the keystone of the arch of financial despotism that enslaves you both."[106] When a leading Black Populist was threatened with lynching, two thousand white farmers responded to Tom Watson's appeal for help to defend him.

Fearing that Populism was a threat to their class rule, the planters resurrected a campaign of violence and intimidation. The cry of "Black domination" was raised to convince poor whites that racial supremacy was in their interests. But the movement kept growing. It collapsed in 1896 when the Populist People's Party decided to back Democratic presidential candidate William Jennings Bryan, based on the argument that he was a lesser evil to Republican McKinley. Bryan adopted the rhetoric of Populism, but he was no populist. His job was to kill the People's Party in a smothering Democratic Party embrace.

With the collapse of the movement in the South, the Southern ruling class used a variety of devices like poll taxes, literacy tests, and property qualifications to disenfranchise Blacks. Poor whites did not benefit from the defeat of Populism. On the contrary, in the process of disenfranchising Blacks, the Southern planters also disenfranchised poor whites. In Louisiana the Black vote declined by 90 percent. The white vote also declined, by 60 percent. This pattern was repeated throughout the South.[107] One Southern newspaper aptly described the move to impose white supremacy as "the struggle of the white people of North Carolina to rid themselves of the danger of the rule of Negroes and the lower class whites."[108]

The Populist movement gives us a glimpse of what enormous changes are possible if the oppressed and exploited unite against their common enemy. But it also explains why the ruling class deploys racism, most often quite successfully—to keep workers divided. The use of Black strikebreakers in the past, for example, was a classic tactic that employers used to divide workers and weaken their organizing efforts. During and immediately after the First World War, for instance, employers saw in Black workers migrating north "the effective means of staving off or preventing the movement toward organization . . . which is now spreading among the foreign worker," explained the manager of a Pittsburgh factory.[109] The steel corporations quite consciously and deliberately used Black strikebreakers to defeat the 1919 steel strike.

There have been high points of class struggle where Black and white workers united to fight their common exploiters. Appeals to racism by lumber mill operators failed to break the unity of thirteen hundred Black and white workers who struck a Louisiana lumber company in 1913; in the end, only violent repression worked. Prior to the strike, Industrial Workers of the World (IWW) leader Big Bill Haywood had succeeded in convincing the Black and white workers of the Southern Lumber Workers union to affiliate to the IWW. In defiance of Jim Crow laws, Black and white workers also agreed to meet in the same hall. "Let the Negroes come together with us," announced the assembled white union members, "and if any arrests are made, all of us will go to jail, white and colored together."[110] In the upsurge of industrial unionism in the 1930s, Black and white unity was commonly forged in struggle. But it didn't come about automatically. It had to be encouraged and fought for. Ferdinand C. Smith, a Black member of the Communist Party and a founding member of the Congress of Industrial Organization's National Maritime Union, was acutely aware of how the employers attempted to use racial animosity to break down labor solidarity. "If the companies show preference for men of one race now, it is only for the time being. Once they get us divided, they will attack one race just as viciously as another. They know that race equality in a trade union is necessary to successful trade unionism—and successful trade unionism is one thing they fear most."[111]

Workers can choose two different responses to the bosses' attempts to divide them. They can accept those divisions, and see lower-paid, more oppressed workers as their competitors. Or they can learn from their own hard experience that the best way to defend themselves is to unite and raise the conditions of all. Obviously, American capitalism would not have survived to this day without succeeding in dividing workers. But every example of real solidarity reminds us of the potential for things to be different. As historian Philip Foner recounted:

> "We are commencing to see a few things," declared a Davenport, Iowa, local of the
> United Brotherhood of Electrical Workers after the employers had taken advantage

of the union's discrimination policy to use Negro workers as strikebreakers. "The prejudice we have held against color is beginning to vanish. A man may be white, black, brown, red or yellow, if he is a toiler he is one of us and part of us, for if his scale of living is lower than ours, our own is not secure, for 'no chain is securer than the weakest link in it.'"[112]

The divisions fostered by the ruling class using racism are not absolute barriers to class unity. We have already spoken of the Populist movement, which demonstrated impressive class solidarity across racial barriers in the Jim Crow Deep South. The United Mine Workers, from its formation in 1890, organized Black and white coalminers in the South, often in the same locals. Half of the UMW members in Alabama were Black, many of the union's officers were Black, and the state's largest local was integrated.[113] The 1912 Lawrence strike—which brought together twenty-five thousand textile workers of twenty-eight different nationalities and who spoke forty-five different dialects—is another example.[114] Foner wrote of Lawrence:

> The spontaneous outburst quickly gave way to a methodical strike organization rarely paralleled in the annals of the American labor movement. . . . A general strike committee of 56 members was set up. The 14 largest nationality groups were each allowed to elect four members. (Later, another nationality was given representation thus increasing the membership to 60.) Of the principal nationalities taking part in the strike, only the Germans were not represented on the committee. . . . The strike committee was the executive board of the strikers, charged with complete authority to conduct the strike, and subject only to the popular mandate of the strikers themselves. All mills on strike and their component parts, all crafts and phases of work, were represented. The committee spoke for all workers.[115]

There have also been periods of intense racism where Blacks felt so cornered, so hounded, and were under such violent attack that separation seemed the only option. This is certainly what gave lift to the mass movement in the early twentieth century behind Marcus Garvey, whose slogan "Up, ye mighty race" inspired millions. But while racism sometimes impels Blacks to organize separately against their oppression, African Americans cannot end racism through their efforts alone. This is not only because Blacks constitute a minority of society; it is also because the Black community is divided by competing class interests. An appeal based on nationalist terms cannot address this division. "As a political current, Black nationalism is extremely heterogeneous, including advocates of Black capitalism, cultural nationalism, reformist politicians, and revolutionaries who oppose the system," notes Ahmed Shawki, author of *Black Liberation and Socialism*. He writes:

> What all varieties of Black separatism share is inconsistency and vacillation. This is necessarily built into all varieties of Black separatism, because neither the analysis nor strategy locate the one agent capable of transforming capitalist society—the working class. So while a separatist strategy can often tap the alienation felt by Blacks, it cannot

provide a solution to the problems that face the mass of Black workers. At times, Black nationalist ideas can be radical in their critique of capitalism as the [Black] Panthers were. But they can also be much more conservative and pro-capitalist, stressing the need for "racial unity" as the basis for Black capitalism.[116]

The civil rights and Black Power movements posed a serious challenge to racism in the United States. Mostly poor and working-class African Americans provided the movement's backbone, though it had the support and participation of many whites, too. In addition to ending legal Jim Crow, these struggles pushed through affirmative action policies aimed at correcting the historic employment and college enrollment imbalance that left Black workers to be "last hired, first fired" and Black students vastly underrepresented in institutions of higher education. They produced sharp increases in social spending, and opened up areas of public employment to Blacks that had been previously closed. The number of Black elected officials tripled between 1969 and 1975.[117]

These struggles did not end racial oppression, however. The civil rights movement lifted up everyone, but it lifted the Black middle class and small Black bourgeoisie far more than it did the majority of poor and working-class Blacks. Today, African Americans still face double the unemployment rate of whites. The national unemployment rate for Black youth ages sixteen to nineteen was 36 percent at the end of 2013.[118] At the height of the recession in 2009, half of all Black men in Milwaukee were out of work.[119] These are official rates that don't take into account the substantial numbers of people who are "discouraged" and have stopped even looking for work. Though they constitute 12 percent of the population, African Americans, as we have seen, make up half of those in prison. And decades after *Brown v. Board of Education*, cities and schools are still heavily segregated in the North and South, with kids of color concentrated in the poorest, least-funded school districts.[120]

That there continue to be major imbalances between the conditions of Black and brown people and white people in the United States cannot be denied. Ruling ideology, accepted by a broad cross-section of society and hammered on in the media now for decades, insists that these imbalances are not the result of systemic oppression, but of personal failure. The dismantling of affirmative action and other programs designed to correct centuries of racial imbalance has been justified deploying the dubious claim that, because of the eradication of the most overt legal forms of discrimination since the 1960s, we now live in a "post racial" society in which no one is disadvantaged anymore because of his or her racial background. Hence, the struggle against racism must not only challenge individual instances of police brutality, combat discrimination, and fight all manifestations of racism—it must also win the battle of ideas and put the blame back where it belongs—on the system.

The end of racial oppression can only come when the system that fosters and depends on it—capitalism—is ended. That requires a body blow delivered by a united working class. Only a conscious, organized battle against racism can foster that kind of unity. Lance Selfa, in an essay on the origins of racism, sums up the matter well:

> First, racism is not part of some unchanging human nature. It was literally invented. And so it can be torn down. Second, despite the overwhelming ideological hold of white supremacy, people always resisted it—from the slaves themselves to white antiracists.
>
> Understanding racism in this way informs the strategy that we use to combat racism. Antiracist education is essential, but it is not enough. Because it treats racism only as a question of "bad ideas" it does not address the underlying material conditions that give rise to the acceptance of racism among large sections of workers. Thoroughly undermining the hold of racism on large sections of workers requires three conditions: first, a broader class fight-back that unites workers across racial lines; second, attacking the conditions (bad jobs, housing, education, etc.) that give rise to the appeal of racism among large sections of workers; and third, the conscious intervention of antiracists to oppose racism in all its manifestations and to win support for interracial class solidarity.[121]

Conclusion

Socialism is not only a theory of the liberation of the working class. It is a theory of the liberation of the working class as the foundation for the liberation of all humanity—and not only from class exploitation, but all forms of oppression. As Lenin writes in *What Is to Be Done?*, "Working-class consciousness cannot be genuine political consciousness unless the workers are trained to respond to all cases of tyranny, oppression, violence, and abuse, no matter what class is affected. . . . The [socialist's] ideal should not be the trade-union secretary, but the tribune of the people, who is able to react to every manifestation of tyranny and oppression, no matter where it appears, no matter what stratum or class of the people it affects."[122]

The idea that Marxism somehow ignores the struggles of the oppressed, especially those struggles that take place outside of the "West," is mistaken. Lenin and the Communist International placed colonial liberation at the center of their strategy for world revolution—linking the struggle for colonial liberation with the workers' struggle in Europe. Trotsky developed his theory of permanent revolution first in relation to Russia. Socialism, he argued, could arrive first in a "backward" country and spread to the more "advanced." But he then applied that argument to China and other colonial struggles in the 1920s. As left-wing sociologist Vivek Chibber argues:

> If you look at the history of Marxism in the twentieth century, it's actually a history of an unceasing engagement with the realities of the nonwestern world. If you think about it, how could it be otherwise? Starting with the revolution in Russia in 1905,

the experience of socialism in the twentieth century has been that the countries where revolutionary movements became the most powerful oftentimes were countries that were not advanced capitalist.

. . . In fact, Marxism is the only theory on the left that has relentlessly and unceasingly engaged with the nonwestern world. The idea that it is a theory that ignores the nonwest or that it imposes western categories artificially, or that it is blind to the realities of the nonwestern world, is pretty far-fetched.[123]

For Marxism, class and oppression cannot be separated, but are part of an integrated and intersecting whole. Oppression cannot be overcome unless capitalism is overthrown. But no successful challenge to capitalism is possible unless it also involves a struggle against oppression in its many forms. This is true not only because without championing these struggles it is impossible to build the kind of unity that is required to challenge the system, but because the struggles of the oppressed have a powerful role to play, as they always have, in the struggle for a different world. Though Lenin was specifically addressing the question of national liberation struggles, his point is more generally applicable:

To imagine that social revolution is conceivable without revolts by small nations in the colonies and in Europe, without revolutionary outbursts by a section of the petty bourgeoisie with all its prejudices, without a movement of the politically non-conscious proletarian and semi-proletarian masses against oppression by the landowners, the church, and the monarchy, against national oppression, etc.—to imagine all this is to repudiate social revolution. So one army lines up in one place and says, "We are for socialism," and another, somewhere else and says, "We are for imperialism," and that will be a social revolution![124]

Revolutionary movements consist in more than simply workers seizing control of production. They are, in Lenin's words, "festivals of the oppressed and exploited," in which all those in society who have been beaten down in various ways rise up and challenge everything that has held them down, crushed their lives, and stultified their personalities.[125]

By definition, sexism, national oppression, or racism affect people of all classes in the oppressed group. But each class experiences oppression differently. Restrictions on abortion and state sterilization programs disproportionately impact working-class and poor women. A wealthy woman will always be able to get the best medical care, including discreet and medically sound abortions—and she can always hire servants to take on the domestic tasks that fall disproportionately on poor and working-class women. The intense racism in the United States means that even a very rich Black man can get pulled over for driving a fancy car ("driving while Black"), but the justice system is far harsher on working-class and poor Blacks than it is on wealthy Blacks. In truth, a Black auto parts worker in Ohio has more in common with his fellow white workers than he does with billionaire Oprah Winfrey or multimillionaire Bill

Cosby. It is no accident that Bill Cosby, a "self-made" man who has shilled for corporate America for decades, is a forceful proponent of the idea that Black people must take "personal responsibility" for their problems. ("It's standing on the corner. It can't speak English. It doesn't want to learn English. I can't even talk the way these people talk," he complained in one of his rants against young Black people.[126]) A hotel maid has more in common with the men she works with than the rich woman whose room she cleans. A native-born worker has more in common with an immigrant worker than he or she does with a native-born boss.

The oppressed must fight to free themselves; but in each struggle of the oppressed, the working class of each oppressed group, people, or nation has an interest in carrying the fight the furthest, that is, beyond the limits its middle-class leaders wish to place on it. The working class is, moreover, the class that is most capable of uniting and providing the social and organizational glue that unites different oppressed peoples together into a struggle for human liberation. A moral identification with the oppressed and a sympathy for capitalism's oppressed victims is a necessary component for building links between various movements and struggles of the oppressed. But it is not sufficient—there must also be a material and social basis, a ground of common interest, that provides the basis for such solidarity. That ground is the common class interests that potentially unite workers of all races, nationalities, ethnicities, languages, and gender identities. "None so fitted to break the chains as they who wear them, none so well equipped to decide what is a fetter," wrote the Irish socialist James Connolly. "But whosoever carries the outworks of the citadel of oppression, the working class alone can raze it to the ground."[127]

Chapter Twelve

Capitalism's Ecological Crisis

The evidence of environmental degradation of our planet as a result of human activity is inescapable. Rising global temperatures—resulting from the increase over the last few centuries, but especially since 1950, in emissions of heat-trapping gases like carbon dioxide (CO_2) and methane into the earth's atmosphere—are having serious consequences for our future on earth.

The rapid melting of arctic ice, which has outpaced all scientific projections, is producing rising sea levels twelve inches above where they were a hundred years ago, and is already threatening some coastal and island communities. Fast-melting glaciers and snow pack in other parts of the world threatens the water supply of major population centers. Warming has created more extreme and less predictable weather patterns—longer droughts and more severe storms, more rapacious wildfires and more devastating floods. It has raised the acidification of oceans and other waterways, and is leading to increasing desertification. It is also stimulating an increase in the frequency and geographical spread of bacterial blights and viral epidemics, reducing biodiversity, and threatening the extinction of species that cannot keep up with the pace of the changes to their habitat.

The burning of fossil fuels, the prime culprit in causing climate change, is fast driving us past a "tipping point" beyond which these non-linear changes become unpredictable and irreversible. We have already blown past 350 parts per million of carbon dioxide in the earth's atmosphere—the figure premiere climate scientist James Hansen projected as the upper limit of safe—reaching 387 ppm in 2009, and cracking 400 (for the first time in three million years) at some measuring stations in 2013.[1]

The means by which heat-trapping gases are captured and removed from the atmosphere—rainforests, woodlands, bogs, and frozen tundra—are fast disappearing as a result of deforestation and warming. More than half of the world's tropical forests are gone.[2] We have reached a point, most scientists agree, where the rise in temperature has created a feedback loop—like the screech that occurs when a microphone is put close to a speaker—that is qualitatively accelerating the rate at which heat-trapping gases like methane and carbon dioxide are leaked into the atmosphere, increasing the pace at which warming, and its damaging effects, unfold.[3]

Climate change is only one aspect of the ecological crisis. There is also the insufficiently regulated pollution of the air, land, waterways, and human beings with industrial, chemical, and biological waste from agriculture, manufacturing, mining, transportation, and extractive industries, which treat the earth as their dumping ground. Exxon's Deepwater Horizon Gulf oil spill in 2010 is only one of the more spectacular and recent examples. Write Fred Magdoff and Brian Tokar on the impact of modern agribusiness:

> The many ecological disasters associated with conventional agricultural production have worsened. These include pollution of groundwater and surface water with nitrates, phosphates, sediments, and pesticides; contamination of food; nutrient depletion on farms that raise crops, even while nutrient-rich wastes accumulate to dangerously polluting levels in large-scale animal production facilities; and increasing spread of antibiotic-resistant microbes due to the routine use of antibiotics in factory-raised livestock.[4]

The very advances made in human productive powers under capitalism that have brought us the possibility of a world without want are also altering our environment in ways that threaten the future viability of life on planet earth. As the renowned environmentalist and activist Bill McKibben notes, "We're moving quickly from a world where we push nature around to a world where nature pushes back—and with far more power."[5]

The impact of global climate change, recognized by virtually the entire scientific community, is making itself so strongly felt that it is impossible to ignore. And yet corporate-funded think tanks spend a great deal of money to convince us that the problem does not exist. Oil giant Exxon-Mobil, for example, spent $27.4 million supporting the climate denial movement between 1998 and 2012 (admittedly small change when compared to the profits of $44.9 billion it made in a single year in 2012!), and the infamous Koch brothers have spent $67 million on climate denial efforts since 1997.[6]

Though there is growing recognition of the problem among the world's leaders, there is little will at the top to take the necessary steps to address it seriously. A series of international meetings over the past few decades to discuss the problem of global climate change, from Kyoto (1997) to Copenhagen (2009) to Warsaw (2013), have failed to adopt workable solutions that have had any meaningful impact. Indeed, the Warsaw conference did not address ways to convert energy use away from coal, whose "burning releases more carbon than other fossil fuels," and increases lung damage, cancer, and acid rain, writes Marxist environmentalist Chris Williams.

> The conference was put on for precisely the opposite reasons. Attendees . . . were there to argue for the future of "clean coal." This technology is known as CCS (carbon

capture and storage). And although it seeks to trap and bury carbon emissions from coal plants, it doesn't exist in any meaningful commercial form. Even some supporters harbor increasing doubts that it ever will be made to work on the scale necessary. But, nevertheless, it is being touted as the way to "safely" continue burning coal. . . .

Rather than raising the level of ambition for deeper emissions cuts and increased funding for developing countries to cope with climate change and transition to alternative energies, countries in the North, responsible for the overwhelming majority of historical emissions to date, are instead further lowering the scope of their commitments.[7]

The decline of cheap, relatively easily extractable oil hasn't meant a shift away from fossil fuels and toward sustainable, renewable energy forms, but toward "unconventional" methods, such as extracting oil from tar sands in Canada, increased offshore and land drilling (notwithstanding the disastrous Exxon gulf oil spill), and hydraulic fracturing ("fracking"), a process involving injecting a mixture of dangerous chemicals, water, and sand into wells at extremely high pressure to extract natural gas. The rapid expansion of this practice, according to the National Resource Defense Council, has resulted in "contaminated water supplies, dangerous air pollution, destroyed streams, and devastated landscapes."[8]

The United States is responsible for 19 percent of global emissions and has no real plans to alter that reality. Notwithstanding his election promises, Obama has rapidly expanded US coal and oil production. Far from being a leader in developing renewal energies and winding down the use of fossil fuels, the United States is once again becoming an energy-producing giant. As McKibben writes,

> If you want to understand how people will remember the Obama climate legacy, a few facts tell the tale: By the time Obama leaves office, the U.S. will pass Saudi Arabia as the planet's biggest oil producer and Russia as the world's biggest producer of oil and gas combined. In the same years, even as we've begun to burn less coal at home, our coal exports have climbed to record highs. We are, despite slight declines in our domestic emissions, a global-warming machine: At the moment when physics tell us we should be jamming on the carbon brakes, America is revving the engine.[9]

Too Many People?

Many people who are concerned about the ecological crisis agree with idea that one of its main causes is that too many people are chasing too few resources, and that each person added to the planet means increasing our damaging "footprint" on earth. The only way to reverse the trend is to reduce consumption and limit population growth, if not cut population numbers outright.

The overpopulation argument has its origin in the theories of the nineteenth-century British economist Thomas Robert Malthus. "Population, when unchecked, increases in a geometrical ratio," he proposed. "Subsistence increases only in an arithmetical ratio."[10] Malthus transferred an observable fact of the nonhuman animal kingdom to human society, without offering a shred of evidence. He used this theory to contend that it was pointless to try to ameliorate the conditions of the poor. "The implications of this line of thought," wrote Engels, "are that since it is precisely the poor who are the surplus, nothing should be done for them except to make their dying of starvation as easy as possible."[11]

Neo-Malthusian explanations for environmental degradation continue to thrive, and are now everyday common sense, an apparently self-evident truth that requires no proof. The publication of Anne and Paul Ehrlich's 1968 book *The Population Bomb* heralded the beginning of an almost continuous alarm on the part of environmentalists over rampant unchecked population growth. In the authors' 1990 sequel, *The Population Explosion*, the alarm became hysteria: "In the six seconds it takes you to read this sentence," they warn, "eighteen more people will be added. Each hour there are 11,000 more mouths to feed; each year, more than 95 million. Yet the world has hundreds of billions *fewer* tons of topsoil and hundreds of trillions *fewer* gallons of groundwater with which to grow food crops than it had in 1968."[12] Without the reduction of population, of resource consumption, and of energy use, they argue, "civilization will collapse."[13] After making this cataclysmic prediction—the beginning of a string of them that never came true—they offer a list of individualistic solutions analogous to trying to collapse a stone wall with a pea shooter: encourage parents to have fewer kids, eat less beef and "more vegetables," wear sweaters and turn down the thermostat, drive a fuel-efficient car, and donate "some of your leisure time to tree planting."[14]

The late Garrett Hardin, a professor of human ecology in California, drew racist conclusions from similar dire predictions: "To survive, rich nations must refuse immigration to people who are poor because their governments are unable or unwilling to stop population growth."[15] He calmly asserted that "freedom to breed is intolerable."[16] Hardin compares the earth to a lifeboat, and makes the assumption that places like the United States and Europe were the "boat" from which the rest of the world should be kept from boarding.

On the most extreme end of this argument are those misanthropic "primitivist" environmentalists who oppose "civilization" of any sort, and believe that we should go back to foraging and hunting, as our ancestors once did.[17] It doesn't take too many seconds of thought to realize that this imagined utopia would be a dystopia for the majority of people on the planet. Non-agricultural foraging could not come close to sustaining the vast majority of human life on the planet. The collapse of civilization—the goal of primitivism—implies the dying off and/or killing of several billion people.

Marx and Engels understood the significance of the fact that for most of human existence we lived in classless, egalitarian, and communal band societies. But rather than proposing the impossible and reactionary—that we go back to ancient communism—they showed how the productive powers and scientific achievements of capitalism, destructive as they were, created the conditions for the "return of modern society to a higher form of the most archaic type—collective production and appropriation."[18]

Before we develop this line of thought further, however, let's look a little deeper into the popular idea that there are "too many people." Some 868 million people in the world go hungry, an estimated 26 percent of the world's children are stunted, and two billion people suffer from one or more micronutrient deficiency.[19] But food production, far from falling behind the population, outstrips it year after year. The United Nations Food and Agricultural Organization estimated in 2005 that world food output per head "has increased steadily over the past 30 years with an average annual growth rate reaching 1.2 percent during the past decade. Both developing and developed countries shared in this expansion, with per capita production growing at higher rates in the developing countries vis-à-vis the developed countries.[20] Enough grain is produced worldwide to feed everyone on the planet.[21] When we throw in other foodstuffs, there is enough to feed double the number of people living in the world today.[22] The sickening irony is that the majority of hungry people on the planet are rural farmers and their families. The growth of production over the last several years in corn and other crops to produce biofuels has driven up food prices and is causing greater hunger. In short, people go hungry not because of absolute shortages of food, but because they can't afford to buy it. To argue otherwise, as neo-Malthusians do, is merely to provide a convenient cover for a system that throws away food to keep prices up rather than feed starving people.

It turns out, in any case, that dire predictions of endless population growth are mistaken. Contrary to the Malthusian claim, population does not grow "exponentially." In 1972 Garrett Hardin, debating socialist environmentalist Barry Commoner, argued that declining birth rates were "fictional." The US birth rate dropped to replacement level that same year, as did birth rates in most countries of the industrialized global North. Several countries, including Germany, Italy, and Japan, are projected to have significantly smaller populations by 2040. In fact, the rate of world population growth, which peaked in 1963, has been slowing down for the last fifty years, and is projected to continue to decline for some time.[23]

In 1844, Engels, in a scathing criticism of Malthus's "vile, infamous theory," noted, "Every adult produces more than he can himself consume."[24] This obvious truth is an ironclad refutation of Malthus. Since every worker can produce "far more than he needs," the "community ought therefore to be glad to furnish him with everything that he needs."[25] The proof of this is the general trend of agricultural production under capitalism, which has dramatically reduced the number of farmers necessary to produce the growing amounts of food needed by the world's burgeoning urban population.

There is no such thing as absolute overpopulation. One has to look at the laws of motion specific to one mode of production to understand its population patterns. Marx criticized Malthus and his theory of population first for giving "brutal expression to the brutal viewpoint of capital"—that it was a piece of capitalist apologetics. But he also dismantled Malthus's arguments, which he exposed as a series of unproven assertions. For Marx, "different modes of social production" produced "different laws of the increase of population and of overpopulation." Malthus, on the other hand, "asserted the fact of overproduction in all forms of society." Malthus, wrote Marx,

> regards *overpopulation* as being *of the same kind* in all the different historic phases of economic development; does not understand their specific difference, and hence stupidly reduces these very complicated and varying relations to a single relation, two equations, in which the natural reproduction of humanity appears on the one side, and the natural reproduction of edible plants (or means of subsistence) on the other, as two natural series, the former geometric and the latter arithmetic in progression. In this way he transforms the historically distinct relations into an abstract numerical relation, which he has fished purely out of thin air, and which rests neither on natural nor on historical laws. He would find in history that population proceeds in very different relations, and that overpopulation is likewise a historically determined relation, in no way determined by abstract numbers or by the absolute limit of the productivity of the necessaries of life, but by limits posited rather by *specific conditions of production*. . . . How small do the numbers which meant overpopulation for the Athenians appear to us!

Overpopulation can only be understood relatively, in relation to the specific society in question and its conditions of production and reproduction. "The overpopulation, e.g., among hunting peoples," Marx continued, "proves not that the earth could not support their small numbers, but rather that the condition of their reproduction required a great amount of territory for few people." Surplus population is therefore purely a relative question, not related "to the means of subsistence as such, but rather the mode of producing them," and "hence also only a *surplus* at this stage of development."[26]

Under capitalism, surplus population is created as a result of the advance of social productivity, not because of any absolute shortage of the means of subsistence. "Surplus population or labor power is invariably tied up with surplus wealth," wrote Engels.[27] Capitalist overpopulation is never overpopulation in relation to available subsistence, but in relation to available employment. As capitalist industry develops, it takes larger and larger amounts of capital to employ smaller and smaller amounts of labor, and market fluctuations in profitability periodically throw workers onto the streets and peasants off the land, to create what Marx called the "reserve army of labor."

As Marx writes in *Capital*, this "surplus laboring population . . . forms a disposable industrial reserve army, . . . a mass of human material always ready for exploitation."[28]

Growth, Population, and Capital Accumulation

It is undeniable that unchecked economic growth in the world today is causing the ecological crisis. Wouldn't having fewer people reduce growth, and therefore, help solve the crisis? The problem with the argument that population equals increased carbon emissions is that not all people are the same. As the authors of the excellent book *Too Many People?* tell us, there is no causal relationship between population density, population growth, and carbon emissions in any single country or region of the planet: "Most of the nations with the highest population growth rates had low growth rates for carbon dioxide emissions, while many of the nations with the lowest population growth rates had high growth rates for carbon dioxide emissions." The truth is that carbon emissions are a problem of rich, industrializing, or already industrialized countries, not poor countries. Moreover, within rich countries, there is no direct correlation between population density and carbon emissions.[29]

The authors subject to withering criticism the population alarmists' usage of per capita statistics to allegedly "prove" the harmful effects of population growth: "Pollution divided by population equals per capita pollution—which leads to the circular claim that per capital pollution times population equals total pollution."[30]

The same circularity afflicts the use of the ratio, first made popular by the Ehrlichs, of IPAT—Impact equals Population times Affluence times Technology—an equation set up to prove what it assumes: that more people using more energy and technology will ruin the planet. This equation has the same problem as the per capita ratio—it is circular: take the total environmental impact and *divide* by the number of people; then take this average and *multiply* it by the number of people—voilà—the "average" impact then becomes what gets added with every "new" person added to the planet. The equation "works" because, as the authors of *Too Many People* note, it isn't a real formula, but an *identity*, something that is "always true by definition," and their definition is "based on their opinion that population growth is the ultimate cause, the universal multiplier, of other problems."[31] The equation assumes, moreover, that the Impact allegedly measured in IPAT is always a negative one. The assumption is that human beings are, by their nature, the enemy of the rest of the natural world from which they have sprung.

These dubious statistical amalgams present us with an abstract, undifferentiated population, giving us the false impression that "emissions are a direct function of population."[32] Per capita figures, however, tell us nothing about who and what is responsible for pollution. "The population is an abstraction," Marx wrote in the *Grundrisse*, "if I leave out, for example, the classes of which it is composed."[33]

It isn't only that a densely populated but barely industrialized country produces less pollution than a highly industrialized country with a low population density. Each country has its own extremes of class and income, where different people hold quite different places in a process of production and distribution. Therefore not every person in the United States is responsible for producing "his" or "her" average carbon dioxide emission. The wealthy capitalist with four houses, a yacht, and a private jet not doubt has a far higher "carbon footprint" than a cashier at Wendy's who walks to work and can barely afford rent. Moreover, the mode of production, over which most of us have no control, is what determines energy use and waste. For example, "99 percent of all solid waste today comes from industrial processes," not from households.[34] The oil, coal, and fracking boom that is currently driving up carbon emissions in the United States represents the "productive consumption" of highly profitable corporations over which most of us have absolutely no control and which we did not cause.[35]

"Growth," like "population," is a superficial and potentially misleading term. What kind of growth? For what purpose and on what basis? In many cases, ecologists argue either that growth is built into what it means to be human, and therefore must be forcibly restrained, or it is something we have more recently become "addicted" to and must seek ways to therapeutically alter. In both cases, there is no clear linkage made between the rampant economic growth we experience and the capitalist mode of production that underlies it.

As discussed earlier, competition drives each individual capitalist to outbid competitors, maximize profits, and continually reinvest in an ever-expanding process of production to cheapen commodities, in an unending cycle only interrupted by periodic crises. Accumulation, unplanned and unchecked growth, is a feature built into the nature of capitalism—and therefore not something that can be altered or opted out of. "The development of capitalist production," writes Marx in *Capital*, "makes it necessary constantly to increase the amount of capital laid out in a given industrial undertaking, and competition subordinates every individual capitalist to the immanent laws of capitalist production, as external and coercive laws."[36] And Engels writes,

> We have seen that the ever-increasing perfectibility of modern machinery is, by the anarchy of social production, turned into a compulsory law that forces the individual industrial capitalist always to improve his machinery, always to increase its productive force. The bare possibility of extending the field of production is transformed for him into a similarly compulsory law. The enormous expansive force of modern industry, compared with which that of gases is mere child's play, appears to us now as a *necessity* for expansion, both qualitative and quantitative, that laughs at all resistance.[37]

Unless the linkage between growth and capital accumulation is made, environmentalists are left seeking changes—cut population, make do with less, change our technologies, do things on a smaller scale and at a slower pace—that fail to confront the underlying economic dynamic that causes the problem in the first place, and whose solutions therefore are either insufficient or, within the confines of capitalism, unrealizable.

Leading environmentalist and activist Bill McKibben argues, for example, "We're so used to growth that we can't imagine alternatives." "For most of human history," he laments, "our society was small and nature was large; in a few brief decades that key ratio has reversed." He urges us to "hunker down," embrace the "slow" and the "small," because "bigness spells trouble."[38] He cites the "too big to fail" financial giants like Citibank and AIG that brought down the financial system as examples of why "bigness" is bad, and contrasts it with the First National Bank of Orwell, Vermont, a small bank that managed to avoid the crash of 2007 and played no role in causing the recession.

But is being slower and smaller, while maintaining capitalism, even possible? Capitalism started with small banks and they got bigger and bigger, just as it started with small companies that got bigger and bigger: this is the logic of capitalist competitive accumulation, which leads to the concentration and centralization of capital. Even if we were able to break up the giant corporations and set up a bunch of smaller ones, which is hardly likely, the economic logic of capitalist competition would start the process all over again. Capitalist competition, Marx presciently observed in the 1860s, "always ends in the ruin of many small capitalists."[39] In short, McKibben offers what Marx would have called a "petty-bourgeois" solution, "cramping the modern means of production and of exchange within the framework of the old property relations that have been, and were bound to be, exploded by those means."[40]

This analysis of the problem reveals a gap between an understanding of the *science* of climate change and the *political economy* of climate change. Beyond a recognition that current climate change is caused by constant economic expansion, it gets no further, offering a description rather than an explanation of the problem. It doesn't advance the analysis very far to say that we have a "growth addiction," or to say that it is part of our nature to constantly expand production. Anyone can see that economic growth is an intrinsic part of our modern world—but it hasn't always been so. To understand why there is a "growth" dynamic requires an understanding of the class nature of capitalism and of the market-driven mechanisms that compel capitalists toward relentless accumulation. Growth is a product not of generic human activity, but of a particular sort of human activity determined by a set of social relations—capitalism—that must be transformed for that sort of activity to change.

Yet nowhere does the word *capitalism* appear in McKibben's book. Indeed, all the solutions he offers to "growth" assume the continued existence of capitalism, equate socialism with the Stalinist bureaucratic state, and portray Marx as a supporter of unchecked industrial growth: "Karl Marx as much as Adam Smith thought we'd end up in a material paradise," he writes. "Richard Nixon and Nikita Krushchev sparred over whose system would produce better appliances."[41] Indeed, it is a common theme among many environmentalists that Marxists share a "worship" of growth per se, refuse to accept environmental limits on economic growth, and advocate the "domination" of humans over nature.[42]

Marx, Engels, and Ecology

Far from seeing the natural world as something to be dominated or exploited, Marx and Engels saw human beings as a part of nature. They sought to heal the rift between man and nature, and saw the only means to achieve this was by ending capitalism and replacing it with the socialism of the associated producers. Marx writes: "From the standpoint of a higher economic form of society, private ownership of the globe by single individuals will appear quite as absurd as private ownership of one man by another. Even a whole society, a nation, or even all simultaneously existing societies taken together, are not the owners of the globe. They are only its possessors, its usufructuaries, and, like *boni patres familias*, they must hand it down to succeeding generations in an improved condition."[43]

The colossal growth of our productive powers under capitalism depends upon, in the words of Marx, crippling wage labor that reduces the worker to a "mere fragment" of a human being.[44] The aim of socialism is not unchecked "growth" for its own sake, as under capitalism, but the rational use of society's productive capacities, planned according to human need, as Engels writes, to reduce the hours of labor, "offering each individual the opportunity to develop all his faculties, physical and mental, in all directions and exercise them to the full—in which, therefore, productive labor will become a pleasure instead of being a burden."[45] Wealth would no longer be measured in how much profits could be amassed, or in the obscene conspicuous consumption of a tiny minority, but in the well-being, free time, and creativity of us all. Such a society would be antithetical to practices that degraded the natural basis upon which such a society could thrive. Though the founders of modern socialism could not possibly have foreseen the scale of environmental dislocation wrought by modern global capitalism, they were already cognizant of the ways in which capitalist production and accumulation impacted the natural world and our relationship to it.[46]

Human beings are part of nature, and like other species, arise from and interact with it. At the same time, as noted in previous chapters, there is a fundamental difference in the way human beings interact with the natural world. Whereas other animals merely *collect* nature's bounty, human beings also *produce their subsistence* by altering the material wealth provided by nature. In a certain sense, history can be seen as the successive changes wrought in human social relations that hinge on the changes in our means of survival, changes that have increased our ability to transform nature and utilize it to meet our needs, and that in turn have altered our relationship to the natural world.

As noted in an earlier chapter, for Marx and Engels, the rise of class society was a necessary result of the development of a surplus. It therefore has had a historically progressive aspect—it freed a minority from drudgery and facilitated the development of society's productive forces. Yet this "advance," based on the breakup of the old communal forms of life,

> from the very start appear as a degradation, a fall from the simple moral greatness of the old gentile society. The lowest interests—base greed, brutal appetites, sordid avarice, selfish robbery of the common wealth—inaugurate the new, civilized, class society. It is by the vilest means—theft, violence, fraud, treason—that the old class-less gentile society is undermined and overthrown. And the new society itself, during all the two and a half thousand years of its existence, has never been anything else but the development of the small minority at the expense of the great exploited and oppressed majority; today it is so more than ever before.[47]

What distinguished capitalism from previous class societies is that it was based upon the forcible separation of the mass of the population from the land in order to create a pauperized source of "free" wage labor, and the concentration of property in the hands of a small minority of exploiters—what Marx called the "release of the worker from the soil as his natural workshop."[48] Human beings no longer directly produce their means of life, which is mediated through the wage relationship. They become separated from the original source of their existence—the land. The process of peasant dispossession continues to this day. In Africa, Asia, and Latin American peasants continue to be driven off the land by the millions, to become poor slum-dwellers surviving at the margins of urban life or as the landless rural poor, of which there are a billion today.[49]

Under capitalism, workers become alienated from the processes and products of their own labor, which stand before them as alien forces standing over them and apart from them. As a system geared toward the production of exchange value, and of profit, capitalism alienates workers not only from the means of production and the products of labor but also from their natural environment. Marx referred to this as a "metabolic rift"—a disruption of the natural metabolism between human beings and nature. The growth of great urban centers "disturbs the metabolic interaction between man and the earth, i.e., it prevents the return to the soil of its constituent elements consumed by man in the form of food and clothing; hence it hinders the operation of the eternal natural conditions for the lasting fertility of the soil." Industrial farming techniques, while at first "increasing the fertility of the soil," in the long run ruined the "long-lasting sources of that fertility." Capitalism thus undermined both "the soil and the worker."[50]

Thus while capitalism created conditions for a society of freedom, based upon the rational use of labor and resources, it did so at the expense of the well-being of both the worker and of nature. Socialism would lead to the restoration of a more rational connection between human beings and nature—for example, the abolition of the distinction between town and country. In the *Manifesto* Marx and Engels include the following in their list of measures to be taken by a workers' state: "combination of agriculture with manufacturing industries; gradual abolition of all the distinction between town and country by a more equable distribution of the populace over the country." And in *Anti-Dühring* Engels writes that the

> abolition of the antithesis between town and country is not merely possible. It has become a direct necessity of industrial production itself, just as it has become a necessity of agricultural production and, besides, of public health. The present poisoning of the air, water and land can be put an end to only by the fusion of town and country; and only such fusion will change the situation of the masses now languishing in the towns, and enable their excrement to be used for the production of plants instead of for the production of disease.[51]

Of course, as Engels explains, industry and agriculture cannot be made to "dovetail harmoniously" without the implementation of "one single vast plan"—something precluded by capitalism, a system characterized by competition, breakneck accumulation, and an absence of rational planning.

Capitalism represents, on the one hand, a tremendous advance in production, in the ability of human beings to understand nature's laws and use them to enhance their own productive powers. Yet this development does not come as part of a harmonious plan driven by human needs. Capitalists only care that "the social effects of human actions in the fields of production and exchange that are actually intended" are examined, and even here the "intended" effects are motivated solely by "the profit to be made on selling," wrote Engels in his essay "The Part Played by Labor in the Transition from Ape to Man."[52]

The unplanned, profit-driven nature of production leads capitalists to blindly pursue its ends without paying attention to their long-term or secondary consequences. "What cared the Spanish planters in Cuba," wrote Engels, "who burned down forests on the slopes of the mountains and obtained from the ashes sufficient fertilizer for one generation of very highly profitable coffee trees—what cared they that the heavy tropical rainfall afterwards washed away the unprotected upper stratum of the soil, leaving behind only bare rock!"[53] Haiti was once one of the lushest islands in the Caribbean and at one time the world's most profitable slave colony. Today, much of it is also "barren rock."

"Let us not . . . flatter ourselves overmuch," Engels therefore warned, "on account of our human victories over nature. For each such victory nature takes its revenge on us. Each victory, it is true, in the first place brings about the results we expected, but in the second and third places it has quite different, unforeseen effects which only too often cancel the first."[54] Indeed, capitalists have not the least interest in handing the earth over to our descendants in "an improved condition." Their concern is solely with profit, and as such do not include in the formation of "value" anything they can snatch "free" from nature. They regard the wealth provided by the earth—land, air, water, its flora and fauna, and its minerals—as much as possible as a free source from which they draw at will and without regard to its effects. And they consider nature also as a place to dump whatever waste products they cannot reapply to profitable enterprises.

We could cite many more alarming, earth-threatening examples since Engels's day demonstrating the reckless disregard for the environment by shortsighted, greedy capitalists. But his words —which flatly contradict the view that Marxists favor human "domination" over nature—are just as apt and extremely relevant today: "Thus at every step we are reminded that we by no means rule over nature like a conqueror over a foreign people, like someone standing outside nature—but that we, with flesh, blood and brain, belong to nature, and exist in its midst, and that all our mastery of it consists in the fact that we have the advantage over all other creatures of being able to learn its laws and apply them correctly."[55]

Market Solutions?

The institutions that are in a position to act as stewards of our environment—corporations, governments, and the military—fail to do so because, first of all, it goes against the very nature of the system: like trying to get wolves not to hunt. Even when breakneck accumulation produces catastrophe right in front of them, capitalists are not willing to absorb the costs associated with either preventing or fixing the damage they do. Governments are beholden to corporate interests, and so the regulation they do attempt is by and large too little, too late. It's not just that corporations are unwilling to foot the bill for the environmental damage they cause; they also spend a great deal of money on lobbyists to prevent or, when that fails, to dilute environmental regulation that would hold them accountable for their polluting behavior.

It is only when environmental degradation and resource shortages impinge on their own profit interests that they are willing to make any changes, and by that point the changes, premised on continuing a system that is the cause of the damage in the first place, are insufficient to substantially reverse the damage already caused. Indeed, the same melting of the arctic ice that has scientists so alarmed is viewed by mining and energy corporations as well as US, European, and Russian officials as a great opportunity, opening up a vast new frontier of mineral and fossil fuel exploration and extraction.[56]

The cause of the environmental crisis is not "bad business practices," which assumes that there is something called "good business practices," but the *everyday* practice of business. That is why market "solutions" to the crisis will always fail. They assume that it is possible to harmonize profit maximization with environmental responsibility.

Carbon trading and other schemes assume that the very mechanisms of market competition that are driving us to planetary disaster can be somehow manipulated in a way to trick capitalists into behaviors that help the planet.

Take just one problem: fossil fuels. This is one of the largest and most profitable industries in the planet upon which the wheels of production, commerce, and transportation turn. Phasing it out would require massive retooling, reorganization, and the development and adoption of viable alternatives. This would require international planning and expenditure on a colossal scale. So long as pumping and selling oil and gas remains profitable, any such transformation will meet with opposition from the oil and gas industry. Clearly this is not about to be accomplished within the boundaries of capitalism with anything close to the scale and speed necessary to make a difference.

Thus the elements that are required for solving the crisis—such as coordinated global planning, a massive increase in the regulation and taxation of industries, the curtailment of accumulation, the immediate phasing out of fossil fuels and their replacement by renewable energies—fly directly in the face of capitalist logic and capitalist interests.[57]

Live Simply?

One of the most popular reactions to society's problems, and one popular among some activists, is to withdraw, to create a small oasis of "correct living" through vegetarian co-ops, anarchist collectives, small organic farms, and the like. Sometimes, the same people who seek to create these spaces of alternative living also get involved in public protests, seeing no contradiction in doing both—fighting the powers that be for something better, but also creating alternatives in the here and now. The idea is that we should all "live simply" by not consuming too much, consuming better, and not buying things that are wasteful or harmful.

This isn't an argument against anyone deciding to make personal changes that suit them. People should have the right to eat and live as they please. But can such choices have any significant social and ecological impact? In order to create a long-term, sustainable environment for human life on the planet, far more is required than individuals deciding to drive fuel-efficient cars or taking time out to plant trees.

What motivates people to decide to change their lifestyle is their genuine alarm at the emptiness of consumer capitalism. But this choice is a luxury to the vast majority of the world's population. For this majority, the question is not what lifestyle to choose, but figuring out how to get by. Half the world's population lives on less than two dollars a day, and 1.35 billion live on $1.25 a day or less.[58] Even in the United States, the richest country in the world, the US Census Bureau counts 46.5 million poor people[59]—and a more reasonable measure of poverty would put this figure significantly higher.[60] Many more live on the edge of poverty, one paycheck away from disaster. Even better-paid workers are mired in debt and overworked. Workers have little time to figure out how to reconfigure their lifestyles. And even if they did, the kinds of changes necessary require fundamental reconfiguring that cannot be altered by individual consumer choices.

The worst environmental problems can't possibly be solved by individual consumer choices. You may choose not to drive a car—if you can figure out how to get to work in a city without a decent public transportation system. But what impact will this have when power plants burn coal and the national transportation system consists of fleets of diesel trucks spewing filth into the air? Someone may eat organic food free of pesticides and chemical fertilizers. But organic food is out of the price range of the majority of people; it is a growing niche market, not part of a plan to create sustainable agricultural practices.

More importantly, individual consumer choice is not the key determinant as to what is produced and how, which are the decisions that most impact the environment. Economists and pundits across the spectrum are fond of calling the United States a *consumer society*, and place a great deal of emphasis on "consumer choice." They present the purchase of commodities as if it were the equivalent of a vote in a democratic election (not realizing what little impact voting has on real political decision-making). Like *growth* and *waste*, "consumer choice" is a misleading phrase that fails to capture the underlying dynamic of capitalism.

As our discussion on economics in chapter 4 noted, under capitalism workers use their wages to purchase commodities so that they and their families can survive; the commodities are bought and personally consumed as use-values. Capitalists, however, do not care in the least about use-values except insofar as they are sellable on the market for profit. Indeed, the lower the quality of the goods they can get away with selling, the better. Moreover, a great deal of consumption under capitalism is not the personal consumption of workers spending their wages, but the *productive consumption* of capitalists buying necessary inputs toward the final products that they will end up selling at a profit.

Beyond our basic human needs, what constitutes a "need" is historically and culturally determined. Paleolithic hunters needed bows and arrows, we don't. We need electricity, cell phones, and tractors, but not canoes or wooden ploughs. Capitalism adds another dimension: the manufacture of new needs and desires in order to sell more products and services. Corporations spend billions yearly on advertising to convince us to buy whatever it is they are selling. They make things that need replacing quickly so they can sell more and more; this is the strategy everyone knows as planned obsolescence.

A great deal of what we are sold bears little relationship to human need by any rational measure. Marx recognized this as early as 1844, when he wrote that for the capitalist "the extension of products and needs becomes a *contriving* and ever-calculating subservience to inhuman, sophisticated, unnatural and imaginary appetites." In order to extend their markets and sales, capitalists must constantly contrive and manufacture new wants and needs, blurring the distinction between them. "Every product is a bait," Marx continues, "with which to seduce away the other's very being, his money; every real and possible need is a weakness which will lead the fly to the glue-pot."[61]

The relatively recent successful marketing of bottled water is a case in point. People in the United States drink more than half a million bottles of water every week, with the mounds of plastic bottle waste finding its way into the nation's landfills and oceans. Studies show that there is no difference between bottled water and tap water. Advertisers and marketers, looking for ways to recover losses from declining soda revenues, began portraying tap water as dangerous and using advertising to associate bottled water with fresh lakes, springs, and eternal health, thus convincing us that it is worth paying for bottled drinking water rather than getting it out of a tap.[62]

Clearly, no one "needs" nutritionally harmful processed foods. But the food industry has invested large sums of money into crafting and promoting, particularly to children, addictive junk foods and sugary drinks for the sole purpose of raking in profits. The food industry has a phrase for the perfect addictive combination of sweet and salty—the "bliss point"—that makes their products irresistible. These capitalists care not a jot about the negative health impacts of their products, though, as a cynical public relations exercise, companies like McDonald's and Coke sign on to initiatives promoting exercise and health. The food industry has been able to market unhealthy "convenience food" successfully not only through advertising and manipulation of taste buds, but also because of the time and financial constraints placed on working-class families trying juggle kids and work.[63] The brilliance of capitalism is that the food industry, having wrecked the health of millions, can now create a new "niche" market selling "healthy" products, as well as diet goods and drugs to deal with medical implications stemming from obesity, thus creatively expanding their opportunities for gain.

"Desire is socially constructed," write authors Kenneth Gould, David Pellow, and Allan Schnaiberg, "and material desires are largely constructed by material producers. The transformation of socially constructed material desire into human need is a result of social processes, which are heavily influenced by those who control production decisions." The authors continue, "Decisions about types of technologies, the use of labor, and volumes of production are made outside the realm of consumer decision-making."[64]

World capitalism is a highly integrated system of production and exchange heavily dependent on fossil fuels, and driven by profit and loss calculations. These calculations are not based on "giving the people what they want," but on convincing people what they should buy. What we are given a "choice" to buy is shaped not only by the limitations of our income, but by the constraints, already established by the system, on what is available. To paraphrase Marx, people make purchasing choices, but not in conditions of their own choosing. Writes Michael Dawson in his book *The Consumer Trap*, "Corporations plan, design, and sell goods and services according to their own profit requirements, without providing any means of subjecting basic productive priorities to popular debate and vote."[65]

The danger of focusing on individual choices is that it can end up blaming the victims—the people who are most hurt by the system—whereas the root of the problem is the way production is organized, not what people choose or don't choose to buy. As the English writer William Morris put it so eloquently.

> It is profit which draws men into enormous unmanageable aggregations called towns, for instance; profit which crowds them up when they are there, into quarters without gardens or open spaces; profit which won't take the most ordinary precautions against wrapping a whole district in a cloud of sulphurous smoke; which turns beautiful rivers into filthy sewers; which condemns all but the rich to live in houses idiotically cramped and confined at the best, and at the worst, in houses for whose wretchedness there is no name.[66]

As individuals, and as consumers, we do not possess the power to alter this. We do, however, have the power as activists, and as workers, to change it. The struggle in Bolivia in 2000 against privatization of the water system is a good example. Millions of Bolivian workers, peasants, and poor people took to the streets and forced the government to back down on its plans to hand the country's water systems over to the American-owned Bechtel Corporation. Activists understood that Bechtel would have massively increased the cost of water for Bolivians. Routing the government's plans not only achieved what individual consumer choices never could have—after all, you can't decide not to consume water—but mass struggle raised the possibility of collective solutions.

There has been a growing awareness of the ecological disaster toward which we are hurtling—and a growing willingness to fight it. In Canada, First Nations activists in 2012 initiated a struggle against a new law lifting environmental protections and opening up Indian land to plunder of its resources by oil and mining interests, starting with a hunger strike by Chief Theresa Spence of the Attawapiskat Cree band. The struggle captured international attention, and spread to Native and environmental activists in the United States. In Canada, "It has captured the imagination of Native and non-Native people alike . . . and has succeeded in uniting a number of diverse constituencies, including public-sector workers and environmentalists," writes one commentator, in part because the bill not only attacks First Nations but also raises the retirement age of public workers and creates a two-tiered pension system. The potential for uniting workers and oppressed people in struggle is exemplified by the letter written by the Canadian Postal Workers in support of Chief Spence's hunger strike:

> We honor you, Chief Spence, driven to this measure, and with humility and gratitude thank you for your courageous defense of the knowledge you have kept alive,

for trying to protect places that future generations will enjoy, and though it is maybe not your intent, to know that your actions are now speaking for all of us, for everyone who wants and deserves a sustainable way of life in harmony and respect with the earth. We add our name to those who will not stand for taking away sovereignty and the inherent right to land and resources from First Nations peoples in this abusive and indefensible relationship.[67]

In the United States, too, the environmental movement has picked up steam, angered by the lack of movement on climate change and the Obama administration's backtracking. On February 11, 2013, the environmental activist organization begun by Bill McKibben, 350.org, held a mass protest for climate change action in Washington that drew almost fifty thousand, along with dozens of smaller protests across the country. The organization also held sizable protests across the country in September to demand a halt to TransCanada corporation's Keystone XL pipeline, which will be used to transport oil from the tar sands of Alberta, Canada, and crude oil from the northern United States through six states to refineries in Texas. The pipeline threatens farmers' land and wildlife in the areas through which it runs, while creating relatively few jobs, and it facilitates more extraction of Alberta tar-sands oil, "one of the most polluting and carbon-intensive fuels in the world."[68]

The scale of the ecological crisis, along with the growing resistance, is prompting a more activist, and therefore more radical, turn among more mainstream environmentalists and scientists. McKibben was an environmentalist writer for years before he realized that there had to be mass action to bring about substantial change, and he is increasingly frustrated by Obama's support for fracking and the Keystone pipeline. James Hansen, a longtime climate scientist, left his job at NASA to give himself more time to be involved in protests. Michael Mann, director of the Earth System Science Center at Pennsylvania State University, wrote in the January 2014 *New York Times*, "In my view, it is no longer acceptable for scientists to remain on the sidelines."[69] Hansen and Mann are, to quote Canadian writer Naomi Klein, "part of a small but increasingly influential group of scientists whose research into the destabilization of natural systems—particularly the climate system—is leading them to similarly transformative, even revolutionary, conclusions."[70]

James Gustave Speth, a founder of the National Research Defense Council, who served as President Jimmy Carter's environmental adviser, as an adviser to the Clinton administration's first transition team, and as an administrator of the UN Development Program in the 1990s, wrote a book in 2008 explaining his radical shift in outlook on the environment. "Most of us with environmental concerns," he writes in the preface, "have worked within the system, but the system has not delivered. The mainstream environmental community as a whole has been the 'ultimate insider.' But it is time for the environmental community—indeed, everyone—to step outside the system and develop a deeper critique of what's going on."[71] According to Speth, we need more "impractical," "radical" answers. "And if some of these answers seem radical or far-fetched today, then I say wait until tomorrow. Soon it will be abundantly clear that it is business as usual that is utopian, whereas creating something very new and different is a practical necessity."[72] The problem is capitalism:

> These features of capitalism, as they are constituted today, work together to produce an economic and political reality that is highly destructive of the environment. An unquestioning society-wide commitment to economic growth at almost any cost; enormous investment in technologies designed with little regard for the environment; powerful corporate interests whose overriding objective is to grow by generating profit, including profit from avoiding the environmental costs they create; markets that systematically fail to recognize environmental costs unless corrected by government; government that is subservient to corporate interests and the growth imperative; rampant consumerism spurred by a worshipping of novelty and by sophisticated advertising; economic activity so large in scale that its impacts alter the fundamental biophysical operations of the planet—all combine to deliver an ever-growing world economy that is undermining the planet's ability to sustain life.[73]

As if frightened by his radical turn, Speth shrinks back from its logic. He opposes not capitalism, but capitalism "as it is constituted today."[74] He proposes "non-socialist" solutions—a differently constituted capitalism that dispenses with its "growth" fetish, and adopts more regulated markets, with consumers that engage in more "mindful consumption." But as we have seen, the "growth fetish" is built into the very nature of capitalism.[75]

Creating a Sustainable World

If this chapter has convinced you of anything, it should be that you should be frightened by our ecological crisis, not the social revolution that will be necessary to solve it. For if Speth is right, what is required is nothing short of a revolutionary reconstitution of society—"a complete revolution in our hitherto existing mode of production, and simultaneously a revolution in our whole contemporary social order," as Engels concluded.[76] The point is not to leave nature alone like some pretty postcard, but to transform human social relations and thereby our relationship to nature. In the words of Chris Williams, "Every single facet of industrial life—energy production most urgently, but also transportation, housing, trade, agriculture, manufacture of commodities, and waste production and treatment—all require gigantic systemic change and complete structural reorganization. It will be nothing short of totally remodeling the world on a social, political, technological, cultural, and infrastructural level."[77]

We can adopt new technologies that capture solar, wind, wave, and geothermal energy. We can replace the car with efficient forms of public rail transportation. The large industrial farming model based on monoculture, mechanization, chemical fertilizers, pesticides, and genetic alteration of seeds has increased yields, but at a high environmental cost, from pollution to food quality. But alternatives can be adopted that are both environmentally sustainable and capable of feeding billions of people. Several studies show that farms using methods like intercropping (growing more than one crop simultaneously), and the use of animal fertilizer, employing combinations of modern and traditional techniques, can produce a total output greater than that of large mechanized monoculture farms while improving soil quality. We can reorganize and integrate food production so that more of it is locally grown and consumed, and animal waste, rather than polluting the environment, serves as fertilizer.[78]

In the production process, by building things to last, we can minimize and reduce waste, and the necessity of continually exploiting new resources and energy to make more. We can eliminate the production of useless, wasteful products, including nuclear weapons, tanks, and hair spray. And with more sensible planning, we can devise more creative ways to recycle materials. We can replant forests, and regenerate land ruined by industrial and military activity.

The same scientific knowledge that is used to produce things in ways that recklessly pollute the earth could, under different circumstances, be used to create a more harmonious balance between human beings and our environment. It is simply not profitable for capitalism to do so. It is this reality that has caused so many to recognize that it is in the interests of capitalists to "privatize the gains" and "socialize" the losses, whereas it is in our interests to socialize everything.

But the answer isn't simply using different technology. Capitalism's drive to accumulate will continue long after oil production becomes too cost prohibitive, so long as capitalism is still around. As drastic changes in our environment unfold, capitalists will look for alternative forms of energy and adapt new forms of industrial and agricultural production. They will be driven to do so out of their own profit interests rather than those of ordinary people. But they will do so only in the face of disasters so great that governments are forced to intervene to ensure the conditions of capital accumulation in general are possible, and only insofar as they do not interfere with profit-making. They will do so, moreover, because of the division of the world into competing states, in a wasteful, uncoordinated way. In the meantime, corporations will continue to squeeze every last drop of profit from fossil fuels, and will continue to consider nature as a source of free raw materials and as a sink for their waste products. Capitalists and their states are incapable of doing anything in a planned, sensible, and timely enough manner to avert the many coming disasters that their actions have caused. Technological fixes won't matter if the same economic logic that has driven us to the abyss is not overturned.

These needs, which can only be satisfied in a fully cooperative, socialist world, do not all imply "growth" as it is understood and carried through under capitalism.

Certainly, in a socialist society there may be an increase in the production of some things—like healthy foods and shelter—in order to ensure that those deprived of real necessities of life under capitalism get them, but rational scientific planning will also entail the curtailment of growth in other areas—and its restructuring in all areas. Efficient use of materials and energy to maximize quality of life rather than maximize profit—measured not in how many "things" we have, but in the things described above—is possible only in a rationally planned society.

Meeting human needs and enhancing the quality of lives of all human beings on the planet does not require rampant growth, any more than solving our climate crisis necessitates some kind of equality of suffering or belt-tightening. Human needs are not reducible to immediate physical needs such as quality and sufficient food and shelter, clean air and water—though these needs must be met first before other problems can be tackled.

There are also our sexual needs. Alienated and stunted sexuality prevents the full enjoyment by human beings of each other. There are also mental and spiritual needs that are closely associated, but not reducible, to our physical needs. Lack of open and green space, and attractive art and architecture designed to facilitate our comfort, harm our sense of well-being. The lack of control over our work and its products— feeling chained to a "job"—converts work from a real *need* that satisfies us to merely a means to an end: a way to get money to buy our necessities. Lack of control over virtually every aspect of our life outside of work also engenders a sense of helplessness and alienation. Leisure time, direct participation in the important decisions of community and society, comprehensive education, the ability to move from one type of work to another, and from one creative endeavor (or whim) to another—these are human needs by any rational measure, and are only luxuries in a capitalist world.

Chapter Thirteen

Imagine . . . the Socialist Future

"We know what you're against. What are you *for*?" is a question often asked of socialists. Socialism can be summed up simply. These words by Eugene Debs are clear and elegant:

The earth for all the people! That is the demand.

The machinery of production and distribution for all the people! That is the demand.

The collective ownership and control of industry and its democratic management in the interests of all the people! That is the demand.

The elimination of rent, interest and profit and the production of wealth to satisfy the wants of all the people! That is the demand.

The end of . . . class rule, of master and slave, of ignorance and vice, of poverty and shame, of cruelty and crime. . . . That is the demand.[1]

Socialism cannot come from "readymade utopias" or blueprints, but must be created by workers themselves. That doesn't mean, however, that we have no idea what a future socialist society would be like or how it might develop.

The initial basis for socialism is the working-class solidarity that is forged in struggle prior to workers coming to power. In these struggles, backward ideas begin to break down. The mass struggles that are necessary to bring down the old order are also necessary to begin the process of creating a different human being. But this is only the starting point. Socialism will be created by people emerging from a system that stunted and suppressed their human potential. Only over a long transition period will a new generation of people be raised who are free from these old constraints and distortions.

"What we have to deal with here," wrote Marx, "is a communist society, not as it has *developed* on its own foundations, but, on the contrary, just as it *emerges* from capitalist society; which is thus in every respect, economically, morally, and intellectually, still stamped with the birthmarks of the old society from whose womb it emerges."[2]

Hence we cannot immediately leap straight into a completely communist society. There must be a transition period in which the old is dissolved, broken apart, and reshaped, and new social relations and habits of intercourse gradually emerge. "Between capitalist and communist society there lies the period of the revolutionary transformation of the one into the other," wrote Marx. "Corresponding to this is also a political transition period in which the state can be nothing but *the revolutionary dictatorship of the proletariat*."[3] So the second premise of socialism is that workers have risen up, formed new institutions of democratic rule, have seized power, and are therefore in a position from which they can start to reshape society.

The aim of socialism is to do away with all class distinctions and create a society whereby the state—an instrument of class domination—gradually fades away. As Engels wrote, "The proletariat seizes the public power, and by means of this transforms the socialized means of production, slipping from the hands of the bourgeoisie, into public property."[4]

Having gained power, the working class then uses that power, first to ensure that the old order cannot gain a foothold again. Though this new workers' state represents the interests of the majority, it must still use coercion, where necessary, to suppress those who would use violence to attempt to restore the old exploitive relations in society. But this task fades as does the resistance of the old exploiters, giving way to the difficult but more rewarding task of social metamorphosis. The new workers' state must begin implementing a series of reforms that, step by step, abolish profit and the market and replace it with conscious, democratic planning. "The proletariat will use its political supremacy to wrest, by degree, all capital from the bourgeoisie," Marx and Engels wrote in the *Manifesto*,

> to centralize all instruments of production in the hands of the state, i.e., of the proletariat organized as the ruling class; and to increase the total productive forces as rapidly as possible.
>
> Of course, in the beginning, this cannot be effected except by means of despotic inroads on the rights of property, and on the conditions of bourgeois production; by means of measures, therefore, which appear economically insufficient and untenable, but which, in the course of the movement, outstrip themselves, necessitate further inroads upon the old social order, and are unavoidable as a means of entirely revolutionizing the mode of production.[5]

Some of these measures might include: introducing a progressive income tax against the rich; establishing free education at all levels; abolishing advertising and all other wasteful and costly diversions, with the use of these funds going toward health, education, and artistic needs; instituting free abortion on demand and free child care provisions; confiscating all empty houses and mansions of capitalist developers and the rich in order to house the poor and homeless; establishing free kitchens to feed the hungry; immediately reducing the workday and providing jobs for the unemployed; creating a community police force on a rotating, elected basis.

The market and money cannot be done away with at one stroke. But the workers' state can nationalize the banks and place them under workers' control, and redirect funds into much-needed state projects, like building a better public transportation system. Money can be transformed from a means of profit-making into a means of accounting for what is produced and how it is distributed. If at first workers' control at the workplace means exercising control over management, over time it would develop into a system of workers' management. The associated producers, organized into a democratic system of councils, would begin to reorganize production and distribution according to a rational plan that meets human need.

Although inequality cannot be abolished all at once, a number of measures could be implemented to uproot it. Special organizations could be created to wipe out discrimination in the education system, and various affirmative action programs could be stepped up on a qualitatively more intensive level to provide opportunities for education and equal participation in society for all, regardless of race, nationality, sex, or language. Education could be provided in all languages, and could be designed to allow individuals to switch jobs, moving from intellectual to manual work with ease. At first, workers may need to exercise joint control over technicians, engineers, and planners, some (but not all) who may still hanker for the privileges they received under capitalism. But the extensive reorganization of education and the production process would give everyone the opportunity to pursue a variety of jobs, gradually weakening the barrier between mental and manual labor, and providing an environment in which the full potential of every individual is given the means to develop.

Committees of workers and technicians would begin to reengineer production so that everything was produced to last, and with the best materials. Society would seek out ways to make production processes and energy use as ecologically sustainable as possible. Productivity would advance to the point that the workday could be reduced to three or four hours. In a socialist society, improvements in labor productivity would be a means to shorten the workday to a minimum in order to free people up as much as possible to devote their energies to other pursuits, including participating in the running of society. Moreover, since workers would own and control the labor process as well as its results, work would no longer have the sense of emptiness it possesses today. Instead of workers dreaming of Fridays and working only in order to receive a paycheck, work would be a source of fulfillment. The mad intensity of work today, whose pace is a physical and mental health issue for millions, would be humanized in a society where workers control the nature and pace of work collectively.

When the resistance of the old ruling classes is gone, so too is the need for the state. With the abolition of class distinctions comes what Engels called "the withering away of the state." Since the state is an instrument for the enforcement of class oppression, the dissolution of class divisions renders the state obsolete. The coercive apparatus of state repression disappears, leaving only purely administrative tasks such as the postal service, transportation, and maintaining the power grid.

What replaces the state is the free association of people—communism. Society is administered according to a plan, but there is no need for organized coercion, because everyone gives what she can and takes what she needs. Society might freely choose or pick volunteers to handle small-scale threats of violence, for example from emotionally distressed individuals, or to defuse drunken brawls. But because society is not divided into classes, this coercion would be incidental rather than systematic, and could be handled without the need for "special bodies" of armed people.

Only in such a consciously and democratically planned and administered society can the potentialities slumbering in the millions of people oppressed and stunted by capitalism have a chance to flourish. In this higher phase of communist society, wrote Marx,

> after the enslaving subordination of the individual to the division of labor, and therewith also the antithesis between mental and physical labor, has vanished; after labor has become not only a means of life but life's prime want; after the productive forces have also increased with the all-around development of the individual, and all the springs of co-operative wealth flow more abundantly—only then can the narrow horizon of bourgeois right be crossed in its entirety and society inscribe on its banners: From each according to his ability, to each according to his needs![6]

The Necessity of Socialism

Two conditions, the world's material abundance and class solidarity, make socialism possible; a third condition, the threat of social and environmental ruin, makes it imperative.

The resources are there in abundance. Workers make the rich fabulously rich while the majority live in want, and the balance is becoming more and more skewed. In 1999, the assets of the two hundred richest people in the world (more than $1 trillion) were more than the combined income of 41 percent of the world's population. Today, the richest eighty-five people on the planet have as much wealth as the poorest *half* of humanity.[7] A fraction of the wealth of these individuals could eliminate many of the problems facing the poor. The *1994 UN Human Development Report* estimated that just 12 percent of military spending in the developing countries (not including the far larger military budgets of the United States and other more developed countries) could provide health care for the one billion people who lack access to it; eliminate severe malnutrition in the 192 million children that suffer from it; and provide safe drinking water for all.[8]

We stand on either a threshold or a precipice. Either we move forward to socialism or the world faces unimaginable barbarism that could come in many forms: nuclear holocaust, environmental disasters, or the return of 1930s-style depression. Capitalism condemns itself as a system, in the prophetic words of Marx, because in the midst of the riches labor creates, the capitalist class cannot even assure the survival of humanity, let alone the survival of the poor.

> And here it becomes evident, that the bourgeoisie is unfit any longer to be the ruling class in society, and to impose its conditions of existence upon society. . . . It is unfit to rule because it is incompetent to assure an existence to its slave within his slavery, because it cannot help letting him sink into such a state, that it has to feed him, instead of being fed by him. Society can no longer live under this bourgeoisie, in other words, its existence is no longer compatible with society.[9]

The alternative is socialism. Shorn of the baggage that socialism never asked to carry, it is an attractive idea. It is not a dream concocted in the head of a utopian thinker: It was born in the collective action of workers themselves, as the experience of Eugene Debs showed. He first toyed with the idea of going into Democratic Party politics before he became a socialist. But his experience as a trade union organizer changed him. As leader of the newly formed American Railway Union, Debs led a strike of workers at the Pullman Sleeping Car Company in 1894. The strike spread throughout the nation, becoming a national boycott of Pullman cars involving 150,000 workers. The government stepped in on behalf of the employers and declared the strike illegal because it was obstructing delivery of the US mail (the government was deliberately attaching mail trains to Pullman cars so they would have this excuse). The government sent in federal troops, and the strike was broken—twenty-five strikers were killed, and Debs was imprisoned for six months. Debs learned that the government—its army, its courts—serves the employers. He learned that the employers will go to any lengths to try and stop workers from organizing and fighting for what is right. "In the gleam of every bayonet and the flash of every rifle the class struggle was revealed," he later explained. "This was my first practical lesson in socialism, though wholly unaware that it was called by that name."[10]

In every struggle, there are many people who go through the kinds of experiences that Debs went through. Whether they fall back into obscurity, returning to the dull routines of daily life, or become active socialists dedicated to changing the world for the better depends on the existence of groups of socialists in every workplace and school that can relate to their experiences and transform their unconscious strivings for socialism into a conscious commitment to its achievement.

The Hydra of Social Revolution

When we look at how beaten down it seems sometimes that ordinary people are, we make the mistake of believing that this is a permanent state of affairs, when in reality it is only one aspect of a complex and contradictory reality. When people are finally driven to do something—to fight back—we are again reminded of the other aspect of the truth, that ordinary people are capable of extraordinary acts of solidarity, heroism, creativity, and energy. When George Orwell went to Barcelona, Spain, in 1936, during the Spanish Civil War, he saw how revolution brought this sense of creative solidarity out in the workers there who had recently seized control of the city:

> It was the first time that I had ever been in a town where the working class was in the saddle. Practically every building of any size had been seized by the workers and was draped with red flags or with the red and black flag of the Anarchists; every wall was scrawled with the hammer and sickle and with the initials of the revolutionary parties. . . . Every shop and cafe had an inscription saying that it had been collectivized; even the bootblacks had been collectivized and their boxes painted red and black. Waiters and shop-walkers looked you in the face and treated you as an equal. Servile and even ceremonial forms of speech had temporarily disappeared. . . . Tipping had been forbidden by law since the time of Primo de Rivera; almost my first experience was receiving a lecture from a hotel manager for trying to tip a lift-boy. There were no private motorcars, they had all been commandeered, and the trams and taxis and much of the other transport were painted red and black. The revolutionary posters were everywhere, flaming from the walls in clean reds and blues that made the few remaining advertisements look like daubs of mud. Down the Ramblas, the wide central artery of the town where crowds of people streamed constantly to and fro, the loud-speakers were bellowing revolutionary songs all day and far into the night. And it was the aspect of the crowds that was the queerest thing of all. In outward appearance it was a town in which the wealthy classes had practically ceased to exist. . . . Practically everyone wore rough working-class clothes, or blue overalls or some variant of militia uniform. All this was queer and moving. There was much in this that I did not understand, in some ways I did not even like it, but I recognized it immediately as a state of affairs worth fighting for.[11]

Given half a chance, genuine cooperativeness among workers flourishes, even in dire situations. Larry Bradshaw and Lorrie Beth Slonsky, two medical workers trapped in New Orleans during Hurricane Katrina, expected the media to project heroic images of troops and police, but the official relief effort they experienced was atrociously inadequate:

> What you will not see, but what we witnessed, were the real heroes and sheroes of the hurricane relief effort: the working class of New Orleans.
>   The maintenance workers who used a forklift to carry the sick and disabled. The engineers who rigged, nurtured and kept the generators running. The electricians

who improvised thick extension cords stretching over blocks to share the little electricity we had in order to free cars stuck on rooftop parking lots. Nurses who took
over for mechanical ventilators and spent many hours on end manually forcing air
into the lungs of unconscious patients to keep them alive. Doormen who rescued
folks stuck in elevators. Refinery workers who broke into boat yards, "stealing" boats
to rescue their neighbors clinging to their roofs in floodwaters. Mechanics who helped
hot-wire any car that could be found to ferry people out of the city. And the food
service workers who scoured the commercial kitchens, improvising communal meals
for hundreds of those stranded.[12]

The real looters were not the people helping themselves to food and goods to survive
a disaster, but the government and their corporate friends who have set the whole
system up as a massive looting operation in which the haves take from the have-nots.

Larry and Lorrie Beth helped organize a group of several hundred stranded survivors. Police broke up their first camp at gunpoint. When the group tried to cross
a bridge into the neighboring town of Gretna, a line of cops firing shotguns over
their heads turned them back. But the group held together and in doing so taught
us something about what ordinary people are capable of:

> Our little encampment began to blossom. Someone stole a water delivery truck
> and brought it up to us. Let's hear it for looting! A mile or so down the freeway, an
> Army truck lost a couple of pallets of C-rations on a tight turn. We ferried the food
> back to our camp in shopping carts.
>
> Now—secure with these two necessities, food and water—cooperation, com-
> munity and creativity flowered. We organized a cleanup and hung garbage bags
> from the rebar poles. We made beds from wood pallets and cardboard. We desig-
> nated a storm drain as the bathroom, and the kids built an elaborate enclosure for
> privacy out of plastic, broken umbrellas and other scraps. We even organized a food-
> recycling system where individuals could swap out parts of C-rations (applesauce
> for babies and candies for kids!).
>
> This was something we saw repeatedly in the aftermath of Katrina. When in-
> dividuals had to fight to find food or water, it meant looking out for yourself. You
> had to do whatever it took to find water for your kids or food for your parents. But
> when these basic needs were met, people began to look out for each other, working
> together and constructing a community.[13]

Reading their account of the heroism of ordinary workers and poor people in New
Orleans, I was reminded of the statement the Spanish revolutionary anarchist Bue-
naventura Durruti made to Canadian journalist Pierre van Paasen in 1936, during
the Spanish Civil War. Durruti fought with the Spanish workers against the danger
of Franco's fascist counterrevolution. "You will be sitting on a pile of ruins if you are
victorious," van Paasen told Durruti. He replied:

> We have always lived in slums and holes in the wall. We will know how to accom-

modate ourselves for a time. For you must not forget that we can also build. It is we who built these palaces and cities, here in Spain and America and everywhere. We, the workers. We can build others to take their place. And better ones. We are not in the least afraid of ruins. We are going to inherit the earth. There is not the slightest doubt about that. The bourgeoisie might blast and ruin its own world before it leaves the stage of history. We carry a new world, here, in our hearts. That world is growing in this minute.[14]

But What About . . . ? Answers to Common Arguments Against Socialism

People Are Naturally Competitive

A common argument against the possibility of socialism is that human beings are naturally competitive. But cooperation and altruistic behavior are among the most distinctive features of human life. Without them society could not function. A number of studies bear out the idea that though humans are capable of competitive and selfish behavior, they can be cooperative and altruistic starting from a very early age.[1]

The lavish praise heaped upon rich benefactors and the way their names grace public buildings (well, until corporations started taking over naming rights) gives the impression that the chief charity givers are rich people. Not so. Studies show that the poorest 20 percent of Americans give 2.3 percent of their income to charity, while the richest 20 percent give only 1.3 percent. Of course, 1.3 percent of millions of dollars is a lot easier to publicly flaunt than 2.3 percent of $25,000. The rich do it for show, to demonstrate their high character, when in reality, explains one psychologist, they are "way more likely to prioritize their own self-interests above the interests of other people."[2] Engels sharply expressed his disdain for capitalists' charity, railing: "As though you rendered the proletarians a service in first sucking out their very life-blood and then practicing your self-complacent, Pharisaic philanthropy upon them, placing yourselves before the world as mighty benefactors of humanity when you give back to the plundered victims the hundredth part of what belongs to them!"[3]

Even as it encourages individualist thinking and competition, capitalism is in a certain sense a breeding ground of cooperation. Mass production and distribution would be impossible without it. In every workplace, hundreds and sometimes thousands of people must labor cooperatively to turn out a product. This socialized, cooperative aspect of capitalism is a partial negation of market competition, and it provides the basis for workers' own sense of themselves as a class whose interests compel them to take collective action.

The biggest problem with the "everyone is competitive" argument is that in a society based upon equitable sharing, people won't need to fight over resources. "In the socialist society, when there is plenty and abundance for all," wrote American Trotskyist James Cannon, "what will be the point in keeping account of each one's share, any more than in the distribution of food at a well-supplied family table? You don't keep books as to who eats how many pancakes for breakfast or how many pieces of bread for dinner. Nobody grabs when the table is laden. If you have a guest, you don't seize the first piece of meat for yourself, you pass the plate and ask him to help himself first."[4]

The point is that, under socialism, society's surplus wealth would be collectively used to enhance the welfare of all rather than that of a small group. Why would I steal what was freely available? Such a society may seem too utopian. But as Cannon said of capitalist society, "What's absurd is to think that this madhouse is permanent and for all time."[5]

"Hang on," say the naysayers, "without competition, creativity and invention would stagnate. There would be no incentive to work hard, to achieve." The implication of this, one of the oldest arguments against socialism, is that capitalist market competition is the best and only guarantee of hard work and innovation.

Marx and Engels dealt with the question in *The Communist Manifesto*. "It has been objected," they write, "that upon the abolition of private property all work will cease, and universal laziness will overtake us." Their answer is as simple as it is devastating: "According to this, bourgeois society ought long ago to have gone to the dogs through sheer idleness; for those of its members who work, acquire nothing, and those who acquire anything do not work."[6]

The majority of people do not work for their own benefit, but for the benefit of others. Their only incentive is that without work they cannot survive. Yet there are plenty of examples of people putting in hours of hard work for no financial gain. Anyone involved in high school or community theater can attest to the satisfaction that comes from pouring hours after school or work into making a theatrical production come to life. How many people devote themselves to pursuits like music and art with no expectation of ever being able to give up their "day job"? I myself met many ordinary people in Mississippi and Louisiana in the wake of Hurricane Katrina who came from all over the country to bring supplies and distribute food to the storm's victims. I met a student from a Nashville divinity school who spent hours in the polluted floodwaters of New Orleans helping stranded Katrina victims onto dry land from rescue boats. Those boats had been donated or commandeered by concerned citizens.

Nor can the argument be leveled that socialism takes incentive away because it doesn't allow for personal possessions. It is only property used to exploit others that socialism prohibits. Socialism will allow for people to have more, not less, of the things that enhance their lives, like leisure time, good quality food and shelter, access to art and culture, and so on. The incentive to invent better technology will remain, and be enhanced without the profit motive, because such inventions will improve everyone's quality of life.

Workers Can't Run Society

A further argument against socialism is that the majority, the working class, is incapable of ruling collectively. We need educated, intelligent experts to run such a complex system. The legendary stupidity of George W. Bush, whose rich parents and crony friends bought him passing grades and much more, is a strong argument against this view. "I think we are welcomed," said Bush, when asked about Vice President Dick Cheney's predictions that Iraqis would greet US troops with open arms. "But it was not a peaceful welcome."[7] When Brazilian president Luiz Inácio Lula da Silva showed him a map of Brazil, Bush exclaimed, "Wow! Brazil is big."[8]

There are many other examples that could be cited of presidents, industrialists, and bureaucrats with limited, or nonexistent, abilities. "Howard Hughes was another mediocrity," wrote Paul Foot.

> He started life as a playboy and ended it as a lunatic. He had no ability at all. Yet through a mixture of luck and the ability to read a balance sheet, Hughes became the boss of a gigantic financial and industrial empire. He was able, almost alone, to nominate the President of the United States, Richard Nixon, who also had no ability, knowledge or skill of any kind. Howard Hughes designed an aeroplane which crashed and directed a film which was a monumental failure. He couldn't do anything which mattered. Yet *he* made the decisions. The list is endless. Successful capitalists, almost to a man, are not people with any natural ability. Yet they decide what the experts do.[9]

Most people at the very top of society, the multimillionaires and billionaires, play no direct function in society's running—they merely collect the rewards of ownership. The ruling class today has become entirely parasitic, siphoning wealth but serving no useful social function. As early as 1881, Frederick Engels wrote that the capitalists had ceased even their former supervisory role over the production process. "The social function of the capitalist here has been transferred to servants paid by wages; but he continues to pocket, in his dividends, the pay for those functions though he has ceased to perform them." The capitalist's function is merely to "speculate with his shares on the Stock Exchange." Engels concludes, "Thus we find that, not only can we manage very well without the interference of the capitalist class in the great industries of the country, but that their interference is becoming more and more a nuisance. Again we say to them, 'Stand back! Give the working class the chance of a turn.'"[10]

Bankers and investors don't make steel. It hardly takes intellectual brilliance for someone who inherits a million dollars to double or triple it. Society could do away with the ruling class and suffer no more than when an appendix is removed from a human body. But do workers possess the capacity to rule? Won't they still depend on experts? Often it is workers' own hard-won, firsthand knowledge that engineers and managers use to figure out how to improve production, that is, to squeeze as much out of workers as possible. Not to deny the genius of a Newton or an Einstein, but "if science is understood in the fundamental sense of *knowledge of nature*," writes Clifford Connor in his *People's History of Science*, "it should not be surprising to find that it originated with the people closest to nature: hunter-gatherers, peasant farmers, sailors, miners, blacksmiths, folk healers, and others forced by the conditions of their lives to wrest the means of their survival from an encounter with nature on a daily basis."[11]

There are many examples of workers demonstrating admirably their ability to run their workplaces under their direct control and supervision. From the Paris Commune to the Russia Revolution, from the Spanish Civil War to the Argentinazo of 2001, workers in struggle have, for various reasons and under various guises, seized control of their workplaces and have attempted to run them, and in some cases, link them together with workers in other concerns. During the rebellion in Argentina in 2001, there were dozens of factory takeovers, the most famous being that of workers at Zanon ceramics (renamed FaSinPat—Fábrica Sin Patronas [factory without bosses]), a factory in Nequén, and the Brukman textile factory in Buenos Aires. Workers at these and other "recovered" factories proved that they could take over and run operations successfully through democratic assemblies. "Without workers," one of the workers at Zanon explained in 2002, "a factory does not function. But without bosses, yes, it functions—and very well indeed! With all the other comrades we are going to demonstrate that the nation functions with the hands of working people and not with the thieving hands of the politicians."[12]

It would be wrong to think, however, that workers could become the masters of society simply by taking over workplaces, one at a time. As Marina Kabat explains, the worker-controlled factories in Argentina were "subdued by the dynamics of capitalism," which continued to exist outside the factory walls and imposed conditions on each enterprise over which the workers within them had no control. Debt obligations, outdated equipment, the need to secure loans, find markets, purchase inputs, and to indemnify the former owners, forced these enterprises to behave like typical capitalist firms or go under. Many couldn't survive. "Others managed to persist," writes Kabat, "but at the price of self-exploitation of the workers."[13]

As Rosa Luxemburg noted, a worker-owned enterprise or cooperative must, if it is to survive, impose on itself the same exploitative conditions that exist in capitalist-owned enterprises. Workers in such an enterprise are, she wrote, "faced with the contradictory necessity of governing themselves with the utmost absolutism. They are obliged to take toward themselves the role of capitalist entrepreneur—a contradiction that accounts for the usual failure of production cooperatives, which either become pure capitalist enterprises or, if the workers' interests continue to predominate, end by dissolving."[14]

The failure or incorporation of worker-owned enterprises is not proof that workers can't run society, but that their attempts to create islands of control and self-management will be thwarted unless they are able to unite and centralize their efforts, taking command of all aspects of production and distribution. For this, workers must seize political power, without which they cannot be in a position to reorganize the economy as a whole.

Of course creating a new society does not mean making immediate administrators and planners out of waiters and nurses. But given the opportunity, everyone is capable of learning the scientific, administrative, and mathematical skills necessary to play a direct role in running society, just as in pre-class society knowledge of terrain, plants, and animals, or of tool-making, was shared by the group, and not treated as the monopoly of a minority. As Lenin wrote a few weeks before the October Revolution:

> We are not utopians. We know that an unskilled laborer or a cook cannot immediately get on with the job of state administration. In this we agree with the Cadets, with Breshkovskaya, and with Tsereteli. We differ, however, from these citizens in that we demand an immediate break with the prejudiced view that only the rich, or officials chosen from rich families, are capable of *administering* the state, of performing the ordinary, everyday work of administration. We demand that *training* in the work of state administration be conducted by class-conscious workers and soldiers and that this training be begun at once, i.e., that a *beginning* be made at once in training all the working people, all the poor, for this work.[15]

Experts and scientists would still be needed for a time even under socialism, until the education system was improved so that the majority received education that today is only reserved for the privileged few. For a time, workers would have to exercise democratic control over the bookkeepers, managers, and engineers. But with society's vast resources diverted toward education, the distinctions between mental and manual work would break down, and the majority would be capable of doing many different kinds of jobs, from manual work to scientific work to administrative work. If workers, through their own directly elected representatives, were to seize control of production, no doubt mistakes would be made. But they would be the mistakes of the collective rather than the blind workings of the market—and could quickly be remedied by experience.

Take Chicago. Today, the priorities of the rich shape the city's policies. For example, at the very time that he was closing dozens of public schools, Mayor Rahm Emanuel announced in summer 2013 plans to use $33 million in tax money to help fund the building of a new basketball stadium at DePaul, a private university.[16] If the workers of Chicago ran the city, instead of corporate bigwigs and their corrupt political hirelings, they would immediately begin solving the city's most pressing problems. The homeless would be quickly housed in unused homes and empty apartments, excess hotel space, and the requisitioned second and third homes of the rich. Meanwhile, unemployed construction workers would be organized to begin building houses. The ill-gotten gains of the city's patricians and their hangers-on would be seized and used to feed the hungry, improve dilapidated schools and build new ones, provide better park services, update and extend transportation, and create real after-school programs for *all*. The run-down, destroyed ghettos of the West Side would become beautiful neighborhoods by redirecting the millions used to line the pockets of bureaucrats, corporations, and real-estate developers. Real jobs (and real job training) would be made available to the thousands of young unemployed African Americans, Latinos, and poor whites who have been left to languish in the streets or in prison, where their great human potential is wasted.

On a national level, billions earmarked for the utter waste of weapons of mass destruction would be diverted into projects that benefit the mass of the population. The solution to homelessness is simple—build homes for the homeless. But in our society nothing is done if it isn't profitable. In a society run by the collective producers, these problems can be solved because social need, rather than the market, will determine how decisions are made. In any case, better to do the right thing, even if at first inexpertly and badly, than to do the wrong thing well.

Capitalism Is More Efficient and Less Bureaucratic Than Socialism

This is premised on the idea, of course, that the Soviet Union was socialist, which it wasn't. While Russian state-capitalism had some of its own peculiar bureaucratic inefficiencies, capitalism in the West hardly evaded similar problems.

But before we can proceed with an answer, we have to interrogate the term *efficient*. In a very limited sense, capitalist enterprises are devoted to efficiency, that is, saving time by figuring out ways for more work to get done at less expense. From the standpoint of human need, however, capitalism is extremely inefficient. Capitalism creates and depends on unemployment, which is a waste of human labor. Nor is it efficient by any logical measure to produce things that wear out or break down more quickly than necessary, and yet this is as common under capitalism as boosting productivity. Corporations martial batteries of consultants and engineers to discover the most efficient way to produce television ads, SUVs, the umpteenth brand of soda, or cruise missiles—never stopping to consider whether, from the standpoint of human need, they are worth producing at all.

The irony of all the talk about how competition encourages efficiency is that monopoly capitalism has, to an important degree, suppressed competition and replaced it with domination and manipulation of markets by handfuls of corporate giants in each industry—the partial suppression of the competitive mechanisms that bourgeois economists spend so much time praising.

Perhaps the most egregious example today of capitalist waste and inefficiency is the financial sector. In the United States alone, the total bank bailout was estimated to be about $29 trillion.[17] That money could have been allocated for any number of useful purposes, like providing clean drinking water to the 1.75 billion people in the world who lack it. This could be accomplished at the bargain price of $10 billion per year for ten years—"about 1.2% of the world's total annual military expenditures," reports UNESCO.[18]

Capitalism certainly doesn't mean less bureaucracy. In *The Eighteenth Brumaire*, Marx wrote that the rise of capitalism did not lead to the diminution of the size of the bureaucratic and military machinery of the state, but to its "perfection." It has from that time on swallowed up a greater and greater portion of society's resources. The US military budget comes to mind.

Proponents of neoliberal ideology harp on about getting the government out of business, yet their ideas fail utterly to describe current reality. Amid all the talk about the declining role of the state, state expenditure as a percentage of GDP has dramatically increased over the last quarter century. A 1997 World Bank report showed that in OECD countries, which include the United States, state spending as a percentage of GDP grew from 10 percent in 1913, to 20 percent in 1960, to 50 percent in 1995. Since then, there has been a slight shrinkage, dropping in the United States, for example, from 37 percent in 1995 to 36.4 percent in 2009.[19]

In spite of the move away from public ownership and toward private ownership, governments around the world have continued to take taxpayers' money and essentially use it to subsidize and bail out private industry, and to enhance the instruments of management, surveillance, repression, and war. Neoliberalism does not really mean "small" government; it means a restructuring of public services, the closer integration of state and business interests, and the enhancement of state power—all of which requires more, not less, bureaucracy.

What about bureaucracy in private industries? "No private enterprise," wrote economist Ludwig von Mises, an advocate of free-market capitalism at a time when Keynesianism ruled the roost, in 1944, "will ever fall prey to bureaucratic methods of management if it is operated with the sole aim of making profit."[20] According to von Mises, only government interference in this process created bureaucracy.

The truth is very different. Corporate bureaucracy is not a product of "state interference" in the free market, but of the concentration and centralization of capital, the growth of the world market, and with it, the development of monopoly control of entire industries and markets by handfuls of giant transnational corporations. These companies compete on an international market, but must also engage in large-scale internal planning that involves armies of lawyers, managers, supervisors, lobbyists, and consultants.

Corporations rely on a large number of management and supervisory personnel beyond simply the task of coordination. Supervisory personnel aren't really necessary for the work to be done right—after all, workers know how to do their jobs better than anyone else—but in order to have eyes on the labor process and impose discipline on workers. The larger the workforce, the more bloated becomes management, and the more layered the hierarchy. The number of private nonfarm supervisory employees in the United States grew from 4.7 million in 1948 to 17 million in 1994, and the percentage of administrative and managerial employees in the country grew from 6.6 percent in 1960 to 13 percent in 1989. And though "corporate downsizing" became the watchword in the 1990s, the percentage of private nonfarm "executive, administrative, and managerial" personnel grew from 12.6 percent in 1989 to 13.2 percent in 1994.[21]

According to author David Gordon, "The larger the number of employees working under an individual executive, especially in direct staff positions, the greater his or her clout." These self-perpetuating management structures tend to create an ever-increasing number of hierarchical rungs on the corporate ladder in order to keep rewarding managers with advancement.

If anything, free-market neoliberalism, with its open nod toward the goodness of rampant unregulated greed, breeds corporate bureaucratism. The profit motive creates a culture of corruption and cronyism in which various players are constantly seeking ways to get their hands on a share of the wealth drawn from the sweat of the workers employed by the particular firm and from state funds. Wherever profits are overflowing, there are hangers-on, crony friends, and "consultants" feeding at the trough. The history of US business is full of stories of big businesses, and even entire industries, that, drunk with the success of a certain organizational and business model, develop bloated, complacent bureaucracies that are then jolted by new competition from unexpected quarters to revise and restructure.

A look at the health care system in the United States completely destroys the argument that private is less bureaucratic than public. The private, for-profit health care industry in the United States generates a massive bureaucracy whose sole purpose is to perform the paperwork involved in ensuring that revenues and profits flow to the "right" people.

A 2004 study by Harvard Medical School researchers and Public Citizen found that the health care bureaucracy cost the United States $399.4 billion, and that a national health insurance system could save at least $286 billion annually on paperwork alone. That would be enough money to provide all of the forty-three million uninsured in the United States, plus provide full prescription drug coverage for everyone in the nation.[22]

The study found that bureaucracy accounts for 31 percent of US health care spending, whereas in Canada, whose national health care system still hangs on, bureaucracy accounts for only 16.7 percent of health care spending and manages to provide more health services per dollar spent.

The health care business is probably the most distressing example of what happens when we "let the market decide" what is efficient and inefficient. Health care for profit means delivering the least amount of health care service possible and selling the service for as much as possible. HMOs deny people access to important medical procedures because they want to maximize their profits or, alternatively, prescribe billable procedures that are unnecessary. Insurance companies refuse coverage to those who need it the most—the chronically ill—because it isn't profitable. Richard Scott, president of the now notorious Columbia/HCA hospital chain, compares health care to fast food: "Do we have an obligation to provide health care for everybody? Where do we draw the line? Is any fast-food restaurant obligated to feed everybody who shows up?"[23]

A nationally funded and planned health care system in the United States would deliver more service for less cost. But then again, health care in the United States isn't about helping people, but about a tiny number of capitalists making a large amount of money. Obama's health care plan mandating that people buy private insurance, sadly, does not change this reality.

Socialists Believe That the Ends Justify the Means

In one of our many fruitless arguments, I remember my father attacking Marxism for believing that "the ends justify the means." By this, he meant that Marxists have no moral scruples and will stop at nothing to achieve their goals. Ironically, this is the same person who once told me, with a straight face, that the United States had to drop the atomic bomb on Hiroshima and Nagasaki "to save lives."

In fact, every ruling class in the world operates on the assumption that the ends justify the means. In every war, these rulers risk the lives of millions of ordinary soldiers in the pursuit of their goals. The US government stands poised to use the world's most terrible weapons of mass destruction if it deems their use necessary. Asked by a reporter in 1995 if US-imposed economic sanctions against Iraq that had killed half a million Iraqi children were "worth it," Madeleine Albright, then the US ambassador to the UN, responded that "the price, we think, is worth it."[24] The end justified the means.

"The ruling class," wrote Russian revolutionary Leon Trotsky in his book *Their Morals and Ours*, "forces its ends upon society and habituates it to considering all those means which contradict its ends as immoral. That is the chief function of official morality."[25] It is therefore "immoral" to kill in peacetime, but a sacred duty to kill in wartime. It is impermissible for strikers to use force to stop a scab crossing a picket line, but perfectly acceptable for a police officer to use force to break up that same picket line. The president can decry a US school shooting massacre on one day, and order a drone strike on a village in Yemen the next.

CIA and military leaders defend lying and deception as indispensable means to confuse and disorient other governments, while children are told that lying and cheating is immoral. The 1936 Flint sit-down strikers could not have won a victory over the auto bosses if they had not employed deception, creating a diversion that led law enforcement officials and company goons to the wrong plant, while workers occupied another plant.

The real question for socialists is this: What justifies the ends? In the US Civil War, for example, both sides engaged in similar acts of violence. But one side was fighting to defend slavery and the other to end it. In Russia, the soldiers who turned on their officers and joined the working-class struggle to overthrow tsarism were justified, whereas the officers who defended the tsar by shooting at workers were not. As Trotsky wrote: "Armies in combat are always more or less symmetrical; were there nothing in common in their methods, they could not inflict blows upon each other."[26]

If all lying and violence are considered out of bounds, then of course humanity must renounce revolution and accept things as they are. In practice, not even struggles committed to nonviolence can refrain from it in the face of the violence committed against them. During the civil rights movement, for example, nearly all the Black Student Nonviolent Coordinating Committee (SNCC) activists in the Deep South, facing the daily threat of deadly white violence, were armed.[27] The Deacons of Defense, an armed self-defense group, protected many nonviolent protests from the Klan and racist police.[28]

Nevertheless, we cannot for a minute forget that not only the aims but also the methods that ordinary people use in fighting for their freedom are fundamentally different from the methods of the ruling class. Workers' power depends on collective rather than individual action, democratic debate and action rather than mutual deceit. While it may be tactically necessary to lie to the bosses during a strike, mass movements must not lie to themselves.

Ends and means are dialectically interrelated. The violence of a revolution, though necessary to break the will of the dominant classes, does not *prefigure* the future society that it aims to establish—that is, one that is free of all coercion. Nevertheless, as the failure of the Russian Revolution shows, the means must be subordinated to the ends.

If a workers' state, in its desperate isolation, requires too much coercion to maintain its rule, then the means can overwhelm and smother the ends.

"A means can only be justified by its end," concluded Trotsky. "But the end in turn needs to be justified."[29] For Marxists,

> The end is justified if it leads to increasing the power of humanity over nature and to the abolition of the power of one person over another. Permissible and obligatory are those and only those means, we answer, which unite the revolutionary proletariat, fill their hearts with irreconcilable hostility to oppression . . . imbue them with consciousness of their own historic mission, raise their courage and spirit of self-sacrifice in the struggle. Precisely from this, it flows that not all means are permissible. When we say that the end justifies the means, then for us, the conclusion follows that the great revolutionary end spurns those base means and ways which set one part of the working class against other parts; or attempt to make the masses happy without their participation; or lower the faith of the masses in themselves and their organization, replacing it by worship for the "leaders."[30]

Marxism Is "Authoritarian"

This is a common criticism leveled at us by anarchists. On one level, anarchists and Marxists want the same thing—in the words of Italian anarchist Errico Malatesta, a society "without bosses and without gendarmes."[31] Both anarchists and socialists agree that some types of authority—the authority of the rich minority of exploiters over the exploited majority, the authority of the capitalist state—should be abolished. Both oppose the authority of the cop who brutalizes people of color and the poor, the judge who serves the wealthy, and the manager who tries to squeeze more work out of us.

It has been sufficiently elucidated in previous chapters that Marx and Engels did not equate socialism with state ownership. Nevertheless, it is true that they had different attitudes toward the question of authority and the need for a *workers'* state than did anarchists. Whereas anarchists oppose "authority" in general—indeed, seeing it as the chief evil, Marxists are only opposed to certain kinds of authority.

Frederick Engels went to the heart of the question when he wrote about the followers of one of the early founders of anarchism, Mikhail Bakunin, "As soon as something displeases the Bakuninists," wrote Engels, "they say: it's *authoritarian*, and thereby imagine that they have damned it forever." But some kind of authority, no matter what type of society we are discussing, is indispensable. As Engels argued, "No joint action of any sort is possible without imposing on some an extraneous will, i.e., an authority. Whether it is the will of a majority of voters, of a leading committee or of one man, it is still a will imposed on the dissentients; but without that single and directing will, no cooperation is possible."[32] Engels asked if Bakunin would get on a train if the switchmen and conductors could come and go as they pleased and weren't willing to abide by strict scheduling, safety, and operational rules.

The question of how to transform society comes down to one of power—the power of the majority of ordinary workers versus the power of big corporations and the institutions they rely on to rule. We therefore can't agree with the argument made by anarchists that power (and what is power if not authority?) corrupts those who use it. The problem is that, in our society, the majority of people are deprived of power—the power to make decisions that affect their lives, the power to determine their own destinies. They should have more power, not less.

Anarchists who sincerely believe in the creative potential of ordinary people to build a new society—a potential that can't be realized unless they use their collective power—can't reconcile this view with the idea that all forms of power corrupt.

In an unequal, class-divided society, authority can't simply be "abolished." If striking workers renounced the authority of the majority over the minority, then they would have to renounce the strike as a weapon. For what is a strike if not the imposition of the authority of the majority who vote to strike over the minority who vote not to strike? And if the workers are to win, they must organize picket lines that are large and militant in order to discourage scabs from exercising their "right" work during the strike.

We could find any number of statements by renowned anarchists, from Proudhon to Emma Goldman to Malatesta, to the effect that it is a principle of anarchism to oppose the imposition of the will of the majority over the minority. Logically, anarchists must also oppose democracy, which by definition is majority rule. In one essay, Goldman is positively disdainful of the masses, arguing, "Always, at every period, the few were the banner bearers of a great idea, of liberating effort. Not so the mass, the leaden weight of which does not let it move," an argument in flat contradictions to anarchism's claim to be against elitism.[33]

Revolutionary "authority"—the imposition of the will of the majority over the minority—is necessary as long as the forces of the old order continue to resist the new. Engels's arguments remain the strongest refutation of the anarchists' blanket condemnation of authority. First, Engels dispels the myth that he and Marx were "state" socialists:

> Why do the anti-authoritarians not confine themselves to crying out against political authority, the state? All Socialists are agreed that the political state, and with it political authority, will disappear as a result of the coming social revolution, that is, that public functions will lose their political character and will be transformed into the simple administrative functions of watching over the true interests of society.

Then he points out that to renounce authority *before* the social revolution means renouncing the social revolution:

But the anti-authoritarians demand that the political state be abolished at one stroke, even before the social conditions that gave birth to it have been destroyed. They demand that the first act of the social revolution shall be the abolition of authority. Have these gentlemen ever seen a revolution? A revolution is certainly the most authoritarian thing there is; it is the act whereby one part of the population imposes its will upon the other part by means of rifles, bayonets and cannon—authoritarian means, if such there be at all; and if the victorious party does not want to have fought in vain, it must maintain this rule by means of the terror which its arms inspire in the reactionaries.[34]

For anarchists, force, authority, and the hierarchical state are the *causes* of class inequality. Abolition of authority is their watchword. For Marxists, the state is a *byproduct* of class antagonism—and can only disappear when class antagonisms disappear. Anarchy—a society without the state—can only come when classes are abolished, not before. Marx and Engels expressed this most clearly: "What all socialists understand by anarchy is this: once the aim of the proletarian movement, the abolition of classes, has been attained, the power of the state, which serves to keep the great majority of producers under the yoke of a numerically small exploiting minority, disappears, and the functions of government are transformed into simple administrative functions."[35]

You Can Be Your Own Boss

A uniquely fluid class system that allows for significant upward mobility is "the promise that lies at the heart of the American dream," according to a *New York Times* study on class in the United States.[36] The ability of the poor and the working class to climb the social ladder has always been exaggerated. But in the early phases of industrial development it had a certain amount of validity. The abundance of cheap land in the West for a time offered workers (but not those who were enslaved) the opportunity to "retire" from wage labor and become farmers. Each new wave of immigrants would start at the bottom, but might dream of improving their lot by moving up and out of the working class. This provided a safety valve preventing the formation of what Engels called a "permanent proletariat."[37] Once westward expansion had completed its course by the end of the 1890s, however, the safety valve was closed.

But the "dream" never disappeared. Being your own boss—starting up a small business where there aren't any foremen or managers bossing you around—continues to be seen as a way out of the working class. The dream is a backhanded acknowledgement of the alienating, tedious, and unrewarding quality of wage labor. But the dream also has an ideological purpose—to promote the idea that individuals can make something of themselves, not through collective struggle, but by dint of individual hard work. Conversely, it reinforces the idea that those who are stuck in the working class or in poverty deserve it because they haven't tried hard enough to get out.

How realistic is it for most workers to become their own boss? There are lots of small businesses in the United States, but they are responsible for only a small part of total employment and total wealth. In the United States, there are 3,551 larger firms that employ twenty-five hundred or more workers, accounting for 37 percent of the total workforce and 43 percent of the total payroll. On the other hand, the 3.75 million businesses that employ nine or fewer workers account for only 11 percent of employment and a paltry 8.7 percent of total payroll.[38]

The problem with the dream of owning your own business is that it is a precarious existence that often ends in bankruptcy. Only half of newly created small businesses are still in business after four years. Indeed, every year about as many small businesses close as are created. In 2004, for example, in the midst of an economic expansion, 580,900 new small businesses opened, but 576,200 closed—34,317 of these ended in bankruptcy.[39]

For millions of people, the dream of ownership means pouring your life savings into a business venture that requires endless work and the constant threat of failure to show for it. The small number of those lucky enough to grow into real businesses end up surviving by exploiting other workers—profiting from the difference between labor's output and labor's pay. That is, by becoming their own boss, they also became someone else's boss.

According to the *New York Times* study, income mobility in the United States has been on the decline for the last three decades. In the past, notes one Michigan economist cited in the study, "People would say, 'Don't worry about inequality. The offspring of the poor have chances as good as the chances of the offspring of the rich.' Well, that's not true. It's not respectable in scholarly circles anymore to make that argument."[40]

Of course there is some income mobility. In fact, capitalism relies on it for its survival, both practically and ideologically. But that mobility has limits. According to one study, one out of three people whose families were in the top one percent of income distribution are making at least $100,000 in family income by age thirty, whereas only one out of twenty-five people who grew up in the bottom half of income distribution have reached that income level by age thirty.[41]

Income inequality, moreover, has grown substantially over the past decades. According to the Economic Policy Institute, "The top 10% of the income distribution has claimed almost two-thirds of the gains to overall incomes since 1979, with the top 1% alone claiming 38.7% of overall gains."[42] According to Sharon Smith, "This is . . . the first generation of young workers in U.S. history that faces a substantially lower standard of living than their parents."[43]

The ultimate argument against the dream of upward mobility for the majority is the fact that the economy is a social pyramid—lots of room at the bottom, very little room at the top. The vast majority of workers in the United States, just like workers everywhere else, can only advance through joint struggle with their class, not by trying to climb out of that class.

Radical Ideas Are Foreign to the United States

There is a long history in the United States of propaganda claiming to prove that radicalism and socialism are "foreign imports" into the United States that have never really taken hold. It is true that the United States never had the same size socialist movement compared to Europe. And it is also true that many immigrants came to the United States bringing their radical ideas with them. But really, if we are going to stick to this method, then horses, factories, the steel plow, books, and the English language are also foreign imports. What does that prove? The conditions that prompted workers and oppressed people to fight back in Europe and elsewhere have always been the same ones that have prompted workers to fight back in the United States.

The US working class has a long and rich tradition of struggle and of radicalism. But it has followed a boom and bust pattern: extended periods of surface calm interrupted by huge explosions. The eruption of pent-up anger appears on the surface to come from nowhere, but it has its roots in the preceding period of employer attacks on the working class and its organizations. The attacks, which often involve intense violence directed against strikers and their families, have usually been successful in weakening or destroying unions and crippling the left. The result has been periodic breaks in the organizational and political continuity of the movement. Each new wave of struggle has not necessarily had the benefit of learning from the experiences of previous waves. This herky-jerky history prompted Trotsky to observe, "The American workers are very combative—as we have seen during the strikes. They have had the most rebellious strikes in the world. What the American worker misses is a spirit of generalization, or analysis, of his class position in society as a whole."[44]

Yet having said this, it is important to point out that in every upturn of mass struggle, tens of thousands of workers have embraced socialist ideas and organization. The Socialist Party, for example, peaked at 150,000 members in 1915. Eugene Debs got almost a million votes in his 1912 presidential run. Tens of thousands of workers went through the school of the IWW, and at its height in 1938, the Communist Party (CP) boasted 80,000 members and twice as many close collaborators. In 1969, at the height of radical ferment, FBI director J. Edgar Hoover warned President Nixon that "a recent poll indicates that approximately 25% of the black population has great respect for the Black Panther Party, including 43% of blacks under twenty-one years of age."[45] The American ruling-class tradition is one in which it uses every means at its disposal to divide and weaken the working-class movement—and to try and crush it when it rises up. It is distinct from other ruling classes not in nature, but in degree. The racism it has employed, for example, has historically surpassed that of every other advanced industrial society, with the exception of apartheid-era South Africa. Moreover, the political system it presides over is based on the rule of nearly identical capitalist parties, in which one party masquerades as an ally of workers and the oppressed in order to absorb the movements. And the scale of violence it is willing to use to smash workers' resistance is the most extreme in the industrialized world. These are the real obstacles workers have faced. Yet the bosses would not place these obstacles in front of workers unless the possibility of class unity was a real threat.

The 1930s were a time when the working class had a real opportunity to fulfill its revolutionary potential.[46] The statistics show the scale of the upheaval. Strikes tripled to 1,856 between 1933 and 1934, and peaked in 1937 at 4,470. Union membership rose from 2.6 million in 1934 to 7.3 million in 1938. In 1930, only 50,000 Black workers were in unions. By 1940, half a million were unionized. In 1937, 193,000 workers engaged in 247 sit-down strikes in the aftermath of the Flint strike, and before the year's end half a million workers had engaged in the sit-down tactic. Out of this upheaval came the formation of the mass industrial unions and the Congress of Industrial Organizations.

Communist Party militants played a leading role in many struggles, attracting to their ranks many of the best working-class rebels. The party took on racism head-on—organizing Black sharecroppers in the South, and picketing stores, demanding the hiring of Black workers in New York City. It organized a campaign for justice for the "Scottsboro Boys" (nine young Black men framed for rape in Alabama) that united Blacks and whites in marches and meetings across the country. As a result, thousands of Blacks joined the party, increasing its African American membership in 1938 to about 9 percent of its total membership. It was able to demonstrate, in a society wracked by racism and lynching, not only that Black and white workers could unite in the struggle for common demands, but that white workers could be won to the fight against racism.[47]

But if the CP showed that US workers weren't at all averse to socialism, it also was the single greatest obstacle to building a left challenge to the Democratic Party. The problem was that by the 1930s the CP had ceased to be a genuine revolutionary party. At the height of the struggle in the 1930s, the CP was in its "Popular Front" phase—having been ordered along with other Western Communist Parties to make uncritical alliances with bourgeois parties as part of Stalin's agreement with the Allies against Hitler. In the United States, this meant instructing members to give their full backing to Roosevelt and the Democratic Party. The party that had denounced Roosevelt as "an inspirer of fascism" in 1935 was singing his praises just a year later. Though the Communist Party's members had played a leading role in the sit-down strikes, the party's leadership agreed to throw a wet towel on the struggle. A December 1937 article in the CP's paper, the *Daily Worker*, declared "unequivocally and emphatically that the Communists and the Communist Party had never in the past and do not now in any shape, manner or form advocate or support unauthorized and wildcat action and regard such strikes as gravely injurious . . . to the cause of cooperative action between labor and middle-class groups."[48]

Instead of building a party of workers committed to genuine socialism, the CP helped steer workers away from that alternative, and into the arms of the Democratic Party. When thousands of workers expressed support for a labor party alternative to the Democrats, the CP and the union bureaucracy created fake local labor parties whose purpose was to siphon workers' votes toward Roosevelt's reelection.

US Workers Have It Too Good to Fight

In the period after the Second World War, world capitalism entered an unprecedented boom. For a layer of workers, it seemed that 1930s-style poverty was a thing of the past. Workers could now expect that their children's lives would improve, and their children's after that. Radical ideas seemed unnecessary. Labor unions partnered up with the employers, trading economic benefits for their members in exchange for class peace. The Cold War anticommunist witch hunts, carried through by employers, the state, and the union bureaucracy, purged thousands of socialists and militants from the trade unions and other institutions, severing the connection between the radical traditions of the 1930s and later generations of workers. The tragedy is that the CP contributed to this process. To ingratiate itself with Roosevelt, it applauded repression against other radicals in the labor movement. When it was attacked and vilified by the state and in the unions, it failed to mount any defense. Party activists denied they were members, and some even participated in the redbaiting.

The postwar prosperity prompted a new battery of pundits to herald the end of socialism and the triumph of capitalism, giving rise to new arguments about how workers were too contented to want change. The claim was exaggerated, though it contained a grain of truth. But there were contradictions. The civil rights movement, and later the fight for Black power in the North, was a stark reminder that the "American Dream" never applied to African Americans. These social movements provided the impetus for the anti–Vietnam War movement, the women's movement, and the stirrings of a new labor movement.

The endless prosperity came to an end in the late 1960s, shattering the postwar honeymoon. As crisis began to hit the US economy, and as the social movements peaked, workers began to stir, bucking against both employers and a sclerotic labor bureaucracy that had become proud of its partnership with capital and looked on picket lines with unease. The number of wildcat strikes doubled from one thousand to two thousand through the 1960s. A strike wave in 1970 included a strike by forty thousand miners demanding disability benefits, and postal workers, though legally prohibited from striking, organized a successful two-week national walkout. In the Detroit auto plants, Black workers organized the Dodge Revolutionary Union Movement and other similar organizations to fight racism and demand rights for Black workers. Socialist ideas became attractive again to a layer of students and young working-class activists. There was a real possibility at this point to begin the process of rebuilding a militant, socialist current rooted in the working class.[49] But there was a problem. The bulk of the radicalized activists were attracted to Maoist and Stalinist politics that turned their back on the working class as "bought off," looking instead to third world national liberation movements for inspiration. Some left organizations did make a turn to the working class, but in the mid-1970s economic recession hit and, instead of provoking more working-class rebellion, heralded the beginning of a retreat.

The balance of class forces shifted decisively toward the employers beginning in the late 1970s. Unions, wages, and the social safety net were ravaged while corporations fed at the state trough, courtesy of the working-class taxpayer. As wages and unionization rates declined, there was a tremendous shift of wealth from the poorest to the richest—shown most dramatically by the 354 to 1 ratio of average CEO compensation to average wages in the United States in 2012 (up by 1,000 percent since 1950).[50] This economic offensive was backed up by a right-wing ideological assault that pinned the blame for poverty on the poor themselves. The 1980s became known as the "looting decade."

The collapse of what passed for socialism seemed another dagger in the heart of the left, already battered and demoralized by the Reagan era. After the fall of the Berlin Wall, writes Ahmed Shawki, "Western politicians and the mainstream press were celebrating the miracles of the market system and proclaiming the victory of capitalism over communism. The introduction to the 1989 edition of the annual *Economic Report of the President* proclaimed, 'The tide of history, which some skeptics saw as ebbing inevitably away from Western ideals . . . flows in our direction.'"[51] But the excitement of capitalists and their spokespeople could not conceal the fact that their gain turned out to be a great loss for most people. Continues Shawki, "The much-heralded promises of Western politicians and business leaders at the time of the collapse of the Eastern Bloc in 1989 have given way to the stark realities of a global capitalist system." The stark reality was that in the United States and the rest of the world, inequality grew to staggering proportions while a handful of people became very rich.

Indeed, the period since 1989 has been one that Sharon Smith describes as "the employers' offensive unhinged"—with record profits accompanying a growing race to the bottom for the working class.[52] Anyone who can argue today that the working class is "bought off" simply does not know what happened to the working class at the end of the last century and the beginning of this one. Income inequality, child poverty, and a widespread lack of access to health care are more pronounced in the United States than in all other advanced countries. Conditions that were already appalling before the Great Recession are now even worse, despite the recovery. According to a 2013 report, that gap in wealth between the top 1 percent of US society, defined as families with incomes above $394,000, and the rest of us is greater than it's been in a hundred years. Between 1993 and 2012, the top 1 percent experience real income growth of 86.1 percent, whereas the bottom 99 percent saw its income grow by 6.6 percent. Since the recession, between 2009 and 2012, the top 1 percent had a 31 percent increase in income, while the bottom 99 percent experienced a 0.4 increase.[53]

The very ferocity of the ruling-class attack was bound to provoke a response. As Shawki notes, the "class inequality and social polarization [that] have accelerated over the decade of the 1990s . . . form the underpinnings to a new radicalization."[54] Yet that radicalization, emerging from a long period of defeat for the working class and the left, was at first slow in coming. As Shawki relates, "While the collapse of Stalinism opened up the possibility of rebuilding a genuinely revolutionary socialist movement internationally, it also produced enormous demoralization and confusion within the existing left. . . . Thus, in many countries, the immediate beneficiaries of the end of Stalinism were the defenders of capitalism."[55]

A strike by Teamsters in 1997 was one of many false starts in the return of working-class combativity, gaining popular support but failing to spark further class struggle. Then came the "Battle in Seattle" in 1999, the mass antiwar protest of February 15, 2003, in cities across the country, involving hundreds of thousands of people. The radicalization was knocked back on its heels by the September 11 bombings and the subsequent conservative backlash. Then came the mass immigrant rights upsurge in spring 2006. In Los Angeles alone, a million people—mostly low-paid workers, many of them undocumented, formerly invisible—poured into the streets on two separate occasions in March and May to demand their rights. Almost as many protested in Chicago—I witnessed two of those marches. These were the stirrings of the most downtrodden sections of the working class that have for years not been able to see or feel their own power. Since then, there have been more stirrings: the occupation of the capitol in Wisconsin in 2011 by workers resisting attacks on their unions; the Occupy Movement of 2011, a series of occupations of public spaces and parks that spread from Manhattan to the rest of the United States like wildfire; the national outpouring of outrage at the murder of Trayvon Martin in 2012; and the Chicago teachers' strike in 2013.

Occupy Wall Street, the first mass expression of anger in the wake of the financial crisis and the bank bailout, expressed a basic questioning of the priorities of capitalism. Writes Jen Roesch, a participant in Occupy Wall Street:

> Occupy Wall Street (OWS), and the Occupy movement that rapidly spread across
> the country in late September 2011, marked a watershed moment in the reemer-

gence of mass struggle and radical politics in the United States. In a matter of weeks, decades of accumulated bitterness and discontent found political expression and began to reshape national politics. Prior to Occupy the media had been focused on the right-wing Tea Party, which most narratives portrayed as a grassroots rebellion against "big government." Almost overnight the national conversation was refocused on the idea of the "99 percent vs. the 1 percent." This message helped the movement gain mass support and provided a left-wing focus for people's simmering anger.[56]

The argument of today's pundits is not that the United States is different, but that the rest of the world is now as exceptional, that is, as closed to a socialist alternative, as the United States. In this depressing view, the United States provides the dystopian model—low wages, poor benefits, and inadequate social services—that the rest of the world is bound to follow. This may be a model that capitalists salivate over, but for the majority it is a model to resist. And they are resisting, from Athens to Buenos Aires, from La Paz to Los Angeles. The single biggest obstacle to the development, or the redevelopment, of genuine socialist currents in the United States and elsewhere—Stalinism—is gone; and the claims of capitalism's great triumph look like a cruel joke. In these conditions, genuine socialist ideas can once again begin to take hold and spread.

Workers Don't Have Power Anymore

Some analysts claim we have entered a "post-industrial" society in which automation is shrinking, if not eliminating, the working class. As a result, workers no longer have the power that Marx attributed to them. "Capital has succeeded," writes French radical author André Gorz in 1980, "in reducing workers' power in the production process."[57]

History is full of speculation going back to Marx's day about how machines would someday replace all workers. Marx joked once "how dreadful that would be for capital which, without wage-labor, ceases to be capital!"[58] The point here is that living labor is the source of profits, not machines. Machines, moreover, as Hal Draper notes, "are not programmed to buy their own products and consume them." The tendency toward more machines and less labor "cannot work itself out to the predicted end without bursting the bounds of that system."[59]

After decades of decline in working-class living standards, it is difficult to make the case that workers are too prosperous to want change (see above). Instead, the explanation as to why workers have low unionization and strike rates has shifted onto a different terrain—that restructuring has rendered the working class powerless.

Many of these theories attribute the decline in unionization rates and levels of class struggle in various parts of the world to something not caused by contingent factors—like the shift of production to the non-union South or the unwillingness of the union bureaucracy to give up "partnership" with the employers—but to structural changes in the nature of the working class that render it no longer the central agent of social transformation. Workers today, it is argued, don't make things anymore, their jobs are increasingly precarious, unstable, part time, and without benefits, and there are a growing number of people relegated to a vast informal sector worldwide. These ideas are often attached to analysis of how capitalism has entered a new "weightless" era of global capitalism, an age of "information," of lightning-fast financial transactions, and so on, in which the old production relations no longer apply. Writes author Kevin Doogan,

> Previous periods of capitalist development were powerfully symbolized by steam engines, aircraft and motorcars, and large factories where people had "real jobs" because "they made things." The new capitalist Zeitgeist is captured in global processes, in the instantaneous transfer of capital, planetary flows of information and communication, interconnection and networks. . . . In leaving behind the concrete realities of industrial society the discussion of new capitalism is "dematerialized."[60]

Some argue that as a result of changes in the nature of work under capitalism, in the words of Michael Hardt and Antonio Negri, the industrial working class "has been displaced from its hegemonic position over other forms of labor by immaterial labor."[61] Jodi Dean, author of *The Communist Horizon*, for example, argues, "The changes . . . usually discussed under the headings of deindustrialization, post-Fordism, and the rise of knowledge- or information-based economy, suggest the inapplicability of the figure of the industrial proletariat as the contemporary subject of communism."[62]

We should stop talking about the "working class" at all. Hardt and Negri argue that it should be replaced by the term *multitude*, based on a conception of labor that "cannot be limited to wage labor." For them, class is merely "a collectivity that struggles in common."[63] Dean proposes substituting for *working class* the term *people*, and proposes that "class struggle," rather than referring to the clash between workers and bosses, should now refer to the struggle between "the rich and the rest of us."[64] Author Guy Standing argues that there is a growing new "precariat" class of insecure workers, distinct from the working class.

But precariousness has been the condition of the working class from the moment the first peasants were "suddenly and forcibly torn from their means of subsistence, and hurled as free and 'unattached' proletarians on the labor-market," to quote Marx in *Capital*.[65] The working class, by its nature, is that class that is "freed" from owning property, and is therefore compelled, on pain of starvation, to sell its labor. "This 'free' proletariat could not possibly be absorbed by the nascent manufactures as fast as it was thrown upon the world," wrote Marx. "They were thus "turned *en masse* into beggars, robbers, vagabonds."[66]

As capitalism has changed, so has the composition of the working class. But capitalism, as we've already discussed, depends upon a "reserve army" of the unemployed in order to discipline the class as a whole. Within the working class there is a varying spectrum, from the more stably employed to the precariously employed to the unemployed. But all are part of the working class. The degree to which a section of the working class is able to secure relatively more stable employment—for example, unionized industrial workers in Europe and the United States after World War II—is a product of the class struggle, and, as we have seen, is therefore not a permanent feature of capital-labor relations, but a highly contested one.

In the United States, there has been a considerable rise in the number of part-time workers, from 13.5 percent in 1968 to almost 20 percent today. But it remains the case that at 80 percent, a majority of workers are full-time employees.[67] In any case, there is not a wall between workers with full-time jobs and those without, or between workers with jobs and those without. They are all part of the working class and have the potential, as they always have, to unite and struggle on that basis.

Views like Gorz's, Hardt and Negri's, and Dean's, moreover, are based on the mistaken idea that workers' power depends on the absolute size of the industrial working class. But industrial workers exhibit a concentrated power far beyond what numbers alone would suggest. Surely this is one of the important lessons of the Russian Revolution, in which the industrial working class was less than 2 percent of the total population, but had its hands on the economic jugular of Russian capitalism and played the central role in its downfall. The same logic applies even more so today. The US manufacturing working class alone is six times larger than Russia's in 1917, and it is far more productive.

Undeniably, there has been a relative shift in employment in the United States and other advanced industrial countries since the late 1960s—from industry to the service sector. About a third (32.7 percent) of workers were employed in manufacturing, mining, and construction in 1963, whereas just over a fifth, or 20.8 percent, were employed in this sector thirty years later. By 2004, the figure had dropped to 17 percent.[68] One author estimates that the United States lost "3.5 to 4 million jobs between 1978 and 1982, or one out of every four jobs in large manufacturing facilities."[69] The manufacturing workforce in the United States stood at 22.5 million in 1979, and had dropped to 18.1 million by 2002.

But that isn't the whole picture. While economic restructuring was shrinking the size of the manufacturing workforce in the United States, industrial growth was increasing it dramatically in countries like China, Brazil, Mexico, and South Korea. In South Korea, for example, the size of the manufacturing workforce increased from 1.2 million in 1969 to 4.7 million in 1994.[70] China, which has become the world's industrial workshop, had an estimated eight million workers sixty-three years ago. By 2011, conservative estimates put the number of workers in China at three hundred million—the total population of the United States.[71]

What about in countries where farmers are being driven off the land in droves and into big cities? In these places, the growth of industry does not keep up with the growth of the dispossessed, creating a larger and larger "reserve army." In many of these societies, workers are not the majority, but they can, as in the past, play a powerful, leading role in broader social struggles. South African author Leo Zelig, in reference to the working-class neighborhoods and slums of Soweto in South Africa, notes that, "The jobless and formally employed are not hermetically sealed from each other." "The township," he writes, "might be viewed as a meeting point—indeed a hotbed—for trade unionists, university students, graduates, the unemployed, informal traders. The specter of unemployment infects all layers of society. But these groups are not distinct or permanently cut off from each other, and may be found in the same community and even in the same household supporting and encouraging and influencing each other."[72] This creates the potential for struggles that bring together the unemployed, the informal sector workers, and formally employed workers.

The relative decline in the number of industrial workers in the older industrialized countries is really just another indicator of the increase in labor productivity, a fact that strengthens rather than weakens the potential power of workers at the point of production. In the United States, manufacturing output increased by 44 percent between 1992 and 2002, at the same time that manufacturing employment declined by 7 percent, representing a 55 percent increase in productivity.[73] In the decade of the 2000s, the US economy shed 5.6 million manufacturing jobs, while productivity increased by 38 percent and output remained relatively stable.[74]

The working class consists of more than just industrial workers, and industrial workers are not just factory workers but also transport, communications, and construction workers. To cite Engels in his 1847 *Principles of Communism*, the proletariat is "that class in society which lives entirely from the sale of its labor."[75] White-collar, service, and public-sector workers are thus also part of the working class. Cashiers, nurses, orderlies, janitors, truck drivers, warehouse workers, waiters, sales workers, social workers, schoolteachers, call-center workers—these are people who work for a wage. They are subject to the same logic of exploitation, and share the same interests, as workers in factories, shipyards, mines, warehouses, building sites, and fields.

Though the number of workers engaged in industrial production has declined, the economic weight of industry in the US economy hasn't. As labor analyst Kim Moody notes, "The ratio of service output to goods and structures, as the government measures these, has not changed much in almost half a century." He concludes that the "industrial core remains the sector on which the majority of economic activity is dependent. Hence it is the power center of the system."[76]

The idea that the age of information and the Internet means we are moving away from material production and industry is only plausible for those whose minds are addled by the endless talk of "cloud computing" into thinking that "cloud" is more than a self-serving metaphor. The age of the Internet, computers, and personal electronic devices requires the mining of materials, the construction of components, and the assembly of those devices we all have come to depend on. The Chinese company Foxconn, made famous when several of its workers committed suicide, employs a million workers, almost half of them at one facility in Shenzhen.[77] Then there is the massive use of energy and space devoted to creating the servers that house all the date we use on our personal devices. "At the heart of every Internet enterprise," writes the *New York Times*, "are data centers, which have become more sprawling and ubiquitous as the amount of stored information explodes, sprouting in community after community."[78]

The explanation for organized labor's decline, writes Moody, cannot be attributed to the "rise of a post-industrial economy, the displacement of goods production by that of services, or even by imports or foreign competition more generally. The economy," he continues,

> remains an industrial economy in terms of its final output despite the rise of service jobs. The rise of retail, finance, and producer services industries rests primarily on the growing complexity of both producing and circulating goods. . . . The loss of manufacturing jobs, the only group of industrial jobs to decline, occurred almost entirely in three industrial groups: primary metals, textile products, and garments. Thus, the decline of unionism in such manufacturing industries as auto, rubber, machinery, electrical equipment, and food production, not to mention non-manufacturing industries such as construction, communications, and transportation, is largely explained by geographic shifts within the US and technological displacement, on the one hand, and the failure of the unions to follow the jobs and organize the now nonunion sectors of their industries, on the other hand.[79]

The current weakened condition of the working class, therefore, cannot be attributed to some intrinsic change that has rendered it permanently powerless. Provided workers organize it and manifest it, their power is still as strong as ever. Indeed, capitalist production has become so integrated that a single strike by a few thousand workers at a strategically critical factory can shut down an entire industry. An eighteen-day strike in 1996 of 3,200 workers at a brake parts plant in Dayton, Ohio, for example, forced General Motors to shut down fourteen assembly plants and sixteen parts plants across Mexico, the United States, and Canada, costing the company thirty to forty million dollars per day.[80]

According to Jodi Dean, classes are not materially constituted forces with a particular relationship to the means of production, as Marx argued. "Communism," she therefore insists, is no longer "the mission of the proletariat."[81]

"The challenge for communists is thus not to identify a particular class vanguard but to clarify why communism is the best alternative to capitalism and to participate in organizing and furthering the struggle toward it."[82] Since there are no defined classes, the struggle of "the rest of us" can take lots of different forms that aren't really driven materially by any class interests. Dean seems to have taken us back to the utopians, who look to a better world but fail to put workers at the center of it, or

Bernstein's conception of socialism as a moral imperative rather than one to which workers, because of their position in society, are particularly drawn.

But capitalism remains a system, to quote Engels, where "the capitalist, the owner of the means of production, employs, for wages, laborers, people deprived of all means of production except their own labor-power, and pockets the excess of the selling price of the products over his outlay."[83] This will not change so long as capitalism remains, whatever the composition of the working class at any particular stage of capitalism's history. Hence, when Dean proposes substituting for *working class* the term *people*, she is reverting to populist terminology that blurs class distinctions that are still fundamental to understanding capitalism and what social forces are central to its transformation.

Socialism Will Make Us All the Same

Socialism will make us all like lemmings. This idea, "delicately stoked by the press and television of a capitalist society which is increasingly stamping sameness and conformity on its working people,"[84] was aided by images and stories of people in the so-called communist regimes. We saw people wearing identical clothing, schoolchildren mouthing slogans by rote to the great leader, work and leisure time regimented to the hour, row upon row of drearily identical buildings, the absence of any public debate, and so on.

But the system of totalitarian conformity that Stalin and Mao imposed in the Soviet Union and China respectively had nothing to do with socialism. Rather, it was part of a policy designed to regiment and dragoon the population, as the military does its soldiers, into making the maximum exertion for the purposes of building up industrial and military strength. This swift, blitzkrieg-style industrialization required strict labor discipline. Along with that went an ideology emphasizing national unity, and strict conformity to the dictates of the party bureaucracy, centered around a deified leader—the infamous cult of personality. "Thank you, Comrade Stalin, for our happy childhood," Russian students were required to say in class.[85] One Chinese official sang this "hymn of praise" to Chairman Mao at the 1955 National People's Congress: "The sun shines only in the day, the moon shines only at night. Only Chairman Mao is the sun that never sets."[86]

The irony of the Cold War is that the United States exhibited its own brand of stifling conformity, particularly in the 1950s. The climate of fear surrounding the anticommunist witch hunts, and the sterile clichés offered up by film, television, and advertising of suburban family life, sent a clear message that uniformity was paramount. Never mind that these images didn't really conform to reality. A 1957 novel expresses some of the frustration felt at the sameness of mass-produced suburban tract housing: "In any one of these new neighborhoods, be it in Hartford or Philadelphia, you can be certain all other houses will be precisely like yours, inhabited by people whose age, income, number of children, problems, habits, conversation, dress, possessions and perhaps even blood type are also precisely like yours."[87]

Mass-market capitalism imposes conformity on the majority. This is true both at work and outside work. At work, we are expected to follow strict rules about our time and behavior; and we are expected to follow a dress code. We churn out the same product or perform the same office tasks, day in and day out, with no letup, and we have very little control over the process. Outside of work, we are "mass consumers," coaxed, exhorted, and seduced into showing up in the millions to buy exactly the same product—which advertisers, ironically, often present to us as if we are making a unique choice that expresses our individuality. Hugo Boss encourages is to "Innovate, don't imitate." "There's no one way to do it," announces Levi's, which the last time I checked doesn't custom make most of its jeans.[88] Only the wealthy have the money and leisure to have palaces built by craftsmen, their clothes specially made, to send their kids to the best schools, and to take vacations to interesting places in private jets.

But it does not have to be this way. The alternative is not between two different brands of conformity. In a socialist society, the productive power of society is harnessed to serve everyone's needs. The collective provides the foundation of a flowering of creative expression and individual achievement. Think of it this way: In ancient Athens, the work of a few hundred thousand slaves provided about fifty thousand citizens with the freedom to meet, debate, and make decisions democratically. It allowed the flowering of great philosophy, theater, and art. Imagine now a society where the productive powers of society are so advanced that able-bodied people need only work a few hours every day to provide what is needed by society as a whole. In such a society—a socialist society—everyone will have the leisure time to pursue all sorts of dreams that today are out of reach to all but a minority. As Trotsky wrote:

> Spiritual creativeness demands freedom. The very purpose of communism is to subject nature to technique and technique to plan, and compel the raw material to give unstintingly everything to man that he needs. Far more than that, its highest goal is to free finally and once and for all the creative forces of mankind from all pressure, limitation and humiliating dependence. Personal relations, science and art will not know any externally imposed "plan," nor even any shadow of compulsion. To what degree spiritual creativeness shall be individual or collective will depend entirely upon its creators.[89]

Appendix 2

Study Questions

Introduction
1. Why is Marxism still relevant?

Chapter One: From Millenarianism to Marx
1. Marx wasn't the first socialist. What made his and Engels's socialism different from the earlier socialists?
2. Many people argue that Marxism is "utopian." Is that true? What did Marx and Engels mean by the term?
3. If people are victims of their circumstances, how can they move beyond them? Put another way, if our consciousness is a reflection of the world we live in, how can we possibly change that world?

Chapter Two: Marx's Materialist Method
1. Most people think that the only way to be "objective" and truthful is to be impartial. What do Marxists think about that idea?
2. What is the difference between idealism and materialism?
3. Is there such a thing as "human nature"? And if so, how is it shaped, environmentally or biologically, or both?
4. Can you explain what is meant by the transformation of quantity into quality?

Chapter Three: The Marxist View of History
1. Some historians see human history as a product of changing ideas. What, for Marx, is the starting point for understanding history?
2. Explain the difference between the forces and relations of production.
3. Is Marxism "deterministic"?
4. How and why did class divisions arise? Under what conditions could classes disappear?
5. Discuss the validity of this statement: capitalism is a product of human greed.

Chapter Four: Marxist Economics: How Capitalism Works

1. Explain the labor theory of value.
2. What's wrong with this statement: the value of commodities is determined by their relative scarcity or abundance.
3. Discuss the validity of this statement: the purpose of the market is to ensure that products are properly distributed.
4. Where do profits come from?

Chapter Five: Marxist Economics: How Capitalism Fails

1. How does capitalism get out of slumps?
2. Explain the "tendency of the rate of profit to fall."

Chapter Six: No Power Greater—the Working Class

1. What is the "working class"? Is it anyone who works?
2. What gives wageworkers more potential power compared to slaves or peasants?
3. What did Marx learn from the Paris Commune of 1871?
4. Why do socialists support unions? Are unions enough to fight for socialism?
5. How can workers who today accept life under capitalism come to challenge it?

Chapter Seven: Democracy, Reform, and Revolution

1. We learn in school that the state balances between competing interests. Discuss.
2. How democratic is democracy under capitalism?
3. The left calls the Democratic Party the "graveyard of social movements." What does this mean?
4. Can elections bring socialism?
5. What is the difference between a coup and a revolution?

Chapter Eight: From Marx to Lenin: Marxism and Political Organization

1. Why did Marx think workers needed a political party?
2. What kind of organization was the German SPD? How did it organize?
3. What did Lenin mean by a "vanguard" party?

Chapter Nine: Russia: The God That Failed?

1. What was the difference between the Bolshevik and Menshevik theories about the nature of the Russian Revolution? How did Trotsky's differ from those?
2. What were the main slogans of the Bolsheviks in the revolution?
3. What were the soviets?
4. Why weren't the Bolsheviks able to fulfill their goals? What held them back?
5. Is socialism synonymous with state control of the economy?

Chapter Ten: Imperialism, Nationalism, and War

1. Is war a product of human nature?
2. Compare and contrast Lenin's view of imperialism with Kautsky's theory of "ultra-imperialism." Is imperialism a government policy or a stage of capitalism?
3. What has changed about imperialism since Lenin's day? Do those changes invalidate his theory?
4. Does the United States intervene all over the world to "spread democracy"?
5. Are there such things as "national interests"?
6. Discuss the validity or otherwise of this statement: The integration of the world economy has rendered national states obsolete.

Chapter Eleven: Marxism and Oppression

1. Explain Lenin's views on the right of nations to self-determination.
2. Have women always been oppressed?
3. What is the role of the family under capitalism?
4. Has racism always existed?
5. Does capitalism need racism?
6. How is LGBTI oppression connected to women's oppression?
7. Explain the difference between sex and gender.
8. Evaluate this statement: "Marxism cares more about exploitation than it does oppression."

Chapter Twelve: Capitalism's Ecological Crisis

1. Marxists see abundance as the basis of a socialist society. How can we have abundance without ruining the environment?
2. Are there too many people on the planet?
3. What do socialists say about lifestyle choices? Are they important?
4. Is there something "special" about US history that makes socialism impossible?

Chapter Thirteen: Imagine . . . the Socialist Future

1. What measures would have to be taken by a workers' government to effect a transition toward a socialist society?
2. What did Marx mean by a planned economy?

Further Reading

This book is merely an introduction. Hopefully it has whetted your appetite for more. More ambitious readers can look at the endnotes to discover what books and articles they might be interested in checking out. But for convenience's sake, I've compiled some lists of books and articles I think are good to follow up with after you've read this book. Many of the articles and books by Marx, Engels, Lenin, Luxemburg, Trotsky, and others referenced in this book are available at www.marxists.org. I highly recommend visiting that site. Many books mentioned below are also available for order from Haymarket Books (www.haymarketbooks.org). If there's a book I refer to and you can't find it in either of the above two places, I recommend searching for it on two websites: www.fetchbook.info or www.bookfinder.org. The *Socialist Worker* and *International Socialist Review* websites (www.socialistworker.org and www.isreview.org) are also good places to get both contemporary and historical Marxist theory, analysis, and commentary.

Here is a by-no-means-exhaustive list of books by the classic Marxist writers, as well as some good secondary sources:

By Marx and Engels

The Communist Manifesto: A Road Map to History's Most Important Political Document
Edited and annotated by Phil Gasper (Haymarket Books). The *Manifesto* is where to start. And Gasper's edition, fully annotated to explain the obscure historical references and terms, as well as providing an introduction and supplementary text, is the edition to read.

Socialism: Utopian and Scientific
Written by Engels (culled from a much longer polemical work called *Anti-Dühring*), it is one of the most complete statements of Marx and Engels's materialist conception of history, of class struggle, and of socialism.

The Eighteenth Brumaire of Louis Napoleon

This is one of the finest examples of Marx's incisive contemporary analysis from a materialist perspective. This work contains the famous statement: "Men make their own history, but they do not make it as they please; they do not make it under self-selected circumstances, but under circumstances existing already, given and transmitted from the past."

The Civil War in France

Marx delivered a series of addresses about the Paris Commune of 1871 where he argued that the Commune showed, for the first time, what the "dictatorship of the proletariat" would look like in practice.

The Origin of the Family, Private Property and the State

Though some of the research on which Engels based his theories is now outdated, this remains a groundbreaking explanation of the rise not only of class society but of the oppression of women that accompanied it.

Capital, Volume 1

If you're feeling ambitious, this is the one to read—Marx's road map to understanding the ins and outs of the capitalist system. A bonus is that it is very funny, too.

About Marx and Marxism

Hal Draper's series of volumes, *Karl Marx's Theory of Revolution*, in particular volumes 1 (*State and Bureaucracy*), 2 (*The Politics of Social Classes*), and 4 (*Critique of Other Socialisms*), are an excellent way to delve more deeply into the politics of Marx and Engels. The first part of volume 1 has a particularly good explanation of how Marx became a Marxist, and volume 2 has one of the best expositions of Marx's conception of the working class and of working-class power. John Molyneux's *What Is the Real Marxist Tradition?* (Haymarket) answers the vexing question: How, given all the conflicting ideas claiming the mantle of socialism and Marxism, do we identify the genuine article?

Lenin

The best way to get beyond the absurd myths about Lenin is to read Lenin.

State and Revolution

Here Lenin rescues Marx's argument that workers cannot take over the existing capitalist state, but must erect a new, directly democratic, workers' state on its ruins.

"Left-Wing" Communism: An Infantile Disorder

After the founding of the Communist International in 1919, Lenin started a debate with "ultra left" socialists in Europe who argued that revolutionaries should turn their backs on elections and trade unions. Lenin argued that until a majority of workers were won to the task of overthrowing capitalism, socialists must work inside parliaments and trade unions in order to influence and lead wider layers of workers. But the relevance of Lenin's arguments go far beyond the immediate context of the debate.

Imperialism: The Highest Stage of Capitalism

Lenin explains, in the midst of world war, that capitalism has entered the phase of imperialism, when the world is being carved up between a handful of great powers. For readers who want to delve further into this topic, I recommend Nikolai Bukharin's (one of the Bolsheviks' chief theoreticians) *Imperialism and World Economy*.

Lenin on National Self-Determination

Lenin developed, in many articles, the best and most consistent Marxist position on the right of oppressed nations to self-determination. Among them are *The Right of Nations to Self-Determination* and *The Discussion on Self-Determination Summed Up*. They are excellent places to start in this question, and can be found on the Marxist Internet Archive.

Lenin on the Question of Organization

This, of course, is the most controversial and maligned aspect of Lenin's politics.

Lenin's *What Is to Be Done?* is very much worth reading, but it is not the final statement on his ideas of party organization. The ideas he developed on the question are scattered in many different articles and developed over a period of years. Here are the best places to start: Chris Harman et al., *Party and Class* (Haymarket); Paul LeBlanc, *Lenin and the Revolutionary Party* (Humanities Press); and finally, Tony Cliff, *Lenin: Building the Party* and *All Power to the Soviets* (both from Haymarket). Alexander Rabinowitch's *The Bolsheviks Come to Power*, in glorious detail, completely debunks the myth that the Bolsheviks were a band of conspirators that "imposed" its power over the working class.

In addition to the few I've just mentioned, I'd also recommend Leon Trotsky's *The Young Lenin* and Marcel Leibman's *Leninism under Lenin*. *Lenin* by Georg Lukács is a good short assessment of Lenin's contribution to Marxism.

Trotsky

Trotsky was a prolific writer, but here are a few of his classic works:

The Permanent Revolution and Results and Prospects
This book outlines his classic theory that workers could come to power in a backward country before an advanced one.

My Life
Reading like a great novel, this summary of his life also works as a great political introduction to many ideas and events in the history of the socialist movement in the early twentieth century.

History of the Russian Revolution
Still the best history of any revolution written in any language. Don't be intimidated by its length—over a thousand pages.

The Struggle Against Fascism in Germany
In the early 1930s, Trotsky penned a series of articles analyzing the rise of Hitler and outlining to the German Communists the united front policy necessary to defeat him. These are perhaps the finest writings by a Marxist on current events ever written.

The Revolution Betrayed
Trotsky may have never made a complete break from his belief that, however distorted, Russia's nationalized property made it somehow still a "workers' state." Nevertheless, this remains a masterful analysis of the degeneration of the Russian Revolution, a fierce indictment of the rise of the Stalinist bureaucracy and a ringing defense of genuine Marxism.

Their Morals and Ours
Trotsky takes up the question, Do the ends justify the means?, and in the process writes a tightly argued polemic on the question of Marxism and morality.

Duncan Hallas's *Trotsky's Marxism* (Haymarket) is the best short introduction to Trotsky's politics.

The Prophet Armed, The Prophet Unarmed, and The Prophet Outcast
Isaac Deustcher's trilogy on the life of Trotsky is unsurpassed in the field of political biography. However, as a political corrective (in the last volume Deustcher comes perilously close to apologizing for Stalin's rule), Tony Cliff's four-volume biography

of Trotsky, and in particular *The Darker the Night, the Brighter the Star*, the final volume, is essential reading.

Rosa Luxemburg

Reform or Revolution
The most definitive statement on the need for revolution and the limits of reform as a means for transforming society.

The Mass Strike, the Political Party and the Trade Union
Luxemburg's masterful analysis of the most important weapon in the arsenal of the working class: the mass strike.

Other Readings

These are some books that I would be remiss not to recommend for those trying to expand their knowledge of Marxism and its application to a whole host of important questions:

Subterranean Fire: A History of Working-Class Radicalism in the United States by Sharon Smith (Haymarket Books)

Black Liberation and Socialism by Ahmed Shawki (Haymarket Books)

Women and Socialism by Sharon Smith (Haymarket Books)

Sexuality and Socialism by Sherry Wolf (Haymarket Books)

Ecology and Socialism by Chris Williams (Haymarket Books)

The German Revolution by Pierre Broué (Haymarket Books)

Notes

Introduction to the 2014 Edition

1. Isabel Ortiz, Sara Burke, Mohamed Berrada, Hernan Cortes Saenz, "World Protests 2006–2013 Executive Summary," Initiative for Policy Dialogue, http://policydialogue.org/publications /working_papers/world_protests_2006-2013_executive_summary/.
2. Alexander Eichler, "Young People More Likely to Favor Socialism Than Capitalism: Pew," *Huffington Post*, December 29, 2011.
3. Naomi Klein, "How Science Is Telling Us to Revolt," *New Statesman*, October 29, 2013.
4. Michael Schuman, "Marx's Revenge: How Class Struggle Is Shaping the World," *TIME*, March 25, 2013.

Introduction

1. Daniel Singer, *Prelude to Revolution: France in May 1968*, 2nd ed. (Boston: South End Press, 2002), xxvi.
2. Sombart quoted in Daniel Bell, *The End of Ideology* (New York: Collier Books, 1962), 277.
3. Bell, *The End of Ideology*, 16.
4. Herbert Marcuse, *One Dimensional Man: Studies in the Ideology of Advanced Industrial Society* (Boston: Beacon Press, 1991), 1–2.
5. Some examples of this line of argument, in various permutations, can be found, for example, in: "Marcuse Defines His New Left Line," interview with Marcuse in *The New Left of the 1960s: The Collected Papers of Herbert Marcuse*, ed. Douglass Kellner (New York: Routledge, 2005); Ernest Laclau and Chantal Mouffe, *Hegemony and Socialist Strategy* (London: Verso, 1985); and André Gorz, *Farewell to the Working Class* (London: Pluto Press, 1982). Many other examples could be cited. The most rabidly anti-Marxist tract against the central role of the working class in achieving a new society is Murray Bookchin's nasty little essay, "Listen, Marxist!," in *Post-Scarcity Anarchism* (Buffalo, NY: Black Rose Books, 1986), 193–242.
6. Francis Fukuyama, "By Way of an Introduction," in *The End of History and the Last Man* (London: Penguin, 1992).
7. Global Inequality Data and Chart Pack, inequality.org.
8. United for a Fair Economy staff, *Born on Third Base: What the Forbes 400 Really Says About*

Economic Equality and Opportunity in America (United for a Fair Economy, 2012), 2, http://faireconomy.org/sites/default/files/BornOnThirdBase_2012.pdf.

9.   *United Nations Human Development Report 2010: The Real Wealth of Nations: Pathways to Human Development* (New York: Palgrave MacMillan, 2010), 96.

10. "Trends in CEO Pay," AFL-CIO Executive Paywatch, www.aflcio.org/Corporate-Watch/CEO -Pay-and-the-99/Trends-in-CEO-Pay.

11. Sara Anderson, et al., *Executive Excess 2008: How Average Taxpayers Subsidize Runaway Pay* (Washington, DC: United for a Fair Economy and Institute for Policy Studies, 2008), 9.

12. Ibid., 13.

13. Sara Anderson et al., *Executive Excess 2005: Defense Contractors Get More Bucks for the Bang*, 12th Annual CEO Compensation Survey for the Institute for Policy Studies, August 30, 2005, 14–15, www.faireconomy.org/press/2005/EE2005.pdf.

14. Dave Gilson and Caroline Perot, "It's the Inequality, Stupid!," *Mother Jones*, March–April 2011.

15. Susan Heavy and Lucia Mutikani, "Number of U.S. Poor Holds Steady But Earnings Gap Grows," Reuters, September 12, 2012; Heidi Shierholz and Elise Gould, "Already More Than a Lost Decade," Economic Policy Institute, September 12, 2012.

16. Keeanga-Yamahtta Taylor, "What Has Obama Done for African-Americans?" *Socialist Worker*, May 19, 2011; Shierholz and Gold, "Already More Than a Lost Decade."

17. *United Nations Human Development Report 2003: Millennium Development Goals* (New York: Oxford University Press, 2003), 155.

18. Frederick Engels, "Karl Marx's Funeral," in Karl Marx and Frederick Engels, *Collected Works* (hereafter *MECW*), vol. 24 (New York: International Publishers, 1989), 468. Note: Many of the Marxist works cited in this book can be found at the Marx-Engels Internet archive at www.marxists.org. It is an indispensable resource.

19. Frances Moore Lappé et al., *World Hunger: Twelve Myths* (New York: Grove Press, 1998), 8; *The State of Food Insecurity in the World 2005* (Rome: United Nations Food and Agricultural Organization, 2005), 20.

20. Karl Marx and Frederick Engels, *Manifesto of the Communist Party*, in *The Communist Manifesto: A Road Map to History's Most Important Political Document*, ed. Phil Gasper (Chicago: Haymarket Books, 2005), 72. (Hereafter, *Communist Manifesto*.) This fully annotated edition of the *Manifesto*, complete with an explanatory introduction by the editor and a selection of key excerpts from other works by Marx and Engels, is the best by far.

21. Karl Marx, *Civil War in France: The Paris Commune* (New York: International Publishers, 1989); Frederick Engels, *Socialism: Utopian and Scientific* (New York: International Publishers, 1989); Rosa Luxemburg, *Reform or Revolution*, in *The Essential Rosa Luxemburg*, ed. Helen Scott (Chicago: Haymarket Books, 2008); Leon Trotsky, *The Lessons of October* (London: Bookmarks, 1987); V. I. Lenin, *State and Revolution* (New York: International Publishers, 1994).

22. Lenin, *State and Revolution*, 101.

Chapter One: From Millenarianism to Marx

1.   Quoted in Karl Kautsky, *Foundations of Christianity* (New York: Monthly Review Press, year unspecified), 332.

2.   Jean Froissart rendering a "typical" John Ball sermon, quoted in Norman Cohn, *The Pursuit*

of the Millennium (London: Oxford University Press, 1970), 199.

3.   Quoted in R. B. Rose, *Gracchus Babeuf: The First Revolutionary Communist* (Stanford, CA: Stanford University Press, 1978), 195.

4.   Quoted in Lillian Symes and Travers Clement, *Rebel America: The Story of Social Revolt in the United States* (New York: Harper & Brothers Publishers, 1934), 40.

5.   Quoted in Karl Marx, *Capital: A Critique of Political Economy*, vol. 1, trans. Ben Fowkes (New York: Vintage, 1977), 801. All references hereafter will be to this version of *Capital*, unless otherwise noted.

6.   Fourier, "Degradation of Women in Civilization," in *Women, the Family, and Freedom: The Debate in Documents*, vol. 1, *1750–1880*, Susan Groag Bell and Karen M. Offen, eds., Karen M. Offen, trans. (Palo Alto, CA: Stanford University Press, 1983), 40–41.

7.   Engels, *Socialism: Utopian and Scientific* (New York: International Publishers, 1989), 36.

8.   Quoted in Michael Löwy, *The Theory of Revolution in the Young Marx* (Chicago: Haymarket Books, 2005), 26.

9.   Quoted in Hal Draper, *Karl Marx's Theory of Revolution*, vol. 1, *State and Bureaucracy* (New York: Monthly Review Press, 1977), 38.

10.   Quoted in Löwy, *The Theory of Revolution in the Young Marx*, 27.

11.   Ibid., 39.

12.   Quoted in ibid., 48.

13.   Karl Marx, *Collected Works*, vol. 3 (New York: International Publishers, 1975), 144.

14.   Quoted in Löwy, *Theory of Revolution in the Young Marx*, 65.

15.   Karl Marx, *Collected Works*, vol. 3, 186.

16.   Karl Marx and Frederick Engels, *The German Ideology*, in *Marx-Engels Collected Works* (hereafter *MECW*), vol. 5 (New York: International Publishers, 1976), 49.

17.   Ibid., 36.

18.   Ibid., 38.

19.   The line of argument here is developed in detail in Michael Löwy, *The Theory of Revolution in the Young Marx*, chapter 1.

20.   Quoted in Georgi Plekhanov, "Initial Phases of the Class Struggle Theory," in *Selected Works*, vol. 2 (Moscow: Progress Publishers, 1976), 433–34.

21.   Karl Marx, "Theses on Feuerbach," in *MECW*, vol. 5, 7.

22.   Ibid.

23.   Ibid.

Chapter Two: Marx's Materialist Method

1.   Marx, "Theses on Feuerbach."

2.   Bob Dylan, "Subterranean Homesick Blues," from the album *Bringing It All Back Home*, Columbia Records, 1965.

3.   Karl Marx, *Capital*, vol. 3 (London: Penguin Books, 1981), 953.

4.   Carl Sagan, *Cosmos* (New York: Ballantine Books, 1985), 32.

5.   David B. Resnick, *The Price of Truth: How Money Affects the Norms of Science* (London: Oxford University Press, 2007), 3.

6.   Marx and Engels, *The German Ideology*, 59.

7.   Mike Marquesee, "Attacking the Outside Agitators," *Red Pepper* (September 2005).

8.   Marx, "Postface to the Second Edition," in *Capital*, vol. 1, 97.

9.   V. I. Lenin, "Three Sources and Three Component Parts of Marxism," in *Collected Works* (hereafter *CW*), vol. 19 (Moscow: Progress Publishers, 1977), 23.

10. Marx, "Postface to the Second Edition," 98.

11. Engels, "Ludwig Feuerbach," in *MECW*, 386.

12. Marx, "Theses on Feuerbach," in *MECW*, 6.

13. Plekhanov, "Socialism and the Political Struggle," in *Selected Works*, vol. 1, 90.

14. Leon Trotsky, "Revolution and War in China," in *Leon Trotsky on China* (New York: Monad Press, 1976), 579.

15. Marx and Engels, *The German Ideology*, 37.

16. Peter Dreier, "Reagan's Legacy: Homelessness in America," *Shelterforce*, no. 135 (May/June 2004).

17. Marx and Engels, *The German Ideology*, 24.

18. Karl Marx, "Preface," in *Contribution to a Critique of Political Economy* (Moscow: Progress Publishers, 1977), 21.

19. Frederick Engels, *Anti-Dühring*, in *MECW*, vol. 25 (New York: Progress Publishers, 1987), 87.

20. Marx and Engels, *The German Ideology*, 30.

21. Ibid., 45.

22. For an excellent account of the history of social Darwinism, see Allan Chase, *The Legacy of Malthus: The Social Costs of the New Scientific Racism* (Urbana, IL: University of Illinois Press, 1980).

23. Ibid., 109.

24. Ibid., 329.

25. Richard J. Herrnstein and Charles Murray, *The Bell Curve* (New York: The Free Press, 1994).

26. Stephen Jay Gould, *The Mismeasure of Man* (New York: W. W. Norton, 1996), 28.

27. Quoted in R. C. Lewontin, *Biology as Ideology* (New York: Harper Perennial, 1992), 93.

28. Ibid., 89.

29. Cordelia Fine, *Delusions of Gender: How Our Minds, Society, and Neurosexism Create Difference* (New York: W. W. Norton & Co., 2011), 176.

30. Steven Rose, "Escaping Evolutionary Psychology," in *Alas Poor Darwin: Arguments Against Evolutionary Psychology*, ed. Hilary Rose and Steven Rose (New York: Harmony Books, 2000), 306.

31. Theodosius Dobzhansky, *Mankind Evolving: The Evolution of the Human Species* (New Haven, CT: Yale University Press, 1971), 8.

32. Quoted in Eleanor Burke Leacock, *Myths of Male Dominance* (Chicago: Haymarket Books, 2008), 35.

33. Ibid, 57–58.

34. Ibid, 50.

35. Fine, *Delusions of Gender*, 177.

36. Georgi Plekhanov, "On the Individual's Role in History," in *Selected Philosophical Works*, vol. 2 (Moscow: Progress Publishers, 1976), 313.

37. Frederick Engels, "Ludwig Feuerbach and the End of Classical German Philosophy," in *MECW*, vol. 26 (New York: International Publishers, 1990), 383.

38. Quoted in George Novak, *The Origins of Materialism* (New York: Pathfinder Press, 1971), 97–100.

39. Karl Marx to his father, November 10, 1837, in *MECW*, vol. 1 (New York: International Publishers, 1975), 18.

40. Engels, *Anti-Dühring* (Moscow: Progress Publishers, 1975), 29–30.

41. Engels, "Dialectics," in *Anti-Dühring*, Marxists.org, www.marxists.org/archive/marx/works/1880/soc-utop/ch02.htm.

42. G. W. F. Hegel, "Preface," in *The Phenomenology of Spirit* (New York: Oxford University Press, 1977), 2.

43. H. D. Lewis, ed., *Hegel's Science of Logic*, translated by A.V. Miller (Amherst, NY: Humanity Books, 1999), 370.

44. *Hegel's Phenomenology of Spirit*, translated by A. V. Miller (New York: Oxford University Press, 1977), 6.

45. Marx, *Capital*, vol. 1, 103.

46. Engels, "Ludwig Feuerbach," in *MECW*, 359.

47. Leon Trotsky, "Mr. Baldwin and . . . Gradualness," in *Trotsky's Writings on Britain*, vol. 2 (London: New Park Publications, 1974), 20.

48. Leon Trotsky, *In Defense of Marxism* (New York: Pioneer Publishers, 1942), 53–54.

Chapter Three: The Marxist View of History

1. Marx, *Capital*, vol. 1, 286.

2. Ibid.

3. Ibid., 283.

4. Marx and Engels, *The German Ideology*, 31.

5. Frederick Engels, "Introduction to the English Edition (1892) of *Socialism: Utopian and Scientific*," in *MECW*, vol. 27 (New York: International Publishers, 1990), 289.

6. Karl Marx, "Preface," *Contribution to the Critique of Political Economy*, in *MECW*, vol. 29 (New York: International Publishers, 1987), 263.

7. Karl Marx, *Capital*, vol. 3 (New York: Penguin Books, 1981), 927.

8. Marx, "Preface," *Contribution to the Critique of Political Economy*, 263.

9. Marx and Engels, *Communist Manifesto*, 39–40.

10. Marx, "Preface," *Contribution to the Critique of Political Economy*, 263.

11. Karl Marx, *The Eighteenth Brumaire of Louis Napoleon*, in *MECW*, vol. 11 (New York: International Publishers, 1979), 103.

12. Karl Marx, "Letter to *Otechestvenniye Zapiski*," in *MECW*, vol. 24, 200.

13. Frederick Engels to J. Bloch, September 21, 1890, in *Historical Materialism* (Moscow: Progress Publishers, 1972), 294–96.

14. Marx and Engels, *Holy Family*, 119.

15. Georgi Plekhanov, "Initial Phases of the Theory of the Class Struggle (an Introduction to the Second Russian Edition of the *Manifesto of the Communist Party*), *Selected Philosophical Writings*, vol. 2 (Moscow: Progress Publishers, 1976), 462.

16. Marx, "Preface," *Contribution to the Critique of Political Economy*, 263.

17. Leon Trotsky, "The School of Revolutionary Strategy: Speech at a General Party Membership Meeting of the Moscow Organization," July 1921, in *The First Five Years of the Communist International*, vol. 2 (New York: Monad Press, 1972), 1–3.

18. See Engels, "Ludwig Feuerbach," 387–88.

19. Engels, Introduction to *Dialectics of Nature*, in *MECW*, vol. 25 (Moscow: Progress Publishers, 1987), 330–31.

20. Marx and Engels, *Communist Manifesto*, 39.

21. Frederick Engels, *The Origins of the Family, Private Property and the State*, in *MECW*, vol. 26, 202.

22. Quoted in Paul Lafargue, "Idealism and Materialism in the Conception of History," lecture to the Group of Collectivist Students of Paris, 1895, *Socialist Standard*, May 1915, www.marxists.org/archive/lafargue/1895/xx/idealism.htm#f1.

23. Engels, *Origins of the Family*, 203.

24. Ibid., 158.

25. Irven DeVore et al., *Man the Hunter* (New York: Aldine de Gruyter, 1968), 5–6.

26. Richard B. Lee, "What Hunters Do for a Living, or, How to Make Out on Scarce Resources," in *Man the Hunter*, 371.

27. While inferences can be made from modern foraging societies about our Paleolithic ancestors, it must be done with care, since these societies are affected by the capitalist world that surrounds them and with which they interact. Presumably, however, since modern foragers are pushed to the most marginal lands, ancient hunter-gatherers, given the lower population density and abundance of game and plant life, must have found the search for subsistence relatively easier than the foragers of today found it.

28. A discussion of this topic can be found in a section called "Ancient Poverty or Assumed Affluence," in chapter 12 of Christopher Ryan and Cacilda Jethá, *Sex at Dawn: How We Mate, Why We Stray, and What It Means for Modern Relationships* (New York: Harper Perennial, 2012), Kindle edition. Also see: Jared Diamond, "The Worst Mistake in the History of the Human Race," *Discover Magazine*, May 1987, 64–66, www.ditext.com/diamond/mistake.html.

29. Diamond, "Worst Mistake."

30. See, for example, Ernest Brandewie, "The Place of the Big Man in Traditional Hagen Society in the Central Highlands of New Guinea," in *Anthropological Approaches to Political Behavior*, ed. Frank McGlynn and Arthur Tuden (Pittsburgh: University of Pittsburgh Press, 1991), 62.

31. Marvin Harris, *Cannibals and Kings: The Origins of Cultures* (New York: Vintage, 1977), 113.

32. Engels, *Anti-Dühring*, 167.

33. Ibid.

34. Diamond, "Worst Mistake."

35. Engels, *Socialism: Utopian and Scientific*, 70.

36. Engels, *Origins of the Family*, 173.

37. Ibid., 204.

38. Ibid., 221.

39. Ibid, 212–13.

40. Ibid., 269.

41. Thomas Hobbes, *Leviathan* (New York: Touchstone Books, 1997), 100.

42. Engels, *Origins of the Family*, 270–71.

43. Marx, *Capital*, vol. 1, 874.

44. Ibid., 344.

45. Ibid., 325.

46. Ibid., 874.

47. As Marx noted in an 1877 letter, when the landowning aristocracy dispossessed small farmers in ancient Rome, they became a landless urban "mob," not a wage-working class, while slaves, captured by conquest and sold on the market, became the laborers on the large estates. See "Letter from Marx to Editor of the *Otecestvenniye Zapisky*," November 1877, www.marxists.org/archive/marx/works/1877/11/russia.htm.

48. Ibid., 914.

49. Karl Marx, *Value, Price and Profit*, in *MECW*, vol. 20 (New York: International Publishers,

1985), 129; *Capital*, vol. 1, 876.

50. Ibid., 898.
51. Ibid., 899.
52. Ibid., 925.
53. Marx and Engels, *Communist Manifesto*, 41.
54. Ibid., 875.
55. Ibid., 915.
56. See chapters 4 and 5 of Leonard Thompson, *A History of South Africa* (New Haven, CT: Yale University Press, 2000).
57. Marx and Engels, *Communist Manifesto*, 43.
58. Marx, *Capital*, vol. 1, 926.
59. Marx and Engels, *Communist Manifesto*, 44.
60. Frederick Engels, "The Housing Question," in *MECW*, vol. 23 (New York: International Publishers, 1988), 324–25.
61. Engels, *Anti-Dühring*, 169.

Chapter Four: Marxist Economics: How Capitalism Works

1. David McNally, "Slump, Austerity, and Resistance," *The Crisis and the Left: Socialist Register 2012* (New York: Monthly Review Press, 2011), 37.
2. Karl Marx and Frederick Engels, *The Holy Family*, in *MECW*, vol. 4 (Moscow: Progress Publishers, 1975), 32.
3. Marx, "Postface to the Second Edition," in *Capital*, vol. 1, 97.
4. George Soros, *The New Paradigm for Financial Markets: The Credit Crisis of 2008 and What It Means* (New York: Public Affairs Books, 2008), 53. Soros is critical of this view.
5. Eugene F. Fama, "Random Walks in Stock Market Prices," Selected Papers No. 16, University of Chicago Graduate School of Business, www.chicagobooth.edu/faculty/selectedpapers/sp16.pdf. Fama is one of the founders of the theory.
6. David McNally, *Global Slump: The Economics and Politics of Crisis and Resistance* (Oakland, CA: PM Press, 2011), 111.
7. Lewis Corey, *The Decline of American Capitalism* (New York: Covici-Friede, 1934), 20.
8. Quoted in Joel Geier and Ahmed Shawki, "Contradictions of the 'Miracle Economy,'" *International Socialist Review* 2 (Fall 1997), www.isreview.org/issues/02/miracle_economy.shtml.
9. Simon Clarke, *Marx's Theory of Crisis* (New York, St. Martin's Press, 1994), 1.
10. Olivier Coibion, Yuriy Gorodnichenko, "Does the Great Recession Really Mean the End of the Great Moderation?," *Vox*, January 16, 2010; www.voxeu.org/article/does-great-recession -really-mean-end-great-moderation.
11. Ben Bernanke, "Implications of the Financial Crisis for Economics," September 24, 2010, Board of Governors of the Federal Reserve System, www.federalreserve.gov/newsevents /speech/bernanke20100924a.htm.
12. See, for example, the New School for Social Research's biography of Say at http://cepa .newschool.edu/het/profiles/say.htm, and of James Mill at http://cepa.newschool.edu/het/profiles /jamesmill.htm.
13. Karl Marx, *Capital*, vol. 1, in *MECW*, vol. 36 (New York: International Publishers, 1996), 123.
14. Karl Marx, *Capital: A Critique of Political Economy*, vol. 1, trans. Samuel Moore and Edward Aveling (London: Lawrence and Wishart, 1974), 43. I cite this edition, because the Vintage

edition uses the less poetic phrase, "immense collection of commodities."

15. Karl Marx, *A Contribution to the Critique of Political Economy*, in *MECW*, vol. 29, 270.

16. David Ricardo, *Principles of Political Economy* (New York: E. P. Dutton & Co., 1926), 5.

17. Marx, *Value, Price and Profit*, 118.

18. "Marx to Ludwig Kugelman," in *MECW*, vol. 43 (Moscow: International Publishers, 1988), 69.

19. Marx, *Capital*, vol. 1, 165.

20. Ibid.

21. Ibid.

22. Karl Marx, *Critique of the Gotha Program*, in *MECW*, vol. 24 (New York: International Publishers, 1989), 81.

23. William Shakespeare, *Timon of Athens*, act 4, scene 3, lines 26–29, www.william-shakespeare.info/act4-script-text-timon-of-athens.htm. Marx cites this passage in the 1844 *Economic and Philosophical Manuscripts* as well as in volume 1, chapter 3 of *Capital*.

24. Marx, *Critique of Political Economy*, 276.

25. Marx, *Capital*, vol. 1, 182.

26. Ibid., 159.

27. Marx, *Capital*, vol. 1, 187.

28. Adam Smith, *The Wealth of Nations* (New York: Modern Library, 1937), 13.

29. Marx, *Capital*, vol. 1, 291–92n.

30. Karl Marx, *Grundrisse* (London: Penguin Books, 1973), 83.

31. Bastiat's *Economic Harmonies*, quoted in Nikolai Bukharin, *Economic Theory of the Leisure Class* (New York: Monthly Review, 1973), 41.

32. Marx, *Grundrisse*, 84.

33. Ibid.

34. Paul A. Samuelson and William D. Nordhaus, *Economics* (Boston: Irwin/McGraw-Hill, 1998). This ahistorical, "use-value" way of describing economics is common: "Economics is the study of how people and society end up choosing, with or without the use of money, to employ scarce production resources that could have alternative uses to produce various commodities and distribute them for consumption." (Jae K. Shim and Joel G. Siegel, *Macroeconomics* (New York: Barron's Educational Series, 2005), 2.

35. A. Smith, *Wealth of Nations*, xxxiv.

36. Marx, *Capital*, vol. 1, 254.

37. Marx to Ludwig Kugelman, 68.

38. Marx, *Capital*, vol. 1, Lawrence and Wishart edition, 152.

39. Karl Marx, *Theories of Surplus Value, Part II* (Moscow: Progress Publishers, 1968), 495.

40. Shakespeare, *King Lear*, act 1, scene 1, line 89 (Glasgow: HarperCollins, 1994), 1129.

41. Marx, *Capital*, vol. 1, 280.

42. Ibid., 274.

43. Ibid., 275.

44. Ibid., 301.

45. Ibid., 671–72.

46. John Stuart Mill, *Principles of Political Economy*, vol. 1(New York: D. Appleton and Company, 1883), 495.

47. Ibid., 509.

48. Marx and Engels, *Communist Manifesto*, 44.

49. Marx, *Capital*, vol. 1, 254.

50. Ibid., 742.

51. See Harry Braverman, *Labor and Monopoly Capital: The Degradation of Work in the Twentieth Century* (New York: Monthly Review Press, 1974), chapters 4–8.

52. Dan Labotz, *Rank and File Rebellion* (New York: Verso Press, 1990), 213.

53. Simon Head, "Worse than Wal-Mart: Amazon's Sick Brutality and Secret History of Ruthlessly Intimidating Workers," *Salon*, February 23, 2014, www.salon.com/2014/02/23/worse_than_wal _mart_amazons_sick_brutality_and_secret_history_of_ruthlessly_intimidating_workers.

54. Michel Beaud, *A History of Capitalism, 1500–2000*, trans. Tom Dickman and Anny Lefebvre (New York: Monthly Review Press, 2001), 131.

55. Jan Fagerberg, "Specialization and Growth: World Manufacturing Productivity 1973–1990," paper prepared for "Technology, Employment and European Cohesion" project, April 1999, available at http://meritbbs.unimaas.nl/tser/tser.html.

56. Bureau of Labor Statistics, US Department of Labor, "Steel Manufacturing," *Career Guide to Industries, 2006–07 Edition*, www.bls.gov/oco/cg/cgs014.htm.

57. Marcel Mazoyer and Laurence Roudart, *A History of World Agriculture: From the Neolithic Age to the Current Crisis* (New York: Monthly Review Press, 2006), 24.

58. Karl Marx, *Capital: A Critique of Political Economy*, vol. 1, in *MECW*, vol. 35, trans. Samuel Moore and Edward Aveling (New York: Progress Publishers, 1996), 750. The phrase reads better in the Moore and Aveling translation than in the Vintage version.

59. Fortune 500 statistics, available at http://money.cnn.com/magazines/fortune/fortune500/2013 /full_list/index.html?iid=F500_sp_full; "California poised to move up in world economy rankings in 2013, Center for Continuing Study of the California Economy, July 2013.

60. It should be noted that there has never been such a thing as "free markets." As noted earlier in this book, capitalism from its origins involved cheating, violence, plunder, slavery, and a great deal of state intervention.

61. Anthony P. D'Costa, *The Global Restructuring of the Steel Industry: Innovations, Institutions, and Industrial Change* (New York: Routledge, 1999), 31.

62. A contraction of a statement by Marx and Engels in *The Communist Manifesto*: "The bourgeoisie, wherever it has got the upper hand, has put an end to all feudal, patriarchal, idyllic relations. It has pitilessly torn asunder the motley feudal ties that bound man to his 'natural superiors,' and has left remaining no other nexus between man and man than naked self-interest, than callous 'cash payment,'" Marx and Engels, *Communist Manifesto*, 43.

63. David McNally, *Global Slump: The Economics and Politics of Crisis and Resistance* (Oakland, CA: PM Press, 2011), 54.

64. Ralph Hoppe, "Globalization: The Global Toothbrush," *Spiegel* online international, January 31, 2006.

65. Marx, *Capital*, vol. 1, 568–69.

66. Erik Rauch, "Productivity and the Workweek," http://groups.csail.mit.edu/mac/users/rauch /worktime.

67. Lewis Mumford, *The Story of Utopias* (New York: Boni and Liveright, 1922), 115–16.

68. Marx, *Capital*, vol. 1, 739.

Chapter Five: Marxist Economics: How Capitalism Fails

1. Marx and Engels, *Communist Manifesto*, 47–48.

2. Ibid., 48.

3.   Engels, *Anti-Dühring*, in *MECW*, vol. 25, 263.

4.   The years vary according to which countries are being discussed, but the trends are clear.

5.   Frances Moore Lappé, "The Myth—Scarcity: The Reality—There IS Enough Food," *Institute for Food and Development Policy Backgrounder* 5, no. 1 (Spring 1998).

6.   Karl Marx, *Capital: A Critique of Political Economy*, vol. 3, trans. David Fernbach (London: Penguin, 1991), 367.

7.   Karl Marx, *Theories of Surplus Value, Part II* (Moscow: Progress Publishers 1968), 527.

8.   Ibid., 522.

9.   Marx, *Capital*, vol. 3, 365.

10.   Ibid., 616.

11.   Marx introduces these terms in *Capital: A Critique of Political Economy*, vol. 2, trans. David Fernbach (New York: Penguin Classics, 1993), 471.

12.   Marx, *Capital*, vol. 3, 363.

13.   Ibid., 362.

14.   McNally, *Global Slump*, 46.

15.   Ibid., 47.

16.   Ibid., 48, 49.

17.   David McNally, "From Financial Crisis to World Slump: Accumulation, Financialization, and the Global Slowdown," *Historical Materialism* 17 (2009), 35.

18.   David McNally, "Financial Meltdown: The Sequel," *Socialistworker.org*, September 26, 2011.

19.   Marx, *Capital*, vol. 3, 569.

20.   Ibid., 515.

21.   Ibid., 516.

22.   Marx, *Capital*, vol. 3, 460.

23.   Ibid., chap. 24; I prefer the translation in this version: www.marxists.org/archive/marx/works/1894-c3/ch24.htm.

24.   Ibid.

25.   David McNally, *Global Slump*, 13.

26.   Luxemburg, *Reform or Revolution*, 41–42.

27.   Ibid., 42.

28.   Lee Sustar, "A Guide to the Wall Street Meltdown," *Socialist Worker*, October 6, 2008.

29.   Petrino DiLeo, "The Road to Ruin," *Socialist Worker*, September 28, 2008.

30.   Lee Sustar, "A Guide to the Wall Street Meltdown."

31.   Jacob Leibenluft, "596 Trillion! How Can the Derivatives Market Be Worth More Than the World's Total Financial Assets?," *Slate*, October 15, 2008, www.slate.com/articles/news_and_politics/explainer/2008/10/596_trillion.html.

32.   Bureau of Labor Statistics, "Steel Manufacturing," www.bls.gov/oco/cg/cgs014.htm.

33.   Steven Greenhouse, "Our Economic Pickle," *New York Times*, January 12, 2013.

34.   What Marx has to say about this is a bit more complicated. He calls the ratio of machinery to workers the "technical composition," while the ratio of the value of constant capital to variable capital is the "value composition." The organic composition is actually "the value-composition of capital, inasmuch as it is determined by, and reflects, its technical composition." (*Capital*, vol. 3, chap. 8, in *MECW*, vol. 38, www.marxists.org/archive/marx/works/1894-c3/ch08.htm.) He makes these distinctions because it is conceivable that there could be an increase in the technical composition, but because the new machinery is so cheap, it is possible that the value composition doesn't change, and therefore the organic composition doesn't rise even though

fewer workers are setting more machinery in motion.

35. Roman Rosdolsky, *The Making of Marx's Capital* (London: Pluto Press, 1977), 408.

36. Karl Marx, *Grundrisse* (London: Penguin Classics, 1993), 340.

37. Marx, *Capital*, vol. 3, 354.

38. Marx, *Grundrisse,* 128.

39. For an explanation of the "permanent arms economy" theory, see Michael Kidron, *Capitalism and Theory* (London: Pluto Press, 1974), 19–23. See also Michael Kidron, "A Permanent Arms Economy," *International Socialism* 1, no. 28 (Spring 1967), www.marxists.org/archive/kidron /works/1967/xx/permarms.htm.

40. Marx, *Grundrisse,* 748.

41. Ibid., 749.

42. Marx, *Capital*, vol. 3, 350.

43. Ibid., 358.

44. Leon Trotsky, *The First Five Years of the Communist International* (New York: Pioneer Publishers, 1945), 62.

Chapter Six: No Power Greater—the Working Class

1. Engels, *Anti-Dühring*, 145.

2. Morris Bierbriar, *The Tomb-Builders of the Pharaohs* (Cairo: American University in Cairo Press, 2003), 41.

3. W. W. Tarn, *Hellenistic Civilization* (New York: Meridian, 1975), 199.

4. Little was actually written about Spartacus, whose story Roman historians weren't keen on playing up. See the chapter on Crassus in Plutarch, *The Fall of the Roman Republic: Six Lives*, trans. Rex Warner (Harmondsworth, UK: Penguin, 1972), 122–27.

5. A. L. Morton, *A People's History of England* (London: Lawrence and Wishart, 1996), 102.

6. Leon Trotsky, "Three Concepts of the Russian Revolution," in *Stalin* (New York: Harper & Brothers, 1941), 425.

7. Frederick Engels, "Principles of Communism," in Marx and Engels, *Communist Manifesto*, 128.

8. Marx, *Capital*, vol. 1, 799.

9. Karl Marx, *Economic and Philosophical Manuscripts*, in *MECW*, vol. 3 (New York: International Publishers, 1975), 274.

10. Engels, "Principles of Communism," 135.

11. Eugene Debs, "Class Unionism," in *Debs: His Life, Writings and Speeches* (Girard, KS: Appeal to Reason, 1908), 419.

12. Karl Marx, *The Eighteenth Brumaire of Louis Bonaparte*, in *MECW*, vol. 11 (New York: International Publishers, 1979), 187.

13. Ralph Chapin, "Solidarity Forever." Lyrics can be found in *The IWW Songbook*, available at www.sacredchao.net/iww/index.shtml.

14. V. I. Lenin, "On Strikes," in *CW*, vol. 4 (Moscow: Progress Publishers, 1977), 315.

15. Ibid.

16. Karl Marx, *The Poverty of Philosophy, MECW*, vol. 6 (Moscow: Progress Publishers, 1976), 210–11.

17. Marx and Engels, *Communist Manifesto*, 55–56.

18. Ibid., 56.

19. Karl Marx, *The Poverty of Philosophy*, in *MECW*, vol. 6 (Moscow: Progress Publishers, 1976),

210–11.

20. Eugene Debs, "Unionism and Socialism," in *Debs: His Life, Writings and Speeches*, 127.

21. Marx, *Value, Price and Profit*, 149.

22. Rosa Luxemburg, *The Mass Strike, The Political Party, and the Trade Unions*, in *Rosa Luxemburg Speaks*, 214–15.

23. Debs, "Unionism and Socialism," 129.

24. Union Members Summary, Bureau of Labor Statistics, January 27, 2012, www.bls.gov /news.release/union2.nr0.htm.

25. Raya Dunayevskaya, *Marxism and Freedom* (London: Pluto Press, 1971), 81.

26. Marx and Engels, *Communist Manifesto*, 68.

27. Leon Trotsky, *The Permanent Revolution and Results and Prospects* (New York: Pathfinder Press, 1976), 57.

28. Karl Marx, *The Civil War in France*, in *MECW*, vol. 22 (New York: International Publishers, 1986), 328.

29. Ibid., 329.

30. Ibid., 334.

31. Ibid., 333.

32. Quoted in Edith Thomas, *The Women Incendiaries* (New York: George Braziller, 1966), x.

33. Marx, *Civil War in France*, 331.

34. Frederick Engels, "Introduction to Karl Marx's *Civil War in France*," in *MECW*, vol. 27, 191.

35. Ibid., 189.

36. Ibid., 190.

37. Leon Trotsky, *1905*, trans. Anya Bostock (New York: Random House, 1971), 224.

38. John Reed, "Soviets in Action," *What Next?*, no. 8 (October 1918), www.marxists.org/history /etol/revhist/otherdox/whatnext/reedsovs.html.

39. For further reading on workers' councils after World War II, see Colin Barker, ed., *Revolutionary Rehearsals* (Chicago: Haymarket Books, 2002); Chris Harman, *Class Struggles in Eastern Europe* (London: Bookmarks, 1988).

40. Peter Fryer, *Hungarian Tragedy* (London: Dobson Books, 1956), chapter 5 ("Györ"), paragraphs 2 and 3, www.marxists.org/archive/fryer/1956/dec/5_gyor.htm.

41. Sharon Smith, *Subterranean Fire: A History of Working-Class Radicalism in the United States* (Chicago: Haymarket Books, 2006), 141.

42. Quoted in Harvey O'Connor, *Revolution in Seattle* (New York: Monthly Review Press, 1964), 133.

43. "General Rules and Administrative Regulations of the International Workingmen's Association," in *MECW*, vol. 23, 3.

44. Eugène Pottier, "The Internationale" (English version), June 1871, www.marxists.org/history /ussr/sounds/lyrics/international.htm.

45. Eugene Debs, "Craft Unionism," in *Debs: His Life, Writings and Speeches*, 392–93.

46. Frederick Engels, "Program of the Blanquist Commune Refugees," in *MECW*, vol. 24, 13.

47. Mikhail Bakunin, "Program and Purpose of the Revolutionary Organization of International Brothers," *Selected Writings*, ed. Arthur Lehning (New York: Grove Press, 1973), 180, 172.

48. Engels, "Program of the Blanquist Commune Refugees," 17.

49. Leon Trotsky, "The Bankruptcy of Individual Terrorism" (1909), www.marxists.org/archive /trotsky/1909/xx/tia09.htm.

50. Leon Trotsky, "On Terrorism," in *Marxism and Terrorism* (New York: Pathfinder Press, 1997), 10.

51. Rosa Luxemburg, "Speech to the Founding Convention of the German Communist Party," *Rosa Luxemburg Speaks* (New York: Pathfinder Press, 1980), 419.

52. Michel De Montaigne, "On the Cannibals," in *The Complete Essays* (London: Penguin, 1991), 240–41.

53. George Orwell, *1984* (New York: Signet Classics, 1984), 60.

54. Ibid., 61–62.

55. Ibid., 61.

56. Voltaire, *Candide* (New York: Modern Library, 1918), 2.

57. Leon Trotsky, *History of the Russian Revolution* (Ann Arbor: University of Michigan Press, 1974), xviii.

58. Antonio Gramsci, *Selections from the Prison Notebooks* (New York: International Publishers, 1980), 333.

59. Marx and Engels, *The German Ideology*, 75.

60. Hal Draper, *Karl Marx's Theory of Revolution*, vol. 2 (New York: Monthly Review Press, 1978), 42.

61. Lenin, "On Strikes," 317.

62. V. I. Lenin, "Lecture on the 1905 Revolution," in *CW*, vol. 23 (Moscow: Progress Publishers, 1981), 243.

63. Karl Marx to W. Bracke, May 5, 1875, in *MECW*, vol. 45 (New York: International Publishers, 1991), 70.

64. Trotsky, *History of the Russian Revolution*, xviii.

65. Quoted in Maryam Poya, "Iran 1979: Long Live Revolution! . . . Long Live Islam?," ed. Colin Barker, *Revolutionary Rehearsals* (Chicago: Haymarket Books, 2002), 147–48.

66. Farrell Dobbs, *Teamster Rebellion* (New York: Pathfinder Press, 1981), 50.

67. James W. Loewen, *Lies My Teacher Told Me: Everything Your American History Textbook Got Wrong* (New York: The New Press, 1995), 196.

68. Frederick R. Strobel and Wallace C. Peterson, *The Coming Class War and How to Avoid It: Rebuilding the American Middle Class* (Armonk, NY: M. E. Sharpe, 1999), xii.

69. Zweig, *Working Class Majority*, 19.

70. Barbara Ehrenriech's 1979 study put the figure higher, but she included teachers and social workers in her estimation of the size of what she calls the "professional managerial class." But teachers and social workers are part of the working class by any reasonable assessment. See Pat Walker, ed., *Between Labor and Capital* (Boston: South End Press, 1979).

71. Leon Trotsky, *The Intelligentsia and Socialism* (London: New Park, 1974), 10–11.

72. Ibid., 8.

73. Marx and Engels, *Communist Manifesto*, 78.

74. Draper, *Karl Marx's Theory of Revolution*, vol. 2, 297.

75. Quoted in Alex Callinicos, *South Africa Between Reform and Revolution* (London: Bookmarks, 1988), 64–65.

76. Quoted in Ashwin Desai, "Mandela's Legacy," *International Socialist Review* 35 (May–June 2004).

77. V. I. Lenin, *Two Tactics of Social Democracy in the Democratic Revolution*, in *CW*, vol. 9 (Moscow: Progress Publishers, 1972), 19.

78. Marx and Engels, "Address of the Central Authority to the League," 280.

79. Ibid., 281.

Chapter Seven: Democracy, Reform, and Revolution

1. Robert Dahl, *A Preface to Democratic Theory*, expanded edition (Chicago: University of Chicago Press, 2006), 137.

2. Paul Foot, *The Politics of Harold Wilson* (London: Penguin Books, 1968), 338.

3. G. William Domhoff, "Wealth, Income and Power," Who Rules America?, www2.ucsc.edu /whorulesamerica/power/wealth.html.

4. Joe Nocera, "Romney and the Forbes 400," *New York Times*, September 24, 2012.

5. Marx and Engels, *Communist Manifesto*, 43.

6. Quoted in Leon Trotsky, *Terrorism and Communism* (Ann Arbor, MI: Ann Arbor Paperbacks, 1972), 41.

7. OpenSecrets.org Lobbying Database, www.opensecrets.org/lobby/index.php and Lobbying Spending Database Labor, 2012, www.opensecrets.org/lobby/indus.php.

8. Nicholas Confessore and Jo Craven McGinty, "Obama, Romney and Their Parties on Track to Raise $2 Billion," *New York Times*, October 25, 2012; "Presidential Fundraising and Spending, 1976–2008," OpenSecrets.org (Center for Responsive Politics), www.opensecrets.org /pres08/totals.php?cycle=2004.

9. "Revolving Door: Goldman Sachs," OpenSecrets.org (Center for Responsive Politics), www.opensecrets.org/revolving/search_result.php?priv=Goldman+Sachs.

10. "Undue Influence," Pesticide Action Network, www.panna.org/issues/pesticides-profit/undue -influence.

11. See, for example, *Rolling Stone*'s article on the Gulf Oil spill and the way in which oil and gas interests largely influence the decisions of the Interior Department's Minerals Management Service under both the Bush and Obama administrations: Tim Dickinson, "The Spill, the Scandal, and the President," *Rolling Stone*, June 8, 2010.

12. Michael Parenti, *Democracy for the Few* (New York: St. Martin's Press, 1988), 302.

13. Karl Marx, *The Eighteenth Brumaire of Louis Napoleon*, in *MECW*, vol. 11, 115.

14. Steven Rosenfeld, "Obama's Dismal Civil Liberties Record," *Salon.com*, April 20, 2012, www.salon.com/2012/04/20/obamas_dismal_civil_liberties_record.

15. Quoted in Stephen M. Kohn, *American Political Prisoners: Prosecutions under the Espionage and Sedition Acts* (Westport, CT: Praeger, 1994), 8.

16. Quoted in ibid., 9.

17. See James P. Cannon, *Socialism on Trial* (New York: Pathfinder Press, 1986).

18. Jim Robbins, "Pardons Granted 88 Years after Crimes of Sedition," *New York Times*, May 3, 2006.

19. Quoted in Kohn, *American Political Prisoners*, 114.

20. Eugene Debs, "Canton, Ohio Speech, Anti-War Speech," www.marxists.org/archive/debs /works/1918/canton.htm. Rosa Luxemburg made a similar statement. Bourgeois justice is, she wrote, "like a net, which allowed the voracious sharks to escape, while the little sardines were caught." Rosa Luxemburg, "Against Capital Punishment," *International Socialist Review* 30, no. 1, January–February 1969.

21. Anatole France, *The Red Lily*, e-book, www.gutenberg.org/files/3922/3922.txt.

22. Eugene Debs, "The Role of the Courts," in *Eugene V. Debs Speaks* (New York: Pathfinder Press, 1980), 52.

23. Quoted in Philip S. Foner, *The Great Labor Uprising of 1877* (New York: Pathfinder Press, 1977), 167.

24. "FAMM Facts: Crack vs. Cocaine Sentencing," report, Families Against Mandatory Minimums Web site, 2002, www.famm.org/si_crack_powder_sentencing_fact_sheet.htm.

25. "Three Strikes Law: A Big Error," *Los Angeles Times*, August 19, 2010; "Three Strikes of Injustice," *New York Times*, October 8, 2012.

26. Charles Ferguson, *Predator Nation: Corporate Criminals, Political Corruption, and the Hijacking of America* (New York: Crown Business, 2012), Kindle e-book.

27. Ted Nace, *Gangs of America: The Rise of Corporate Power and the Disabling of Democracy* (San Francisco: Berrett-Koehler, 2003), 8.

28. Kevin Phillips, *The Politics of Rich and Poor* (New York: Random House, 1990), 32.

29. Frederick Engels to Friedrich Adolph Sorge, December 2, 1893, in *Marx and Engels on the United States* (Moscow: Progress Publishers, 1979), 333.

30. Frederick Engels, "Introduction to Karl Marx's *The Civil War in France*," in *MECW*, vol. 27, 189.

31. Eugene Debs, "Outlook for Socialism in the United States," in *Debs: His Life, Writings and Speeches*, 90–91.

32. Richard A. Harris and Sidney M. Milkis, *Remaking American Politics* (Boulder, CO: Westview Press, 1989), 185n.

33. Quoted in C. Vann Woodward, *Tom Watson: Agrarian Radical* (New York: Oxford University Press, 1963), 328. Watson later became a vicious racist.

34. Ibid., 311.

35. Joe Allen, "Vietnam: The War the U.S. Lost: Part II," *International Socialist Review* 33 (January–February 2004).

36. Quoted in Lance Selfa, *The Democrats: A Critical History*, 2nd ed. (Chicago: Haymarket Books, 2012), 93.

37. David Saltonstall, "Obama Has Collected Nearly Twice as Much Money as John McCain," *New York Daily News*, July 1, 2008, www.nydailynews.com/news/politics/barack-obama-collected-money-john-mccain-article-1.351304.

38. Selfa, *The Democrats*, 92.

39. Ibid., 3.

40. Selfa, *The Democrats*, 99.

41. "The Next President of Austerity," *Socialist Worker* online, November 1, 2012.

42. Lee Sustar, "The Austerity vs. Austerity Debate," *Socialist Worker* online, February 27, 2013.

43. Jordan Fabian, "Obama: More Moderate Republican Than Socialist," ABC News, December 14, 2012, http://abcnews.go.com/ABC_Univision/Politics/obama-considered-moderate-republican-1980s/story?id=17973080.

44. Suzy Khimm, "Obama Is Deporting Immigrants Faster Than Bush. Republicans Don't Think That's Enough," *Wonkblog*, August 27, 2012, www.washingtonpost.com/blogs/wonkblog/wp/2012/08/27/obama-is-deporting-more-immigrants-than-bush-republicans-dont-think-thats-enough.

45. Frederick Engels to Friedrich Adolph Sorge, November 29, 1886, in *CW*, vol. 47 (New York: Progress Publishers, 1995), 532.

46. Selfa, *The Democrats*, 10, 26.

47. Karl Marx and Frederick Engels, "Address of the Central Authority to the League," in *MECW*, vol. 10 (New York: International Publishers, 1978), 284.

48. Quoted in Paul D'Amato, "Kucinich: Kerry's Bagman," *International Socialist Review* 37 (September–October 2004).

49. Dennis Kucinich, "A Joint Message with My Friend John Conyers," *Daily Kos*, www.dailykos .com/story/2009/11/05/801123/-A-joint-message-with-my-friend-John-Conyers.

50. Adolph Reed, "Nothing Left: The Long, Slow Surrender of America Liberals," *Harper's*, March 2014.

51. Hal Draper, "Who Is Going to Be the Lesser Evil in 1968?," in *The New Left of the Sixties*, ed. Michael Friedman (Berkeley, CA: Independent Socialist Press, 1972), 57, www.isreview.org /issues/32/draper.shtml.

52. Herbert Haines, *Against Capital Punishment: The Anti-Death Penalty Movement in America, 1972–1994* (New York: Oxford University Press, 1999), 133.

53. "The Sleeping Giant," *New York Times*, editorial, April 29, 2006.

54. Martin Luther King Jr., "Letter from a Birmingham Jail," in *Let Freedom Ring: A Documentary History of the Modern Civil Rights Movement* (Westport, CT: Praeger, 1992), 111.

55. The gist of this section is largely derived from chapter 1 in Hal Draper, "Patterns of Revolution," in his second volume of *Karl Marx's Theory of Social Revolution: The Politics of Social Classes* (New York: Monthly Review), 17–48.

56. Quoted in ibid., 19.

57. Engels, *Anti-Dühring*, 171.

58. Draper, *Karl Marx's Theory of Revolution*, vol. 2, 29.

59. Ibid., 20.

60. Ibid., 31.

61. Eduard Bernstein, *Evolutionary Socialism* (New York: Schocken, 1961), 202.

62. Quoted in John Riddell, ed., *Lenin's Struggle for a Revolutionary International: Documents, 1907–1916* (New York: Monad Press, 1984), 10.

63. Albert Rhys Williams, *Through the Russian Revolution* (New York: Boni and Liveright, 1921), 174.

64. Quoted in James Hinton, *Labour and Socialism: A History of the British Labour Movement, 1867–1974* (Amherst, MA: University of Massachusetts Press, 1983), 149.

65. Luxemburg, *Reform or Revolution*, 56.

66. Fred Branfman, "The Top 10 Most Inhuman Henry Kissinger Quotes," *Alternet*, April 24, 2013, www.alternet.org/world/top-10-most-inhuman-henry-kissinger-quotes.

67. See Tom Lewis, "Chile: The State and Revolution," *International Socialist Review* 6 (Spring 1999) and Mike Gonzales, "Chile 1972–73: The Workers United," in *Revolutionary Rehearsals*, ed. Colin Barker (Chicago: Haymarket Books, 2002), 41–47.

68. Quoted in Paul Ginsborg, *A History of Contemporary Italy: Society and Politics 1943–1988* (London: Penguin Books, 1990), 355.

69. Leon Trotsky, "Whither France?," in *Leon Trotsky on France* (New York: Monad Press, 1979), 45. The original quote (without the ellipsis points) is "do not balk," which must be a mistake either by Trotsky or his translator, since balk means to stop short. If the working class balks (that is, stops short) then the ruling class is not obliged to stop them.

70. See, for example, Marx, *The Eighteenth Brumaire*, in *MECW*, vol. 11, 161.

71. Karl Marx and Frederick Engels, "Circular Letter to Bebel, Liebknecht, Bracke and Others," in *MECW*, vol. 24, 266.

72. Karl Marx, "Address to the Central Committee of the Communist League," in *On Revolution*, ed. Saul K. Padover (New York: McGraw-Hill, 1971), 117.

73. Ibid., 269.

74. Rosa Luxemburg, "Opportunism and the Art of the Possible," *Sächsische Arbeiter Zeitung*, Sep-

tember 30, 1898, Rosa Luxemburg Internet archive, www.marxists.org/archive/luxemburg/1898/09/30.htm.

75. It was a phrase coined by Wilhelm Leibknecht in 1871, quoted in Gary P. Steensen, *Not One Man! Not One Penny! German Social Democracy, 1863–1914* (Pittsburgh, PA: University of Pittsburgh Press, 1981), xi.

76. Quoted in Rosa Luxemburg, "Rebuilding the International," *Die Internationale*, no. 1, 1915, Rosa Luxemburg Internet archive, www.marxists.org/archive/luxemburg/1915/rebuild-int.htm.

77. Ibid.

78. See, for example, Daniel Singer, *Is Socialism Doomed? The Meaning of Mitterand* (New York: Oxford University Press, 1988), and Daniel Singer, *Whose Millennium? Theirs or Ours?* (New York: Monthly Review Press, 1999), 129–49.

79. Daniel Singer, *Is Socialism Doomed?*, 265.

80. Ibid., 267.

81. Ibid.

82. The term "third way" was popularized by Bill Clinton and Tony Blair in the 1990s. Its theorist is Anthony Giddens. See his book, *The Third Way: The Renewal of Social Democracy* (London: Polity Press, 2000).

83. Luxemburg, *Reform or Revolution*, 77–78.

84. Lenin, "Marxism and Reformism," in *CW*, vol. 19 (Moscow: Progress Publishers, 1977), 372.

85. Marx and Engels, *The German Ideology*, 52–53.

86. Trotsky, *History of the Russian Revolution*, xvii.

87. V. I. Lenin, "The Collapse of the Second International," in *CW*, vol. 21 (Moscow: Progress Publishers, 1980), 213–14.

88. Trotsky, *1905*, 102.

89. Trotsky, *History of the Russian Revolution*, 120.

90. Ibid., 121.

91. Ibid., 105.

92. Foner, *The Great Labor Uprising of 1877*, 72.

93. Tony Cliff, *Portugal at the Crossroads*, in *Selected Writings*, vol. 1, 238.

Chapter Eight: From Marx to Lenin: Marxism and Political Organization

1. Karl Marx and Frederick Engels, *The Holy Family*, in *MECW*, vol. 4, 93.

2. Karl Marx, "Introduction," *Contribution to a Critique of Hegel's Philosophy of Law*, in *MECW*, vol. 3, 186.

3. Marx and Engels, *The Holy Family*, 119.

4. Frederick Engels, "On the History of the Communist League," in *MECW*, vol. 26 (New York: International Publishers, 1990), 318.

5. Hal Draper, *Karl Marx's Theory of Revolution*, vol. 1: *The Politics of Social Classes* (New York: Monthly Review, 1978), 53.

6. Antonio Gramsci, *Selections from the Prison Notebooks* (New York: International Publishers, 1980), 197.

7. Draper, *Karl Marx's Theory of Revolution*, 29.

8. Marx, "Introduction," *Contribution to a Critique of Hegel's Philosophy of Law*, 184.

9. Marx and Engels, *Communist Manifesto*, 53.

10. Marx and Engels, "Resolutions of the Conference of Delegates of the International Working Men's Association," in *MECW*, vol. 22 (New York: International Publishers, 1986), 427.

11. Engels, "On the Political Action of the Working Class," in *MECW*, vol. 22 (New York: International Publishers, 1986), 417.

12. Engels, *The Origin of the Family, Private Property and the State* (New York: Progress Publishers, 1985), 232.

13. Engels to Gherson Trier (draft), December 1889, in *MECW*, vol. 48 (New York: International Publishers, 2001), 423.

14. Marx and Engels, *Communist Manifesto*, 58–59.

15. Ibid., 87–89.

16. Marx to Bracke, May 5, 1875, in *MECW*, vol. 45 (New York: International Publishers, 1991), 70.

17. Engels to Florence Kelley-Wischnewetzky, in *MECW*, vol. 47 (New York: International Publishers, 1995), 541.

18. Engels to Florence Kelley-Wischnewetzky, *Marx and Engels on the United States* (Moscow: Progress Publishers, 1979), 317.

19. Letter from Marx to Schweitzer (October 13, 1868), www.marxists.org/archive/marx/works/1868/letters/68_10_13-abs.htm.

20. Engels to August Bebel in Hubertsburg, London, June 20, 1873, www.marxists.org/archive/marx/works/1873/letters/73_06_20.htm.

21. Marx quoted in August H. Nimtz, *Marx and Engels: Their Contribution to the Democratic Breakthrough* (New York: State University of New York Press, 2000), 46.

22. Karl Kautsky, *The Road to Power* (Atlantic Highlands, NJ: Humanities Press, 1996), 38.

23. Quoted in Massimo Salvadori, *Karl Kautsky and the Socialist Revolution, 1880–1938* (London: New Left Books, 1979), 162.

24. Kautsky, "Sects or Class Parties," *Neue Zeit* 13, no. 7 (July 1909): 316–28, www.marxists.org/archive/kautsky/1909/07/unions.htm.

25. "Resolution on Unification and Statements at the London Conference of the International Socialist Bureau, December 14, 1913," in *The Bolsheviks and World War*, Olga Hess Gankin and H. H. Fisher, eds. (Stanford, CA: Stanford University Press, 1940), 94.

26. "Congress Debate on Colonial Policy," in *Lenin's Struggle for a Revolutionary International: Documents, 1907–1916, the Preparatory Years*, John Riddell, ed., (New York: Monad Press, 1984), 10.

27. Pierre Broué, *The German Revolution, 1917–1923* (Chicago: Haymarket Books, 2006), 21, 23.

28. The antiwar resolutions at the Second International's 1907 Stuttgart and 1910 Copenhagen conference can be found in John Riddell, ed., *Lenin's Struggle for a Revolutionary International*, 33 and 70.

29. Quoted in J. P. Nettle, *Rosa Luxemburg*, vol. 1 (London: Oxford University Press, 1966), 375.

30. Ibid., 368.

31. Georg Adler, Peter Hudis, Annelies Laschitza, eds., *The Letters of Rosa Luxemburg* (New York: Verso Press, 2011), 242.

32. Quoted in Broué, *German Revolution*, 35.

33. Nettle, *Rosa Luxemburg*, 430–31.

34. The irony of this is that in Luxemberg's native Poland the Socialist movement (which she was also active in) was split into different factions and organizations.

35. Lenin, "The Proletarian Revolution and the Renegade Kautsky," in *CW*, vol. 28 (Moscow: Progress Publishers, 1981), 112.

36. Lenin, "The Junius Pamphlet," in *CW*, vol. 22 (Moscow: Progress Publishers, 1977), 319.

37. Lenin, *"Left-Wing" Communism: An Infantile Disorder*, in *CW*, vol. 31 (Moscow: Progress Publishers, 1982), 25–26.

38. "The academic historians who laid the basis of the textbook interpretation constituted the first generation in postwar Soviet studies: Leopold Haimson, Alfred G. Meyer, Adam Ulam, Leonard Schapiro, John Keep, Samuel Baron, Allan Wildman, Israel Getzler, Abraham Ascher, Richard Pipes, Jonathan Frankel." Lars T. Lih, *Lenin Rediscovered: "What Is to Be Done?" in Context* (Chicago: Haymarket Books, 2008), 14. Lih also performs a useful exegesis of the genesis of the "Lenin as elitist" formula in his article, "How a Founding Document Was Found, or, One Hundred Years of Lenin's *What Is to Be Done?*," in *Kritika: Explorations in Russian and Eurasian History* 4, no. 1 (2003): 5–49.

39. Lenin, "The Reorganization of the Party," in *CW*, vol. 10 (Moscow: Progress Publishers, 1978), 33.

40. Lenin, "Letter to A. A. Bogdanov and S. I. Gusev," in *CW*, vol. 8, 147.

41. Lenin, "Freedom to Criticize and Unity of Action," in *CW*, vol. 10, 443.

42. Lenin, "The Revolutionary Proletariat and the Right of Nations to Self-Determination," in *CW*, vol. 21 (Moscow: Progress Publishers, 1980), 408.

43. Lenin, "The Urgent Tasks of Our Movement," in *CW*, vol. 4, 370.

44. N. K. Krupskaya, *Reminiscences of Lenin* (New York: International Publishers, 1979), 19.

45. Broué, *The German Revolution,* 12.

46. Moira Donald, *Marxism and Revolution: Karl Kautsky and the Russia Marxists, 1900–1924* (New Haven, CT: Yale University Press, 1993), 39.

47. Quoted in Lenin, "A Protest by Russian Social Democrats," in *Collected Works*, vol. 4, (Moscow: Progress Publishers, 1977), 173–74.

48. Ibid., 176.

49. Ibid., 180.

50. Lenin, "Declaration of the Editorial Board of *Iskra*," www.marxists.org/archive/lenin/works/1900/sep/iskra.htm.

51. Translated and annotated by Brian Pearce, *1903: Second Ordinary Congress of the RSDLP: Complete Text of the Minutes* (London: New Park Publications, 1978), 311.

52. Ibid., 313.

53. Ibid., 327.

54. Lenin, *One Step Forward, Two Steps Back*, in *CW*, vol. 7 (Moscow: Progress Publishers, 1977), 258.

55. Ibid., 258–59.

56. Ibid., 260.

57. Duncan Hallas, "Toward a Revolutionary Socialist Party," in *Party and Class* (Chicago: Haymarket Books, 2003), 45.

58. Lenin, *What Is to Be Done?*, in *CW*, vol. 5 (Moscow: Progress Publishers, 1973), 426.

59. Lenin, "Revolutionary Days," in *CW*, vol. 8 (Moscow: Progress Publishers, 1962), 101.

60. Lenin, "The Two Tactics of Social Democracy in the Democratic Revolution," in *CW*, vol. 9 (Moscow: Progress Publishers, 1972), 113.

61. Lenin, "Revolution Teaches," in *CW*, vol. 9 (Moscow: Progress Publishers, 1972), 148.

62. Lenin, "Argue about Tactics, But Give Clear Slogans!," in *CW*, vol. 9 (Moscow: Progress Publishers, 1972), 262.

63. Lenin, "The Faction of Supporters of Otzovism and God-Building," in *CW*, vol. 16 (Moscow:

Progress Publishers, 1977), 36–37.

64. Quoted in Tony Cliff, *Lenin: Building the Party* (London: Bookmarks, 1994), 250.

65. Ibid., 251.

66. A. S. Martynov, *Two Dictatorships*, quoted in Tony Cliff, "Deflected Permanent Revolution," *International Socialism* 12 (Spring 1963).

67. The irony is that the French Revolution was actually led by the radical petty bourgeoisie, pushed from below by the sansculottes, even though the bourgeoisie was the main beneficiary of the revolution. Neil Davidson's recent articles in *Historical Materialism* are good on this question: "How revolutionary were the bourgeois revolutions?," *Historical Materialism* 13, nos. 3 and 4 (2005). In fact there may never have been a bourgeois revolution actually led by the bourgeoisie.

68. Lenin, "The Democratic Tasks of the Revolutionary Proletariat," in *CW*, vol. 8 (Moscow: Progress Publishers, 1978), 511.

69. Lenin, "Report of the C.C. of the R.S.D.L.P. to the Brussels Conference and Instructions to the C.C. Delegation," in *CW*, vol. 20 (Moscow: Progress Publishers, 1977), 498–99.

70. Neil Harding, *Lenin's Political Thought*, vol. 1: *Theory and Practice of the Democracy Revolution* (Chicago: Haymarket Books, 2009), 263.

71. Ibid., 501.

72. Chris Harman, "Party and Class," in Cliff, Hallas, Harman, Trotsky, *Party and Class* (Chicago: Haymarket Books, 2003), 34.

73. Rosa Luxemburg, "Organizational Questions of Russian Social Democracy," in *The Russian Revolution and Leninism or Marxism?* (Ann Arbor, MI: University of Michigan Press, 1961), 105.

74. Lenin, "The Social Democrats and the Elections in St. Petersburg," in *CW*, vol. 11 (Moscow: Progress Publishers, 1972), 434–35.

75. Trotsky, *What Next? Vital Questions for the German Proletariat*, www.marxists.org/archive/trotsky/germany/1932-ger/next01.htm.

76. Trotsky, "The Class, the Party, and the Leadership" (1940), www.marxists.org/archive/trotsky/1940/xx/party.htm.

77. Colin Barker, "Solidarnosc: From Gdansk to Military Repression," *International Socialism* 15 (Winter 1982): 93.

78. Barker, *Festival of the Oppressed: Solidarity, Reform and Revolution in Poland, 1980–81* (London: Bookmarks, 1986), 150.

79. Trotsky, *History of the Russian Revolution* (Chicago: Haymarket Books, 2008), xvi.

80. Hallas, "Toward a Revolutionary Socialist Party," 38.

Chapter Nine: Russia: The God That Failed?

1. Eugene Debs, "The Day of the People," in *Eugene V. Debs Speaks*, 293.

2. For an excellent account of the party's growth, its debates, and its overall conduct in the months before October, read Alexander Rabinowitch, *The Bolsheviks Come to Power* (Chicago: Haymarket Books, 2004).

3. Morgan Phillips Price, *Dispatches from the Revolution: Russia, 1916–1918* (Durham, NC: Duke University Press, 1998), 81.

4. Russia was still using the Julian calendar.

5. Trotsky, *History of the Russian Revolution*, 378.

6. Ibid., 468.

7. Tsuyoshi Hasegawa, *The February Revolution: Petrograd 1917* (Seattle: University of Wash-

ington Press, 1981), 75.

8.   Quoted in Lionel Kochan, *Russia in Revolution* (New York: New American Library, 1966), 187.

9.   Ibid., 188.

10. Marx and Engels, "Address of the Central Authority to the League," in *MECW*, vol. 10, 281.

11. Trotsky, *History of the Russian Revolution*, 59.

12. Ibid., 57.

13. Trotsky, *History of the Russian Revolution*, xv.

14. Trotsky, *History of the Russian Revolution*, 80–81.

15. See Trotsky, "Dual Power," chapter 11 in *History of the Russian Revolution*.

16. Trotsky, *History of the Russian Revolution*, 159.

17. In particular, members of an organization called the Mezhiarontsy, or Inter-district Committee, which soon joined the Bolshevik Party, played an important role in the streets during February. See Jason Yanowitz, "February's Forgotten Vanguard: The Myth of Russia's Spontaneous Revolution," *International Socialist Review* 75, January–February 2011.

18. Ibid., 167.

19. Ibid., 173.

20. Lenin, The Tasks of the Proletariat in the Present Revolution," in *CW*, vol. 25 (Moscow: Progress Publishers, 1980), 22.

21. Ibid., 23.

22. Lenin, "The Tasks of the Proletariat in Our Revolution," ibid., 85.

23. Quoted in Tony Cliff, *All Power to the Soviets: Lenin, 1914–1917* (Chicago: Haymarket Books, 2004), 110.

24. Quoted in Rabinowitch, *Bolsheviks Come to Power*, 132.

25. Leon Trotsky, *History of the Russian Revolution*, 527.

26. Ibid., 529.

27. Rabinowitch, *Bolsheviks Come to Power*, 148.

28. Ibid., 311–12.

29. John Reed, *Ten Days That Shook the World* (New York: International Publishers, 1982), 292.

30. Lenin quoted in Tony Cliff, *State Capitalism in Russia* (London: Pluto Press, 1974), 144–45. The quote was stricken, according to Cliff, from the fourth edition of volume 25 of Lenin's *Collected Works*.

31. Leon Trotsky, "Three Concepts of the Russian Revolution," appendix, *Stalin* (New York: Harper and Brothers Publishing, 1941), 432. I used this version of the quote because I think it reads better than the Pathfinder translation of Trotsky's 1906 work, *Results and Prospects*, from which it comes.

32. Lenin, *Left-Wing Communism: An "Infantile" Disorder*, in *MECW*, vol. 31 (Moscow: Progress Publishers, 1982), 21.

33. Tony Cliff, *State Capitalism in Russia*, 148.

34. Marx and Engels, *The German Ideology*, 49.

35. Frederick Engels, *The Peasant War in Germany*, in *MECW*, vol. 10, 469–70.

36. See Pierre Broué's masterful history, *The German Revolution* (Chicago: Haymarket Books, 2006).

37. Victor Serge, *Year One of the Russian Revolution* (New York: Holt, Rinehart and Winston, 1972), 79, 89.

38. E. H. Carr, *The Bolshevik Revolution: 1917–1923*, vol. 2 (London: Pelican Books, 1972), 197–98.

39. Lenin, "The New Economic Policy and the Tasks of the Political Education Departments,"

MECW, vol. 33 (Moscow: Progress Publishers, 1980), 65–67.

40. Hallas, "Toward a Revolutionary Socialist Party," 43.

41. Tony Cliff, *Revolution Besieged: Lenin: 1917–1923* (London: Bookmarks, 1987), 110.

42. V. I. Lenin, "Political Report to the Central Committee of the RCP(B)," in *CW*, vol. 33 (Moscow: Progress Publishers, 1980), 288.

43. Leon Trotsky, *The Revolution Betrayed* (New York: Pathfinder Press, 2002), 86.

44. Hallas, "Toward a Revolutionary Socialist Party."

45. Quoted in Alex Nove, *An Economic History of the USSR* (London: Pelican Books, 1982), 189.

46. Rosa Luxemburg, "The Russian Revolution," in *Rosa Luxemburg Speaks*, 394–95.

47. Frederick Engels, *Socialism: Utopian and Scientific*, in *MECW*, vol. 24, 318n.

48. Ibid., 319.

49. Leon Trotsky, "Trade Unions in the Epoch of Imperialist Decay," in *Marxism and the Trade Unions* (New York: Labor Publications, 1973), 17.

50. Quoted in Barker, *Festival of the Oppressed*, 93.

51. Engels, *Socialism: Utopian and Scientific*, 319.

52. For an analysis of the Cuban Revolution and its aftermath, see Sam Farber, *Revolution and Reaction in Cuba, 1933–1960* (Middletown, CT: Wesleyan University Press, 1960); Sam Farber, *The Origins of the Cuban Revolution Reconsidered* (Chapel Hill, NC: University of North Carolina Press, 2006); Sam Farber, *Cuba Since the Revolution of 1959: A Critical Assessment* (Chicago: Haymarket Books, 2011). See also: Paul D'Amato, "Cuba: Image and Reality," *International Socialist Review* 51, January–February 2007.

53. Quoted in Carmelo Mesa-Lago, *Cuba in the 1970s: Pragmatism and Institutionalization* (Albuquerque, NM: University of Arizona Press, 1974), 80.

54. Ibid., 81.

55. Engels, *Socialism: Utopian and Scientific*, in *MECW*, vol. 24, 325.

Chapter Ten: Imperialism, Nationalism, and War

1. Eric Hobsbawm, "War and Peace in the 20th Century," *London Review of Books* 24, no. 4 (February 2002), http://www.lrb.co.uk/v24/n04/hobs01_.html.

2. Michael Ghiglieri, *The Dark Side of Man* (New York: Basic Books, 1999). See chapter 1, "Born to Be Bad?"

3. Richard Wrangham and Dale Peterson, *Demonic Males: Apes and the Origins of Human Violence* (New York: Mariner Books, 1996), 63.

4. Frans de Waal and Frans Lanting, *Bonobo: The Forgotten Ape* (Berkeley and Los Angeles: University of California Press, 1997), 2.

5. Chagnon quoted in Richard H. Robbins, *Cultural Anthropology: A Problem-Based Approach* (Belmont, CA: Wadsworth, 2013), 320.

6. R. Brian Ferguson, "A Savage Encounter: Western Contact and the Yanomami War Complex," R. Brian Ferguson and Neil L. Whitehead, eds., *War in the Tribal Zone: Expanding States and Indigenous Warfare* (Santa Fe, NM: School of American Research Press, 1992), 201.

7. Quoted in Douglas P. Fry, *The Human Potential for Peace: An Anthropological Challenge to Assumptions about War and Violence* (London: Oxford University Press, 2006), 100–1.

8. Cited in ibid., 97.

9. Robert H. Lowie, *Indians of the Plains* (Garden City, NY: The Natural History Press, 1963), 117–18.

10. Quoted in Francis Jennings, *The Invasion of America: Indians, Colonialism and the Cant of Conquest* (New York: Norton, 1976), 150.

11. Quoted in ibid.

12. Ashley Montagu, *Man in Process* (Cleveland, OH: World Publishing Company, 1961), 92.

13. Marx, *Capital*, vol. 1, 915–16.

14. Lance Selfa, "A New Colonial 'Age of Empire'?," *International Socialist Review* 23 (May–June 2002).

15. Stefan Kanfer, *The Last Empire: De Beers, Diamonds, and the World* (New York: Noonday Press, 1993), 116–25.

16. Ibid., 124.

17. Adam Hochschild, *King Leopold's Ghost* (New York, Houghton Mifflin, 1998), 66.

18. Ibid., 165.

19. Ibid., 160.

20. Mike Davis, *Late Victorian Holocausts* (New York: Verso, 2001), 32.

21. Ibid., 311.

22. Sidney Lens, *The Forging of the American Empire* (Chicago: Haymarket Books, 2004), 2.

23. William McKinley, "Remarks to Methodist Delegation," in *The Philippines Reader*, Daniel B. Schirmer and Stephen R. Shalom, eds. (Boston: South End Press, 1987), 22.

24. Luzviminda Francisco, "The Philippine-American War," in *The Philippines Reader*, 17.

25. Ibid., 18–19.

26. Quoted in Helen Scott, "The Mark Twain They Didn't Teach Us in School," *International Socialist Review* 10 (Winter 2000).

27. Scott Nearing and Joseph Freeman, *Dollar Diplomacy* (New York: Modern Reader, 1969), 133, 151; Hans Schmidt, *The United States Occupation of Haiti, 1915–1934* (New Brunswick, NJ: Rutgers University Press, 1995).

28. Quoted in Lens, *Forging of the American Empire*, 195.

29. V. I. Lenin, *Imperialism: The Highest Stage of Capitalism*, in *CW*, vol. 22, 298, 300.

30. See Massimo Salvadori, *Karl Kautsky and the Socialist Revolution, 1880–1938* (London: New Left Books, 1980), 181–203. Kautsky's 1914 article, "Ultra-Imperialism," can be found online at the Marxist Internet Archive, www.marxists.org/archive/kautsky/1914/09/ultra-imp.htm.

31. V. I. Lenin, "Critical Remarks on the National Question," *Questions of National Policy and Proletarian Internationalism* (Moscow: Progress Publishers, 1970), 20.

32. Nikolai Bukharin, *Imperialism and World Economy* (New York: Monthly Review Press, 1973), 106–7.

33. Leon Trotsky, *The Bolsheviki and World Peace* (New York: Boni & Liveright, Inc., 1918), 20–22. This text was also published as "The War and the International," and is available at www.marxists.org/archive/trotsky/1914/war/index.htm.

34. Ibid.

35. For a rundown of US Cold War interventions, see William Blum, *Rogue State: A Guide to the World's Only Superpower* (Monroe, ME: Common Courage Press, 2000); and William Blum, *The CIA: A Forgotten History* (London: Zed Books, 1986).

36. Peter Starck, "World Military Spending Topped $1 Trillion in 2004," Reuters, June 7, 2005.

37. Chalmers Johnson, *The Sorrows of Empire: Militarism, Secrecy, and the End of the Republic* (New York: Metropolitan Books, 2004), 4.

38. Condoleezza Rice, address at the Paul H. Nitze School of Advanced International Studies, Johns Hopkins University, Washington, DC, April 29, 2002.

39. "The President's Real Goal in Iraq," *Atlanta Journal-Constitution*, September 29, 2002.

40. George W. Bush, "President Outlines Priorities," press conference, November 7, 2002, www.whitehouse.gov/news/releases/2002/11/20021107-2.html.

41. William Christie MacLeod, *The American Indian Frontier* (New York: Alfred A. Knopf, 1928), 76.

42. Quoted in "This Isn't Liberation, This Is Conquest," *Socialist Worker*, editorial, April 18, 2003.

43. See, for example, Mohamed M. Ali and Iqbal H. Shah, "Sanctions and Child Mortality in Iraq," *Lancet* 355, no. 9218 (May 27, 2000): 1851–1857,

44. See Lance Selfa, "Eight Years of Clinton-Gore: The Price of Lesser-Evilism," *International Socialist Review* 13 (August–September 2000); Sami Farsoun, "Roots of the American Anti-Terrorism Crusade," in *Civil Rights in Peril: The Targeting of Arabs and Muslims,* ed. Elaine C. Hagopian (Chicago and London: Haymarket Books/Pluto Press, 2004), 133–46.

45. Johnson, *Sorrows of Empire*, 151–52.

46. Ashley Smith, "Obama's New Imperial Strategy," *International Socialist Review* 83, May 2012, www.isreview.org/issue/83/obamas-new-imperialist-strategy.

47. See "Full Text of Obama's Nobel Peace Prize Speech," NBCNews.com, December 10, 2009, www.msnbc.msn.com/id/34360743/ns/politics-white_house/t/full-text-obamas-nobel-peace-prize-speech/#.UPWqXuhU2Xo.

48. Eamon Javers, "Conservative Praise for Nobel Speech," Politico.com, December 10, 2009, http://dyn.politico.com/printstory.cfm?uuid=79BD6E2B-18FE-70B2-A85D3CF476223A56.

49. Quoted in Glenn Greenwald, "Remember When Obama Vowed to Protect Whistleblowers?," *Guardian*, March 15, 2013.

50. Alan Maass, "The National Spying-on-You Agency," *SocialistWorker.com*, June 11, 2013, http://socialistworker.org/2013/06/11/national-spying-on-you-agency.

51. CNN Wire Staff, "Drone Strikes Kill, Maim, and Traumatize Too Many Civilians, U.S. Study Says," CNN.com, September 25, 2012.

52. Quoted in Johnson, *Sorrows of Empire*, 67.

53. Benedict Anderson, "Indonesian Nationalism Today and in the Future," *New Left Review* 235 (May/June 1999).

54. V. I. Lenin, "Who Stands to Gain?," in *CW*, vol. 19, 53.

55. Debs, "The Canton Speech," 260.

56. Lee Sustar, "Globalization: Myths and Realities," *International Socialist Review* 12 (June–July 2000).

57. Ibid.

58. William I. Robinson, *A Theory of Global Capitalism: Production, Class, and State in a Transnational World* (Baltimore, MD: Johns Hopkins University Press, 2004), 16.

59. FDI, especially into developed countries, has plummeted since this book was first written as a result of the Great Recession. In 2012 alone, FDI decline by 18 percent, to $1.35 trillion. Developing countries now account for 52 percent of foreign investment flows. See "World Investment Report 2013," United Nations Conference on Trade and Development.

60. United Nations Conference on Trade and Development, "International Trade Statistics 2009," 10; Richard Baldwin, "The Great Trade Collapse: What Caused It and What Does It Mean?" *Vox*, November 27, 2009, www.voxeu.org/article/great-trade-collapse-what-caused-it-and-what-does-it-mean.

61. United Nations Conference on Trade and Development, "2009 Development and Globalization Facts and Figures," 30.

62. Bruce Upbin, "The 147 Companies That Control Everything," *Forbes*, October 22, 2011, www.forbes.com/sites/bruceupbin/2011/10/22/the-147-companies-that-control-everything); Stefania Vitali, James B. Glattfelder, and Stafano Battiston, "The Network of Global Corporate Control," paper written for the Federal Institute of Technology, Zurich, Switzerland, September 19, 2011.

63. Michael Hardt and Antonio Negri, *Empire* (Boston: Harvard University Press, 2000), xiii–xiv.

64. Quoted in J. Patrice McSherry, "Preserving Hegemony: National Security Doctrine in the Post-Cold War Era," *NACLA Report on the Americas* 24, no. 3 (November/December 2000), 10.

65. Kevin Farnsworth, *Social Versus Corporate Welfare: Competing Needs and Interests Within the Welfare State* (New York: Palgrave MacMillan, 2012), 2.

66. Philip Mattera and Anna Purinton, "Shopping for Subsidies: How Wal-Mart Uses Taxpayer Money to Finance Its Never-Ending Growth," Good Jobs First report, May 2004, www .goodjobsfirst.org/pdf/wmtstudy.pdf.

67. This fact, along with a substantial list of other corporate welfare handouts, can be found at "Two Trillion in Corporate Welfare: Start Here," *Daily Kos*, May 24, 2011, www.dailykos.com /story/2011/05/24/978756/-Two-Trillion-In-Corporate-Welfare-Start-Here.

68. Louise Story, Tiff Fehr, and Derek Watkins, "United States of Subsidies," *New York Times*, December 1, 2012, www.nytimes.com/interactive/2012/12/01/us/government-incentives.html? _r=0#co-kochindustriesinc; Kenneth Thomas, "Libertarian Koch Brothers Have Taken Tens of Millions in Subsidies," *Daily Kos*, May 28, 2013, www.dailykos.com/story/2013/05/28 /1212161/-Libertarian-Koch-brothers-have-taken-tens-of-millions-in-subsidies.

69. Louise Story, "As Companies Seek Tax Deals, Governments Pay High Price," *New York Times*, December 1, 2012, www.nytimes.com/2012/12/02/us/how-local-taxpayers-bankroll -corporations.html.

70. Charles M. Sennott, "The $150 Billion 'Welfare' Recipients: U.S. Corporations," *Boston Globe*, July 7, 1996.

71. Kevin Danaher and Jason Mark, *Insurrection: Citizen Challenge to Corporate Power* (New York: Routledge, 2003), 7.

72. See Keith Rosenthal, "What Do Socialists Say About World Hunger?" *International Socialist Review* 45 (January–February 2006).

73. Ibid.

74. Michael Skapinker, "Worlds Apart: Despite a Wave of Mergers and Acquisitions, the Long-Predicted Global Corporation Remains a Distant Ideal," *Financial Times*, March 1, 2001.

75. Gao Xu, "State-Owned Enterprises in China: How Big Are They?," *World Bank* blog, http://blogs.worldbank.org/eastasiapacific/state-owned-enterprises-in-china-how-big-are-they.

76. Bukharin, *Imperialism and World Economy*, 61–62.

77. Thomas Friedman, "What the World Needs Now," *New York Times*, March 28, 1999.

78. V. I. Lenin, *Imperialism: The Highest Stage of Capitalism*, in *CW*, vol. 22 (Moscow: Progress Publishers, 1977), 295.

79. John Keegan, *A History of Warfare* (New York: Vintage, 1993), 391.

80. Carl von Clausewitz, *On War* (London: Penguin, 1986), 119.

81. Quoted in Phyllis Bennis, *Calling the Shots: How Washington Dominates Today's UN* (New York: Olive Branch Press, 2000), xxiii.

82. Leon Trotsky, *Terrorism and Communism* (Ann Arbor, MI: Anne Arbor Paperbacks, 1972), 63.

83. The statistics vary, but they all paint a picture of complete devastation. See Nick Turse, *Kill Anything That Moves: The Real American War in Vietnam* (New York: Picador, 2013), 10–11.

Turse cites a 2008 study by the Harvard Medical School and the Institute for Health Metrics at the University of Washington.

84. See Stanley Weintraub, *Silent Night: The Story of the World War I Christmas Truce* (New York: Plume Books, 2001).

85. Quoted in Ahmed Shawki, "80 Years Since the Russian Revolution," *International Socialist Review* 3 (Winter 1997).

86. Victor Serge, *Year One of the Russian Revolution*, 325.

87. Engels, "Principles of Communism," in *The Communist Manifesto*, 141.

Chapter Eleven: Marxism and Oppression

1. "Lesbian, Gay, Bisexual, Transgender, Queer and HIV-Affected Hate Violence in 2012," National Coalition of Anti-Violence Programs (New York: NCAVP, 2013), 8, 9, www.avp.org /storage/documents/ncavp_2012_hvreport_final.pdf.

2. Fawn Johnson, "Actually, Obama Has Been Terrible for Immigrants," nationaljournal.com, October 10, 2013.

3. Stephanie M. Schwartz, "The Arrogance of Ignorance: Hidden Away, Out of Sight and Out of Mind," October 15, 2006, http://silvrdrach.homestead.com/Schwartz_2006_Oct_15.html.

4. Allan Chase, *The Legacy of Malthus: The Social Costs of the New Scientific Racism* (Chicago: University of Illinois Press, 1980), 3.

5. Ibid., 20–21.

6. Percy Bysshe Shelley, *The Masque of Anarchy* (London: Reeves and Turner, 1892), 47.

7. Engels to Hermann Schlüter, *Marx and Engels on the United States* (Moscow: Progress Publishers, 1979), 238.

8. Quoted in *Work and Struggle: Voices from U.S. Labor Radicalism*, ed. Paul Le Blanc (New York: Routledge, 2011), 126.

9. Quoted in Francis Fox Piven and Richard Cloward, *Poor People's Movements* (New York: Vintage Books, 1979), 100.

10. Sharon Smith, "Mistaken Identity—or Can Identity Politics Liberate the Oppressed?," *International Socialism* 62 (Spring 1994): 39.

11. Barbara J. Fields, "Slavery, Race and Ideology in the USA," in *Racecraft: The Soul of Inequality in American Life*, Karen F. Fields and Barbara J. Fields (New York: Verso, 2012), 128.

12. Quoted in Cordelia Fine, *Delusions of Gender: How Our Minds, Society, and Neurosexism Create Difference* (New York: W. W. Norton, 2010), xix.

13. Quoted in ibid., xxiii.

14. Michael Albert, "Marxism: Virtues and Problems," *Z* magazine, www.zmag.org/marxismdebate .htm.

15. Quoted in V. I. Lenin, "The Question of Peace," in *CW*, vol. 21, 293.

16. Bebel, *Women Under Socialism*, 6.

17. Karl Marx, *Capital* (New York: Vintage, 1977), 915.

18. Ibid., 918.

19. "Marx to Annenkov, December 28, 1846," in *MECW*, vol. 38 (New York: Progress Publishers, 1982), 101–2.

20. Marx, *Capital*, 925–26.

21. Marx, "Outline of a Report on the Irish Question to the Communist Educational Association of German Workers in London," in *MECW*, vol. 21 (Moscow: Progress Publishers, 1985),

200, 202.

22. See, for example, George W. Bush, "President Addresses the Nation," Washington, DC, September 7, 2003, www.whitehouse.gov/news/releases/2003/09/20030907-1.html.

23. Quoted in Robert Middlekauff, *The Glorious Cause: The American Revolution, 1763–1789* (New York: Oxford University Press, 1982), 372.

24. Ibid.

25. Quoted in V. I. Lenin, "The National Program of the RSDLP," in *Questions of National Policy and Proletarian Internationalism* (Moscow: Progress Publishers, 1970), 10.

26. "A Letter from Debs on Immigration," first published in *International Socialist Review* 11, no. 1 (July 1910), www.marxists.org/archive/debs/works/1910/immigration.htm.

27. Karl Marx, "The General Council to the Federal Council of Romance Switzerland," in *MECW*, vol. 21, 89.

28. Marx, *Capital*, vol. 1, 414.

29. Woodrow Wilson, "Speech on the Fourteen Points," *Congressional Record*, 65th Cong., 2nd sess., 1918, 680–81, www.fordham.edu/halsall/mod/1918wilson.html.

30. In pre-revolutionary Russia, women did not have the right to divorce their husbands. This was granted during the Russian Revolution, on the understanding that it was key to women achieving equality with men.

31. Lenin, "The Question of Nationalities or 'Autonomization,'" in *CW*, vol. 36 (Moscow: Progress Publishers, 1977), 607–8.

32. Lenin, *The Right of Nations to Self-Determination*, 410.

33. Ibid., 7.

34. Ibid., 9.

35. Annie Zirin, "The Hidden History of Zionism," *International Socialist Review*, no. 24, July–August 2004; Lance Selfa, "Zionism: False Messiah," in Lance Selfa, ed., *The Struggle for Palestine* (Chicago: Haymarket Books, 2002), 4.

36. Selfa, "Zionism: False Messiah," 13–14.

37. Noam Chomsky, "The Origins of the 'Special Relationship,'" in *The Essential Chomsky*, ed. Anthony Arnove (New York: W. W. Norton & Company, 2008), 211.

38. Quoted in Jane Degras, ed., *The Communist International, 1919–1943, Documents*, vol. 1 (London: F. Cass, 1971), 143–44.

39. Martha E. Gimenez, "Capitalism and the Oppression of Women: Marx Revisited," *Science & Society* 69, no. 1 (January 2005): 20.

40. See Patricia Draper, "!Kung Women: Contrasts in Sexual Egalitarianism in Foraging and Sedentary Contexts," in Rayna R. Reiter, ed., *Toward an Anthropology of Women* (New York: Monthly Review Press, 1975); Francis Dahlberg, ed., *Woman the Gatherer* (New Haven, CT: Yale University Press, 1981); and Stephanie Coontz and Peta Henderson, *Women's Work, Men's Property* (London: Verso Press, 1986).

41. John D'Emilio and Estelle B. Freedman, *Intimate Matters: A History of Sexuality in America* (New York: Harper and Row, 1988), 8–9.

42. Bronislaw Malinowski, *The Sexual Life of Savages* (New York: Harvest Books, 1929), 3.

43. Ibid., 53, 59.

44. Walter L. Williams, "The 'Two-Spirit' People of Indigenous North Americans," *Guardian*, October 11, 2010.

45. Judith K. Brown, "Economic Organization and the Position of Women Among the Iroquois," *Ethnohistory* 17, no. 3/4 (Summer–Autumn, 1970): 151–67.

46. Engels, *Origins of the Family*, 165.

47. Ibid.

48. Karl Marx, *Capital*, vol. 1, 275.

49. See, for example, Lise Vogel, *Marxism and the Oppression of Women: Toward a Unitary Theory* (Chicago: Haymarket Books, 2014); Sharon Smith, "Theorizing Women's Oppression: Domestic Labor and Women's Oppression," *International Socialist Review* 88, March 2013, http://isreview.org/issue/88/theorizing-womens-oppression-part-1; Tithi Bhattacharya, "What Is Social Reproduction Theory?," *Socialist Worker*, September 10, 2013, http://socialistworker.org/2013/09/10/what-is-social-reproduction-theory.

50. Susan Ferguson and David McNally, "Capital, Labor Power, and Gender Relations," in *Marxism and the Oppression of Women* (Chicago: Haymarket Books, 2013), xxv.

51. Sharon Smith, *Women and Socialism: Essays on Women's Liberation* (Chicago: Haymarket Books, 2005), 85–86.

52. Angela Y. Davis, *Women, Race, and Class* (New York: Vintage, 1983), 229.

53. Engels, *Origin of the Family, Private Property and the State*, chap 2, sec. 4, "The Monogamous Family."

54. Smith, *Women and Socialism*, 55.

55. Angela Davis, *Women, Race, and Class* (New York: Vintage Press, 1983), 231–32.

56. Stephanie Coontz, *The Way We Never Were: American Families and the Nostalgia Trap* (New York: Basic Books, 1992), 11–12.

57. Arlene Skolnick, *Embattled Paradise: The American Family in an Age of Uncertainty* (New York: Basic Books, 1991), 10.

58. Ibid, 9.

59. Laura Basset, "Women Still Earned 77 Cents on Men's Dollar in 2012: Report," *Huffington Post*, September 17, 2013.

60. *Full Report of the Prevalence, Incidence, and Consequences of Violence Against Women: Findings from the National Violence Against Women Survey* (Washington, DC: US Department of Justice Office of Justice Programs, 2000), iii.

61. "Stealing Roe One Law at a Time," *Socialistworker.org*, January 22, 2014.

62. Smith, *Women and Socialism*, 56.

63. Alix Holt, ed. and trans., *Selected Writings of Alexandra Kollontai* (London: Alison and Busby, 1977), 59.

64. Tithi Bhattacharya, "Marissa Mayer, the Family, and Capitalism," *Socialist Worker*, March 14, 2013.

65. Leon Trotsky, *Women and the Family* (New York: Pathfinder, 1986), 29.

66. V. I. Lenin, "A Great Beginning," in *Not by Politics Alone: The Other Lenin*, ed. Tamara Deutscher (Westport, CT: Lawrence Hill & Co., 1983), 215.

67. Leon Trotsky, *The Revolution Betrayed* (New York: Pathfinder Press, 1972), 145.

68. Kathleen Gough, "The Origin of the Family," in *Toward an Anthropology of Women*, ed. Rayna R. Reiter (New York: Monthly Review, 1975), 75.

69. David Greenberg, *The Construction of Homosexuality* (Chicago: University of Chicago Press, 1990), 3.

70. Ibid., 66.

71. Ibid., 65.

72. Fine, *Delusions of Gender*, 230–31.

73. The point is made in John Bosworth, *Christianity, Social Tolerance, and Homosexuality* (Chicago: University of Chicago Press, 1980), 24.

74. Wolf, *Sexuality and Socialism*, 20–21.
75. Jeffrey Weeks, *Sex, Politics, and Society: The Regulation of Sexuality Since 1800* (New York: Longman, 1993), 102.
76. Marx and Engels, *Communist Manifesto*, 43; Karl Marx, *Grundrisse* (London: Penguin, 1993), 83.
77. John D'Emilio, "Capitalism and Gay Identity," in *Making Trouble: Essays on Gay History, Politics, and the University* (London: Routledge, 1992), 7.
78. Ibid., 13.
79. Richard J. Herrnstein and Charles Murray, *The Bell Curve: Intelligence and Class Structure in American Life* (New York: Free Press, 1996).
80. Dobzhansky, *Mankind Evolving*, 21.
81. Phil Gasper, "IQ, Genetics, and Racism," *International Socialist Review* 57, January–February 2008.
82. Barbara J. Fields, "Slavery, Race, and Ideology in the United States of America," *New Left Review*, May–June 1990, 96.
83. Ashley Montagu, *Race and IQ* (New York: Galaxy Books, 1975), 3.
84. Thomas F. Gossett, *Race: The History of an Idea in America* (New York: Schocken Books, 1965), 118.
85. Eric Williams, *Capitalism and Slavery* (New York: Perigee Books, 1980), 7.
86. Betty Wood, *The Origins of American Slavery: Freedom and Bondage in the English Colonies* (New York: Hill and Wang, 1997), 90.
87. Peter Fryer, *Staying Power: The History of Black People in Britain* (London: Pluto Press, 1984), 17.
88. Peter Kolchin, *American Slavery, 1619–1877* (New York: Hill & Wang, 2003), 15.
89. Quoted in Ahmed Shawki, *Black Liberation and Socialism* (Chicago: Haymarket Books, 2006), 34.
90. Lance Selfa, "Slavery and the Origins of Racism," *International Socialist Review* 26 (November–December 2002).
91. Ibid., 318.
92. Allan Chase, *The Legacy of Malthus: The Social Costs of the New Scientific Racism* (Chicago: University of Illinois Press, 1980), 16–17; Randall Hansen and Desmond King, *Sterilized by the State: Eugenics, Race, and the Population Scare in Twentieth-Century North America* (New York: Cambridge University Press, 2013), 249; Relf v. Weinberger, available at www.splcenter.org/get-informed/case-docket/relf-v-weinberger.
93. Karl Marx, "Confidential Communication," in *MECW*, vol. 25, 120.
94. Brian Jones, "How Racism Lives in a Colorblind Society," *Socialist Worker*, December 4, 2012, http://socialistworker.org/2012/12/04/racism-in-a-color-blind-society.
95. The statistics can be found at "Black History Month: Welfare, in Black and White," *Beautiful, Also, Are the Souls of My Black Sisters* blog, February 2, 2009, http://kathmanduk2.wordpress.com/2009/02/02/black-history-month-welfare-in-black-and-white/.
96. NAACP criminal justice fact sheet, www.naacp.org/pages/criminal-justice-fact-sheet.
97. Michael McLaughlin, "Felon Voting Laws Disenfranchise 5.8 Million Americans with Criminal Records: The Sentencing Project," *Huffington Post*, July 12, 2012.
98. Michelle Alexander, *The New Jim Crow: Mass Incarceration in the Age of Colorblindness* (New York: The New Press, 2011), 175.
99. "African-American Economic Gains Reversed by Great Recession," *Huffington Post*, July 10, 2011.

100. Hope Yen, "80 Percent of Adults Face Near-Poverty, Unemployment: Survey," *Huffington Post*, July 28, 2013, www.huffingtonpost.com/2013/07/28/poverty-unemployment-rates_n_3666594.html.

101. Mark Robert Rank, *One Nation, Underprivileged: Why American Poverty Affects Us All* (Oxford: Oxford University Press, 2004), 296n.

102. Quoted in Shawki, *Black Liberation and Socialism*, 66.

103. Quoted in ibid., 72.

104. Ibid., 74.

105. Ibid., 75.

106. Tom Watson, "The Negro Question in the South," in *Contending Voices: Biographical Explorations of the American Past*, vol. 2, ed. John Hollitz (Boston: Wadsworth, 2011), 64.

107. Jack Bloom, *Class, Race & the Civil Rights Movement* (Bloomington: Indiana University Press, 1987), 49.

108. Quoted in Shawki, *Black Liberation and Socialism*, 81.

109. Quoted in Jacqueline Jones, *American Work: Four Centuries of Black and White Labor* (New York: W. W. Norton & Company, 1998), 311.

110. Philip S. Foner, *Organized Labor and the Black Worker* (New York: Progress Publishers, 1981), 116, 117.

111. Ibid., 227.

112. Quoted in Philip S. Foner, *History of the Labor Movement in the United States*, vol. 3 (New York: International Publishers, 1981), 254.

113. Foner, *Organized Labor and the Black Worker*, 82–84.

114. William Haywood, *The Autobiography of Big Bill Haywood* (New York: International Publishers, 1929), 252.

115. Philip S. Foner, *History of the Labor Movement in the United States*, vol. 4 (New York: International Publishers, 1997), 318.

116. Shawki, *Black Liberation and Socialism*, 247–48.

117. Manning Marable, *Race, Reform and Rebellion: The Second Reconstruction and Beyond in Black America, 1945–2006*, 3rd ed. (Jackson: University of Mississippi Press, 2007), 117.

118. "Employment Status of the Civilian Population by Age, Race, and Sex," Bureau of Labor Statistics, www.bls.gov/news.release/empsit.t02.htm.

119. Krissah Thompson, "Black Men Hit Hard by Unemployment in Milwaukee," *Washington Post*, December 14, 2009.

120. "The Schools Chicago Students Deserve: Research-based Proposals to Strengthen Elementary and Secondary Education in the Chicago Public Schools," Chicago Teachers Union, February 2012, www.ctunet.com/quest-center/research/the-schools-chicagos-students-deserve.

121. Selfa, "Slavery and the Origins of Racism."

122. V. I. Lenin, *What Is to Be Done?* (New York: Progress Publishers, 1992), 69.

123. "Marxism, Post-colonial Studies, and the Tasks of Radical Theory," Interview with Vivek Chibber, *International Socialist Review*, Spring 2013.

124. Lenin, "The Discussion of Self-Determination Summed Up," *Collected Works*, vol. 22 (Moscow: Progress Publishers, 1977), 355–56.

125. Lenin, "Two Tactics of Social Democracy in the Democratic Revolution," 113.

126. Bill Cosby quoted in Michael Eric Dyson, "Talking Points," http://www.michaelericdyson.com/cosby/points.html.

127. James Connolly, *The Reconquest of Ireland* (Dublin: New Books, 1972), chap. 6, www.marxists.org/archive/connolly/1915/rcoi/index.htm.

Chapter Twelve: Capitalism's Ecological Crisis

1. James Hansen, *Storms of My Grandchildren: The Truth About the Coming Climate Catastrophe and Our Last Chance to Save Humanity* (New York: Bloomsbury USA, 2009), Kindle edition, preface; David Biello, "400 ppm: Carbon Dioxide in the Atmosphere Reaches Prehistoric Levels," *Scientific American*, May 9, 2013.

2. "Facts about Rainforests," Nature Conservancy, October 6, 2011, www.nature.org/ourinitiatives /urgentissues/rainforests/rainforests-facts.xml.

3. A discussion of "abrupt climate change impacts" can be found here: National Research Council, *Abrupt Impacts of Climate Change: Anticipating Surprises* (Washington, DC: The National Academies Press, 2013).

4. Fred Magdoff and Brian Tokar, *Agriculture and Food in Crisis: Conflict, Resistance, and Renewal* (New York: Monthly Review Press, 2010), 15.

5. Bill McKibben, *Eaarth: Making a Life on a Tough New Planet* (New York: Times Books, 2010), 101.

6. See for example, the Greenpeace report *Dealing in Doubt: The Climate Denial Machine vs. Climate Science*, September 2013, 9, www.greenpeace.org/usa/en/campaigns/global-warming-and -energy/polluterwatch/Dealing-in-Doubt—the-Climate-Denial-Machine-vs-Climate-Science/.

7. Chris Williams, "Warsaw Climate Talks Go Up in Smoke," *Truth-out.org*, November 21, 2013.

8. "Risky Gas Drilling Threatens Health, Water Supplies," National Resource Defense Council, www.nrdc.org/energy/gasdrilling.

9. Bill McKibben, "Obama and Climate Change: The Real Story," *Rolling Stone*, December 17, 2013.

10. Thomas Robert Malthus, *An Essay on the Principle of Population* (New York: W. W. Norton & Company, 1976), 20.

11. Frederick Engels, *Outlines of a Critique of Political Economy*, in *MECW*, vol. 3 (New York: International Publishers, 1975), 437.

12. Paul R. Erlich and Anne H. Erlich, *The Population Explosion* (London: Hutchinson, 1990), 9.

13. Ibid., 224.

14. Ibid., 226–28.

15. Garrett Hardin, *Living Within Limits: Ecology, Economics and Population Taboos* (New York: Oxford University Press, 1993), 294.

16. Garrett Hardin, "The Tragedy of the Commons," in *Valuing the Earth: Economics, Ecology, Ethics*, Herman E. Daly and Kenneth N. Townsend, eds. (Cambridge, MA: MIT Press, 1994), 135.

17. These ideas are put forward, for example, by advocates of "deep green resistance." See *The Derrick Jensen Reader: Writings on Environmental Revolution* (New York: Seven Stories Press, 2012); and Aric McBay, Lierre Keith, and Derrick Jensen, *Deep Green Resistance* (New York: Seven Stories Press, 2011).

18. Karl Marx, "First Draft of Letter to Vera Zasulich," in *MECW*, vol. 24 (New York: International Publishers, 1989), 357.

19. *State of Food and Agriculture, 2013: Food Systems for Better Nutrition* (Rome: UN Food and Agricultural Organization, 2013), ix.

20. UN FAO, Thirty-third Session, "Review of the State of Food and Agriculture," Rome, November 19–26, 2005, www.fao.org/docrep/meeting/010/j6091e/j6091e.htm.

21. Lappé, "The Myth—Scarcity: The Reality—There IS Enough Food."

22. See ibid. and figures from Jean Ziegler, the UN's Special Rapporteur on the Right to Food,

cited in Eulàlia Iglesias, "UN Food Expert Condemns U.S. Tactics in Iraq," InterPress Service, November 12, 2005.

23.   Ian Angus and Simon Butler, *Too Many People? Population, Immigration, and the Environmental Crisis* (Chicago: Haymarket Books, 2011), 66.

24.   Engels, *Outlines of a Critique of Political Economy*, in *MECW*, vol. 3, 438.

25.   Ibid.

26.   Marx, *Grundrisse*, 604–8.

27.   Engels, *Outlines of a Critique of Political Economy*, 438.

28.   Marx, *Capital*, vol. 1, chap. 25, sec. 3, "Progressive Production of a Relative Surplus Population or Industrial Reserve Army," www.marxists.org/archive/marx/works/1867-c1/ch25.htm#S3.

29.   Angus and Butler, *Too Many People?* , 42–43.

30.   Ibid. 44.

31.   Angus and Butler, *Too Many People?*, 48.

32.   Jeff White quoted in ibid., 45

33.   Karl Marx, *Grundrisse* (New York: Penguin Books, 1993), 100.

34.   Angus and Butler, *Too Many People?*, 138.

35.   Brad Plumer, "After Years of Decline, U.S. Carbon Emissions Rose 3 Percent in 2013, *Wonkblog*, January 13, 2014, www.washingtonpost.com/blogs/wonkblog/wp/2014/01/13 /after-years-of-decline-u-s-carbon-emissions-rose-2-percent-in-2013.

36.   Marx, *Capital*, vol. 1, 739.

37.   Engels, *Anti-Dühring*, 315.

38.   McKibben, *Eaarth*, 103–6.

39.   Marx, *Capital*, vol. 1, 777.

40.   Marx and Engels, *Communist Manifesto*, 76.

41.   McKibben, *Eaarth*, 147.

42.   This is discussed in Paul Burkett, "Marx's Vision of Sustainable Human Development," *Monthly Review* 25, no. 5, October 2005.

43.   Marx, *Capital*, vol. 3, 776.

44.   Marx quoted in Engels, *Anti-Dühring*, 339.

45.   Engels, *Anti-Dühring*, 338.

46.   Marx and Engels's insights on capitalism and the environment are scattered throughout different texts, from Marx's *Capital* (mostly volumes 1 and 3) and the *Grundrisse* to Engels's *Anti-Dühring, Dialectics of Nature*, and *The Housing Question*. A good place to get a handle on their views is to read John Bellamy Foster, *Marx's Ecology* (New York: Monthly Review, 2000); John Bellamy Foster, Brett Clark, and Richard York, *The Ecological Rift: Capitalism's War on the Earth* (New York: Monthly Review, 2010); Paul Burkett, *Marxism and Ecological Economics* (Chicago: Haymarket Books, 2005); Paul Burkett, *Marx and Nature: A Red and Green Perspective* (Chicago: Haymarket Books, 2014); Joel Kovel, *The Enemy of Nature* (London: Zed Books, 2007); Chris Williams, *Ecology and Socialism: Solutions to Capitalist Ecological Crisis* (Chicago: Haymarket Books, 2010); and Howard L. Parsons, *Marx and Engels on Ecology* (Westport, CT: Greenwood Press, 1977).

47.   Engels, *Origin of the Family*, 204.

48.   Quoted in John Bellamy Foster, *Marx's Ecology*, 170.

49.   See, for example, Farshad Araghi, "The Great Global Enclosure of Our Times: Peasants and the Agrarian Question at the End of the 20th Century," in *Hungry for Profit: The Agribusiness Threat to Farmers, Food, and the Environment* (New York: Monthly Review, 2000), 157.

50. Karl Marx, *Capital*, 637–38.

51. Engels, *Anti-Dühring*, 341.

52. Ibid., 463.

53. Engels, "The Part Played by Labor in the Transition from Ape to Man," in *MECW*, vol. 25, 461.

54. Ibid., 460–61.

55. Ibid., 461.

56. Chris Arsenault, "World Powers Scramble for Arctic Oil and Gas," *Al-Jazeera English*, December 1, 2010.

57. For a development of these arguments in much more detail, see Richard Smith, "Green Capitalism: The God That Failed," *Truthout*, January 9, 2014, www.truth-out.org/news/item /21060-green-capitalism-the-god-that-failed.

58. *United Nations Human Development Report 2005: International Cooperation at the Crossroads*, 4, http://hdr.undp.org/reports/global/2005; "Hunger Notes: 2013 World Poverty Facts and Statistics," www.worldhunger.org/articles/Learn/world%20hunger%20facts%202002.htm.

59. US Census Bureau, *Income, Poverty, and Health Insurance Coverage in the United States, 2012*, www.census.gov/hhes/www/hlthins/data/incpovhlth.

60. The Census Bureau's poverty threshold for a family of four was a pitiful $23,021 in 2012— enough for one person to barely get by.

61. Karl Marx, "Human Requirements and Division of Labor under the Rule of Private Property," in *Economic and Philosophical Manuscripts of 1844*, www.marxists.org/archive/marx/works /1844/manuscripts/needs.htm.

62. Lara Hernández Anton, "The Story of Bottled Water," http://welearntoday.com/the-story-of-bottled-water.

63. "Salt, Sugar, Fat: NY Times Reporter Michael Moss on How the Food Giants Hooked Americans on Junk Food," Michael Moss interview, *Democracy Now!*, March 1, 2013, www.democracynow .org/2013/3/1/salt_sugar_fat_ny_times_reporter.

64. Kenneth Gould, David Pellow, and Allan Schnaiberg, "Interrogating the Treadmill of Production: Everything You Wanted to Know about the Treadmill but Were Afraid to Ask," revised paper from Madison symposium on the treadmill of production, December 29, 2003, www.sociology.northwestern.edu/people/faculty/documents/schnaiberg/21 .INTERROGATINGTHETREADMILL.pdf.

65. Quoted in Angus and Butler, *Too Many People?*, 170.

66. William Morris, "How We Live and How We Might Live," lecture delivered to the Hammersmith Branch of the Socialist Democratic Federation, Hammersmith, UK, November 30, 1884, www.marxists.org/archive/morris/works/1884/hwl/hwl.htm.

67. Quoted in Brian Ward, "Canada Is 'Idle No More,'" *Socialistworker.org*, January 9, 2013, http://socialistworker.org/2013/01/09/canada-is-idle-no-more.

68. National Wildlife Federation, "Keystone XL Pipeline," www.nwf.org/What-We-Do/Energy -and-Climate/Drilling-and-Mining/Tar-Sands/Keystone-XL-Pipeline.aspx.

69. Michael E. Mann, "If You See Something, Say Something," *New York Times*, January 17, 2014.

70. Naomi Klein, "How Science Is Telling Us All to Revolt," *New Statesman*, October 29, 2013.

71. James Gustave Speth, *The Bridge at the End of the World: Capitalism, the Environment, and Crossing from Crisis to Sustainability* (New Haven, CT: Yale University Press, 2008), Kindle edition, xiii.

72. Ibid., xiii–xiv.

73.   James Gustave Speth, *The Bridge at the End of the World*, 8.
74.   James Gustave Speth, "Global Warming and Capitalism," *Nation*, September 17, 2008.
75.   Quoted in Foster, Clark, and York, *The Ecological Rift*, 163.
76.   Ibid., 462.
77.   Williams, *Ecology and Socialism*, 217.
78.   See ibid., and also Miguel A. Altieri, "Agroecology, Small Farms, and Food Sovereignty," in Magdoff and Tokar, *Agriculture and Food in Crisis*, chap. 14.

Chapter Thirteen: Imagine . . . the Socialist Future

1.   Debs, "Unionism and Socialism," 154–55.
2.   Karl Marx, "Critique of the Gotha Program," in *MECW*, vol. 24, 85–86.
3.   Ibid., 95.
4.   Engels, "Socialism: Utopian and Scientific," in *MECW*, vol. 24, 325.
5.   Marx and Engels, *Communist Manifesto*, 69–70.
6.   Marx, "Critique of the Gotha Program," 87.
7.   *UN Human Development Report 1999*, 29, http://hdr.undp.org/reports/global/1999/en/; "Wealth of 85 Richest People Equal to That of Poorest 3.5bn: Oxfam Report Finds Growing Inequality Driven by Power Grab by Wealthy Elites," *Irish Times*, January 20, 2014.
8.   *UN Human Development Report 1994*, 50, http://hdr.undp.org/reports/global/1994/en/.
9.   Marx and Engels, *Communist Manifesto*, 56–57.
10.   Debs, *Eugene V. Debs Speaks*, 47.
11.   George Orwell, *Homage to Catalonia* (New York: Mariner Books, 1980), 4–5.
12.   Larry Bradshaw and Lorrie Beth Slonsky, "The Real Heroes and Sheroes of New Orleans," *Socialist Worker*, September 9, 2005.
13.   Ibid.
14.   Quoted in Abel Paz, *Durruti: The People Armed* (New York: Black Rose Books, 1977), 229.

Appendix 1: But What About . . . ?
Answers to Common Arguments Against Socialism

1.   See, for example, Michael Tomasello, *Why We Cooperate* (Boston, MA: MIT Press, 2009); Robert W. Sussman and C. Robert Cloninger, *Origins of Altruism and Cooperation* (New York: Springer, 2011).
2.   Ken Stern, "Why the Rich Don't Give to Charity," *Atlantic*, March 20, 2013.
3.   Frederick Engels, *The Conditions of the Working Class in England* (1845), chap. 13, www.marxists.org/archive/marx/works/1845/condition-working-class/ch13.htm.
4.   James P. Cannon, "What Will Socialism in America Look Like?," in *Speeches for Socialism* (New York: Pathfinder Press, 1971), 405–6.
5.   Ibid., 406.
6.   Marx and Engels, *Communist Manifesto*, 63.
7.   "President Bush on Iraq, Katrina, and the Economy," George W. Bush interview by Brian Williams, *NBC Nightly News*, NBC, December 12, 2005, www.nbcnews.com/id/10439994/ns/nbc_nightly_news_with_brian_williams/t/president-bush-iraq-katrina-economy/.
8.   Elisabeth Bumiller and Larry Rohter, "Bush's Vision for Latin America: He Calls for Strong Democracies in Response to Leftists," *San Francisco Chronicle*, November 7, 2005.
9.   Paul Foot, *Why You Should Be a Socialist* (London: Socialist Workers Party, 1977), chap. 3,

www.marxists.org/archive/foot-paul/1977/wysbas/index.htm.

10. Engels, "Social Classes: Necessary and Superfluous," in *MECW*, vol. 24, 417.

11. Clifford D. Conner, *A People's History of Science* (New York: Nation Books, 2005), 2.

12. Quoted in James Cockroft, "Argentina: Workers' Control and the Crisis, Part I," *Against the Current* 103, March–April 2003, www.solidarity-us.org/site/node/634.

13. Marina Kabat, "Argentinian Worker-Taken Factories: Trajectories of Workers' Control under the Economic Crisis," in *Ours to Master and to Own: Workers' Control from the Commune to the Present*, Emmanuel Ness and Dario Azzellini, eds. (Chicago: Haymarket Books, 2011), 365.

14. Rosa Luxemburg, *Reform or Revolution*, in *The Essential Rosa Luxemburg*, 80–81. (Hereafter *Reform or Revolution*.)

15. V. I. Lenin, "Can the Bolsheviks Retain State Power?," October 1, 1917, www.marxists.org /archive/lenin/works/1917/oct/01.htm.

16. Ben Strauss, "Critics Say Chicago Shouldn't Aid DePaul Arena with Closing," *New York Times*, June 23, 2013.

17. Gjohnsit, "The Total Cost of the Bank Bailout," *Daily Kos*, February 20, 2013, www.dailykos.com /story/2013/02/20/1188374/-The-true-cost-of-the-Bank-Bailout#.

18. "Eliminating Unhealthy Water/Providing Clean Water for All," UNESCO's World Game Institute, www.unesco.org/education/tlsf/mods/theme_a/interact/www.worldgame.org/wwwproject /what04.shtml.

19. World Bank, *The State in a Changing World*, World Development Report (London: Oxford University Press, 1997), 2; "Government at a Glance 2009," OECDiLibrary, "General Government Expenditure as a Percentage of GDP (2006)," www.oecd-ilibrary.org.

20. Ludwig von Mises, "Bureaucracy," 1944, Ludwig von Mises Institute, http://mises.org /etexts/mises/bureaucracy/section4.asp.

21. David Gordon, *Fat and Mean: The Corporate Squeeze of Working Americans and the Myth of Managerial Downsizing* (New York: The Free Press, 1996), 46–52.

22. David U. Himmelstein et al., "The Cost to the Nation, the States and the District of Columbia, with State-Specific Estimates of Potential Savings," Public Citizen, www.citizen.org /publications/release.cfm?ID=7271.

23. Quoted in Jamie Court and Francis Smith, *Making a Killing: HMOs and the Threat to Your Health* (Monroe, ME: Common Courage Press, 1999), chap. 3, www.makingakilling .org/chapter3.html.

24. Madeleine Albright, interview by Leslie Stahl, *60 Minutes*, CBS, May 12, 1996.

25. Leon Trotsky, *Their Morals and Ours* (New York: Pathfinder Press, 1992), 20–21.

26. Ibid., 14.

27. Clayborne Carson, *In Struggle: SNCC and the Black Awakening of the 1960s* (Cambridge, MA: Harvard University Press, 1981), 164.

28. Charles R. Sims, Deacons of Defense leader from Bogalusa, Louisiana, in Howell Raines, *My Soul Is Rested: The Story of the Civil Rights Movement in the Deep South* (London: Penguin Books, 1987), 416–23.

29. Trotsky, *Their Morals and Ours*, 48.

30. Ibid., 49.

31. Errico Malatesta, "Anarchist Propaganda," Anarchist Library, http://theanarchistlibrary.org/library/errico-malatesta-anarchist-propaganda.

32. Engels to P. Lafargue, December 30, 1871, in *Anarchism and Anarcho-Syndicalism* (Moscow: Progress Publishers, 1972), 58.

33. Emma Goldman, "Minorities versus Majorities," in *Anarchism and Other Essays* (Old Chelsea Station, NY: Cosimo, Inc., 2005), 81.

34. Engels, "On Authority," in *Anarchism and Anarcho-Syndicalism*, 103.

35. Karl Marx and Frederick Engels, "Fictitious Splits in the International," *Anarchism and Anarcho-Syndicalism*, 74.

36. "Class Matters" series, *New York Times*, April–May 2005, www.nytimes.com/pages/national/class/index.html.

37. Frederick Engels, "Appendix to the American edition of *The Condition of the Working Class in England*," in *MECW*, vol. 26, 403.

38. US Small Business Administration, "Employer Firms, Establishments, Employment, and Annual Payroll Small Firm Size Classes, 2003" table, www.sba.gov/advo/research/us_03ss.pdf.

39. US Small Business Administration, "Frequently Asked Questions," http://app1.sba.gov/faqs/faqindex.cfm?areaID=24. These statistics are misleading because they consider a small business any firm that employs fewer than five hundred workers. The businesses that have the most difficulty surviving, however, are the small "mom and pop" stores, restaurants and local shops, and businesses run by individuals out of their homes.

40. Quoted in Janny Scott and David Leonhardt, "Shadowy Lines That Still Divide," in the "Class Matters" series, *New York Times*, May 15, 2005.

41. David Leonhardt, "In Climbing Income Ladder, Location Matters," *New York Times*, July 22, 2013.

42. Economic Policy Institute, "Income Inequality," in *The State of Working America*, http://stateofworkingamerica.org/inequality/income-inequality.

43. Smith, *Subterranean Fire*, 300.

44. Leon Trotsky, "American Problems," *Writings of Leon Trotsky, 1939–1940* (New York: Pathfinder Press, 1973), 335.

45. Quoted in Dick Cluster, *They Should Have Served That Cup of Coffee* (Boston: South End Press, 1979), 44.

46. Facts and quotes in this section, unless otherwise cited, come from Sharon Smith, "Depression Decade: The Turning Point," in *Subterranean Fire*, 102–52.

47. Paul D'Amato, "The Communist Party and Black Liberation in the 1930s," *International Socialist Review* 1, Summer 1997.

48. Bert Cochran, *Labor and Communism: The Conflict That Shaped American Unions* (Princeton, NJ: Princeton University Press, 1977), 138.

49. See Smith, *Subterranean Fire*, 219–23.

50. "CEO-to-Worker Pay Ratio Ballooned 1,000 Percent Since 1950: Report," *Huffington Post*, April 30, 2013.

51. Ahmed Shawki, "Between Things Ended and Things Begun," *International Socialist Review*, June–July 2001.

52. Smith, *Subterranean Fire*, 298.

53. Emmanuel Saez, "Striking It Richer: The Evolution of Top Incomes in the United States (updated with 2012 provisional estimates)," September 2013. A link to the article can be found at http://articles.latimes.com/2013/sep/11/nation/la-na-nn-income-inequality-20130910.

54. Shawki, "Between Things Ended and Things Begun."

55. Ibid.

56. Jen Roesch, "The Life and Times of Occupy Wall Street," *International Socialism* 135, www.isj.org.uk/index.php4?id=821&issue=135.

57. André Gorz, *Farewell to the Working Class: An Essay on Post-Industrial Socialism* (Boston: South End Press, 1980), 28.

58. Quoted in Hal Draper, *Karl Marx's Theory of Revolution: The Politics of Social Classes* vol. 2 (New York: Monthly Review Press, 1978), 576.

59. Ibid.

60. Kevin Doogan, *The New Capitalism* (Malden, MA, Polity Press, 2009), 228–35.

61. Antonio Negri and Michael Hardt, *Multitude: War and Democracy in the Age of Empire* (London: Penguin Books, 2004), 223.

62. Jodi Dean, *The Communist Horizon* (London: Verso, 2012), 77.

63. Hardt and Negri, *Multitude*, 104, 105.

64. Dean, *Communist Horizon*, 82.

65. Marx, *Capital*, vol. 1, chap. 26, www.marxists.org/archive/marx/works/1867-c1/ch26.htm.

66. Ibid., chap. 28, www.marxists.org/archive/marx/works/1867-c1/ch28.htm.

67. Doug Short, "The Full Time–Part Time Employment Ratio Shows Little Improvement," January 10, 2014, www.advisorperspectives.com/dshort/commentaries/Full-Time-vs-Part-Time-Employment.php.

68. Barry Bluestone, "Economic Inequality and the Macrostructuralist Debate," in *Political Economy for the 21st Century: Contemporary Views on the Trend of Economics*, ed. Charles J. Whalen (Armonk, NY: M. E. Sharpe, 1995), 177; Kim Moody, *US Labor in Trouble and Transition: The Failure of Reform from Above, the Promise of Revival from Below* (London: Verso, 2007), 37.

69. Cited in Barry Bluestone and Bennett Harrison, *The Great U-Turn: Corporate Restructuring and the Polarizing of America* (New York: Basic Books, 1988), 37.

70. "Total Employment by Economic Activity, Republic of South Korea," International Labor Organization Web site, http://laborsta.ilo.org.

71. Zhang Yaozu, "Notes on the Transformation and Development of the Chinese Working Class During the Past 60 Years," *China Left Review* 4, 2011, http://chinaleftreview.org/?p=474.

72. Leo Zelig, "Introduction," in *Class Struggle and Resistance in Africa*, ed. Leo Zelig (Chicago: Haymarket Books, 2010), 17.

73. "The Productivity Surge," *Washington Times*, November 3, 2002.

74. James Sherk, "Technology Explains Drop in Manufacturing Jobs," Heritage Foundation, October 12, 2010, www.heritage.org/research/reports/2010/10/technology-explains-drop-in-manufacturing-jobs.

75. Frederick Engels, *Principles of Communism* (London: Pluto Press, 1971), 5.

76. Moody, *US Labor in Trouble and Transition*, 39.

77. Joel Johnson, "1 Million Workers. 90 Million iPhones. 17 Suicides. Who's to Blame?," *Wired Magazine*, February 28, 2011.

78. James Glanz, "The Cloud Factories: Data Barns in a Farm Town, Gobbling Power and Flexing Muscle," *New York Times*, September 23, 2012.

79. Moody, *US Labor in Trouble and Transition*, 245.

80. Keith Bradsher, "Strikes' Effect Widely Felt in Auto Plants," *New York Times*, March 12, 1996; "The General Motors Strike," *New York Times*, March 23, 1996.

81. Dean, *Communist Horizon*, 83.

82. Ibid., 84.

83. Engels, *Socialism: Utopian and Scientific*, 1892 English Introduction, www.marxists.org/archive/marx/works/1880/soc-utop/int-mat.htm.

84. Foot, *Why You Should Be a Socialist*, chap. 3.

85. Quoted in Robert C. Tucker, *Stalin in Power: The Revolution from Above, 1929–1941* (New York: Norton, 1990), 282.

86. Quoted in Ygael Gluckstein, *Mao's China* (Boston: Beacon Press, 1957), 379.

87. John Keats, *The Crack in the Picture Window* (New York: Houghton Mifflin, 1957), xi.

88. Thomas Frank and Matt Weiland, *Commodify Your Dissent: Salvos from the Baffler*, chap. 1, www.nytimes.com/books/first/f/frank-dissent.html.

89. Leon Trotsky, *The Revolution Betrayed*, 180.

Index

About the Author

© Jeffrey Boyette

Paul D'Amato is editor of the quarterly US journal *International Socialist Review* (www.isreview.org) and a frequent contributor to *Socialist Worker* (www.socialist-worker.org). D'Amato is a long time socialist and activist and he lives in Chicago.